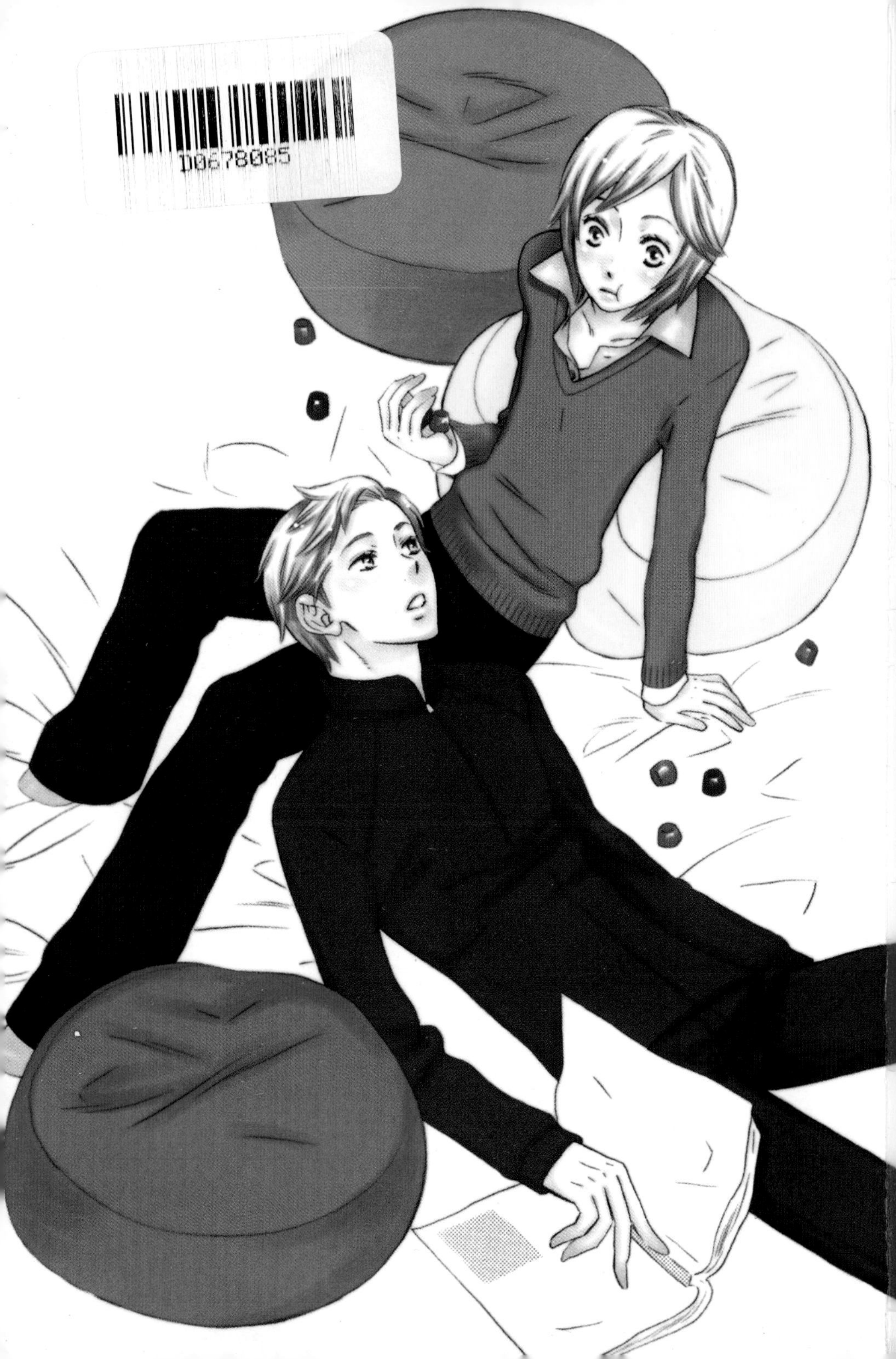

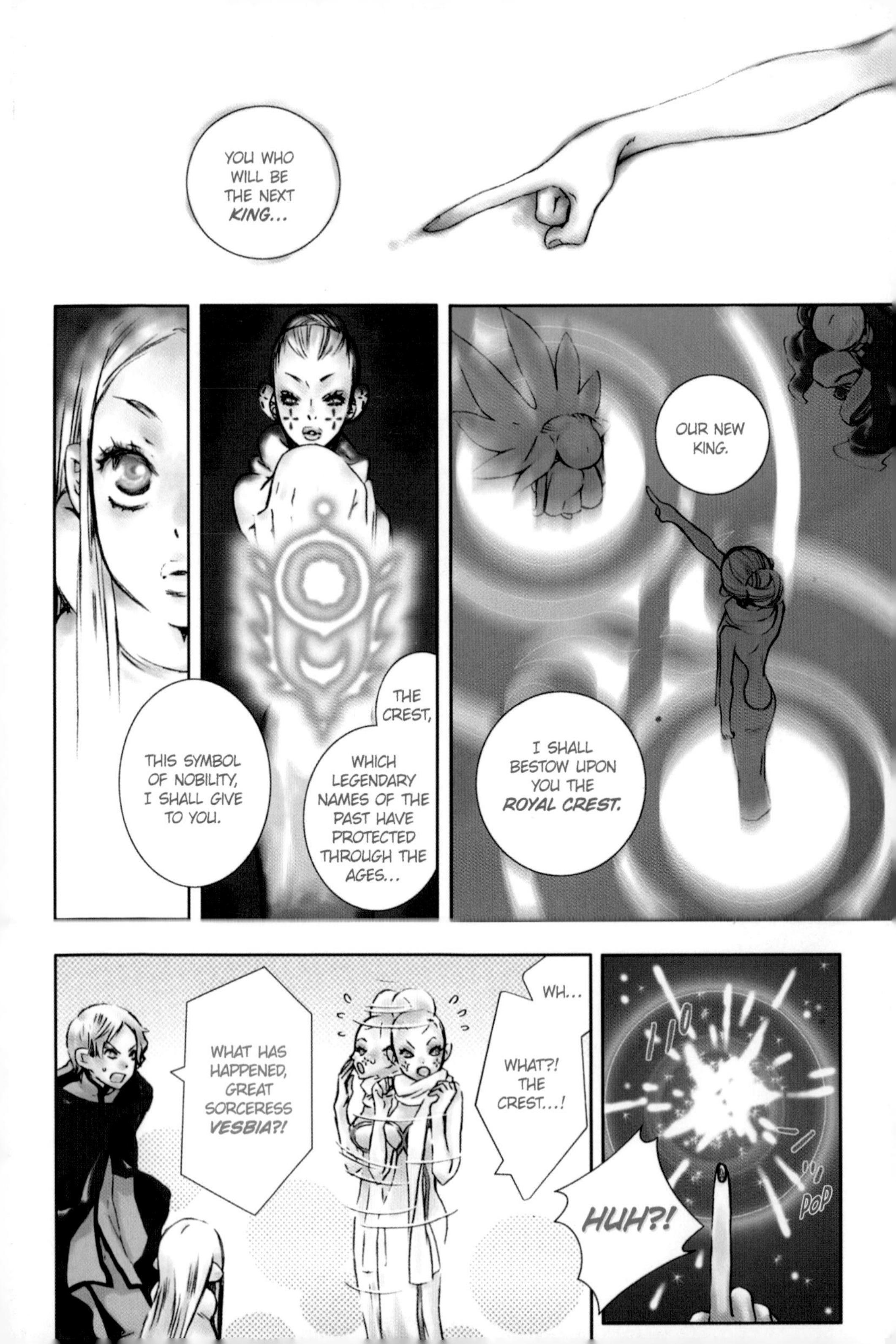
YOU WHO WILL BE THE NEXT KING...
OUR NEW KING.
I SHALL BESTOW UPON YOU THE ROYAL CREST.
THE CREST,
WHICH LEGENDARY NAMES OF THE PAST HAVE PROTECTED THROUGH THE AGES...
THIS SYMBOL OF NOBILITY, I SHALL GIVE TO YOU.
POP
HUH?!
WH...
WHAT?! THE CREST...!
WHAT HAS HAPPENED, GREAT SORCERESS VESBIA?!

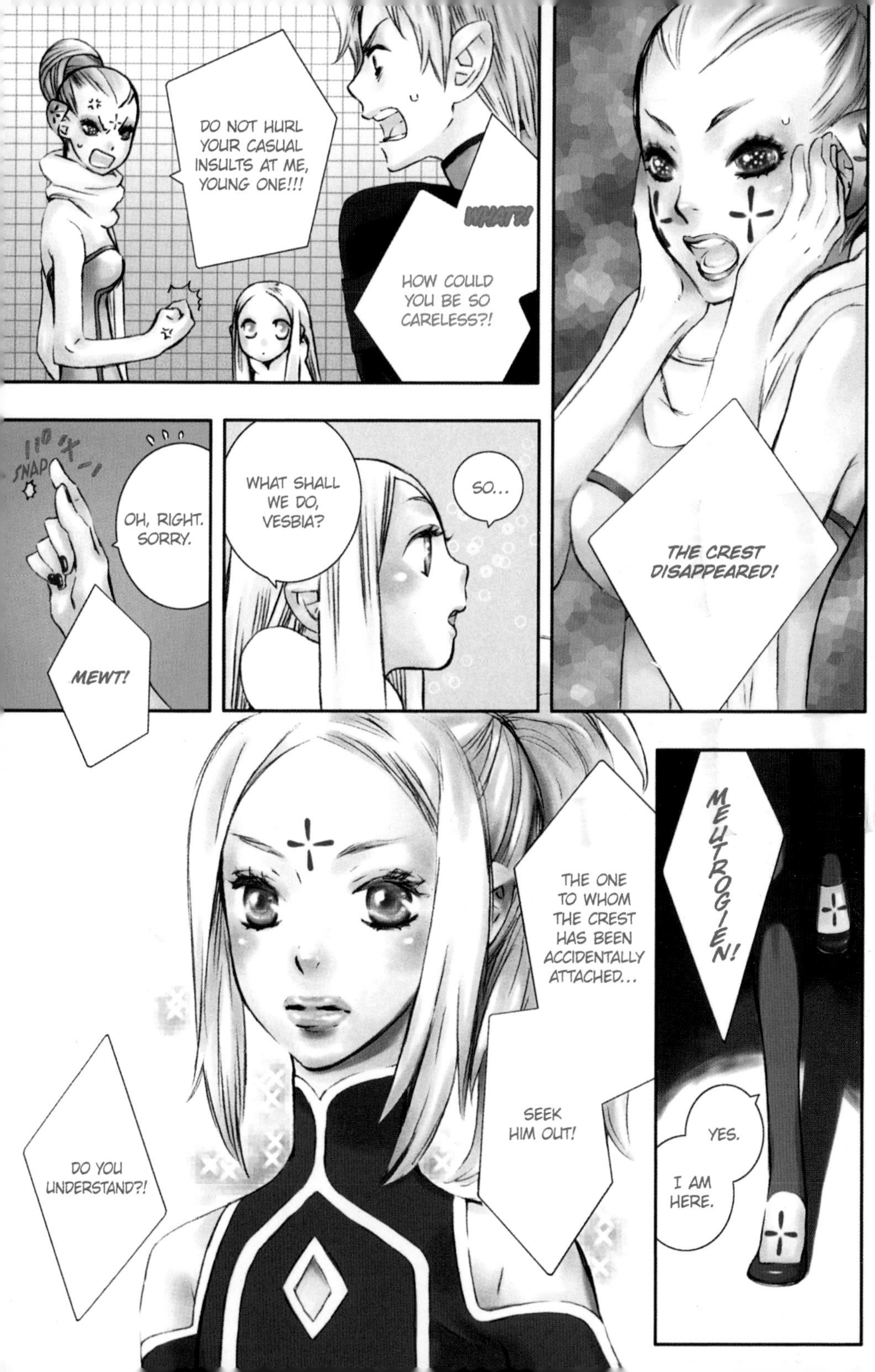
THE CREST DISAPPEARED!
WHAT?!
HOW COULD YOU BE SO CARELESS?!
DO NOT HURL YOUR CASUAL INSULTS AT ME, YOUNG ONE!!!
SO...
WHAT SHALL WE DO, VESBIA?
OH, RIGHT. SORRY.
SNAP
MEWT!
MEUTROGIEN!
YES.
I AM HERE.
THE ONE TO WHOM THE CREST HAS BEEN ACCIDENTALLY ATTACHED...
SEEK HIM OUT!
DO YOU UNDERSTAND?!

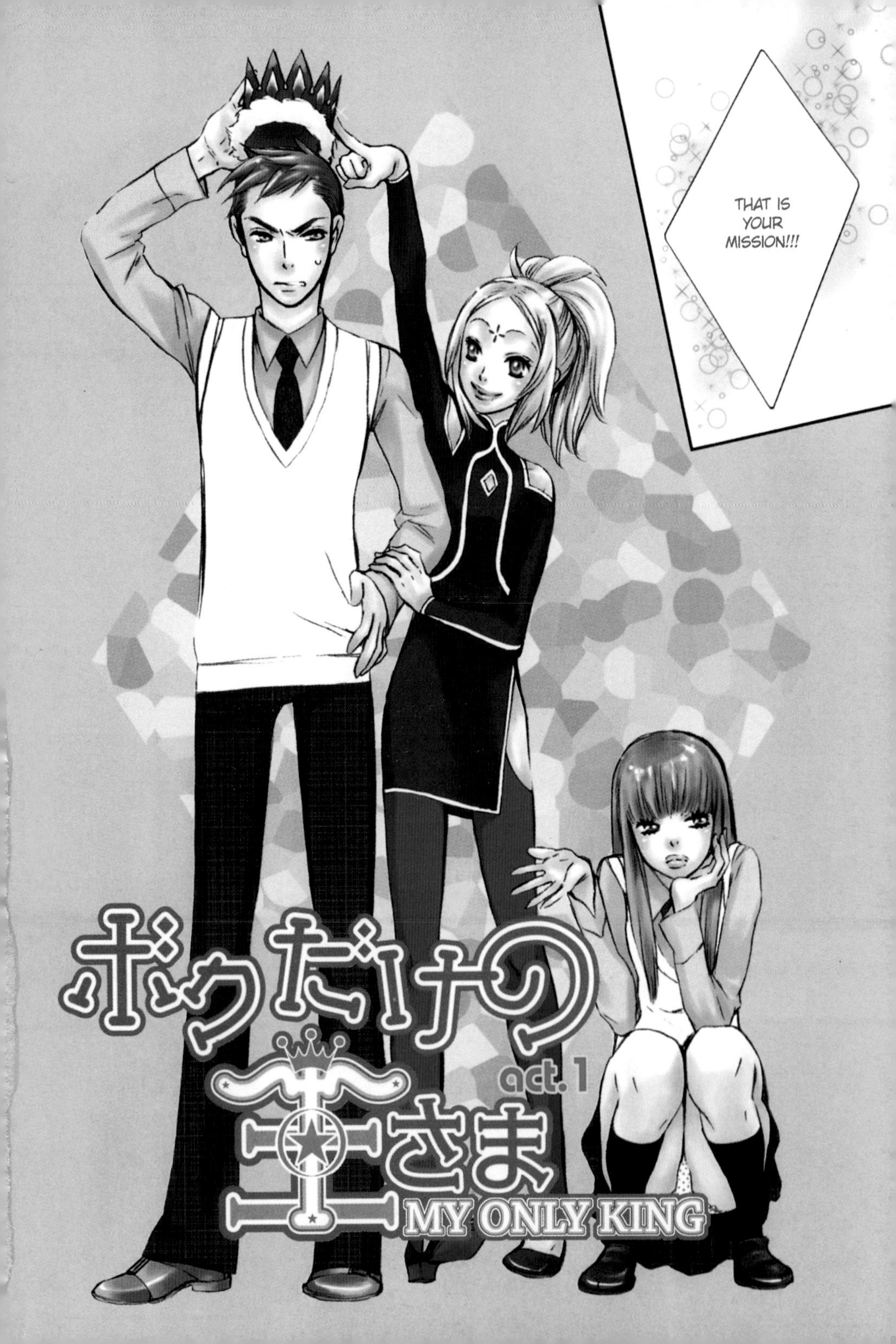
THAT IS YOUR MISSION!!!
ボクだけの王さま
act.1
MY ONLY KING

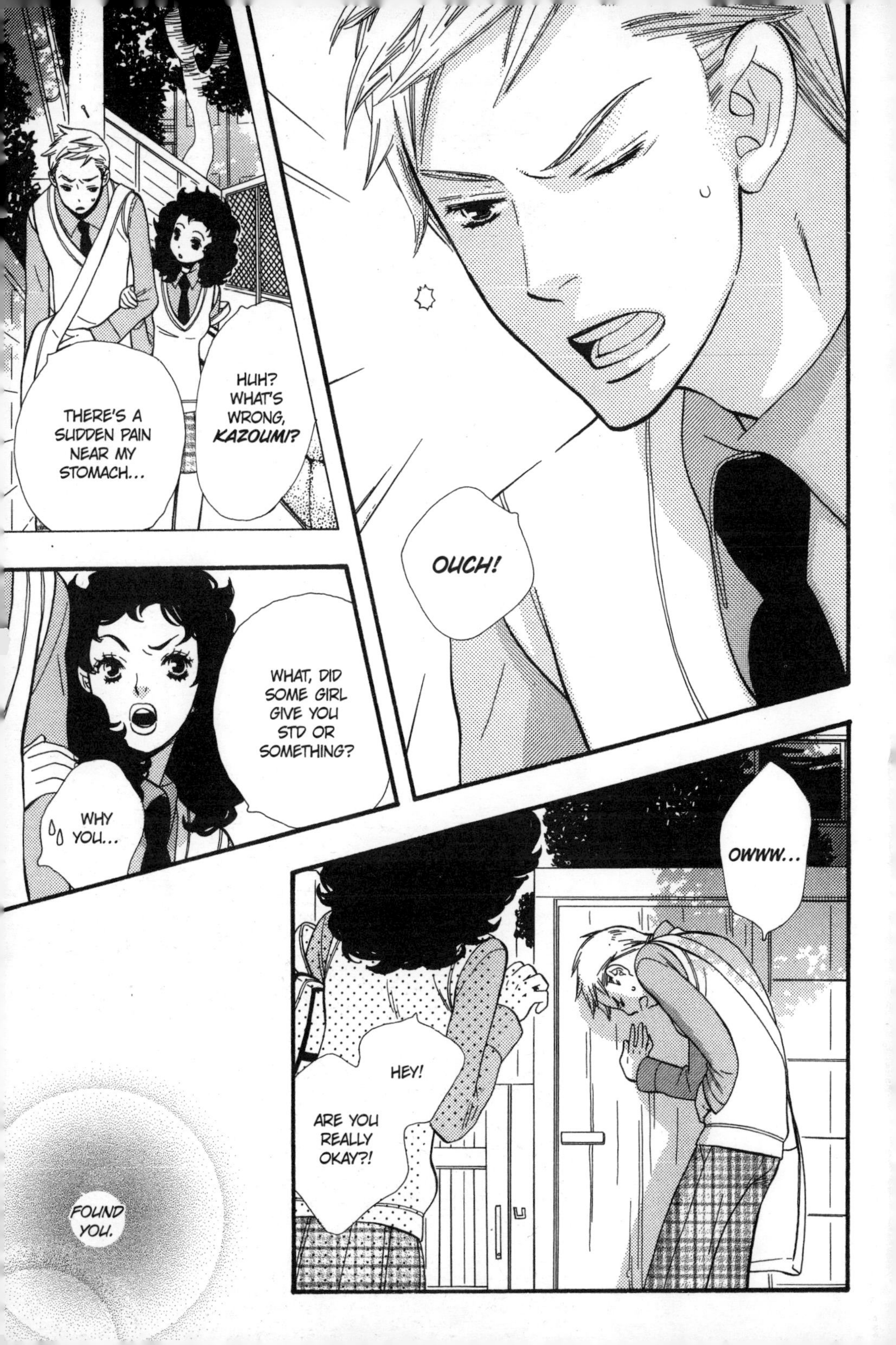
OUCH!
HUH? WHAT'S WRONG, KAZOUMI?
THERE'S A SUDDEN PAIN NEAR MY STOMACH...
WHAT, DID SOME GIRL GIVE YOU STD OR SOMETHING?
WHY YOU...
OWWW...
HEY!
ARE YOU REALLY OKAY?!
FOUND YOU.

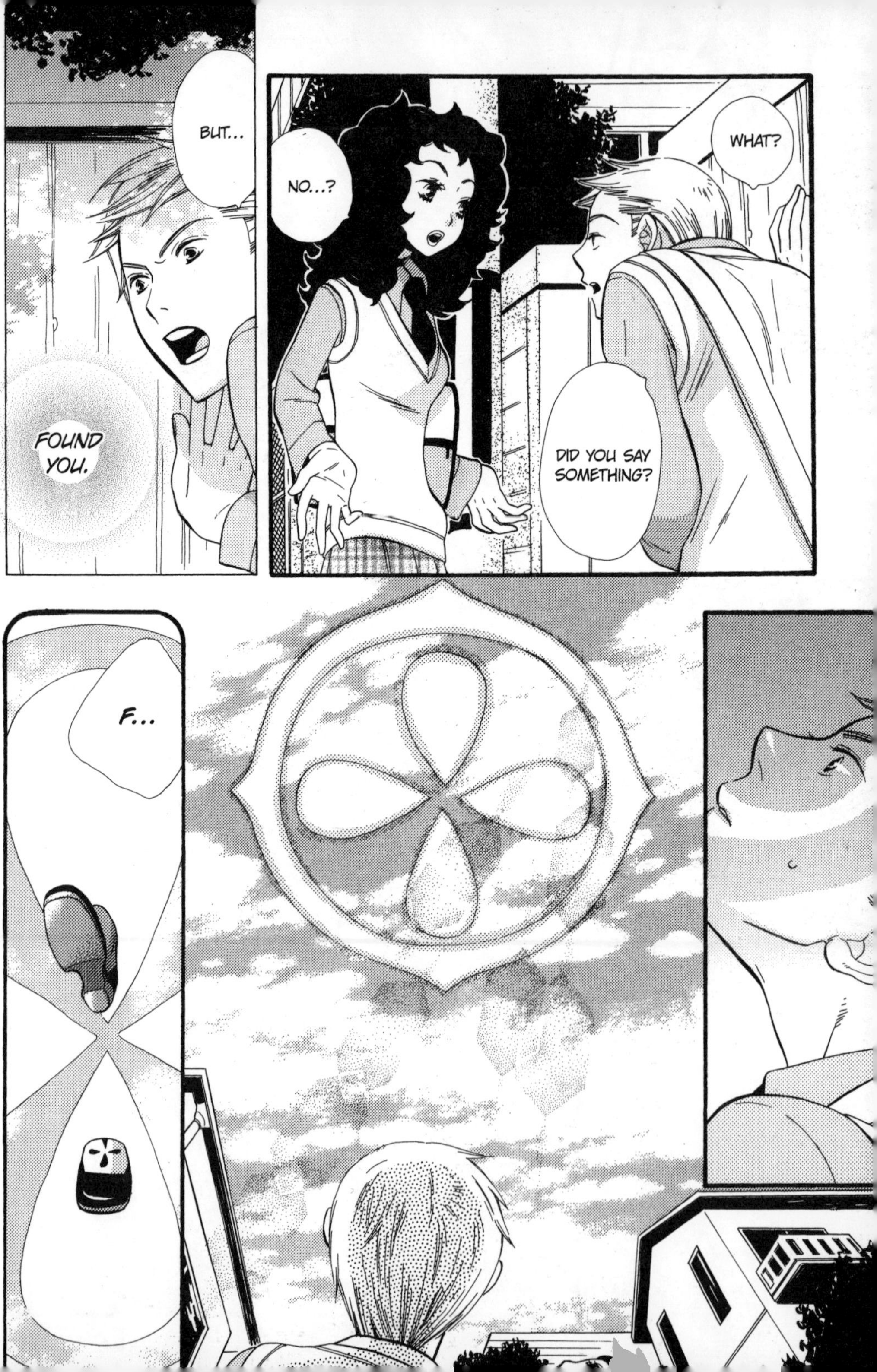
WHAT?
DID YOU SAY SOMETHING?
NO...?
BUT...
FOUND YOU.
F...

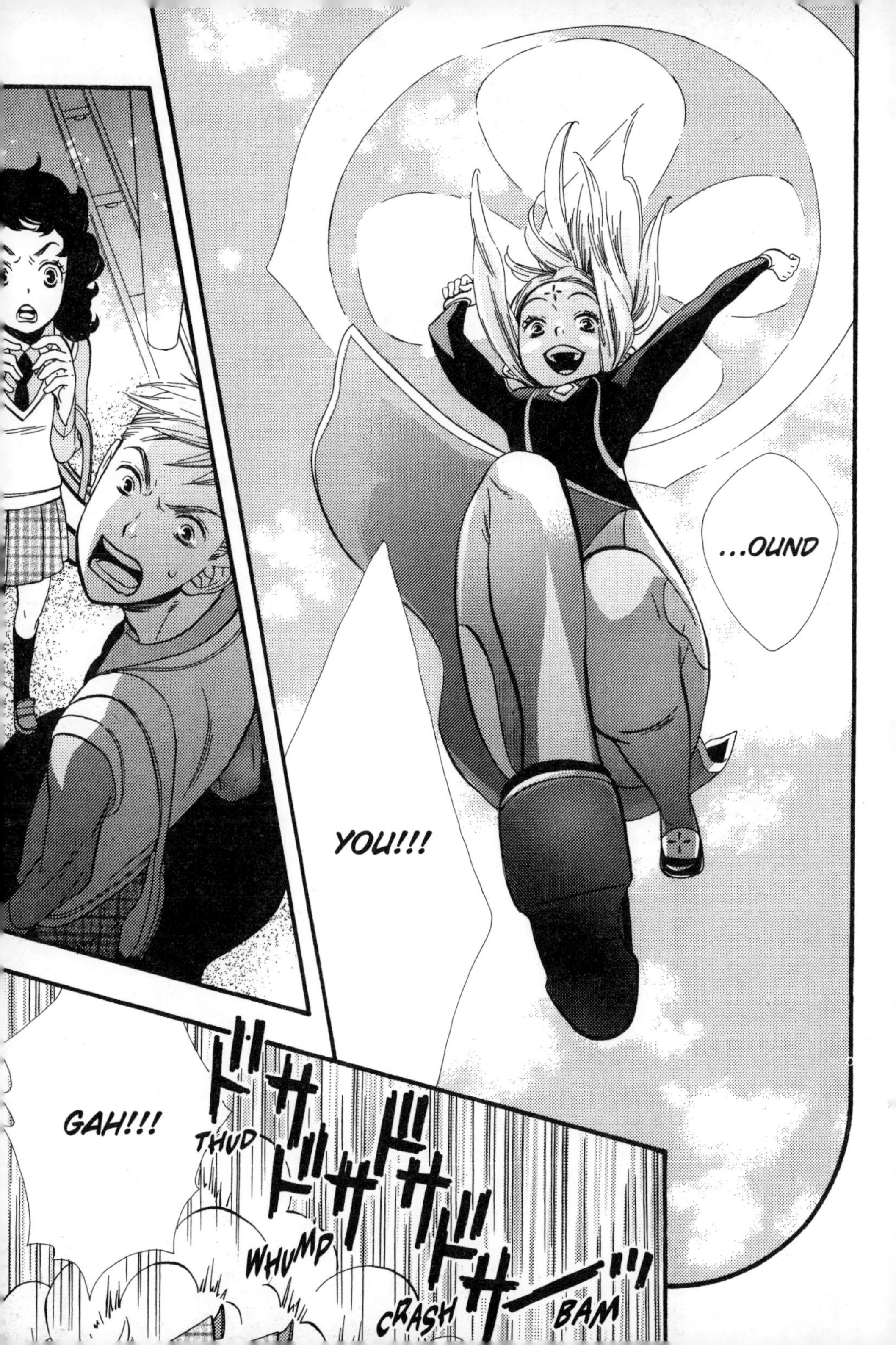
...OUND
YOU!!!
GAH!!!
THUD
WHUMP
CRASH
BAM

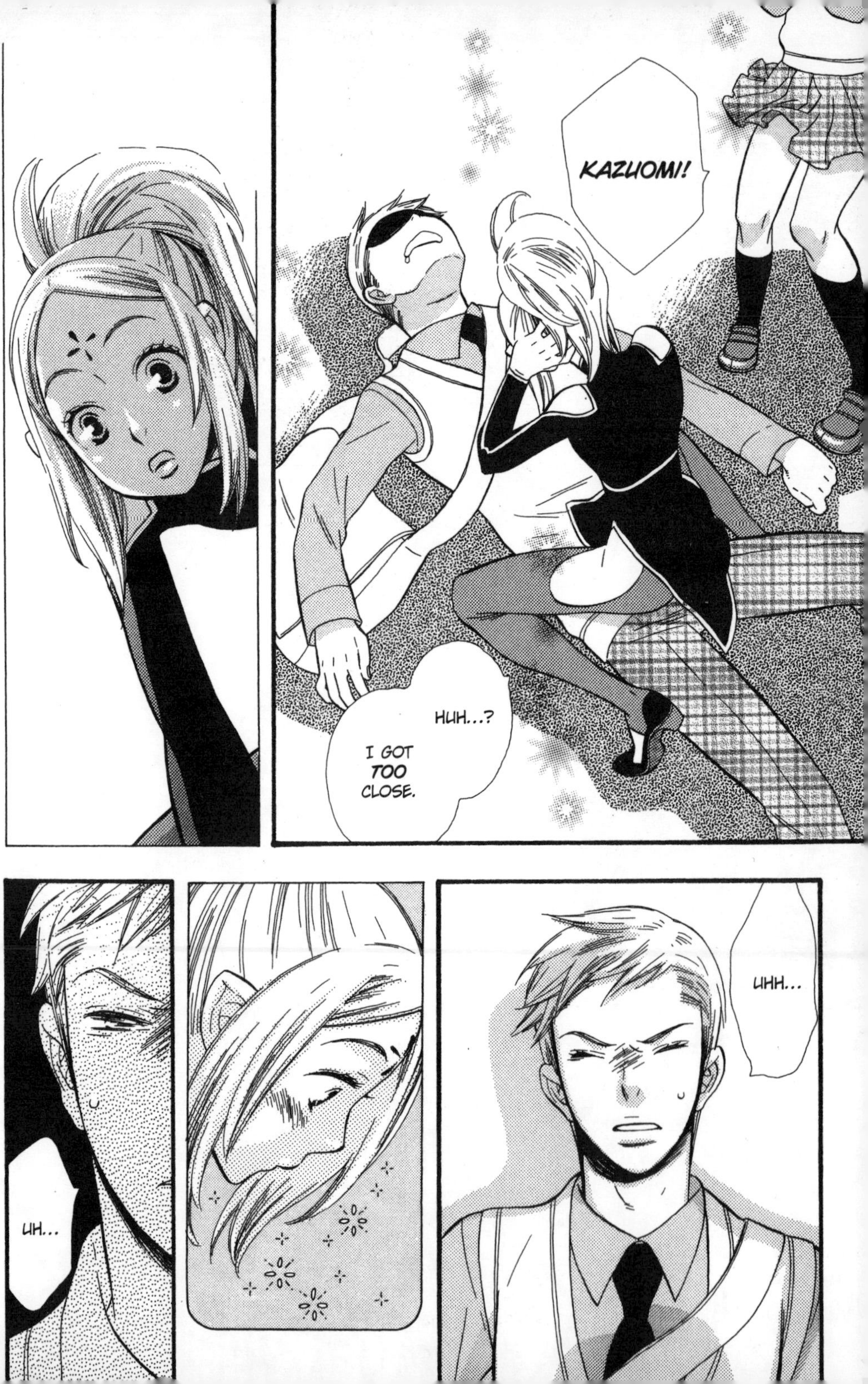
KAZUOMI!
HUH...?
I GOT TOO CLOSE.
UHH...
UH...

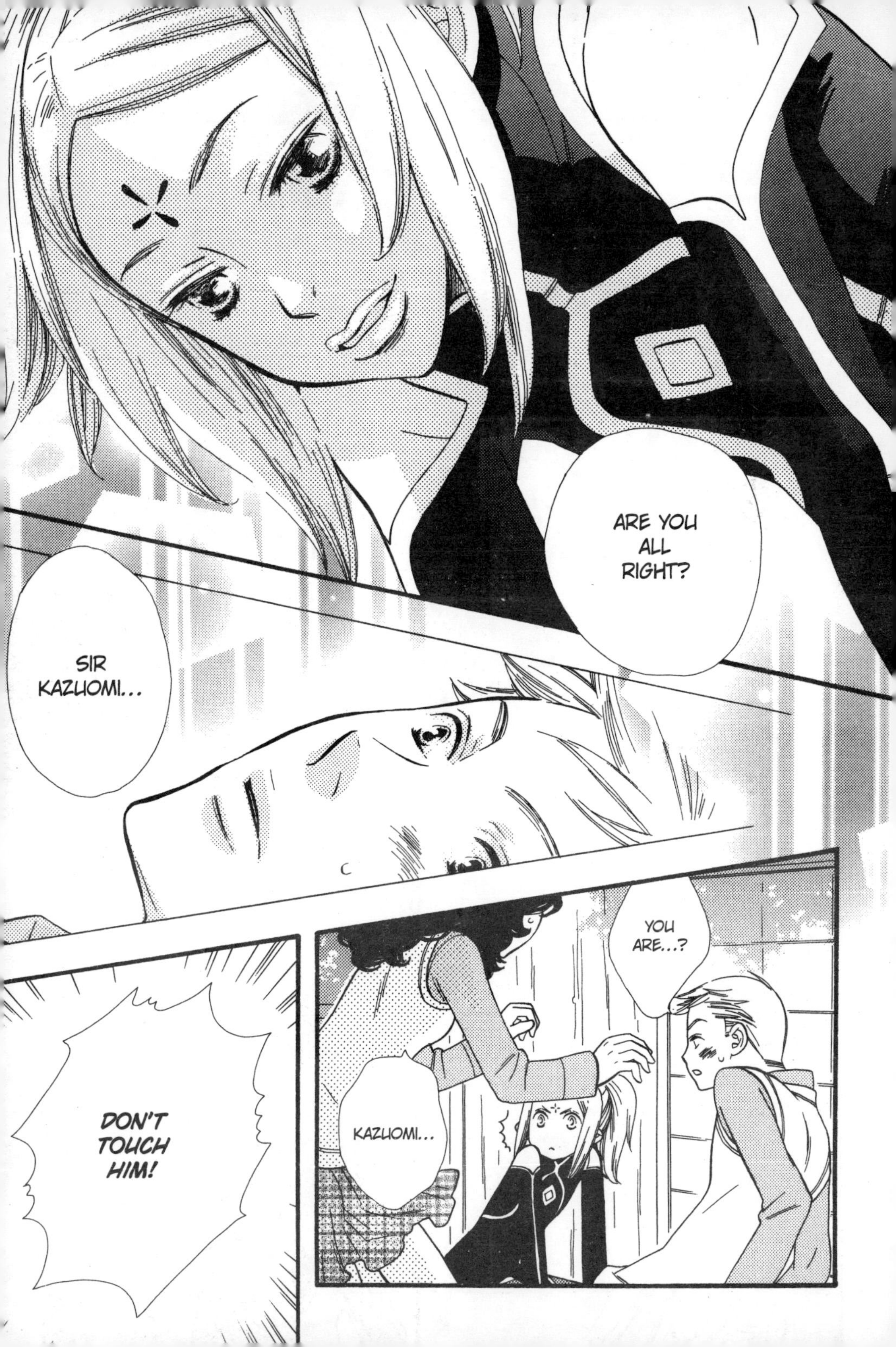
ARE YOU ALL RIGHT?
SIR KAZUOMI...
YOU ARE...?
KAZUOMI...
DON'T TOUCH HIM!

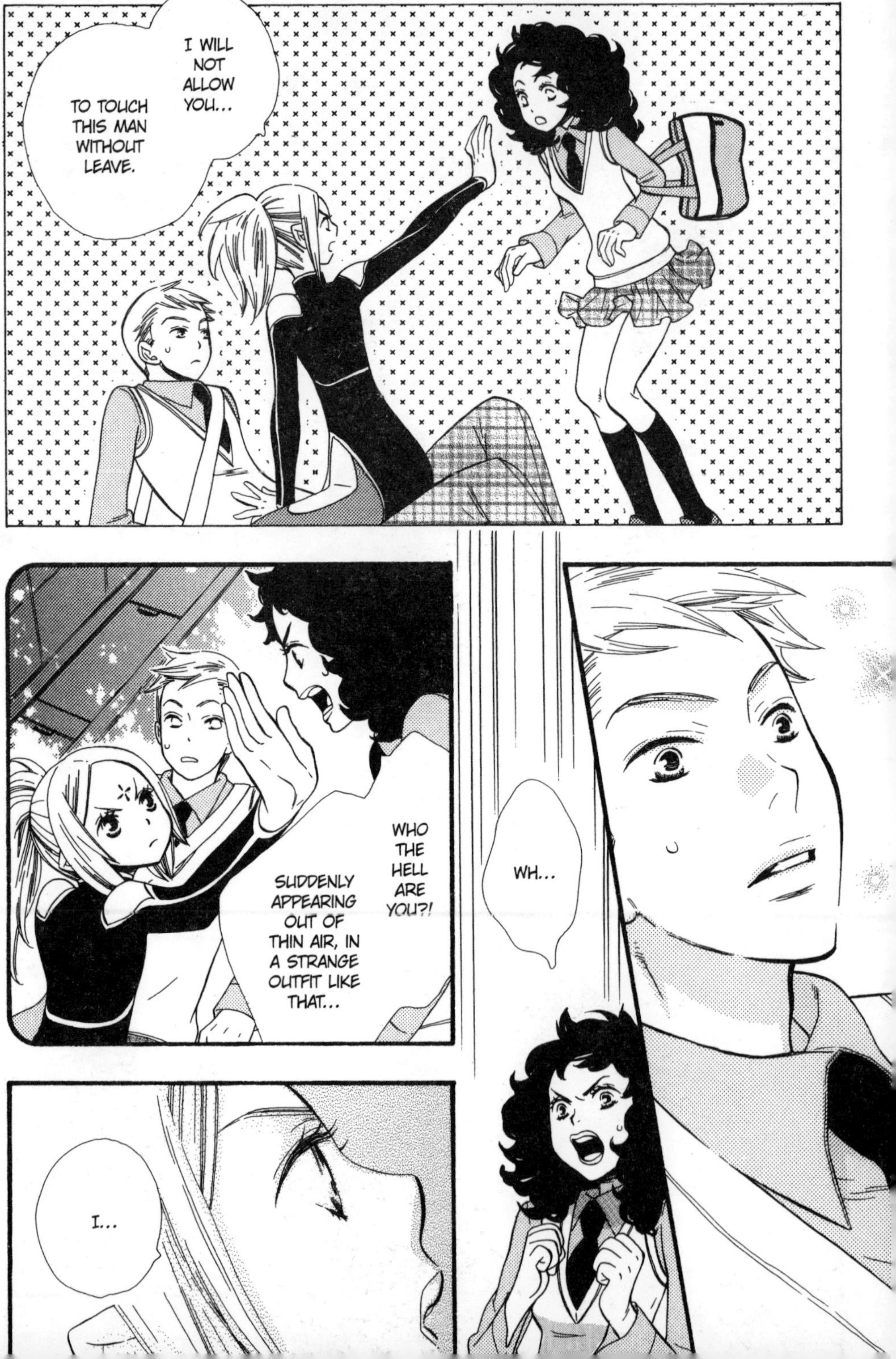
I WILL NOT ALLOW YOU...
TO TOUCH THIS MAN WITHOUT LEAVE.
WH...
WHO THE HELL ARE YOU?!
SUDDENLY APPEARING OUT OF THIN AIR, IN A STRANGE OUTFIT LIKE THAT...
I...

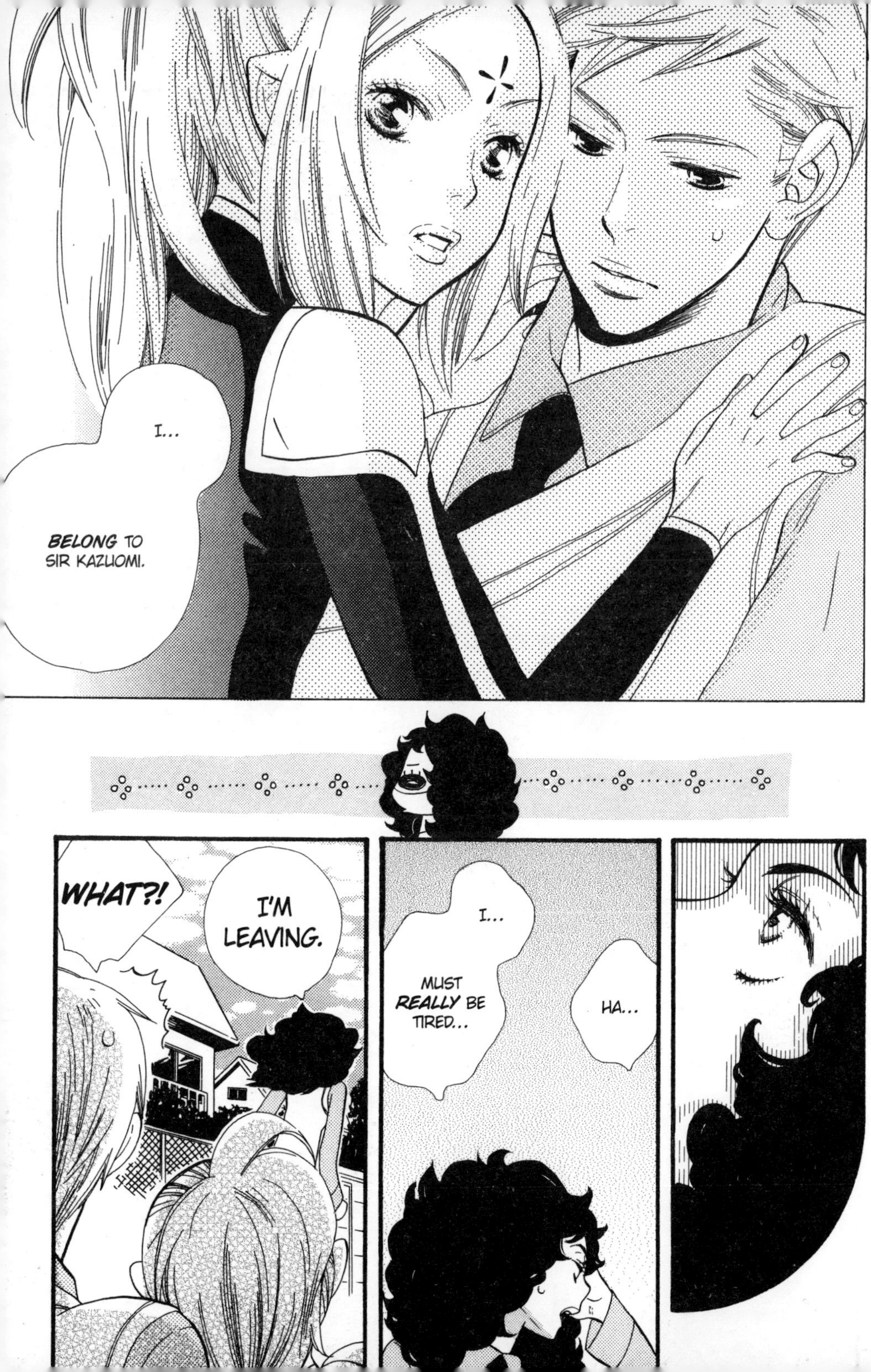
I...
BELONG TO SIR KAZUOMI.
I...
MUST REALLY BE TIRED...
HA...
I'M LEAVING.
WHAT?!

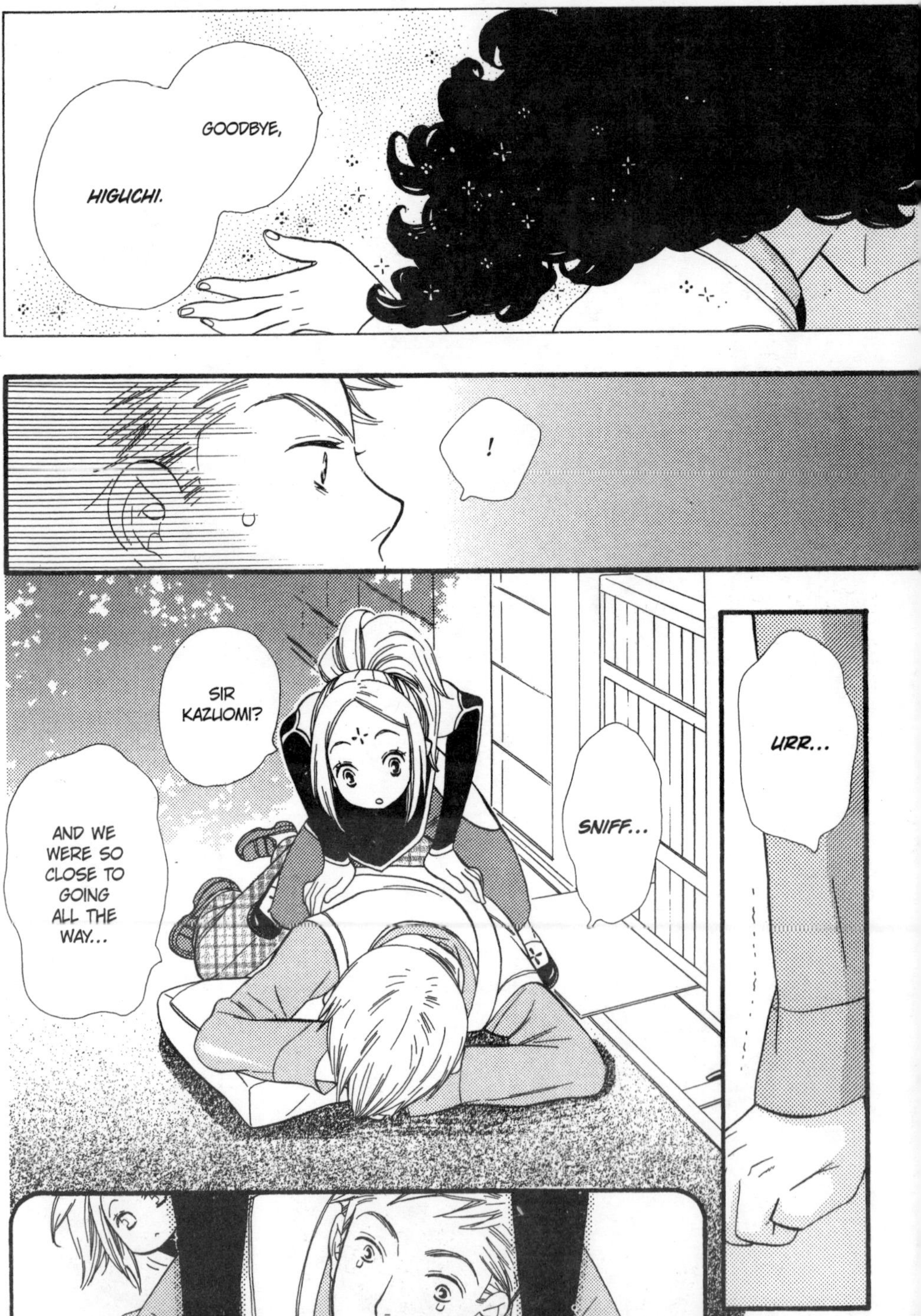
GOODBYE, HIGUCHI.
!
URR...
SNIFF...
SIR KAZUOMI?
AND WE WERE SO CLOSE TO GOING ALL THE WAY...

WHAT ARE YOU DOING, BIG BRO?

LYING IN THE STREET...

MAKOTO...

SORRY TO HAVE DELAYED MY INTRO-DUCTION.

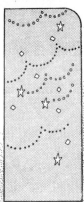

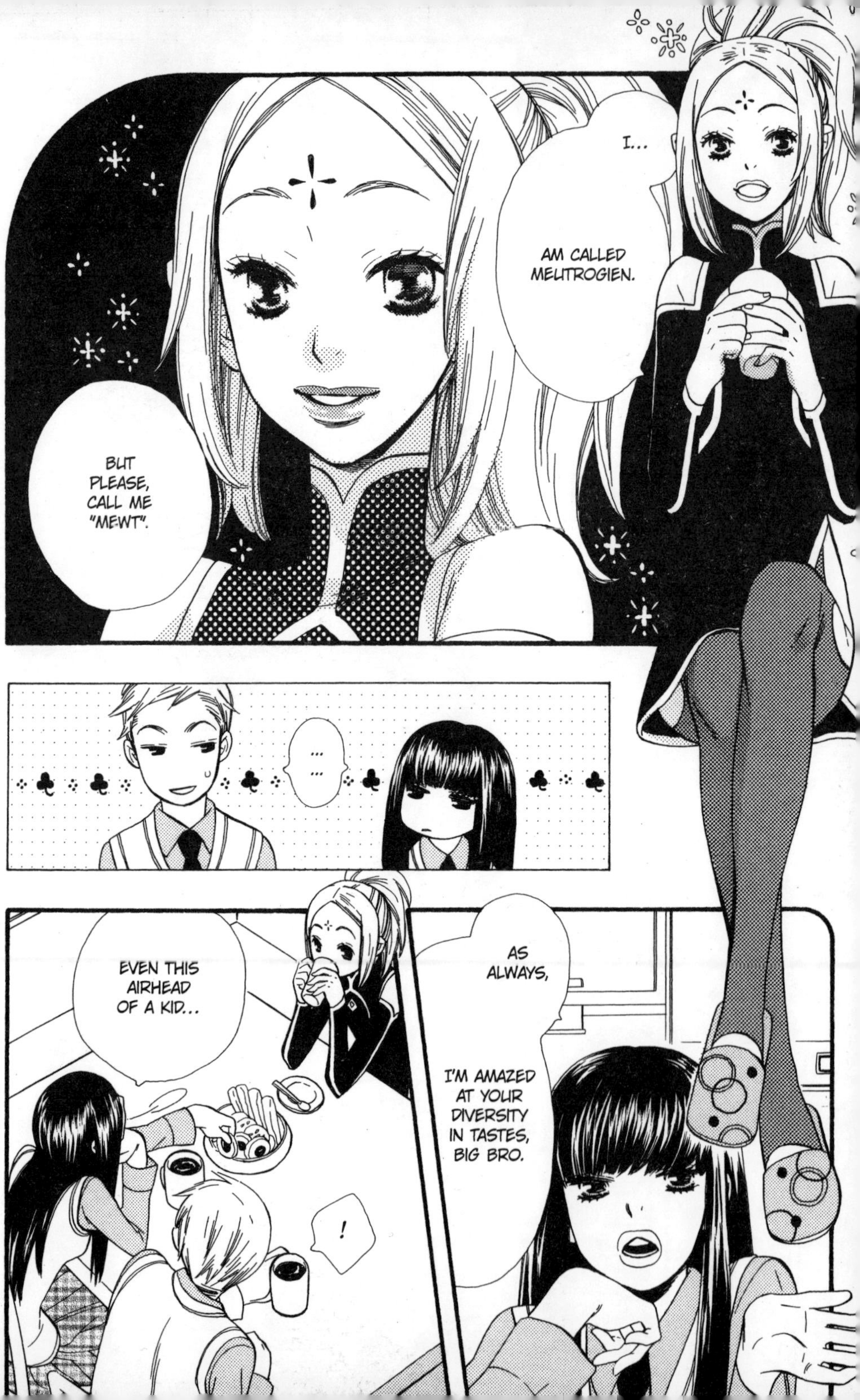
I...
AM CALLED MEUTROGIEN.
BUT PLEASE, CALL ME "MEWT".
... ...
AS ALWAYS,
I'M AMAZED AT YOUR DIVERSITY IN TASTES, BIG BRO.
EVEN THIS AIRHEAD OF A KID...
!

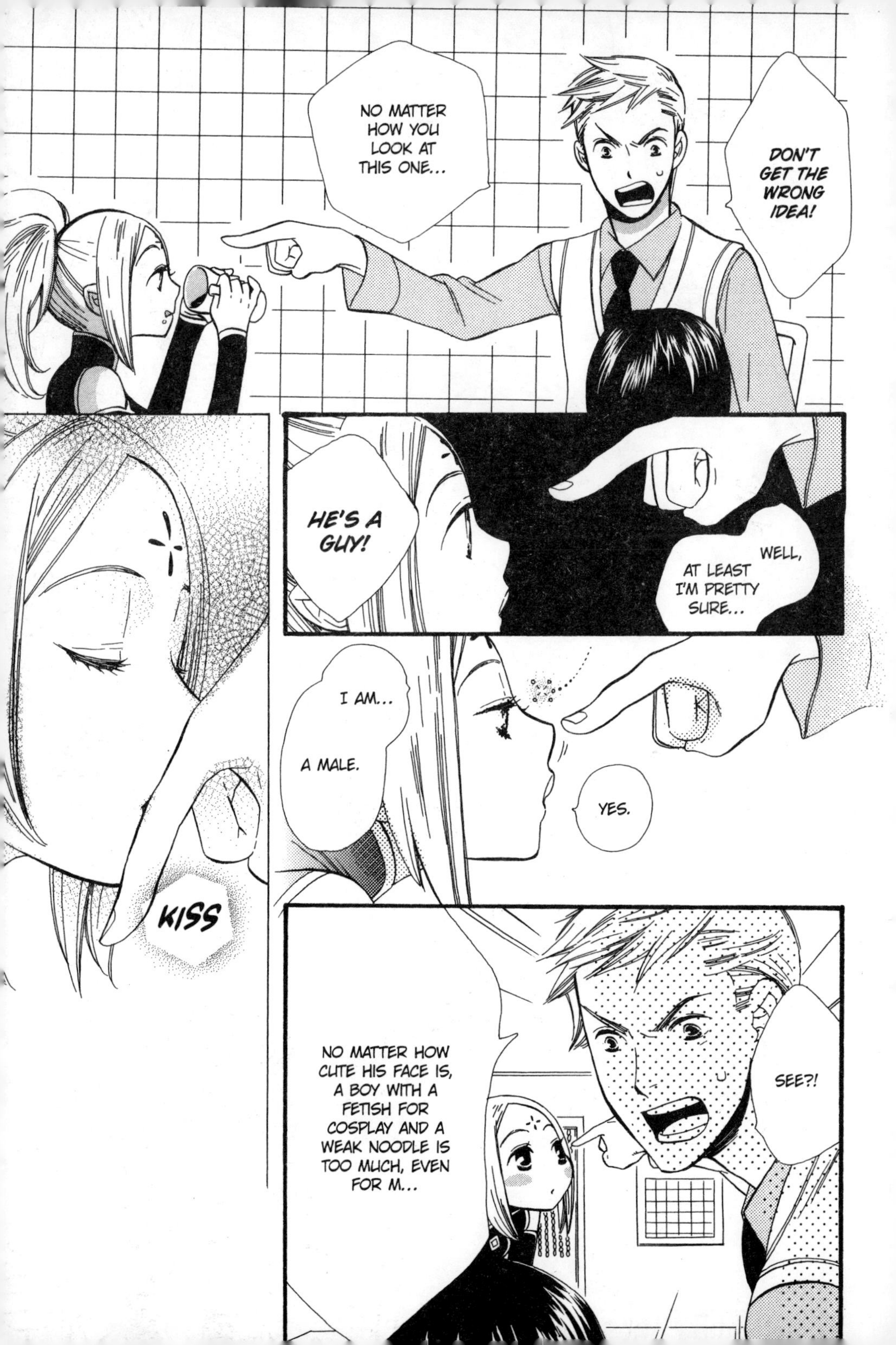
DON'T GET THE WRONG IDEA!
NO MATTER HOW YOU LOOK AT THIS ONE...
HE'S A GUY!
WELL, AT LEAST I'M PRETTY SURE...
YES.
I AM...
A MALE.
KISS
SEE?!
NO MATTER HOW CUTE HIS FACE IS, A BOY WITH A FETISH FOR COSPLAY AND A WEAK NOODLE IS TOO MUCH, EVEN FOR M...

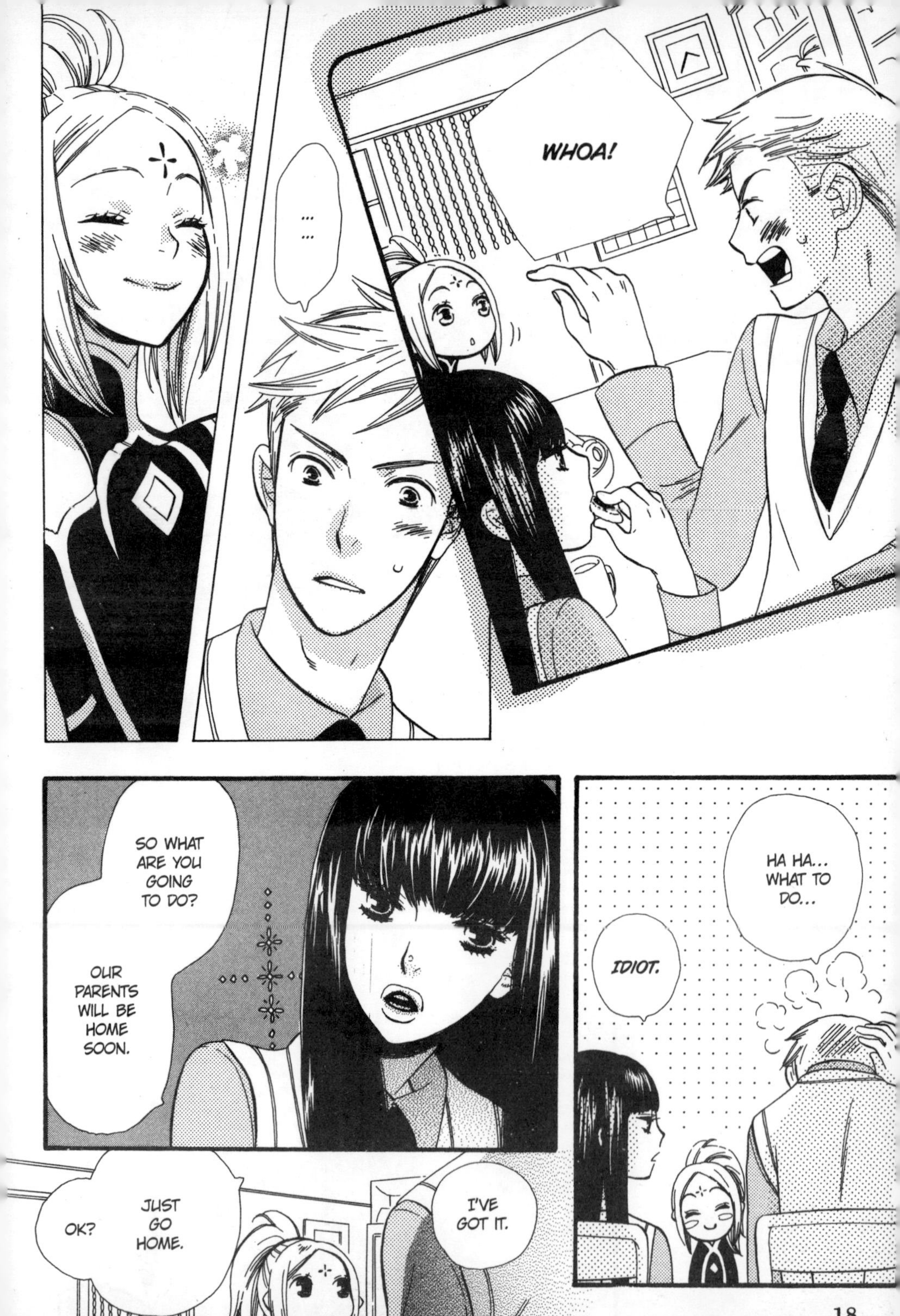
WHOA!
... ...
HA HA... WHAT TO DO...
IDIOT.
SO WHAT ARE YOU GOING TO DO?
OUR PARENTS WILL BE HOME SOON.
I'VE GOT IT.
JUST GO HOME.
OK?

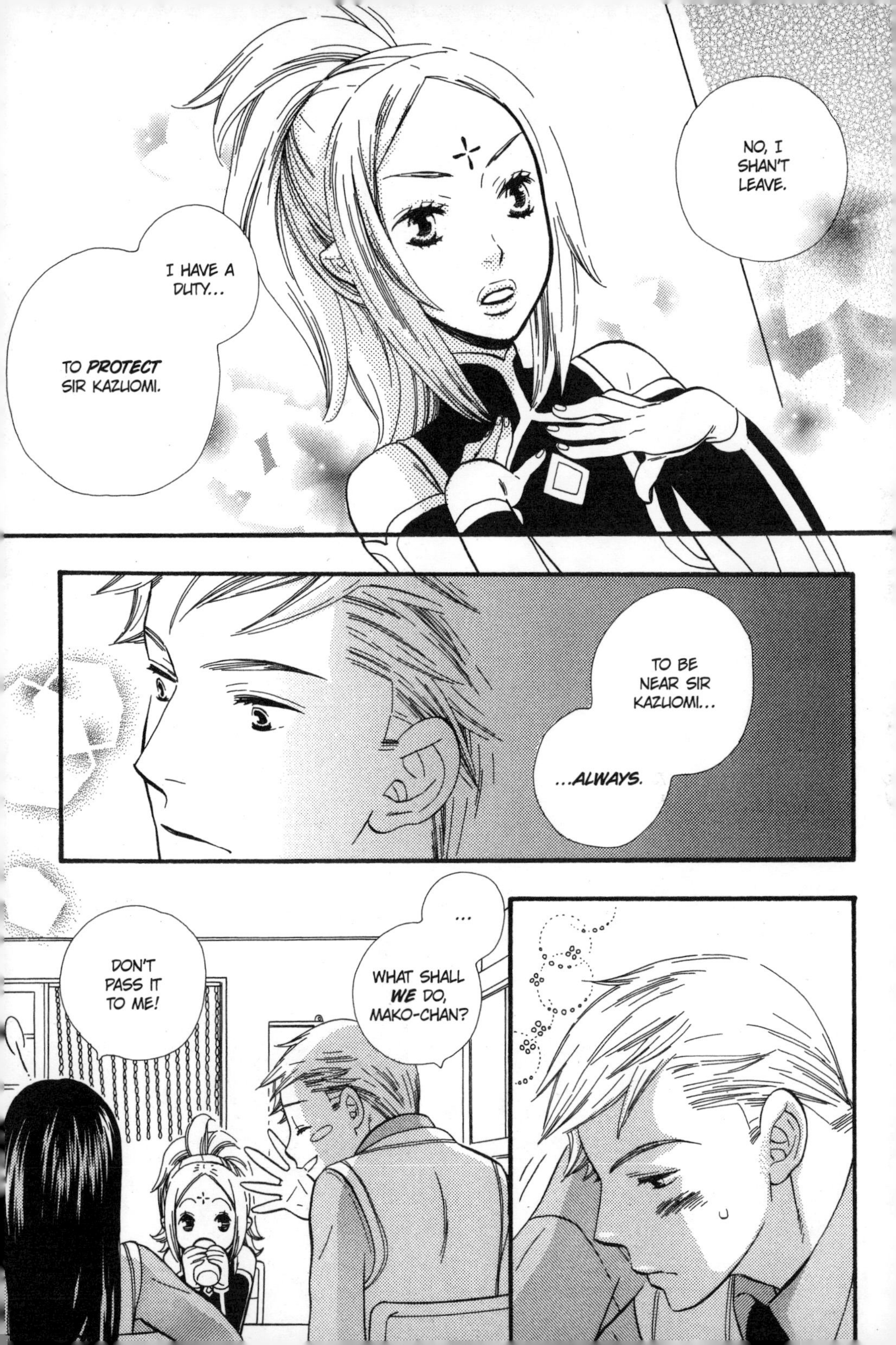
NO, I SHAN'T LEAVE.
I HAVE A DUTY...
TO *PROTECT* SIR KAZUOMI.
TO BE NEAR SIR KAZUOMI...
...*ALWAYS*.
...
WHAT SHALL *WE* DO, MAKO-CHAN?
DON'T PASS IT TO ME!

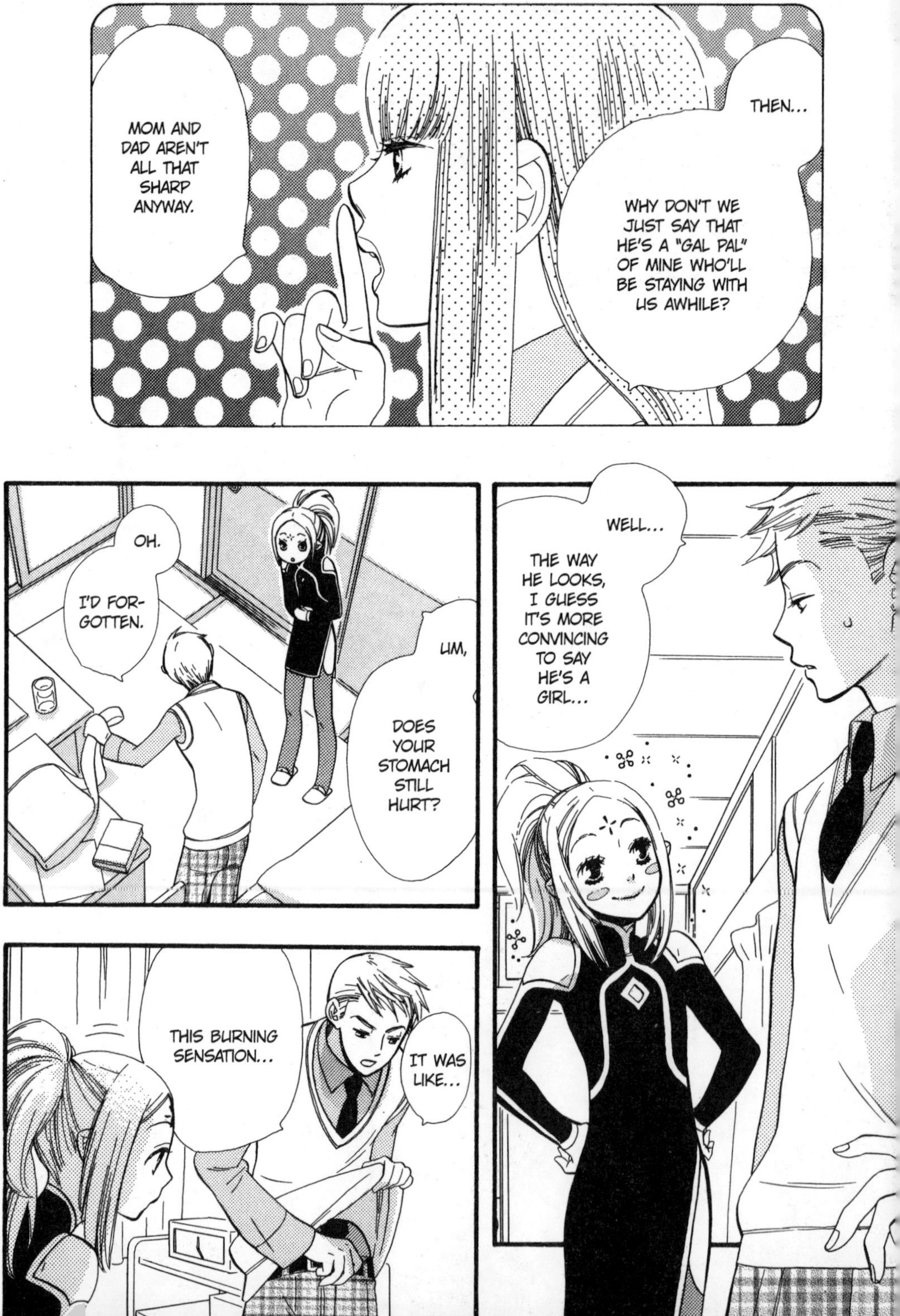
THEN...
WHY DON'T WE JUST SAY THAT HE'S A "GAL PAL" OF MINE WHO'LL BE STAYING WITH US AWHILE?
MOM AND DAD AREN'T ALL THAT SHARP ANYWAY.
WELL...
THE WAY HE LOOKS, I GUESS IT'S MORE CONVINCING TO SAY HE'S A GIRL...
UM,
DOES YOUR STOMACH STILL HURT?
OH.
I'D FOR-GOTTEN.
IT WAS LIKE...
THIS BURNING SENSATION...

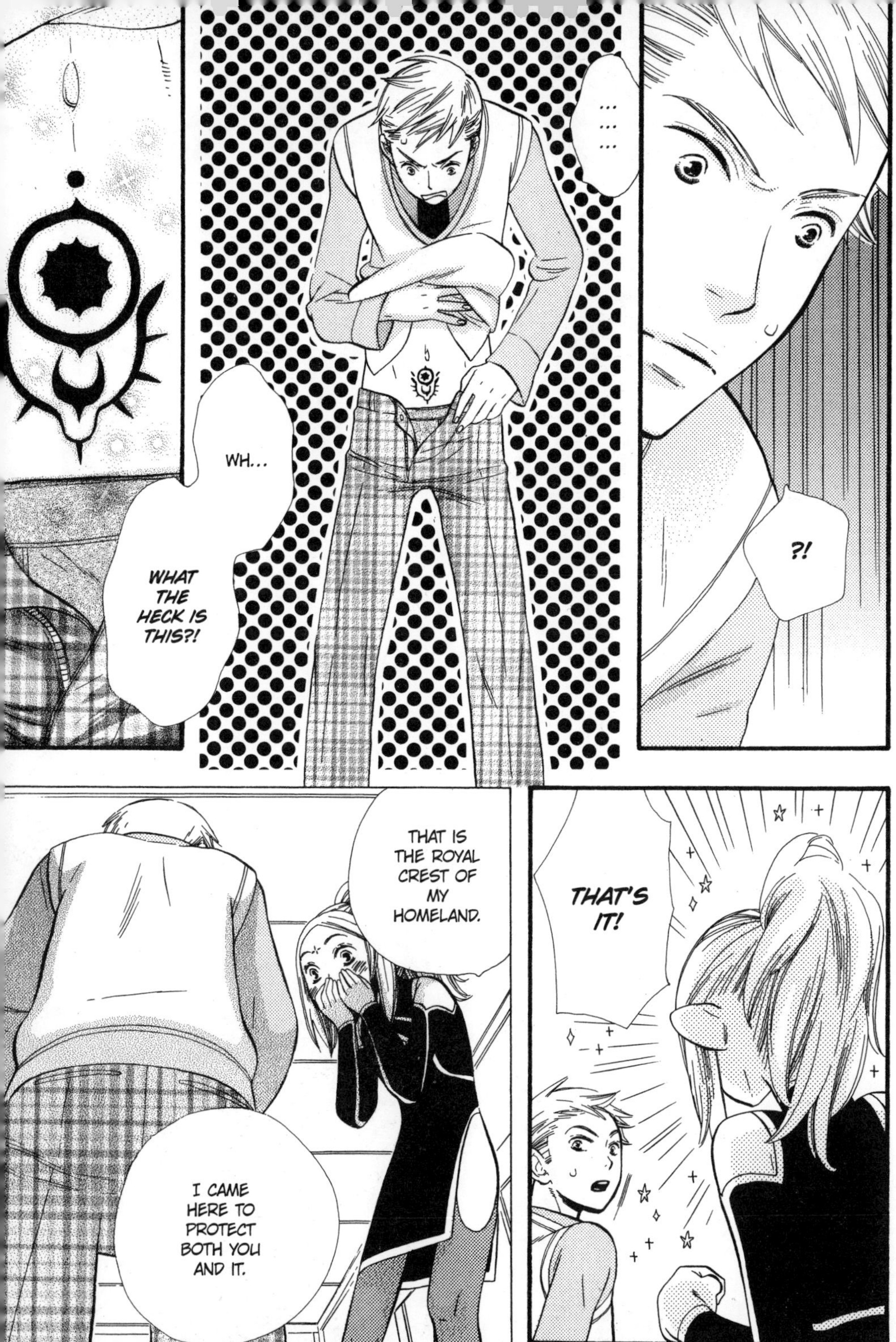
……
?!
WH…
WHAT THE HECK IS THIS?!
THAT'S IT!
THAT IS THE ROYAL CREST OF MY HOMELAND.
I CAME HERE TO PROTECT BOTH YOU AND IT.

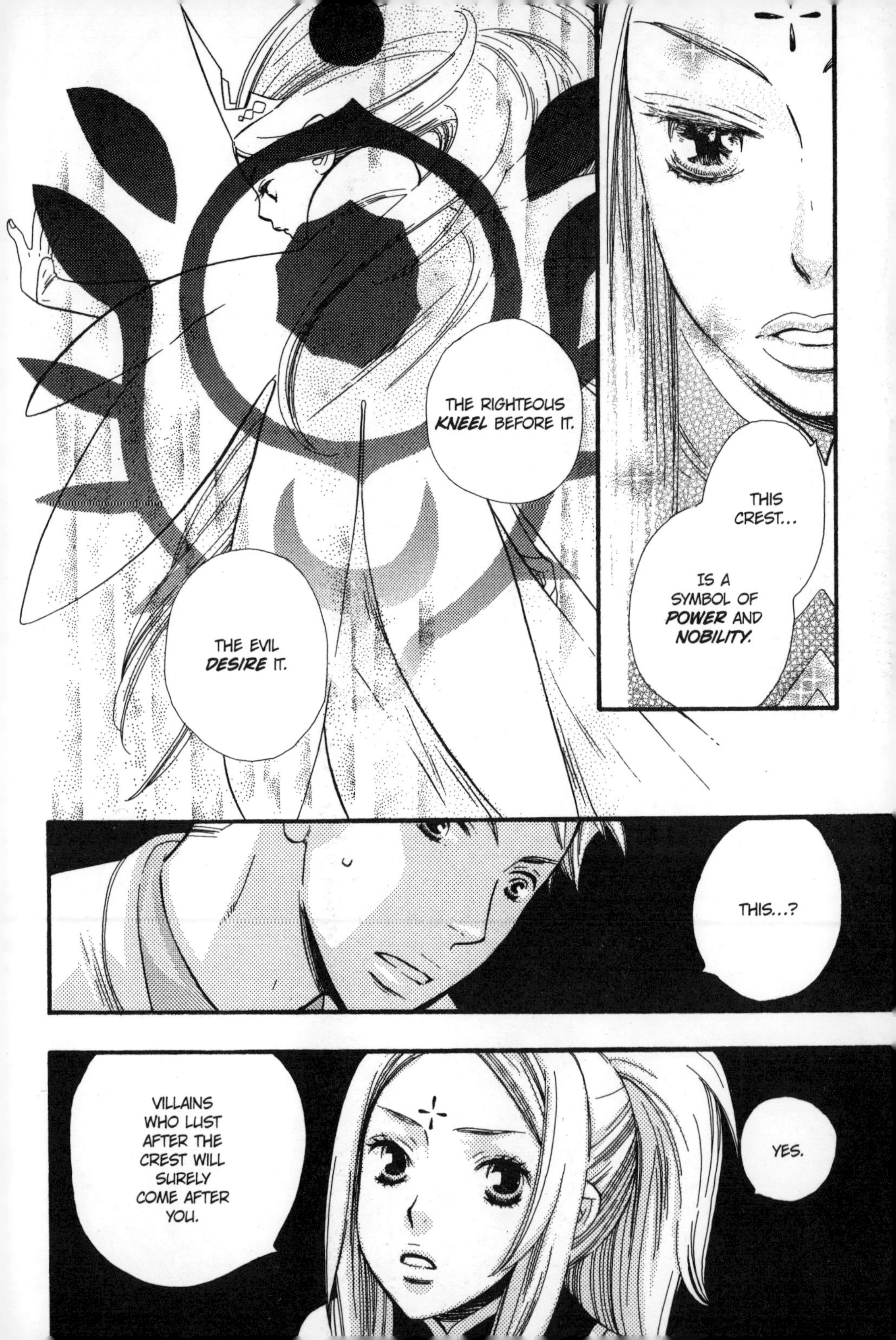
THIS CREST...
IS A SYMBOL OF POWER AND NOBILITY.
THE RIGHTEOUS KNEEL BEFORE IT.
THE EVIL DESIRE IT.
THIS...?
YES.
VILLAINS WHO LUST AFTER THE CREST WILL SURELY COME AFTER YOU.

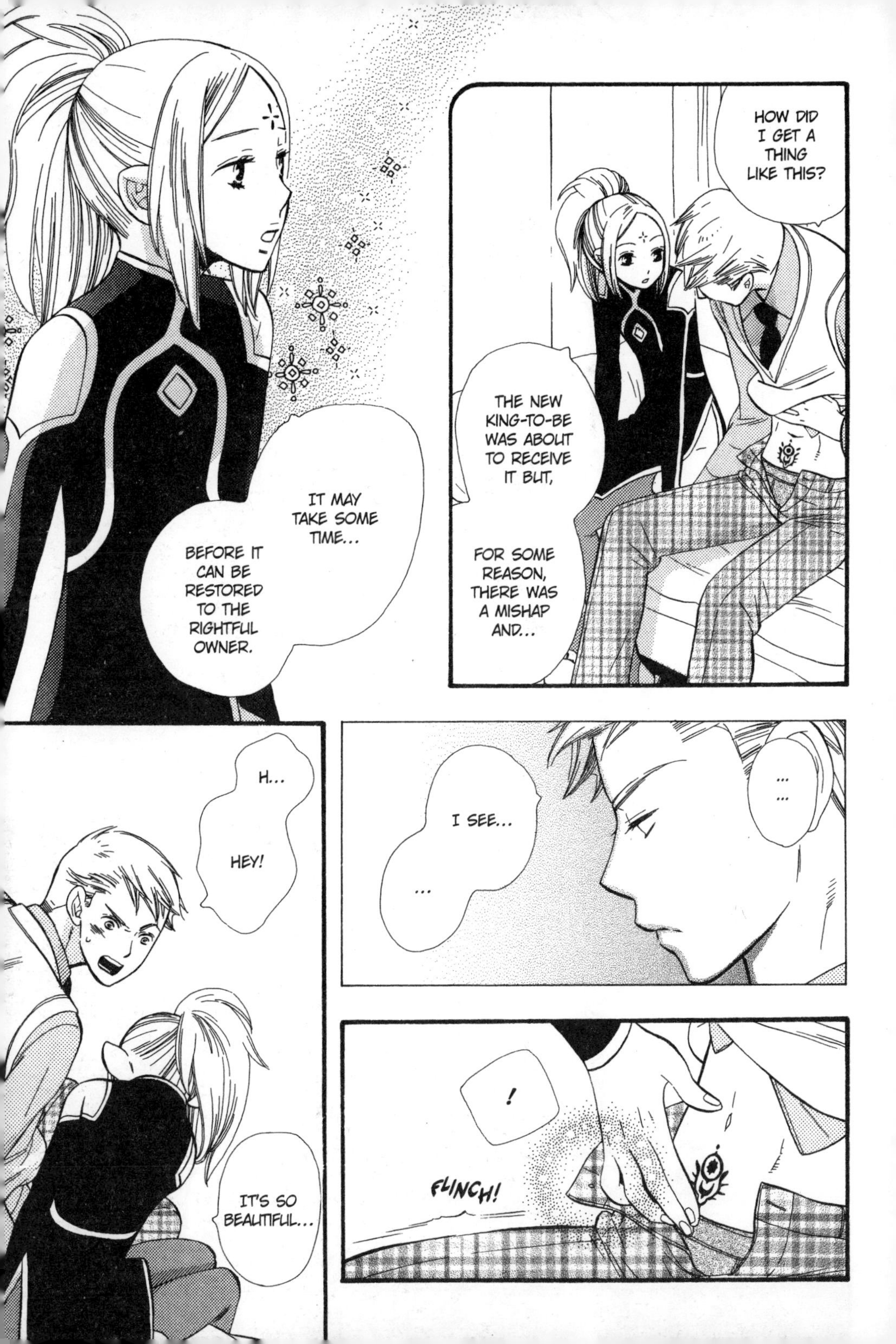
HOW DID I GET A THING LIKE THIS?
THE NEW KING-TO-BE WAS ABOUT TO RECEIVE IT BUT,
FOR SOME REASON, THERE WAS A MISHAP AND...
IT MAY TAKE SOME TIME...
BEFORE IT CAN BE RESTORED TO THE RIGHTFUL OWNER.
... ...
I SEE...
...
!
FLINCH!
H...
HEY!
IT'S SO BEAUTIFUL...

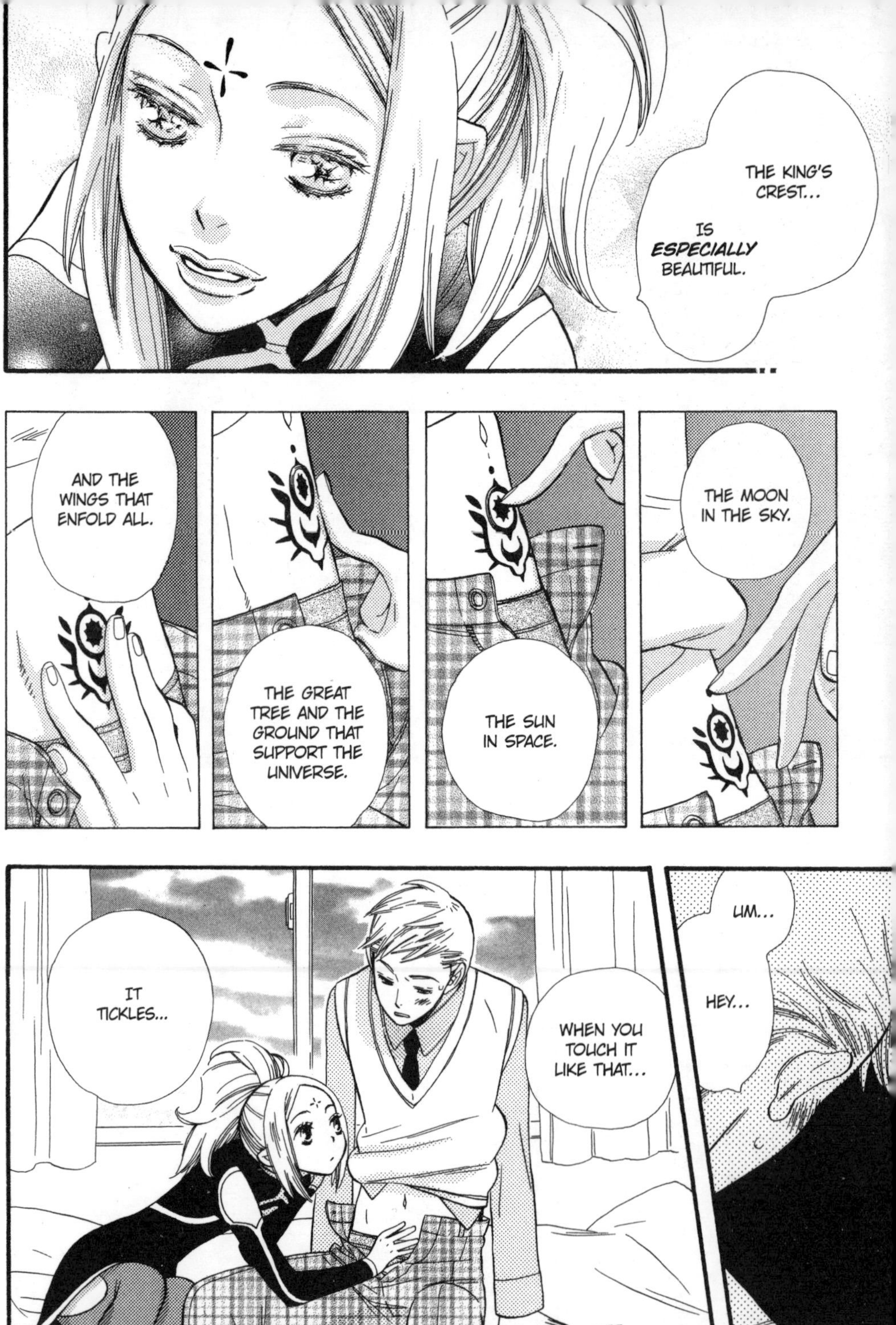
THE KING'S CREST...
IS ESPECIALLY BEAUTIFUL.
THE MOON IN THE SKY.
THE SUN IN SPACE.
THE GREAT TREE AND THE GROUND THAT SUPPORT THE UNIVERSE.
AND THE WINGS THAT ENFOLD ALL.
UM...
HEY...
WHEN YOU TOUCH IT LIKE THAT...
IT TICKLES...

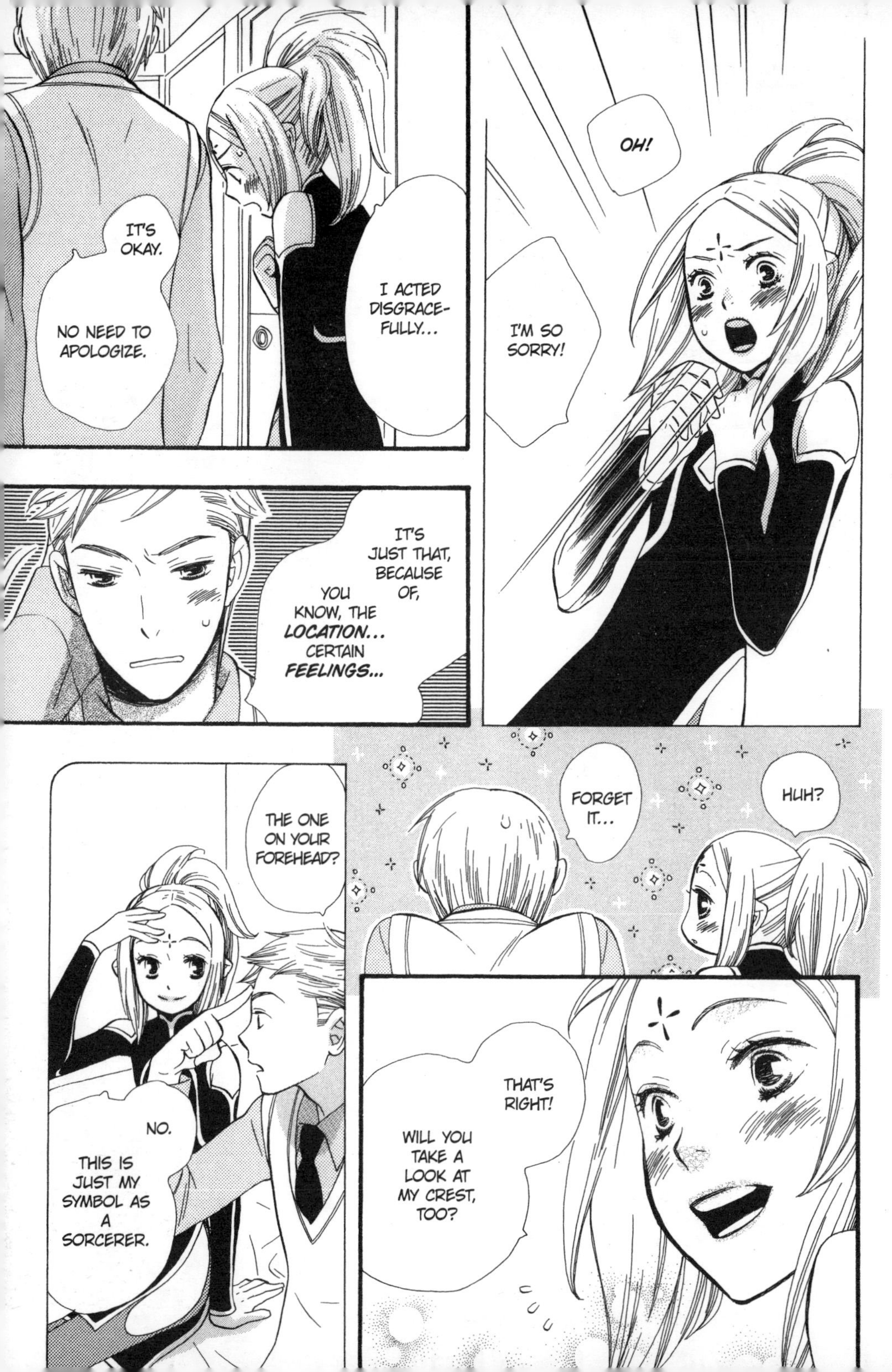
OH!
I'M SO SORRY!
I ACTED DISGRACE-FULLY...
IT'S OKAY.
NO NEED TO APOLOGIZE.
IT'S JUST THAT, BECAUSE OF,
YOU KNOW, THE **LOCATION...** CERTAIN **FEELINGS...**
HUH?
FORGET IT...
THAT'S RIGHT!
WILL YOU TAKE A LOOK AT MY CREST, TOO?
THE ONE ON YOUR FOREHEAD?
NO.
THIS IS JUST MY SYMBOL AS A SORCERER.

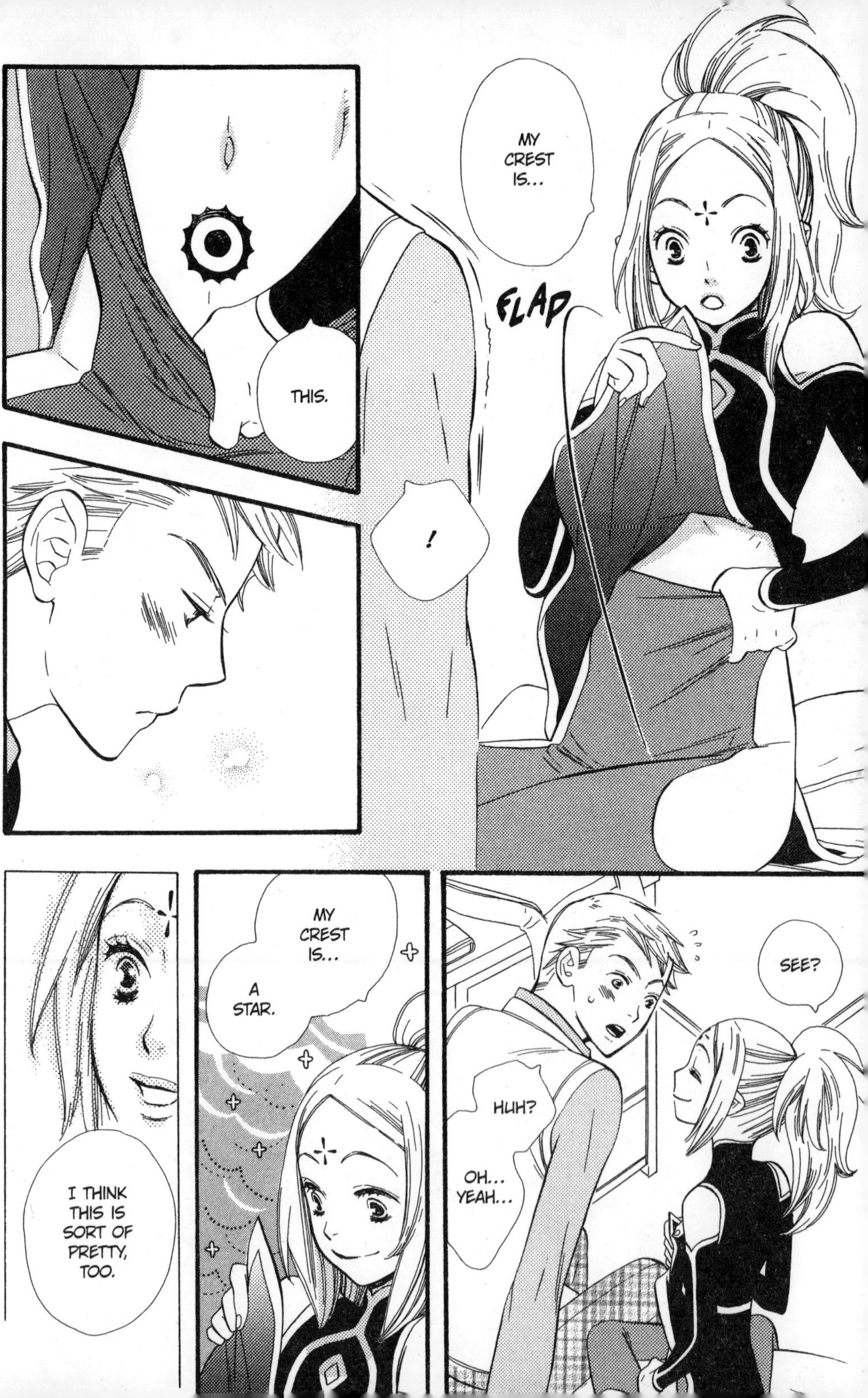
MY CREST IS...
FLAP
THIS.
!
SEE?
HUH?
OH... YEAH...
MY CREST IS...
A STAR.
I THINK THIS IS SORT OF PRETTY, TOO.

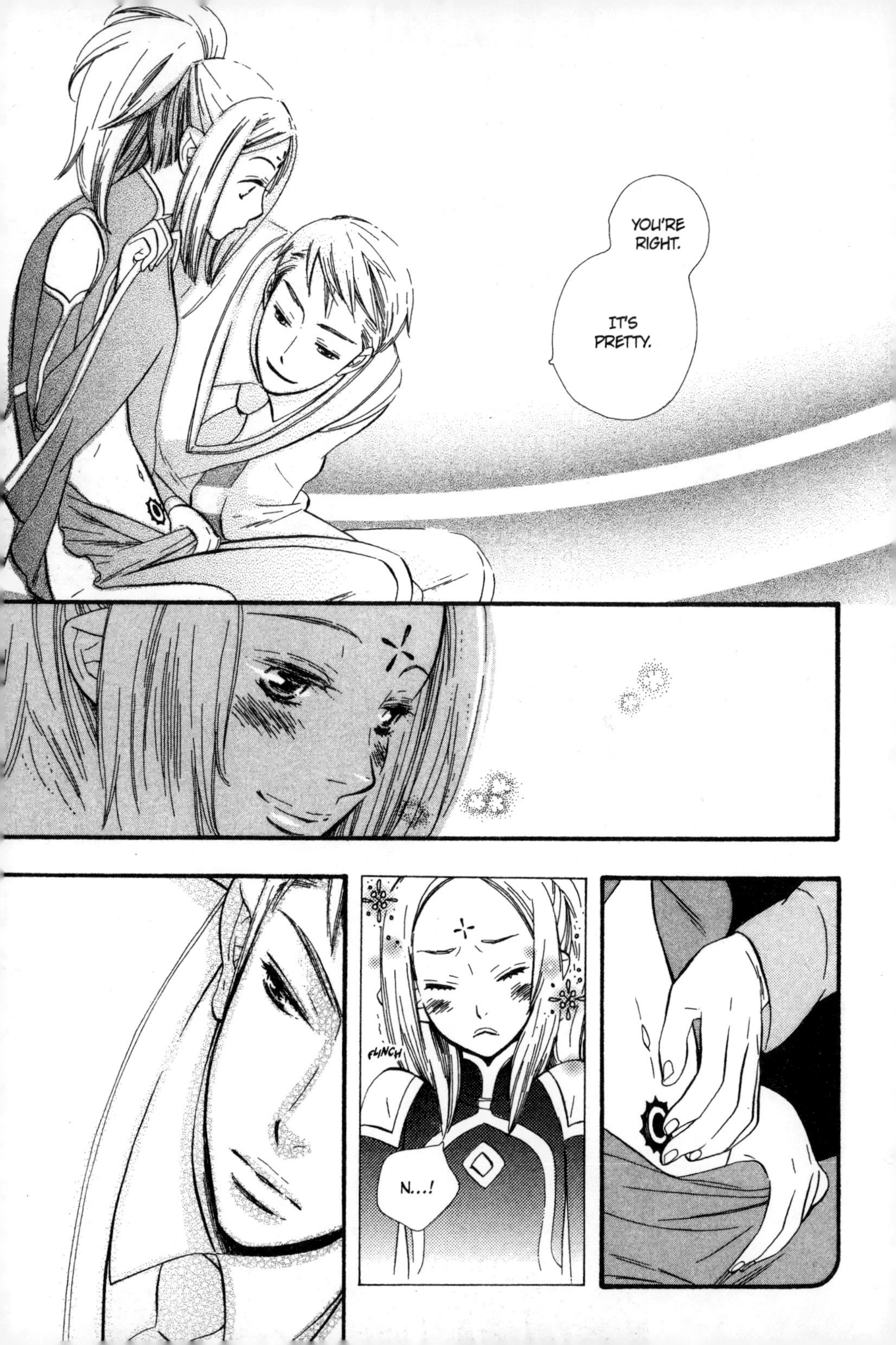
YOU'RE RIGHT.
IT'S PRETTY.
FLINCH
N...!

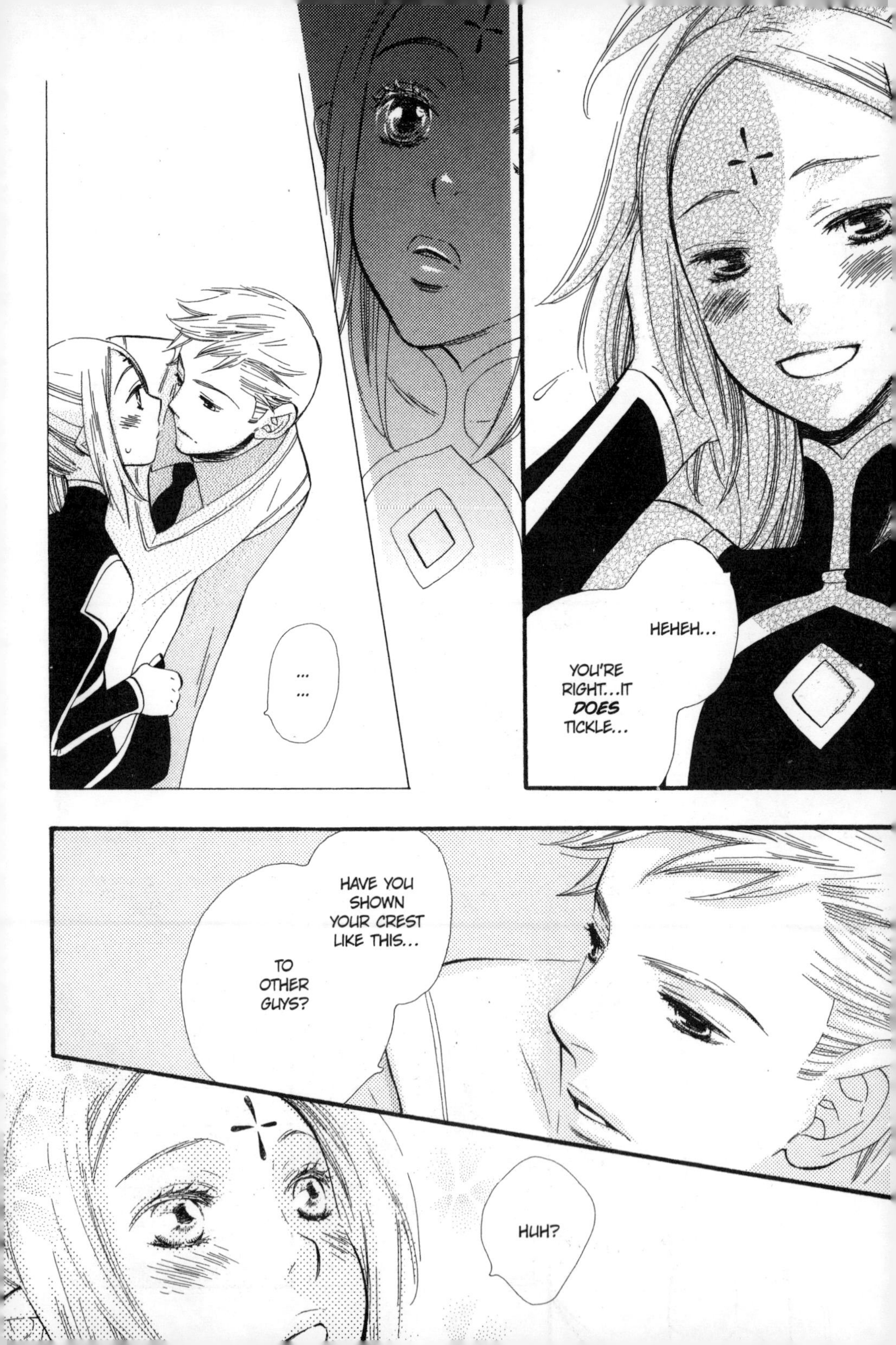
HEHEH...
YOU'RE RIGHT...IT **DOES** TICKLE...
... ...
HAVE YOU SHOWN YOUR CREST LIKE THIS...
TO OTHER GUYS?
HUH?

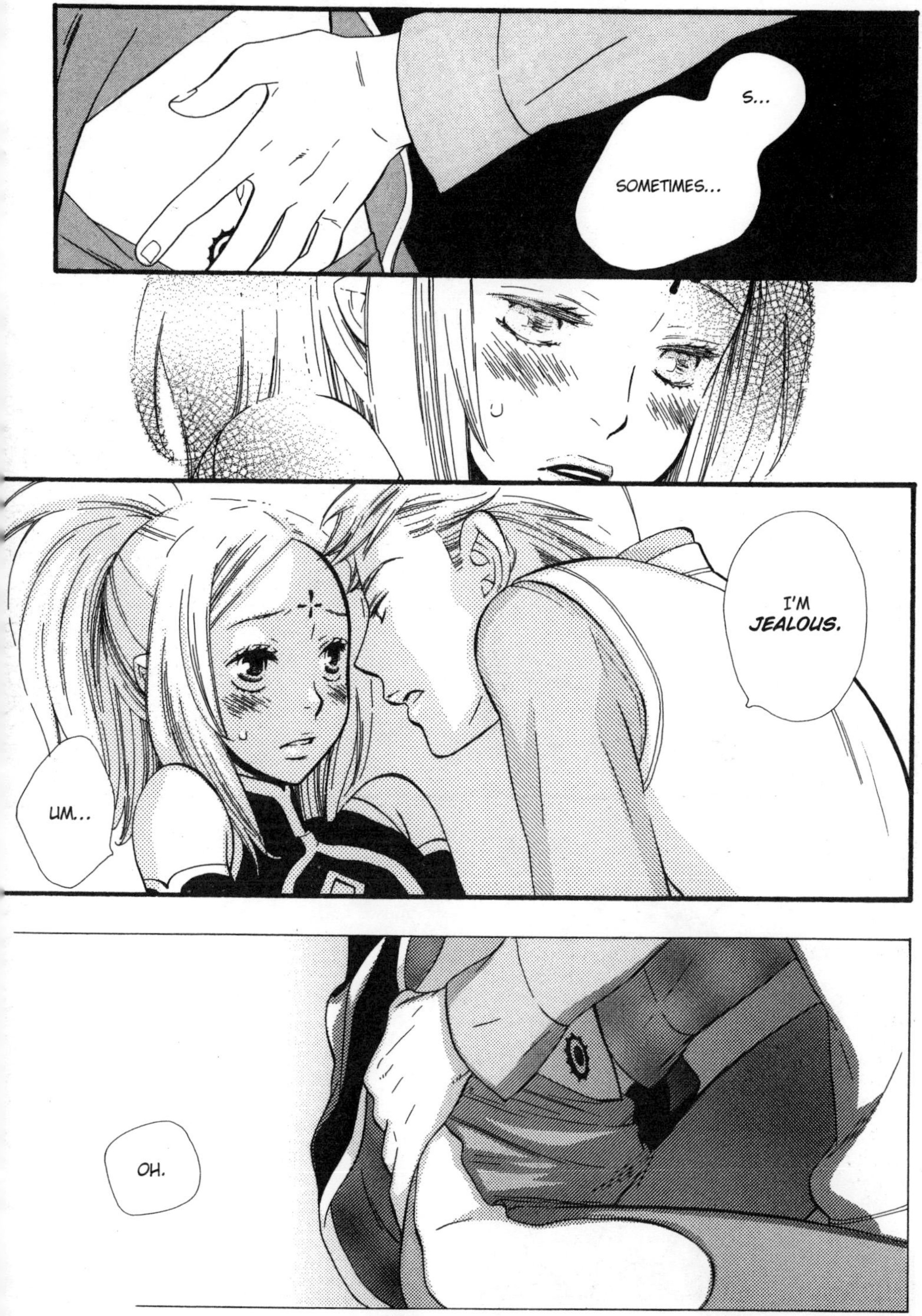
S...
SOMETIMES...
I'M JEALOUS.
UM...
OH.

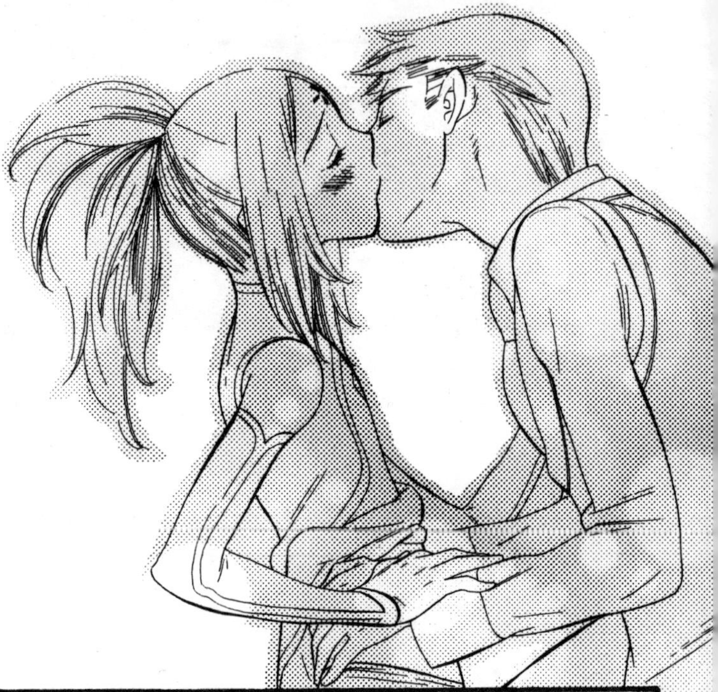

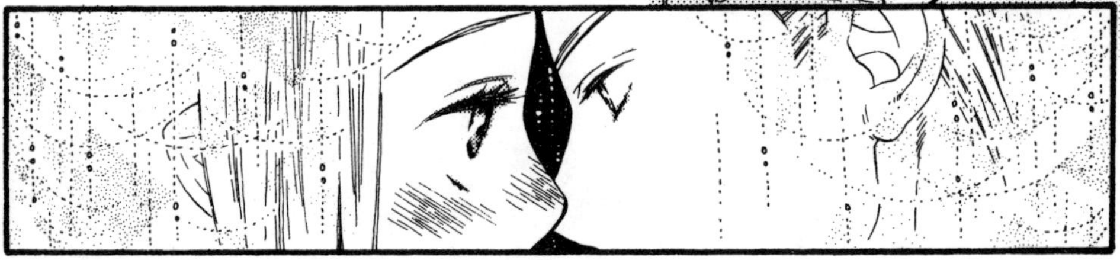

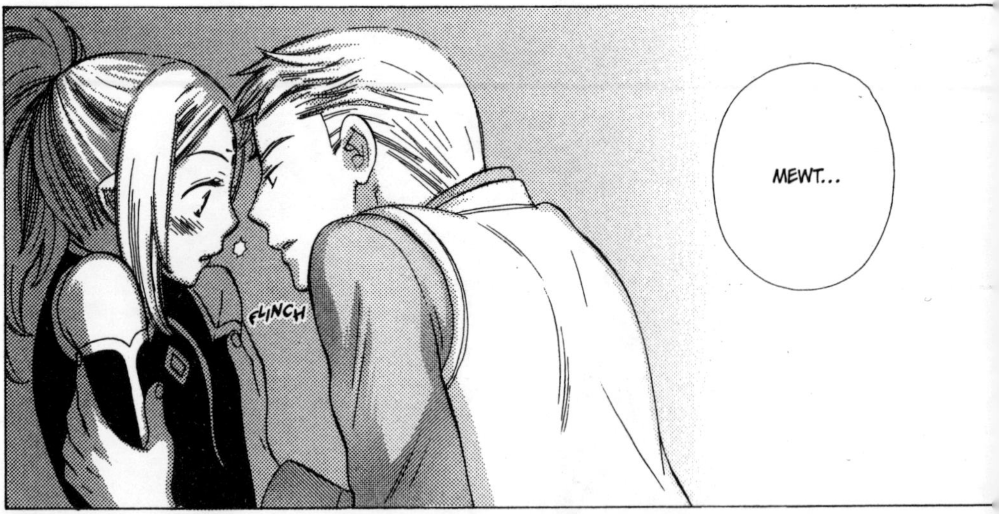
MEWT...
FLINCH

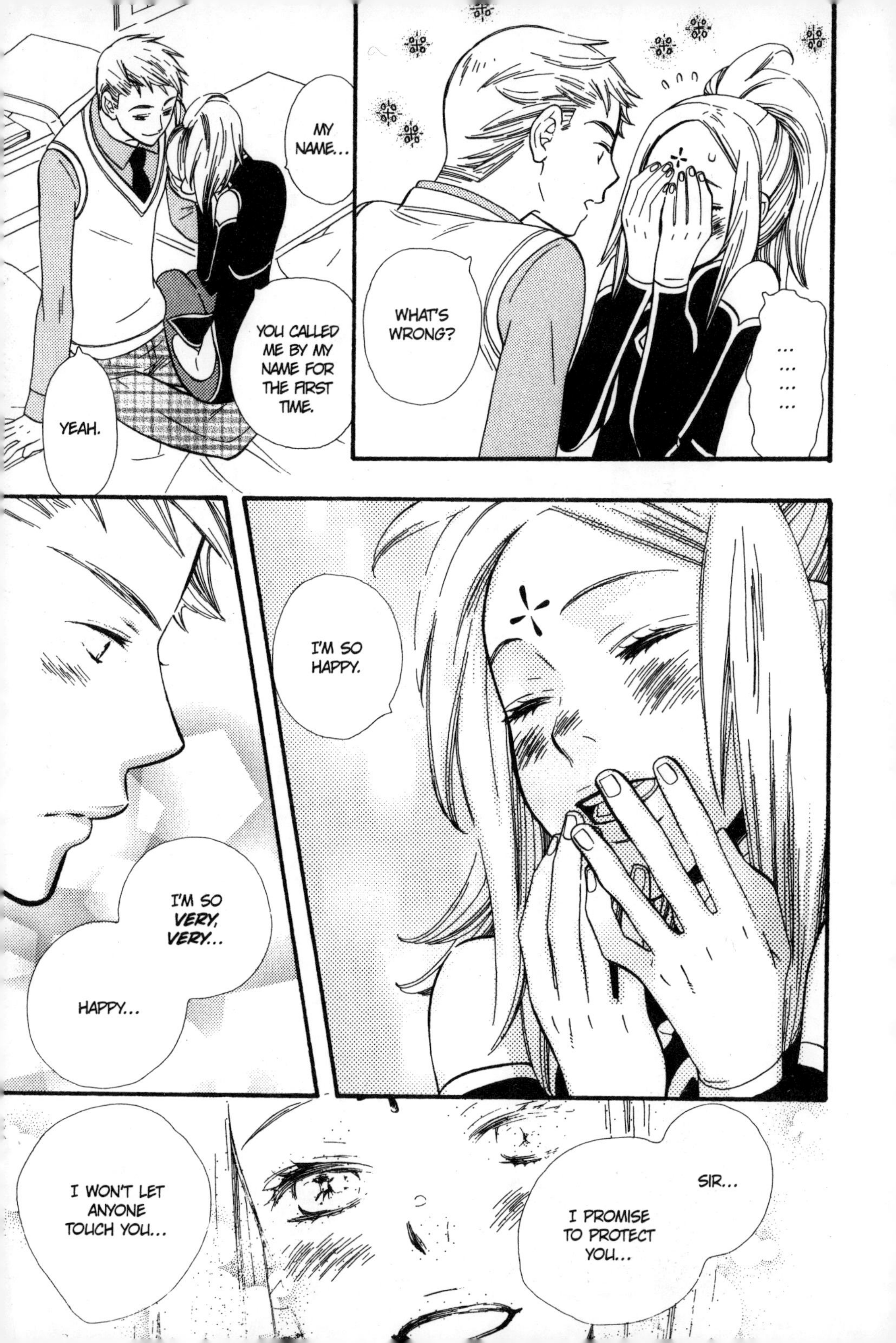
WHAT'S WRONG?
......
MY NAME...
YOU CALLED ME BY MY NAME FOR THE FIRST TIME.
YEAH.
I'M SO HAPPY.
I'M SO VERY, VERY...
HAPPY...
SIR...
I PROMISE TO PROTECT YOU...
I WON'T LET ANYONE TOUCH YOU...

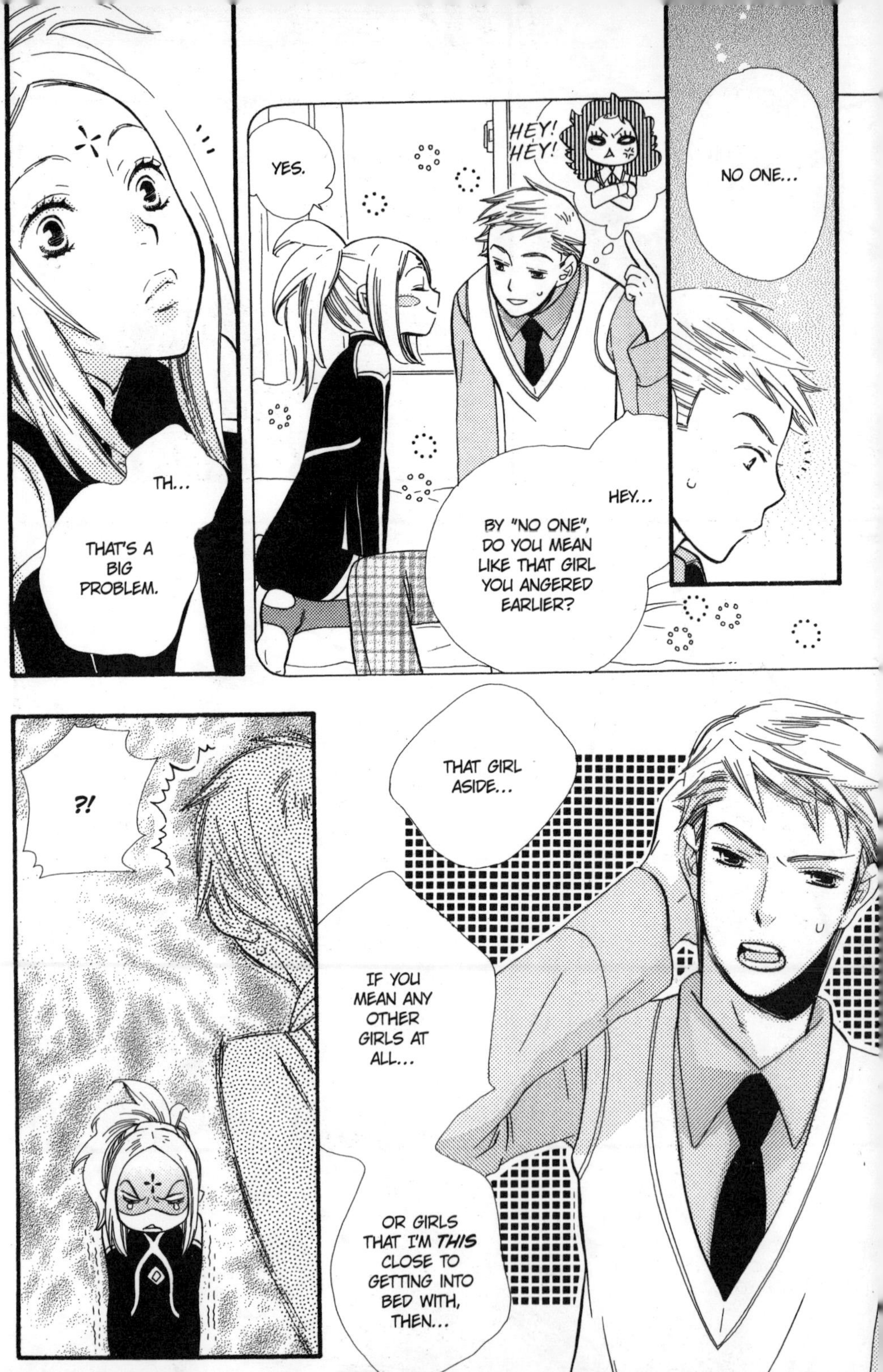
NO ONE...
HEY! HEY!
YES.
HEY...
BY "NO ONE", DO YOU MEAN LIKE THAT GIRL YOU ANGERED EARLIER?
TH...
THAT'S A BIG PROBLEM.
THAT GIRL ASIDE...
IF YOU MEAN ANY OTHER GIRLS AT ALL...
OR GIRLS THAT I'M *THIS* CLOSE TO GETTING INTO BED WITH, THEN...
?!

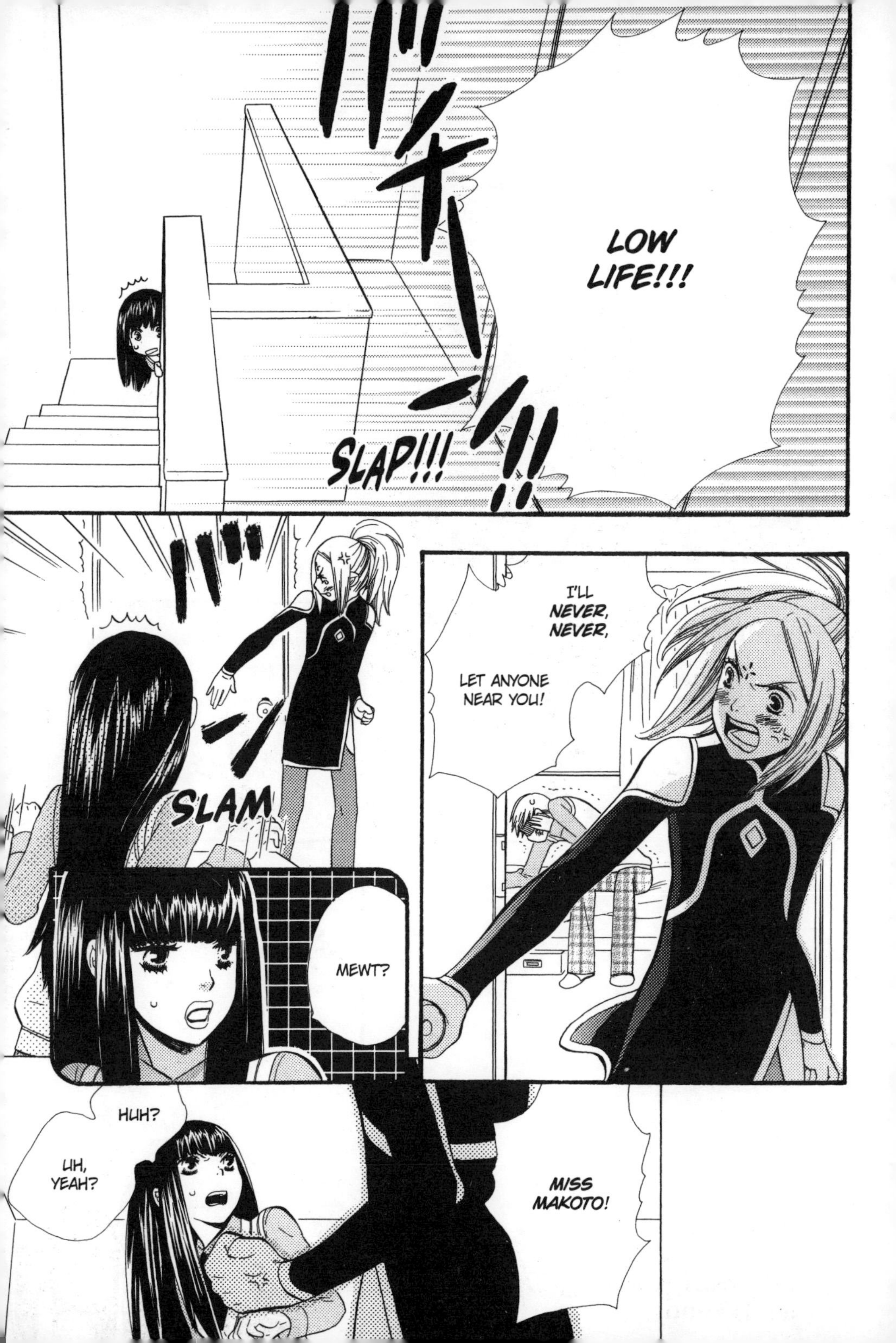
LOW LIFE!!!
SLAP!!!
I'LL NEVER, NEVER,
LET ANYONE NEAR YOU!
SLAM
MEWT?
MISS MAKOTO!
HUH?
UH, YEAH?

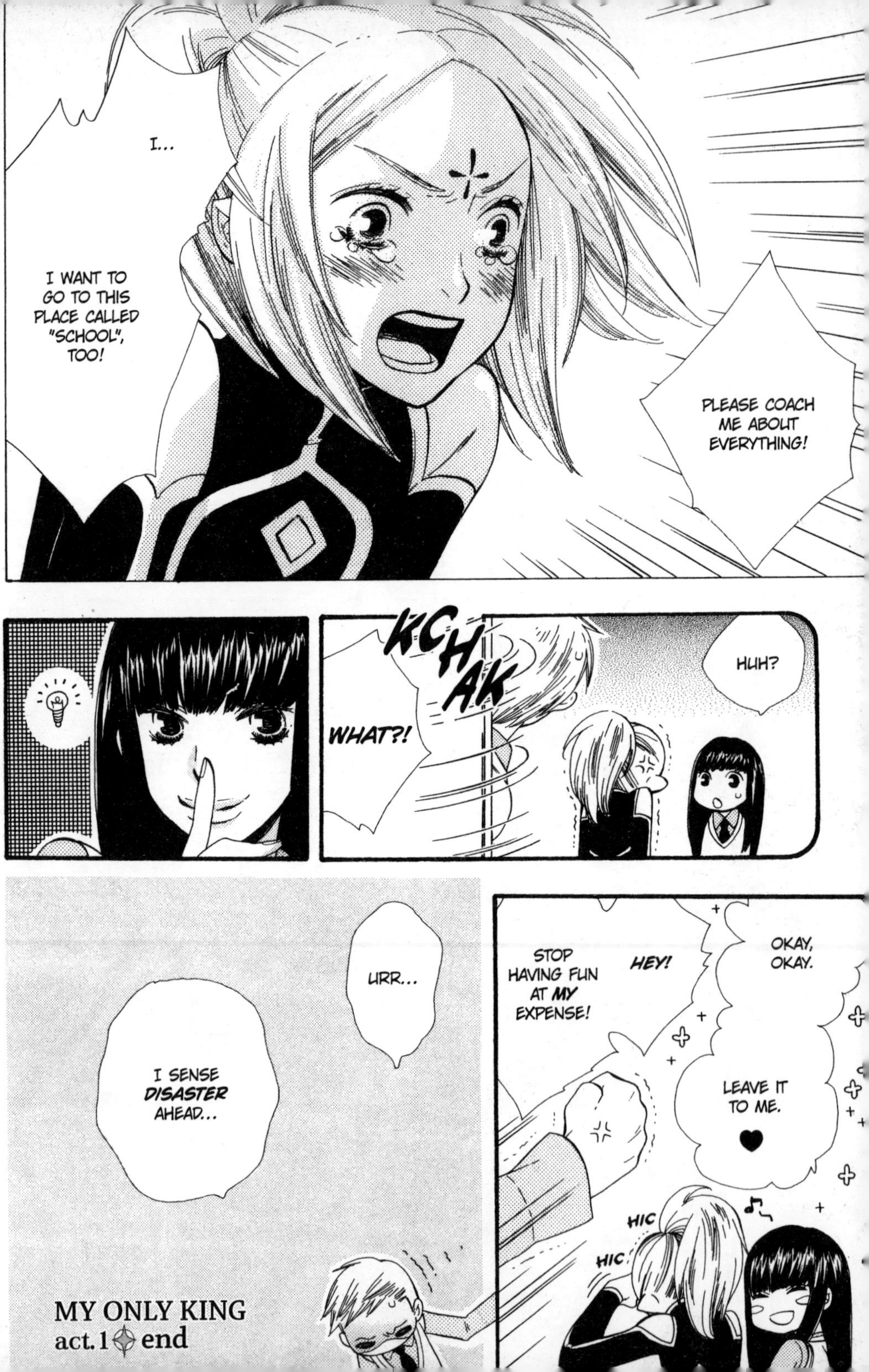
I...
I WANT TO GO TO THIS PLACE CALLED "SCHOOL", TOO!
PLEASE COACH ME ABOUT EVERYTHING!
KCHAK
WHAT?!
HUH?
HEY!
STOP HAVING FUN AT MY EXPENSE!
OKAY, OKAY.
LEAVE IT TO ME.
HIC
HIC
URR...
I SENSE DISASTER AHEAD...
MY ONLY KING
act.1 end

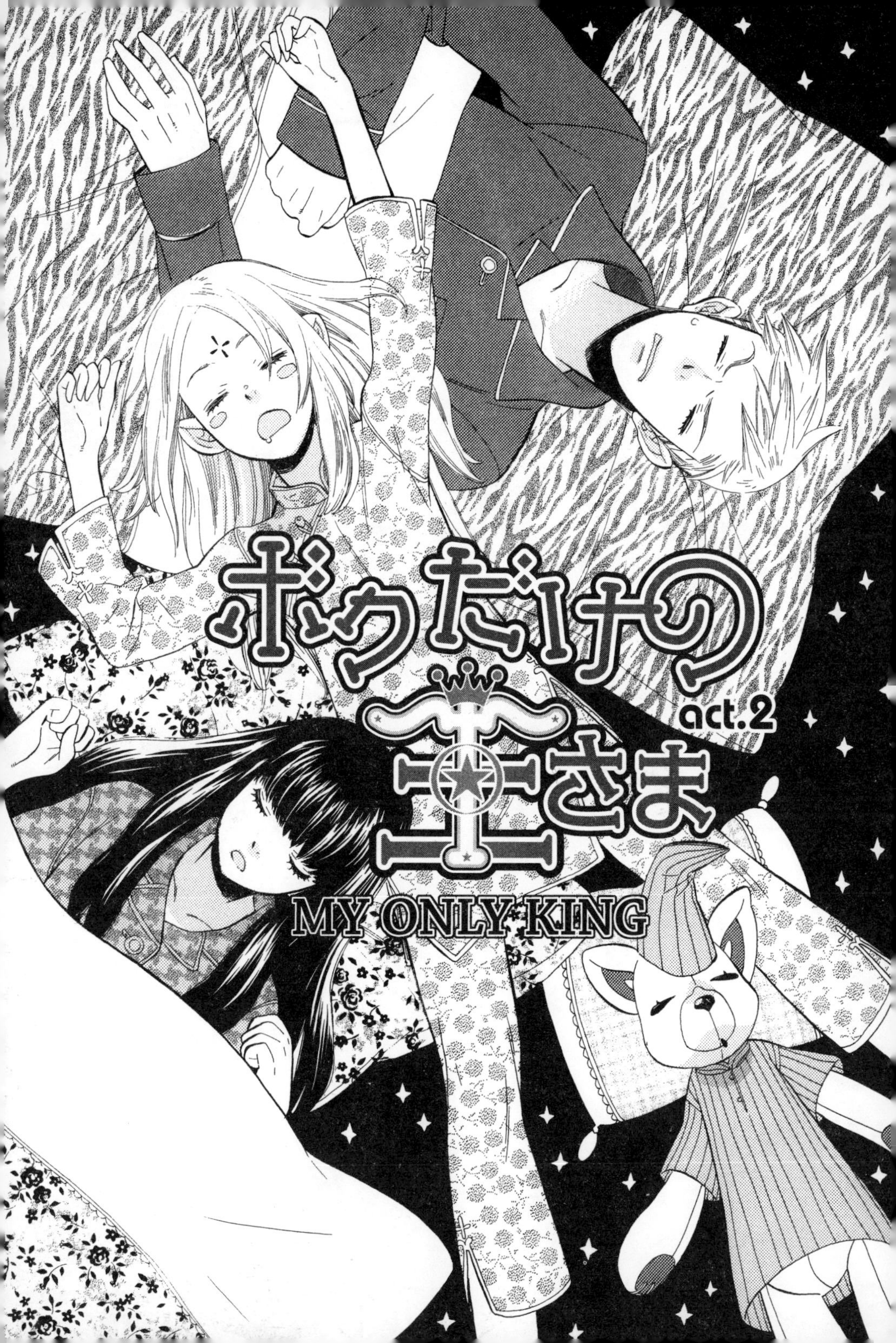
ボクだけの王さま
act.2
MY ONLY KING

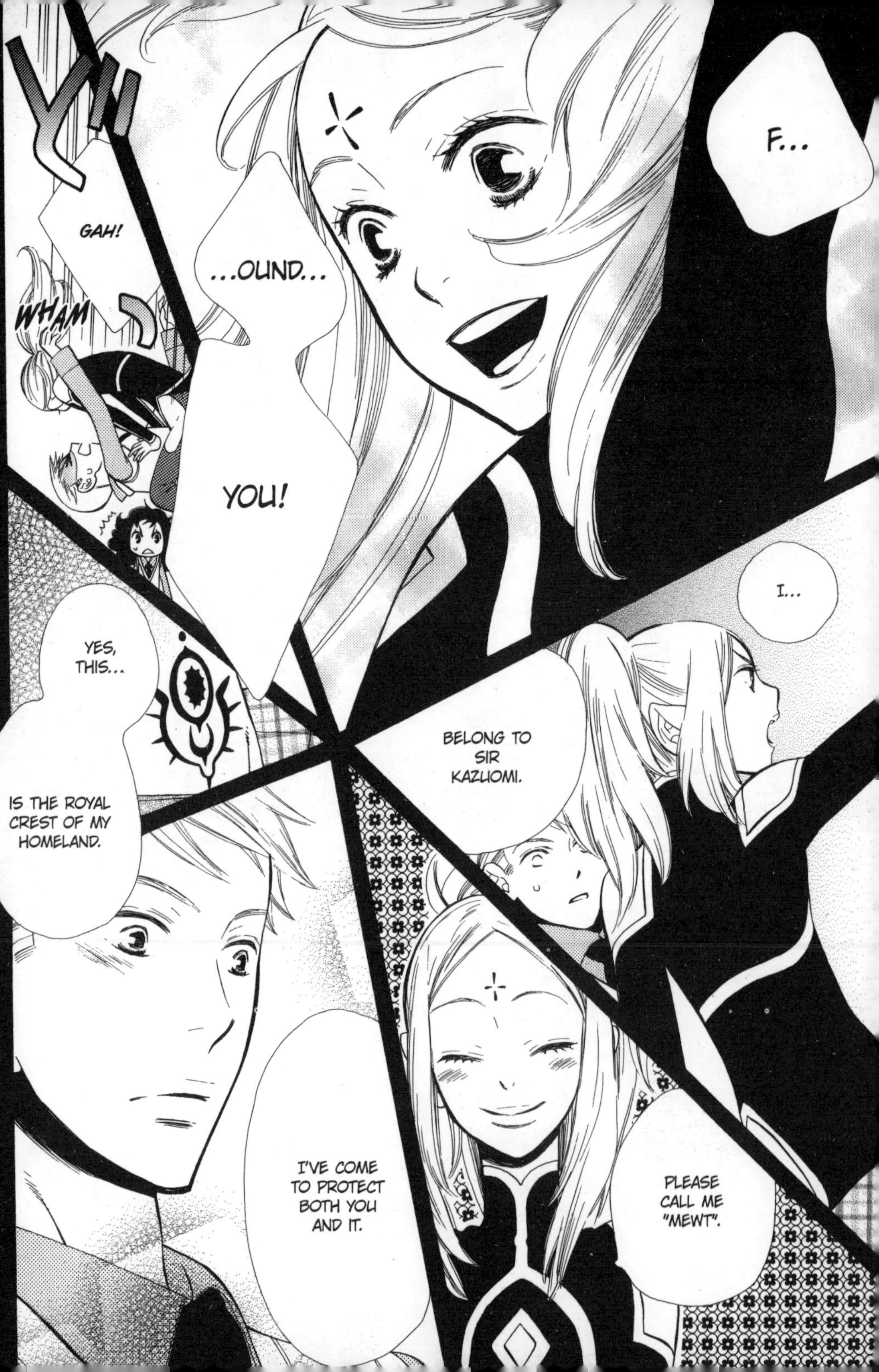
F...
...OUND...
YOU!
YANK
GAH!
WHAM
I...
BELONG TO SIR KAZUOMI.
YES, THIS...
IS THE ROYAL CREST OF MY HOMELAND.
PLEASE CALL ME "MEWT".
I'VE COME TO PROTECT BOTH YOU AND IT.

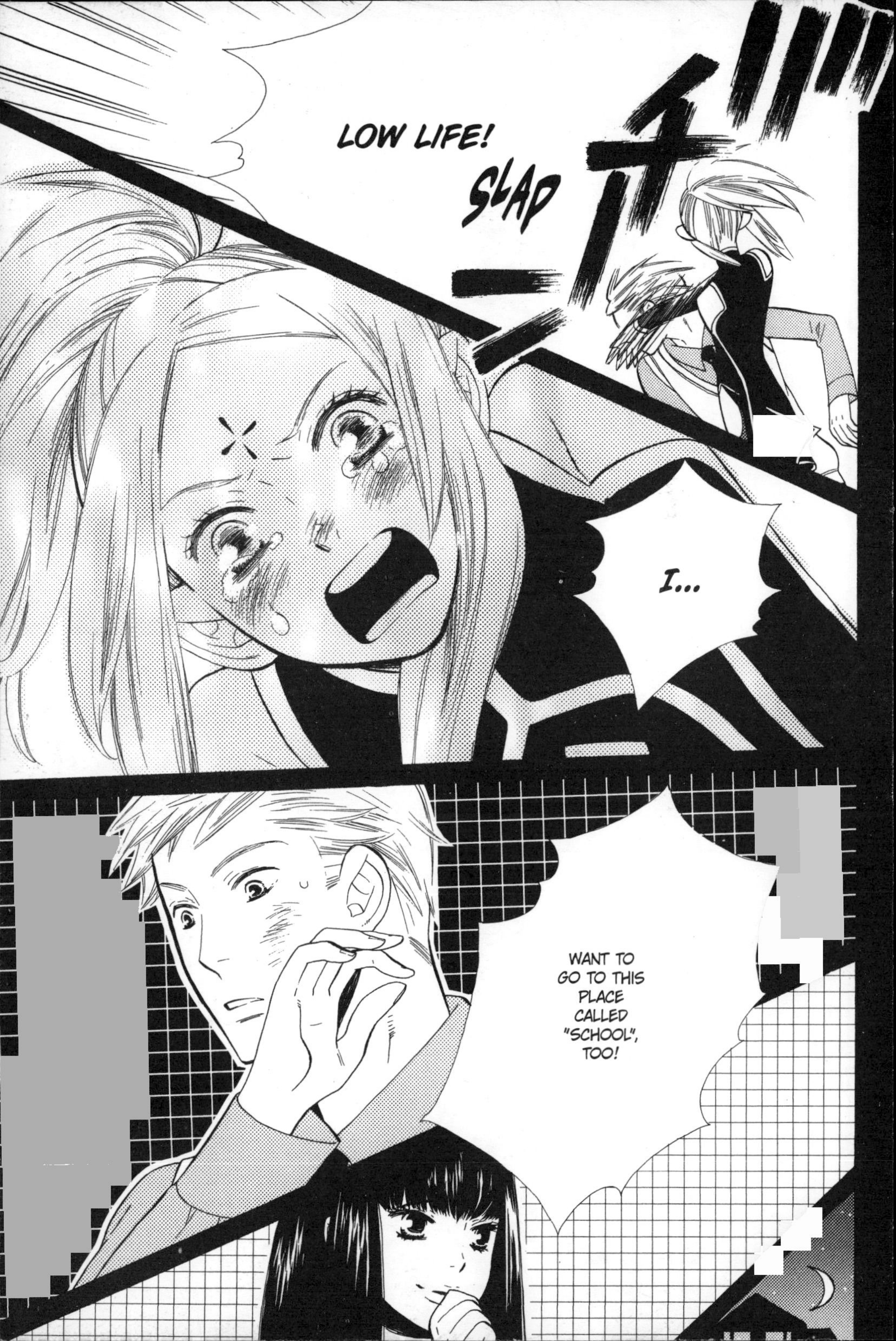
LOW LIFE!
SLAP
I...
WANT TO GO TO THIS PLACE CALLED "SCHOOL", TOO!

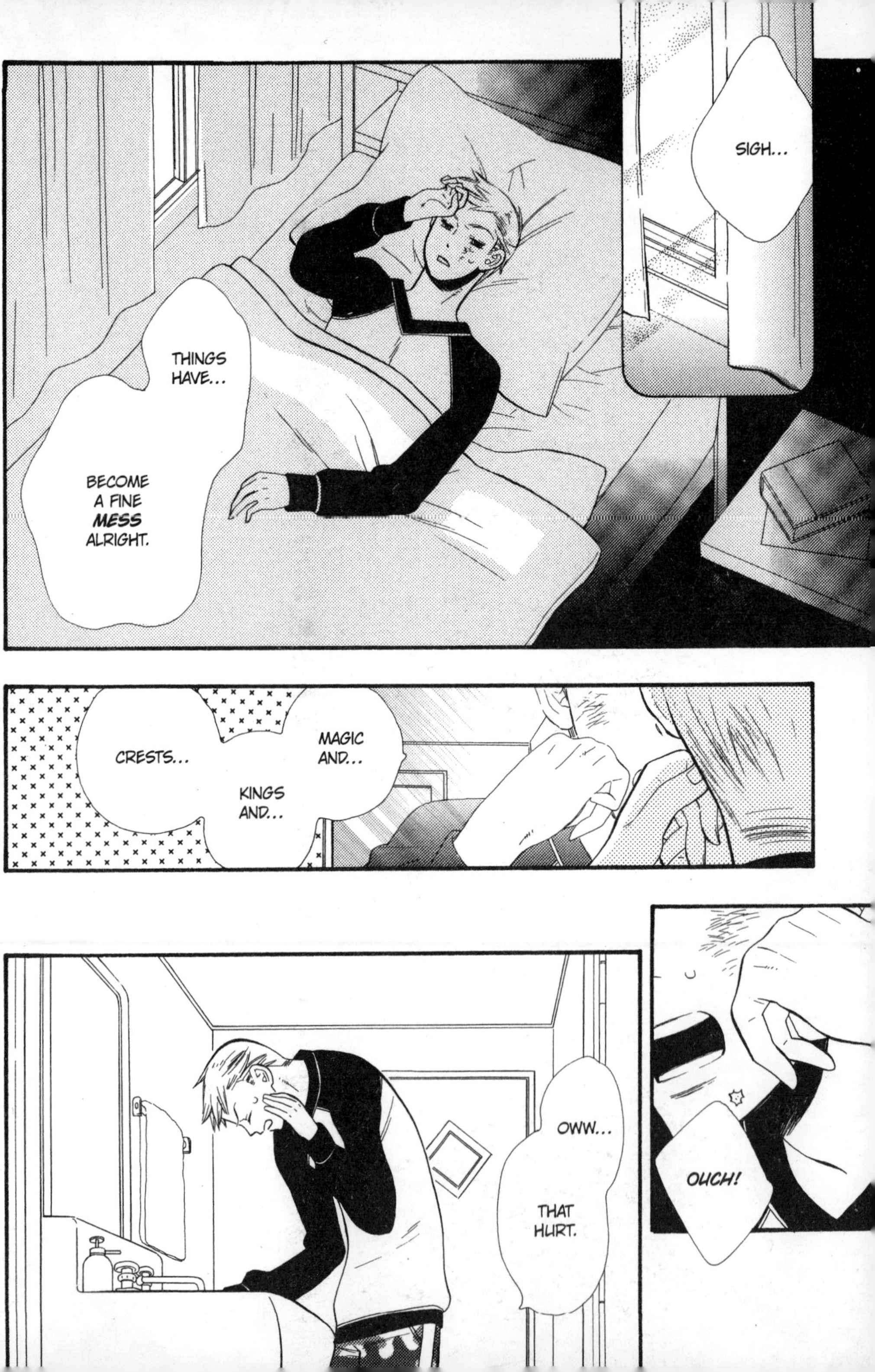
SIGH...
THINGS HAVE...
BECOME A FINE **MESS** ALRIGHT.
MAGIC AND...
KINGS AND...
CRESTS...
OUCH!
OWW...
THAT HURT.

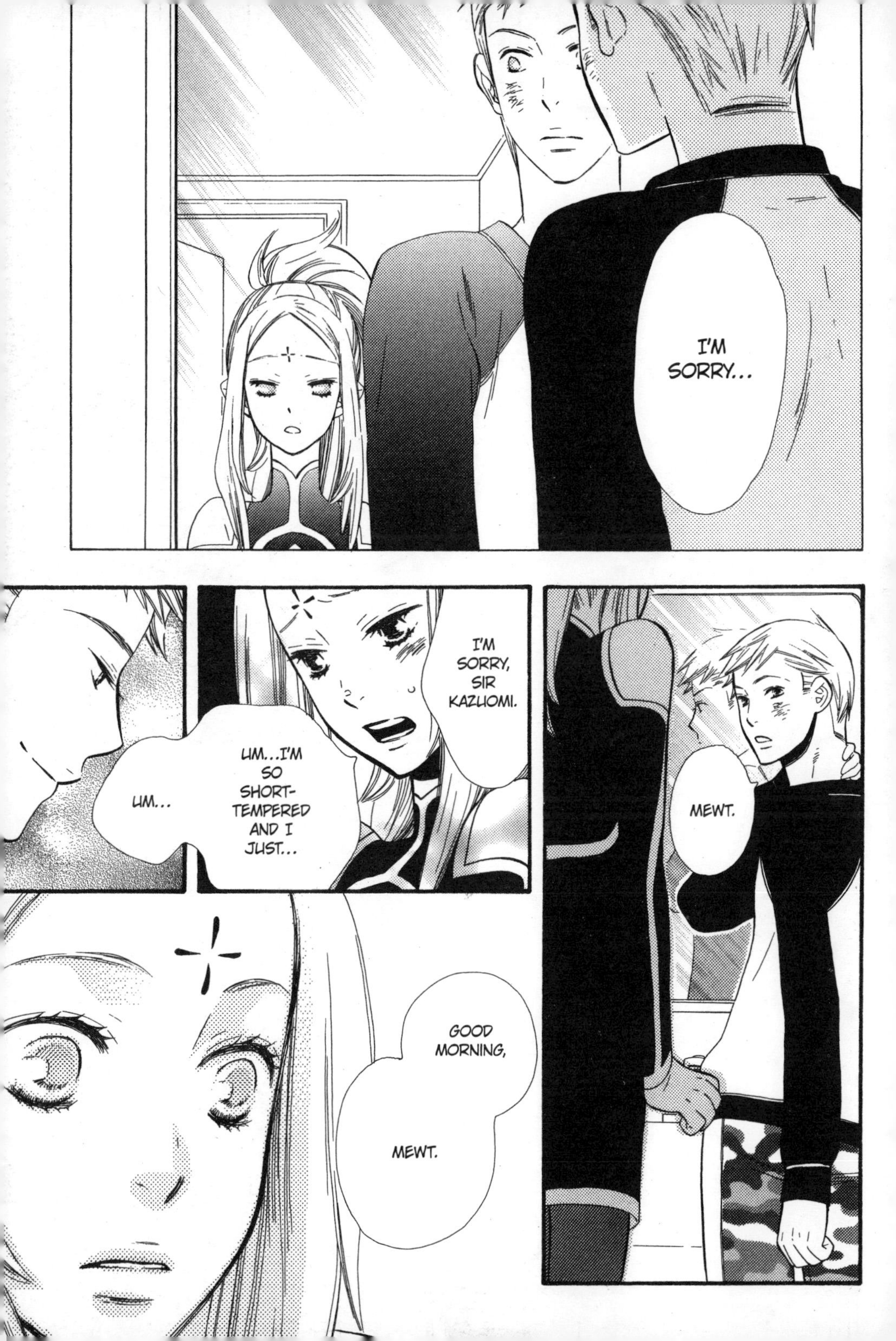
I'M SORRY...
MEWT.
I'M SORRY, SIR KAZUOMI.
UM...I'M SO SHORT-TEMPERED AND I JUST...
UM...
GOOD MORNING,
MEWT.

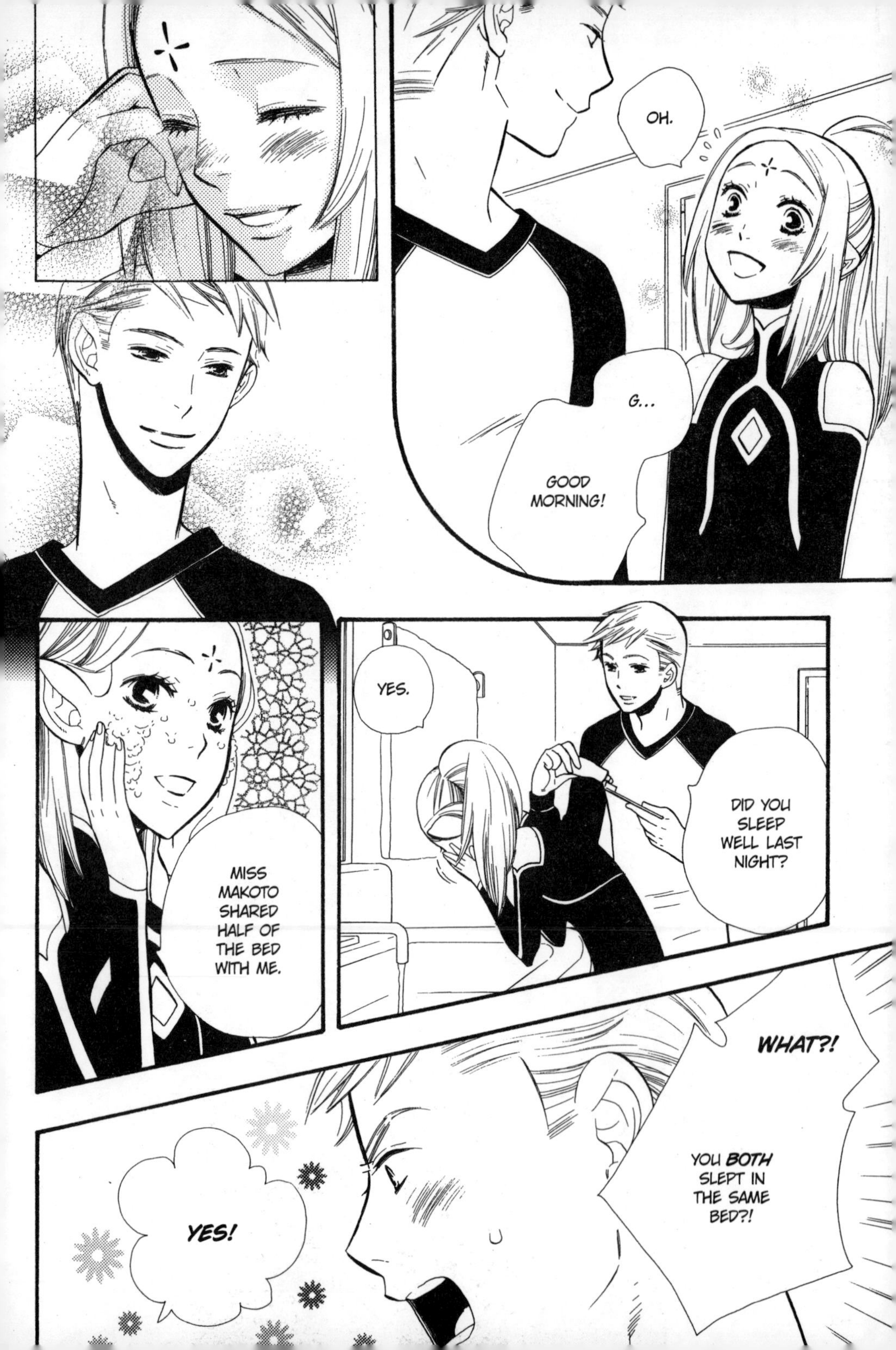
OH.
G...
GOOD MORNING!
DID YOU SLEEP WELL LAST NIGHT?
YES.
MISS MAKOTO SHARED HALF OF THE BED WITH ME.
WHAT?!
YOU BOTH SLEPT IN THE SAME BED?!
YES!

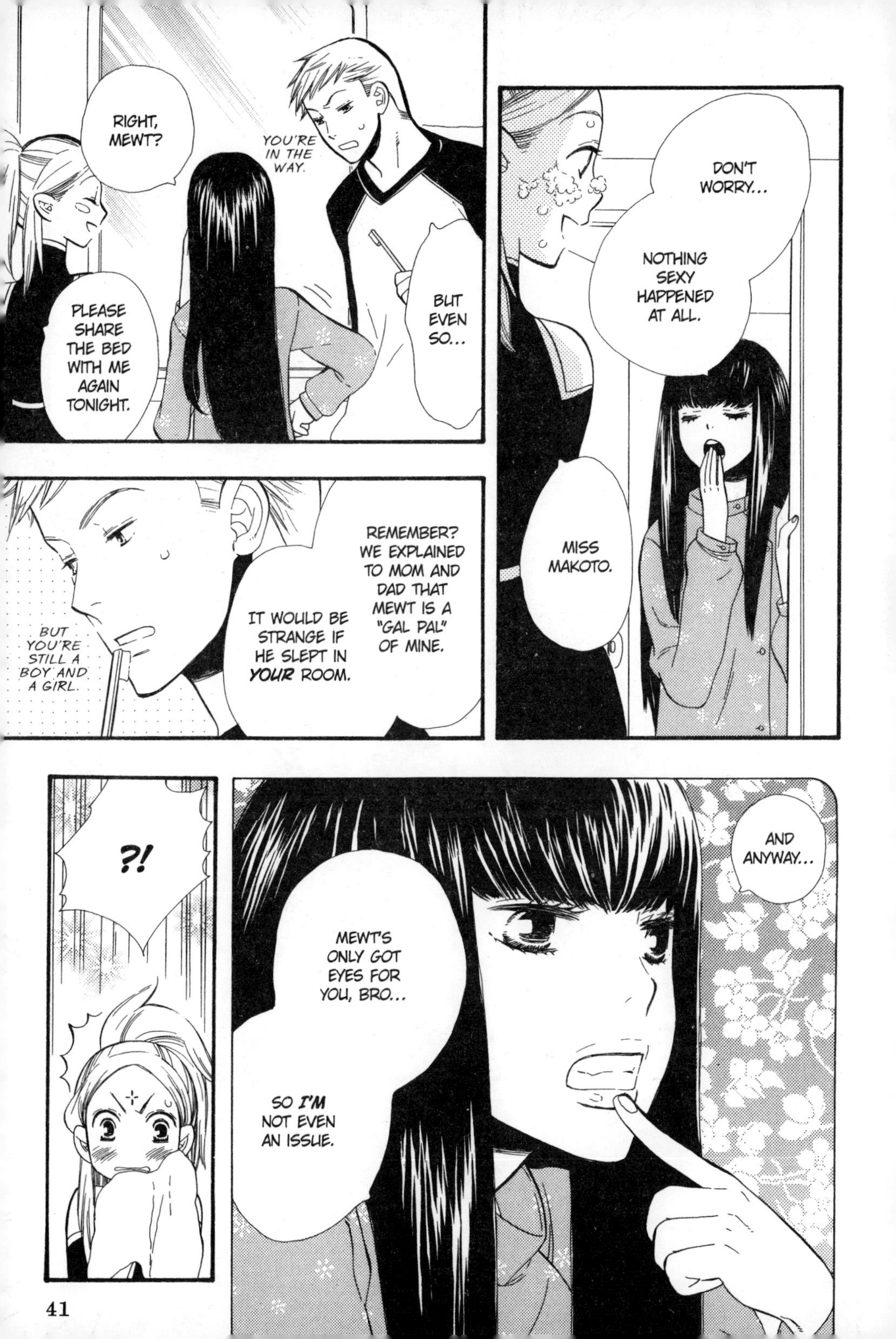
DON'T WORRY...
NOTHING SEXY HAPPENED AT ALL.
MISS MAKOTO.
RIGHT, MEWT?
YOU'RE IN THE WAY.
PLEASE SHARE THE BED WITH ME AGAIN TONIGHT.
BUT EVEN SO...
REMEMBER? WE EXPLAINED TO MOM AND DAD THAT MEWT IS A "GAL PAL" OF MINE.
IT WOULD BE STRANGE IF HE SLEPT IN YOUR ROOM.
BUT YOU'RE STILL A BOY AND A GIRL.
AND ANYWAY...
MEWT'S ONLY GOT EYES FOR YOU, BRO...
SO I'M NOT EVEN AN ISSUE.
?!

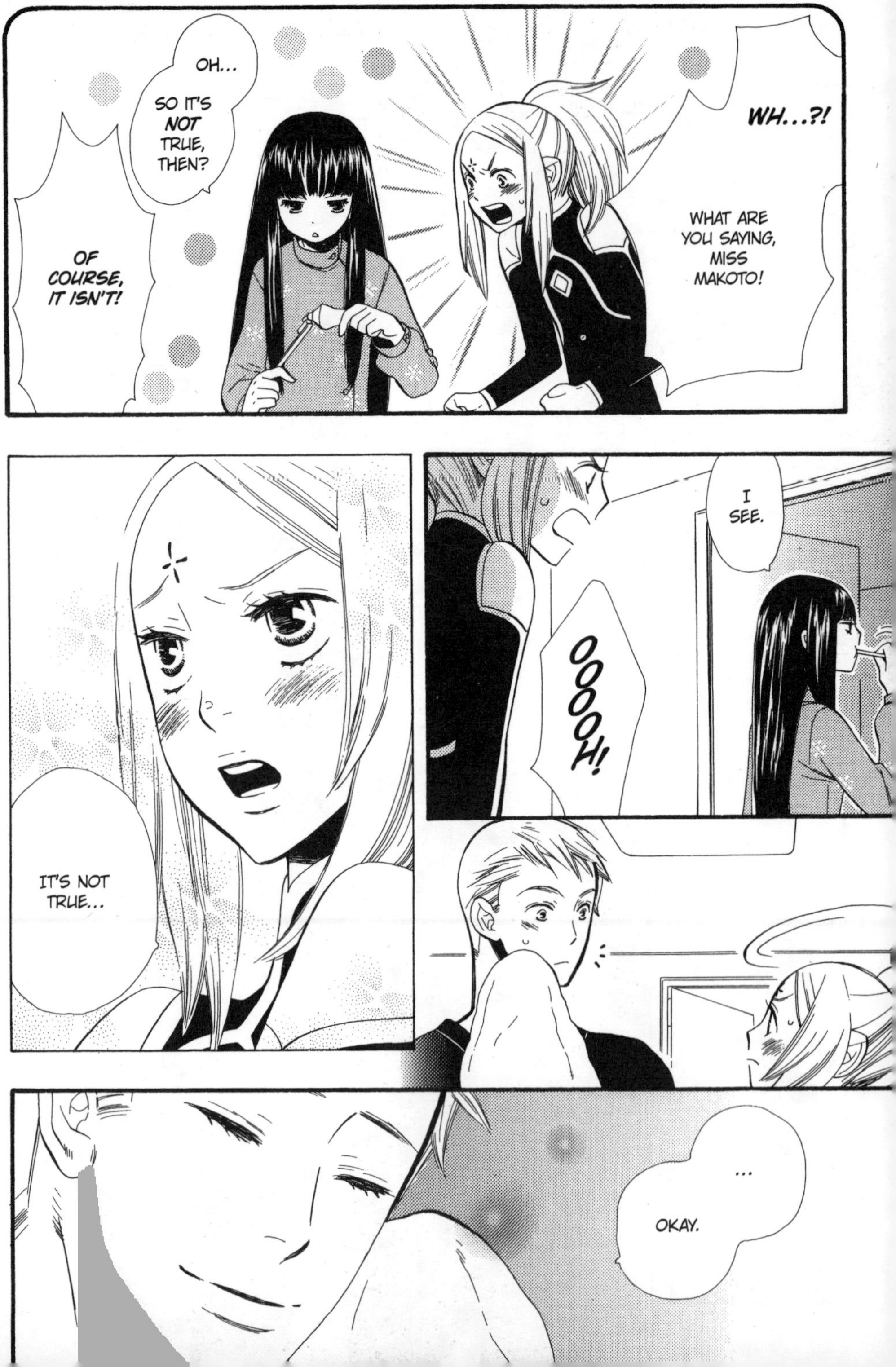
WH...?!
WHAT ARE YOU SAYING, MISS MAKOTO!
OH... SO IT'S NOT TRUE, THEN?
OF COURSE, IT ISN'T!
I SEE.
OOOOOH!
IT'S NOT TRUE...
... OKAY.

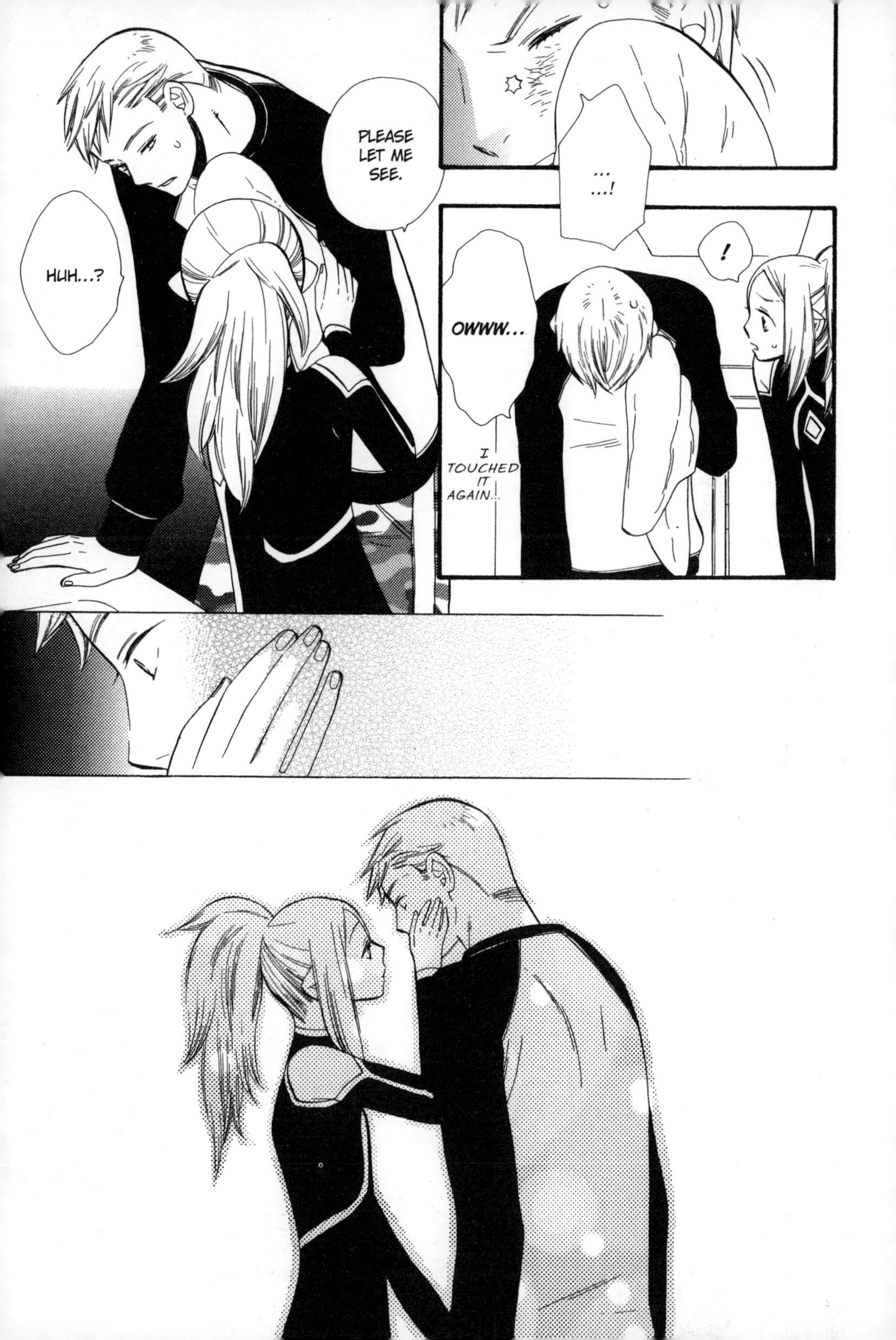
...
...!
!
OWWW...
I TOUCHED IT AGAIN...
PLEASE LET ME SEE.
HUH...?

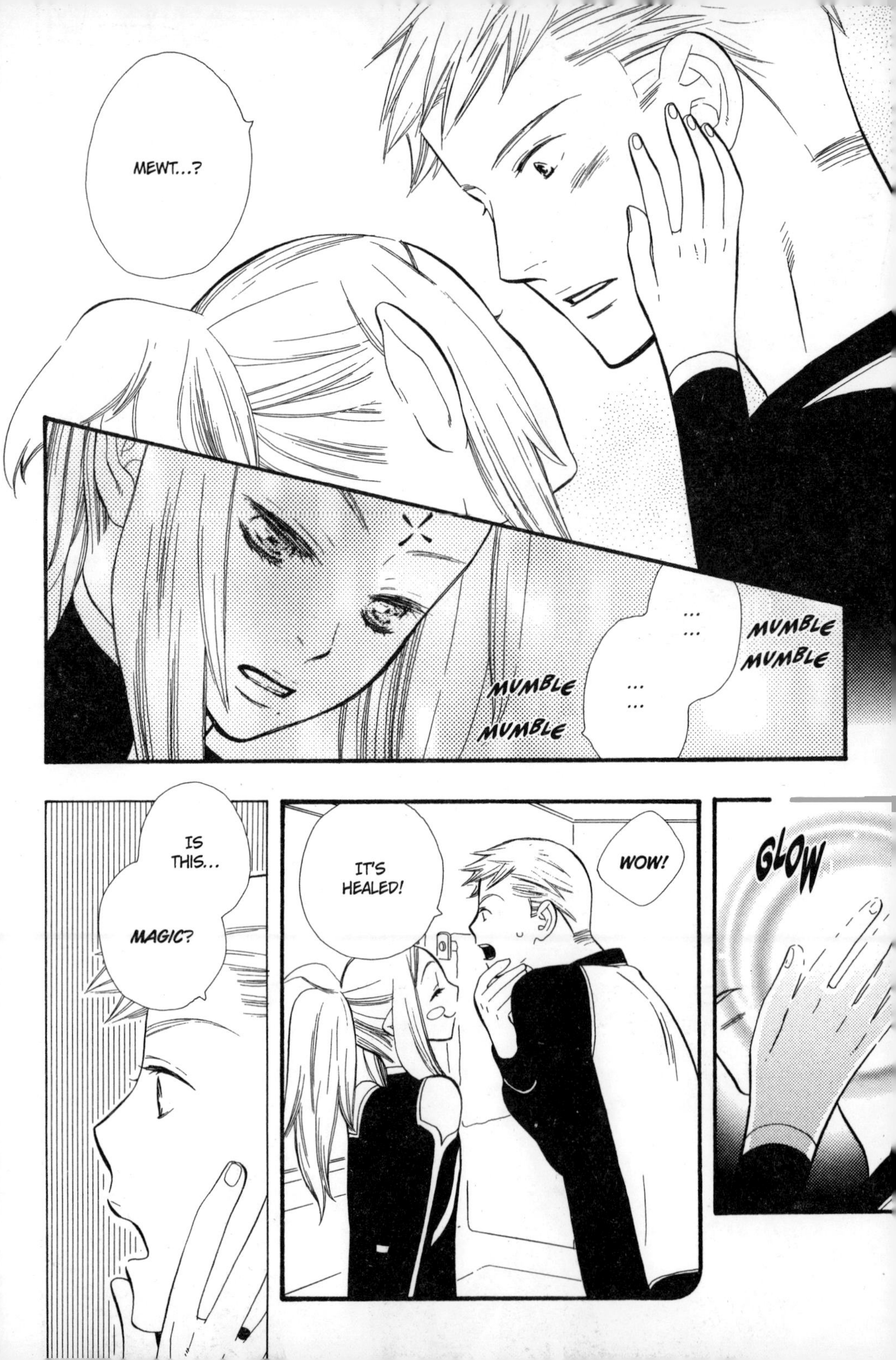
MEWT...?
MUMBLE MUMBLE
...
...
...
...
MUMBLE MUMBLE
GLOW
WOW!
IT'S HEALED!
IS THIS...
MAGIC?

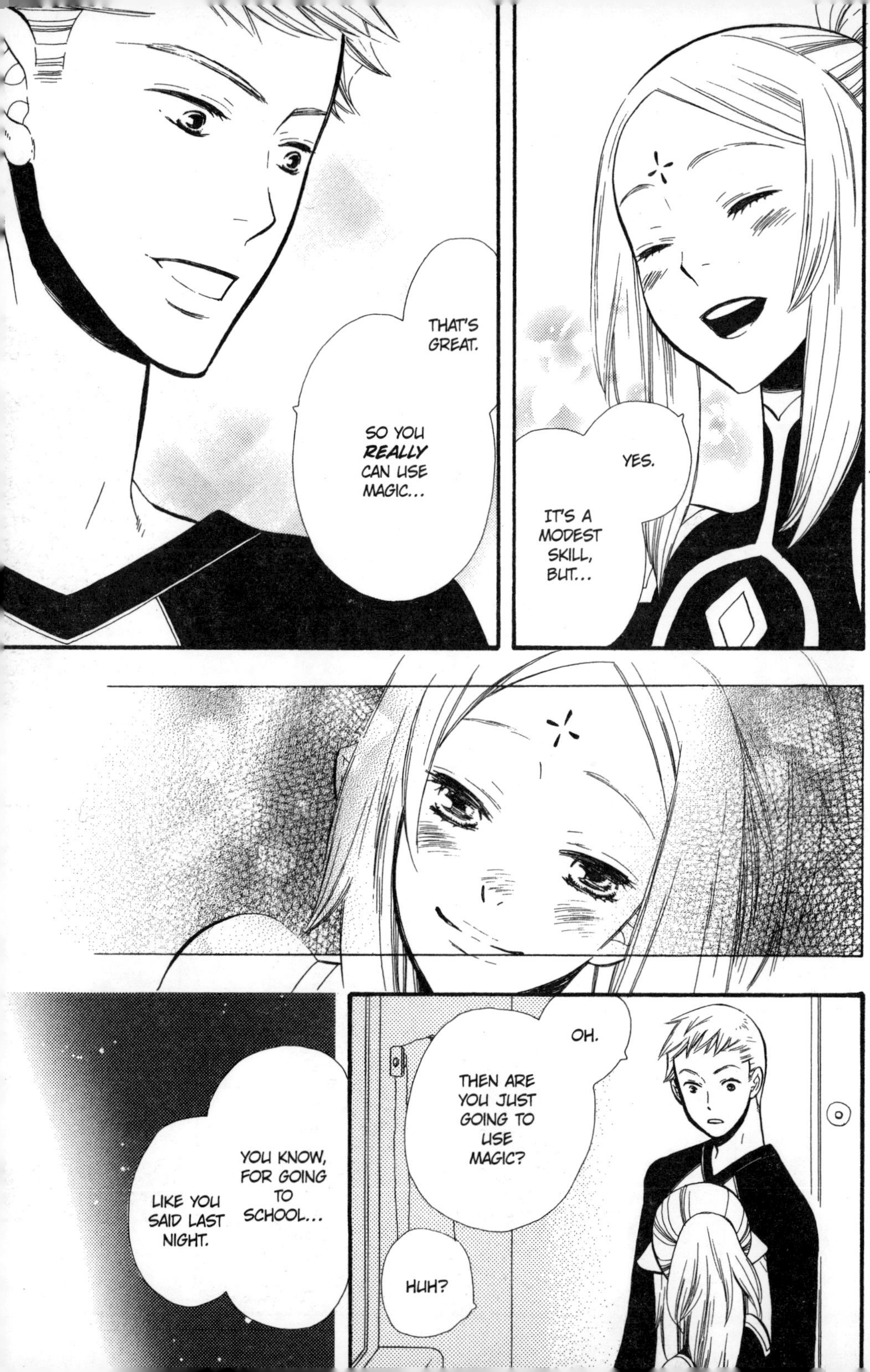
YES.
IT'S A MODEST SKILL, BUT...
THAT'S GREAT.
SO YOU *REALLY* CAN USE MAGIC...
OH.
THEN ARE YOU JUST GOING TO USE MAGIC?
HUH?
YOU KNOW, FOR GOING TO SCHOOL...
LIKE YOU SAID LAST NIGHT.

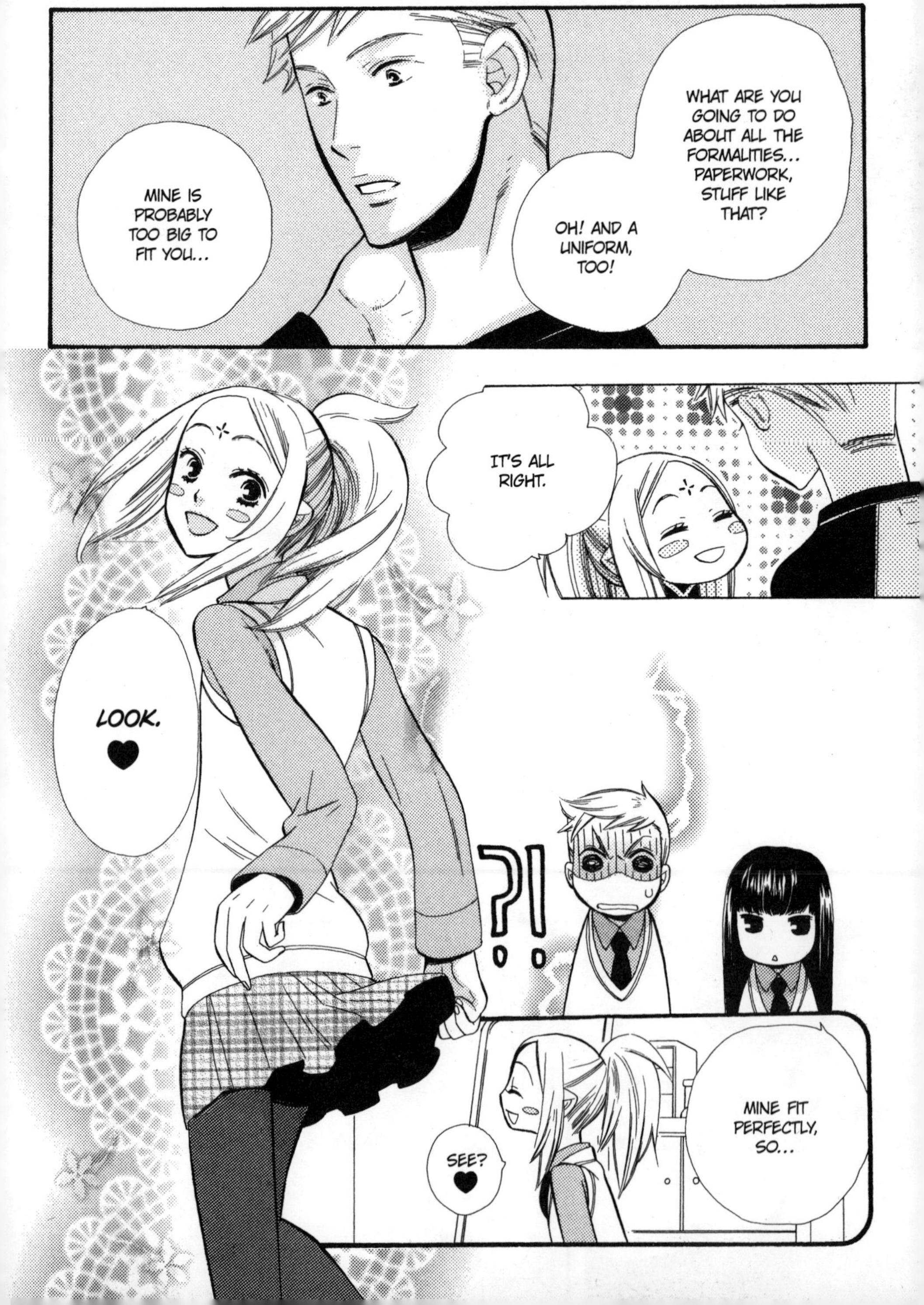
WHAT ARE YOU GOING TO DO ABOUT ALL THE FORMALITIES... PAPERWORK, STUFF LIKE THAT?
OH! AND A UNIFORM, TOO!
MINE IS PROBABLY TOO BIG TO FIT YOU...
IT'S ALL RIGHT.
MINE FIT PERFECTLY, SO...
SEE? ♥
LOOK. ♥
?!

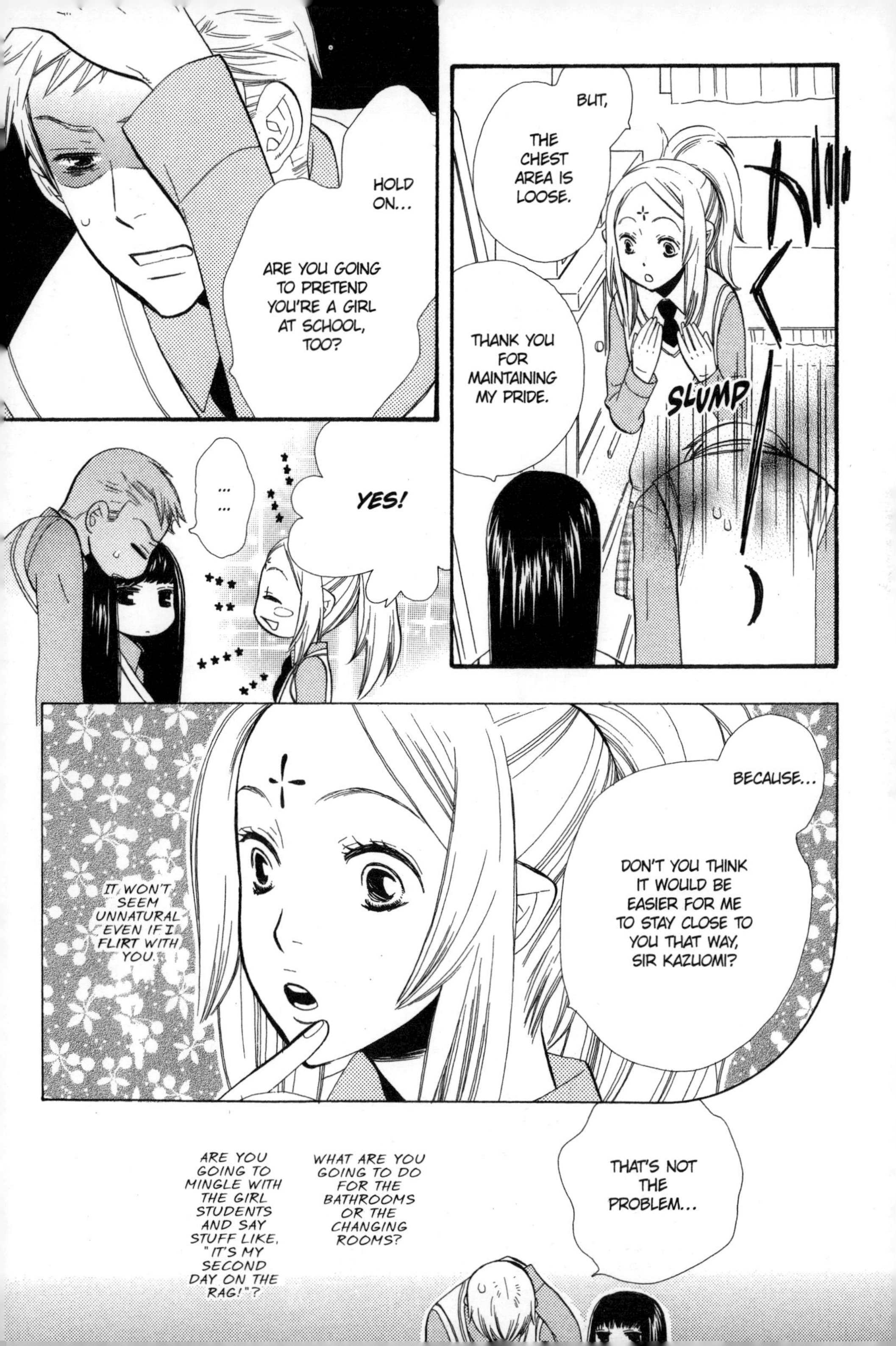
BUT,
THE CHEST AREA IS LOOSE.
THANK YOU FOR MAINTAINING MY PRIDE.
SLUMP
HOLD ON...
ARE YOU GOING TO PRETEND YOU'RE A GIRL AT SCHOOL, TOO?
YES!
......
BECAUSE...
DON'T YOU THINK IT WOULD BE EASIER FOR ME TO STAY CLOSE TO YOU THAT WAY, SIR KAZUOMI?
IT WON'T SEEM UNNATURAL EVEN IF I FLIRT WITH YOU.
THAT'S NOT THE PROBLEM...
WHAT ARE YOU GOING TO DO FOR THE BATHROOMS OR THE CHANGING ROOMS?
ARE YOU GOING TO MINGLE WITH THE GIRL STUDENTS AND SAY STUFF LIKE, "IT'S MY SECOND DAY ON THE RAG!"?

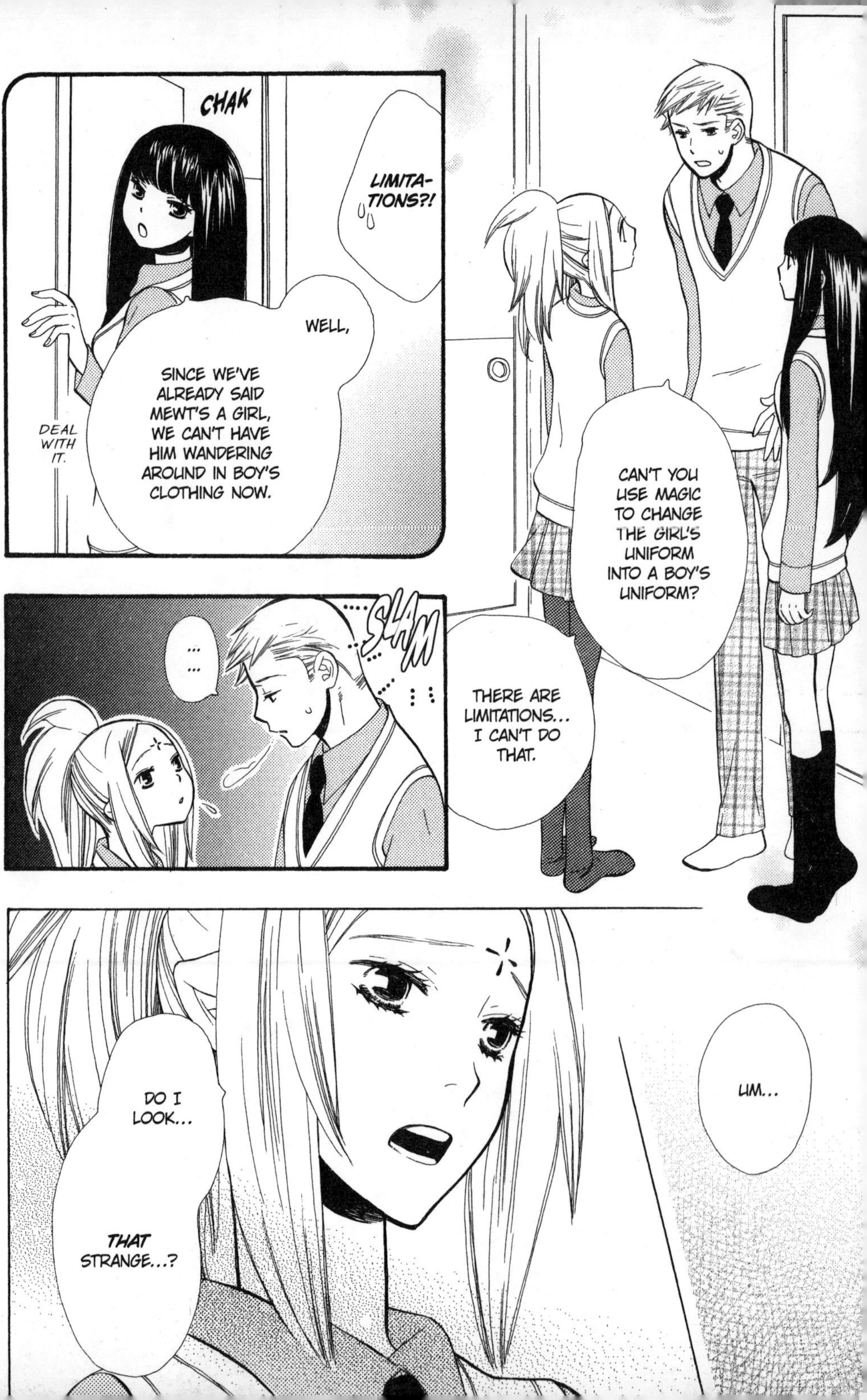
CAN'T YOU USE MAGIC TO CHANGE THE GIRL'S UNIFORM INTO A BOY'S UNIFORM?
THERE ARE LIMITATIONS... I CAN'T DO THAT.
CHAK
LIMITA-TIONS?!
WELL,
SINCE WE'VE ALREADY SAID MEWT'S A GIRL, WE CAN'T HAVE HIM WANDERING AROUND IN BOY'S CLOTHING NOW.
DEAL WITH IT.
SLAM
......
UM...
DO I LOOK...
THAT STRANGE...?

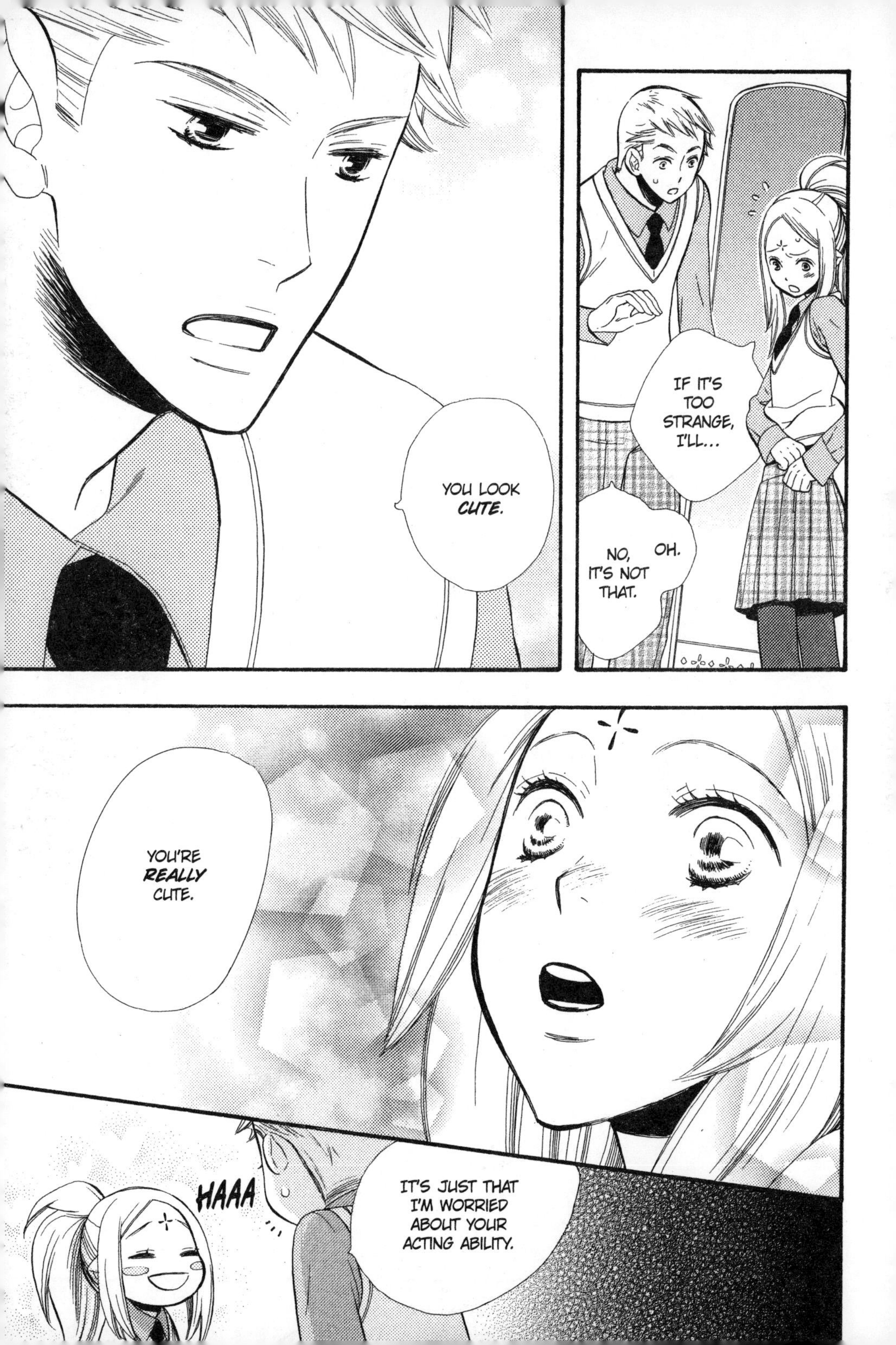
IF IT'S TOO STRANGE, I'LL...
OH.
NO, IT'S NOT THAT.
YOU LOOK *CUTE.*
YOU'RE *REALLY* CUTE.
IT'S JUST THAT I'M WORRIED ABOUT YOUR ACTING ABILITY.
HAAA

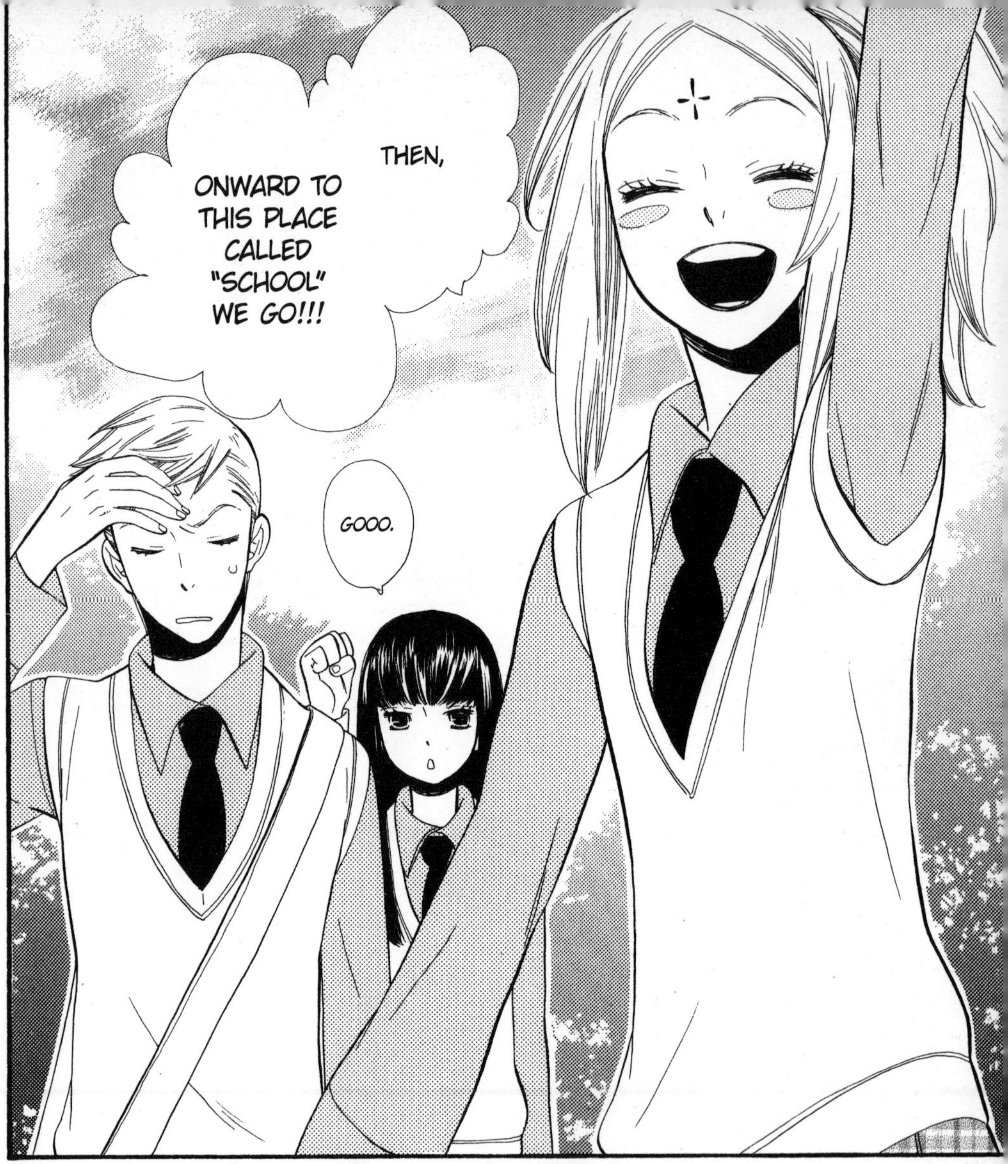
THEN,
ONWARD TO THIS PLACE CALLED "SCHOOL" WE GO!!!
GOOO.

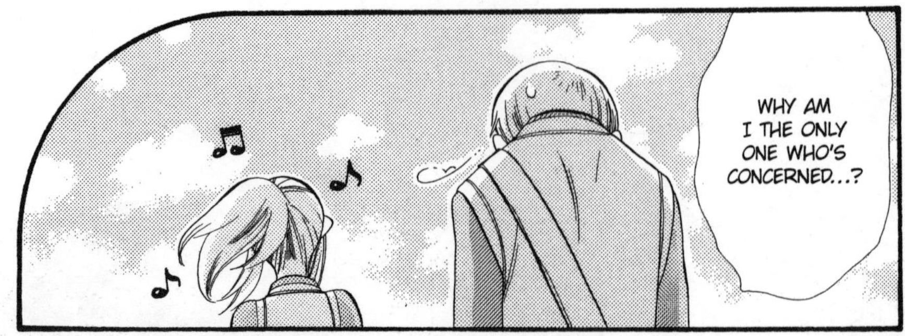
WHY AM I THE ONLY ONE WHO'S CONCERNED...?

MY ONLY KING act.2 end

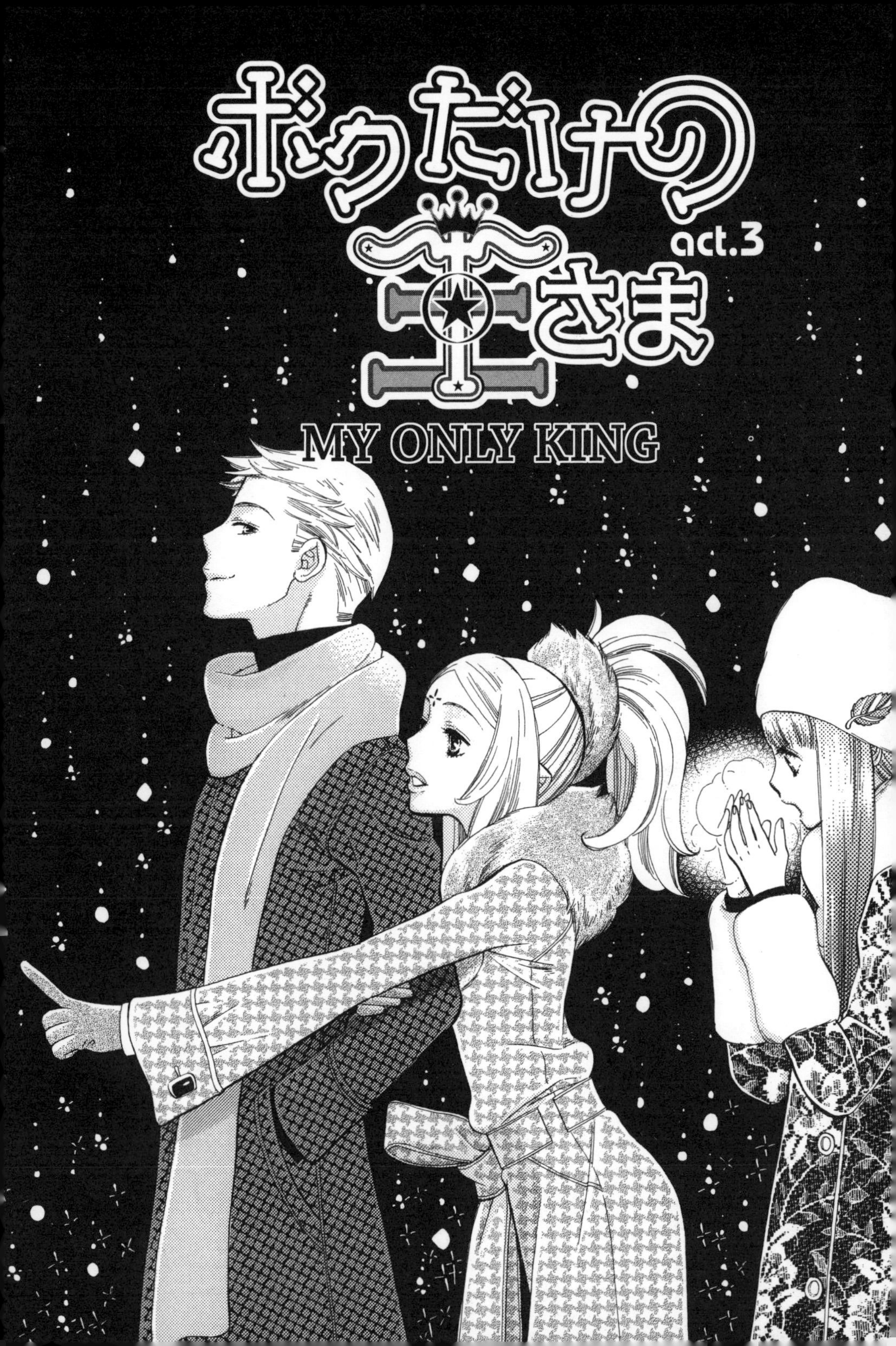
ボクだけの王さま
act.3
MY ONLY KING

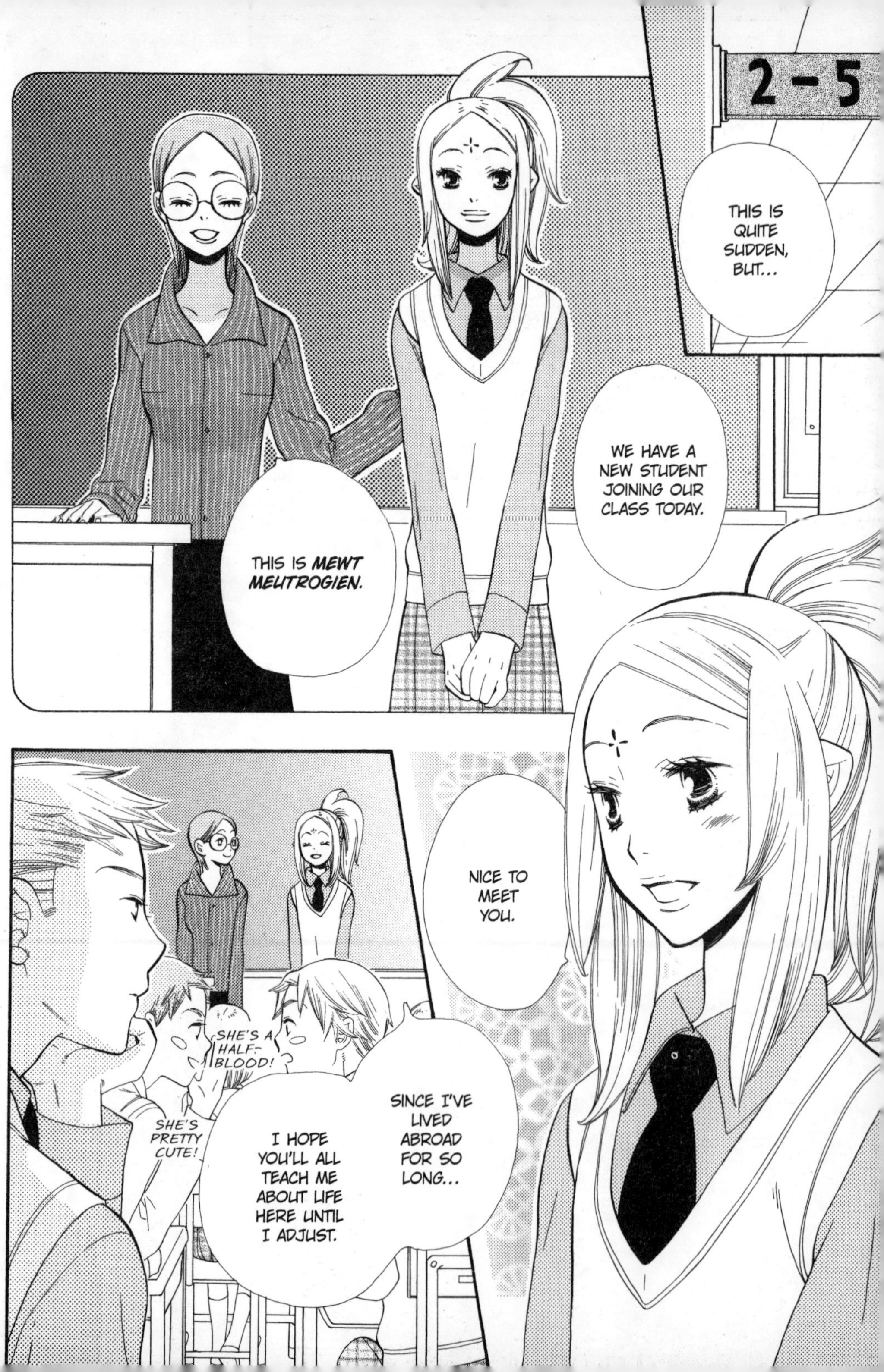
2-5
THIS IS QUITE SUDDEN, BUT...
WE HAVE A NEW STUDENT JOINING OUR CLASS TODAY.
THIS IS **MEWT MEUTROGIEN.**
NICE TO MEET YOU.
SINCE I'VE LIVED ABROAD FOR SO LONG...
I HOPE YOU'LL ALL TEACH ME ABOUT LIFE HERE UNTIL I ADJUST.
SHE'S A HALF-BLOOD!
SHE'S PRETTY CUTE!

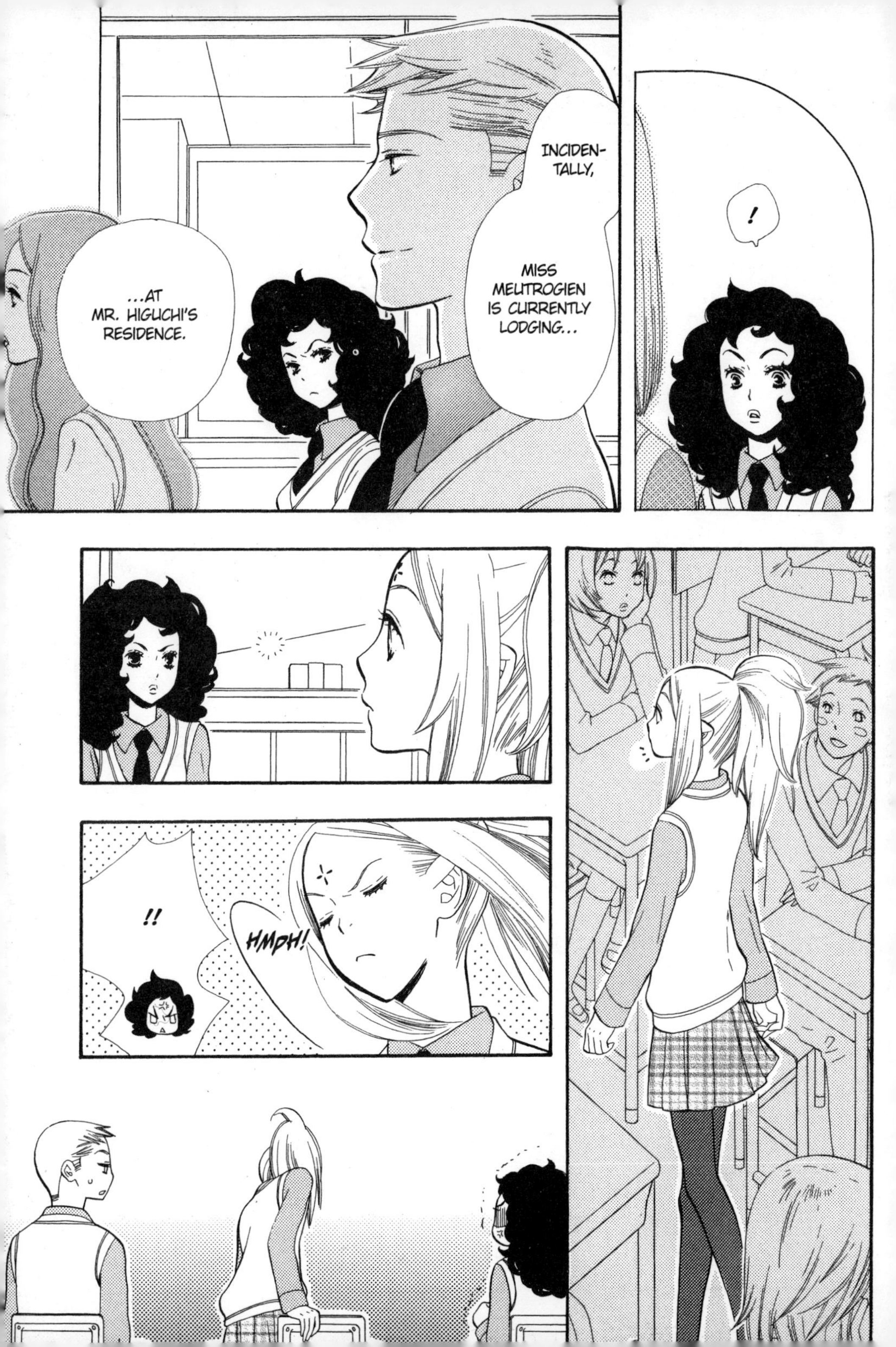
INCIDEN-
TALLY,
MISS MEUTROGIEN IS CURRENTLY LODGING...
...AT MR. HIGUCHI'S RESIDENCE.
!
!!
HMPH!

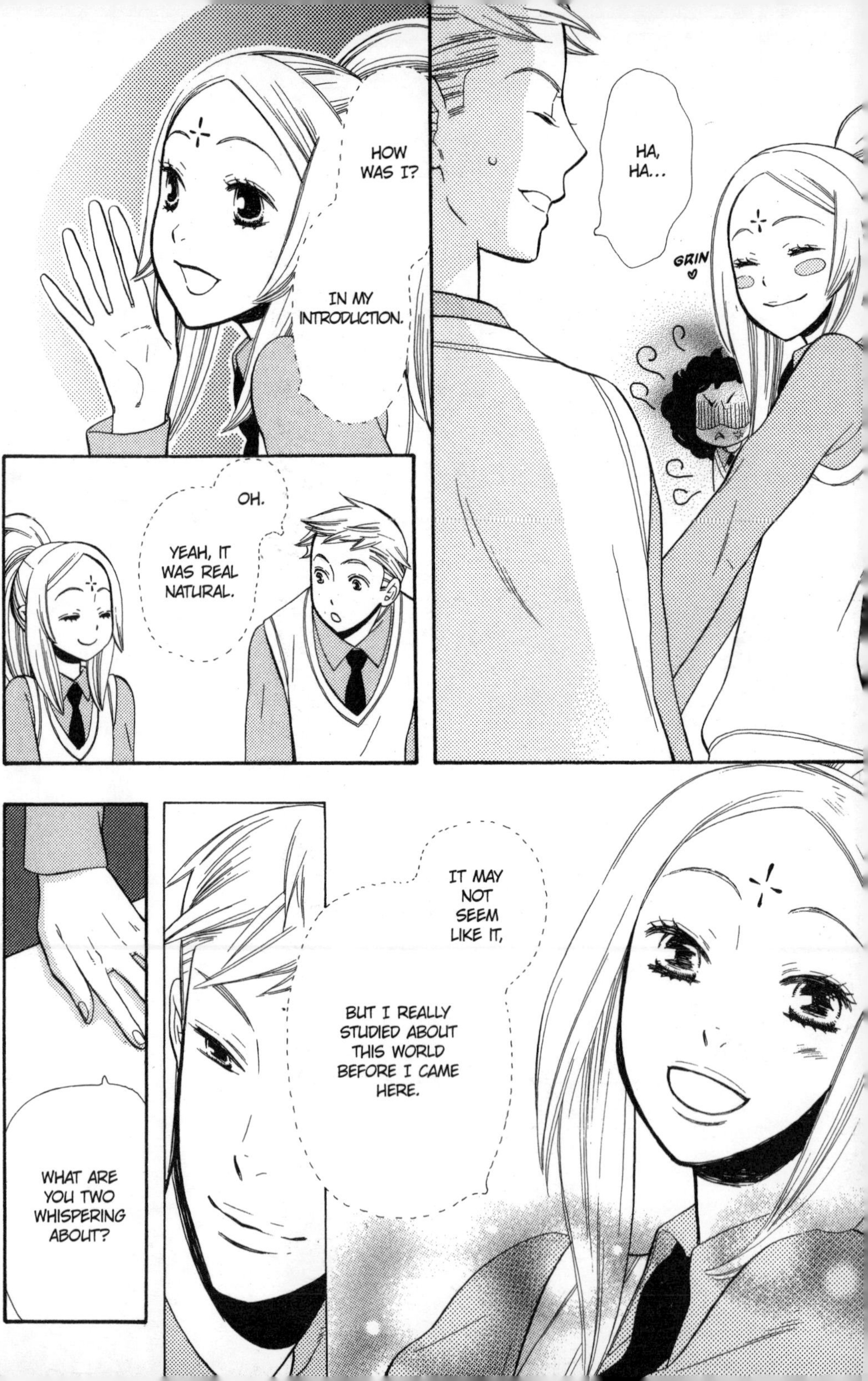
HA, HA...
GRIN
HOW WAS I?
IN MY INTRODUCTION.
OH.
YEAH, IT WAS REAL NATURAL.
IT MAY NOT SEEM LIKE IT,
BUT I REALLY STUDIED ABOUT THIS WORLD BEFORE I CAME HERE.
WHAT ARE YOU TWO WHISPERING ABOUT?

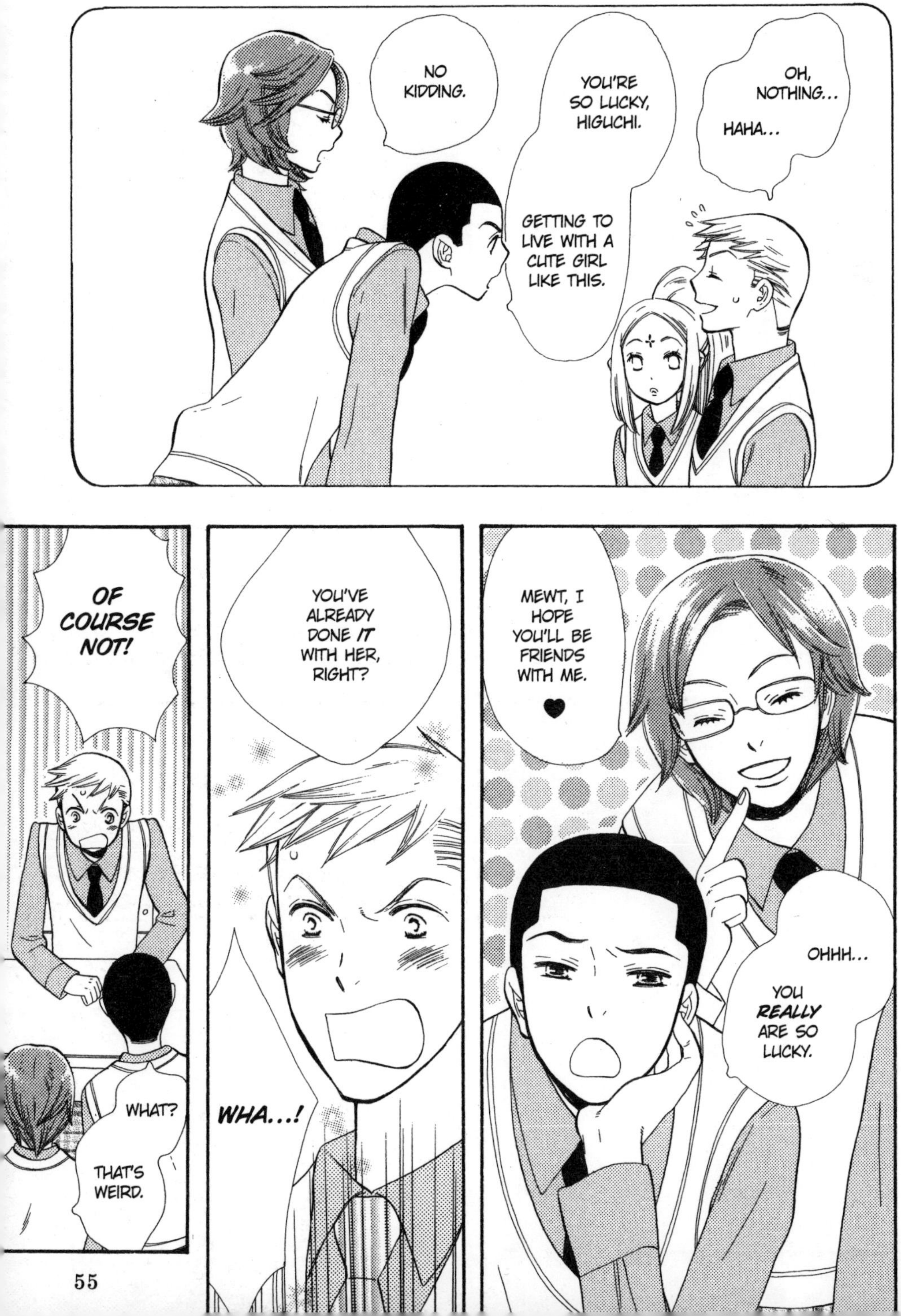
OH, NOTHING... HAHA...
YOU'RE SO LUCKY, HIGUCHI.
GETTING TO LIVE WITH A CUTE GIRL LIKE THIS.
NO KIDDING.
MEWT, I HOPE YOU'LL BE FRIENDS WITH ME. ♥
OHHH... YOU *REALLY* ARE SO LUCKY.
YOU'VE ALREADY DONE *IT* WITH HER, RIGHT?
WHA...!
OF COURSE NOT!
WHAT? THAT'S WEIRD.

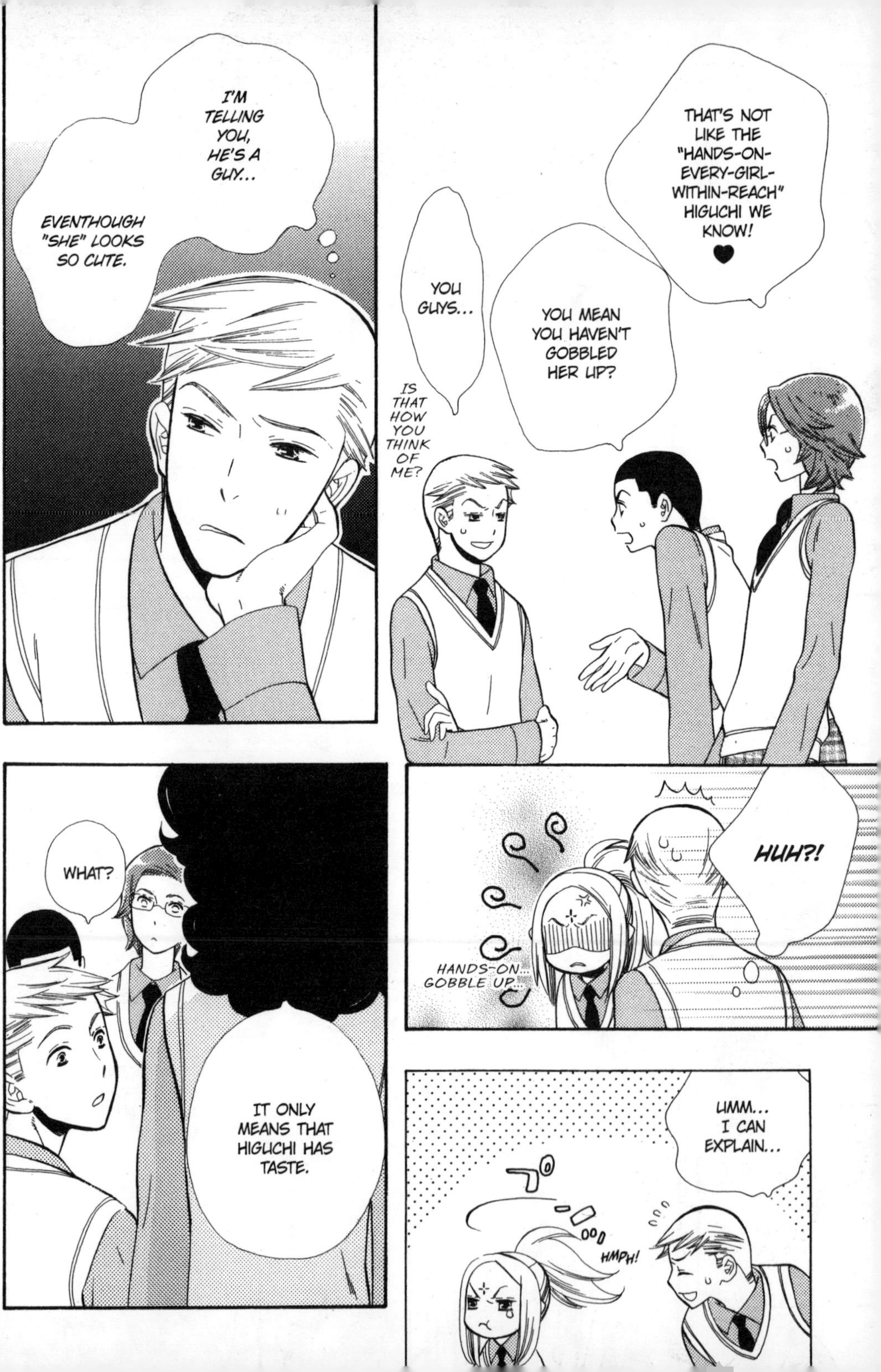
THAT'S NOT LIKE THE "HANDS-ON-EVERY-GIRL-WITHIN-REACH" HIGUCHI WE KNOW! ♥
YOU MEAN YOU HAVEN'T GOBBLED HER UP?
YOU GUYS...
IS THAT HOW YOU THINK OF ME?
I'M TELLING YOU, HE'S A GUY...
EVENTHOUGH "SHE" LOOKS SO CUTE.
HUH?!
HANDS-ON... GOBBLE UP...
UMM... I CAN EXPLAIN...
HMPH!
WHAT?
IT ONLY MEANS THAT HIGUCHI HAS TASTE.

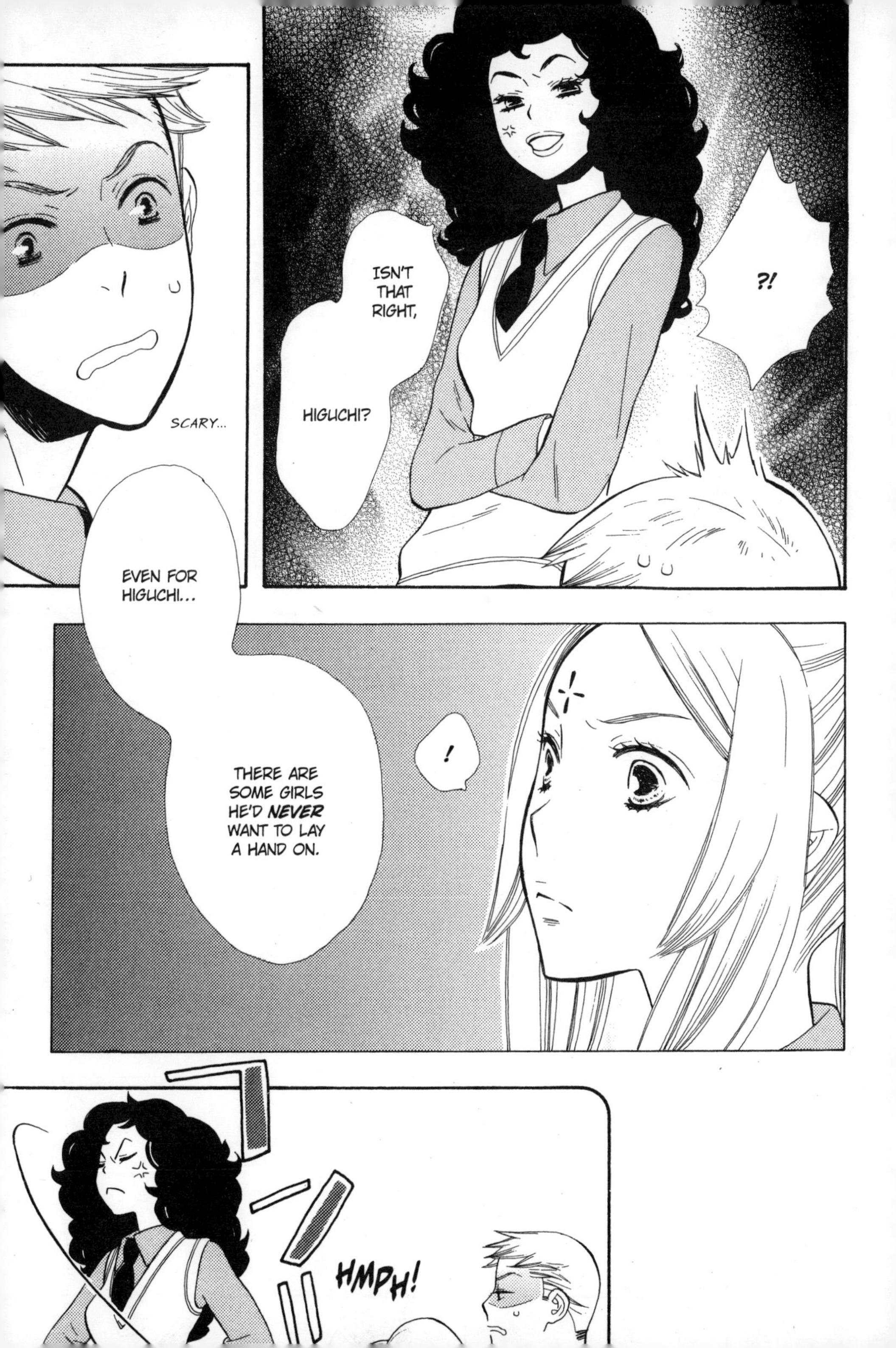
?!
ISN'T THAT RIGHT, HIGUCHI?
SCARY...
EVEN FOR HIGUCHI... THERE ARE SOME GIRLS HE'D ***NEVER*** WANT TO LAY A HAND ON.
!
HMPH!

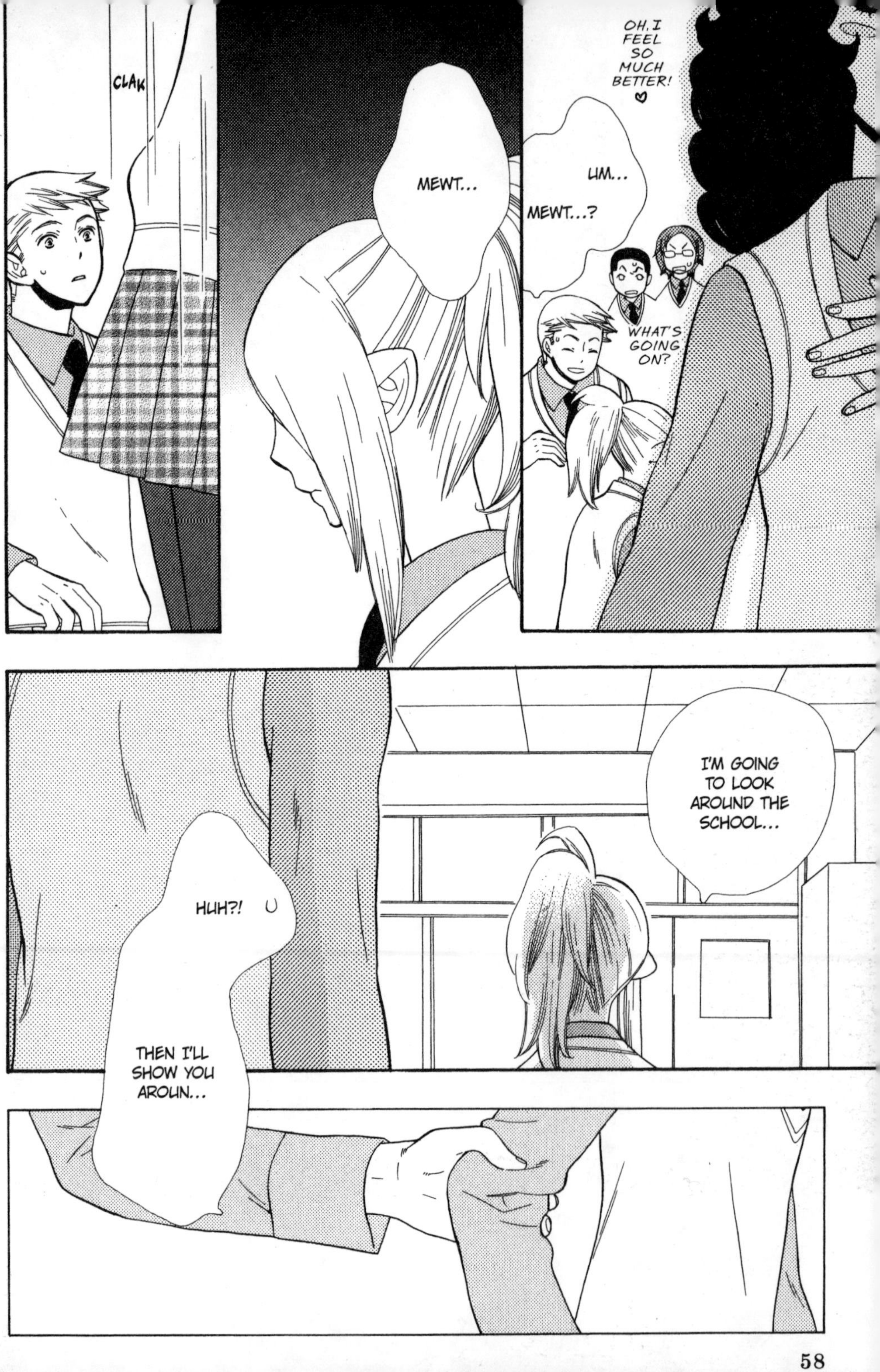
OH, I FEEL SO MUCH BETTER!
UM... MEWT...?
WHAT'S GOING ON?
MEWT...
CLAK
I'M GOING TO LOOK AROUND THE SCHOOL...
HUH?!
THEN I'LL SHOW YOU AROUN...

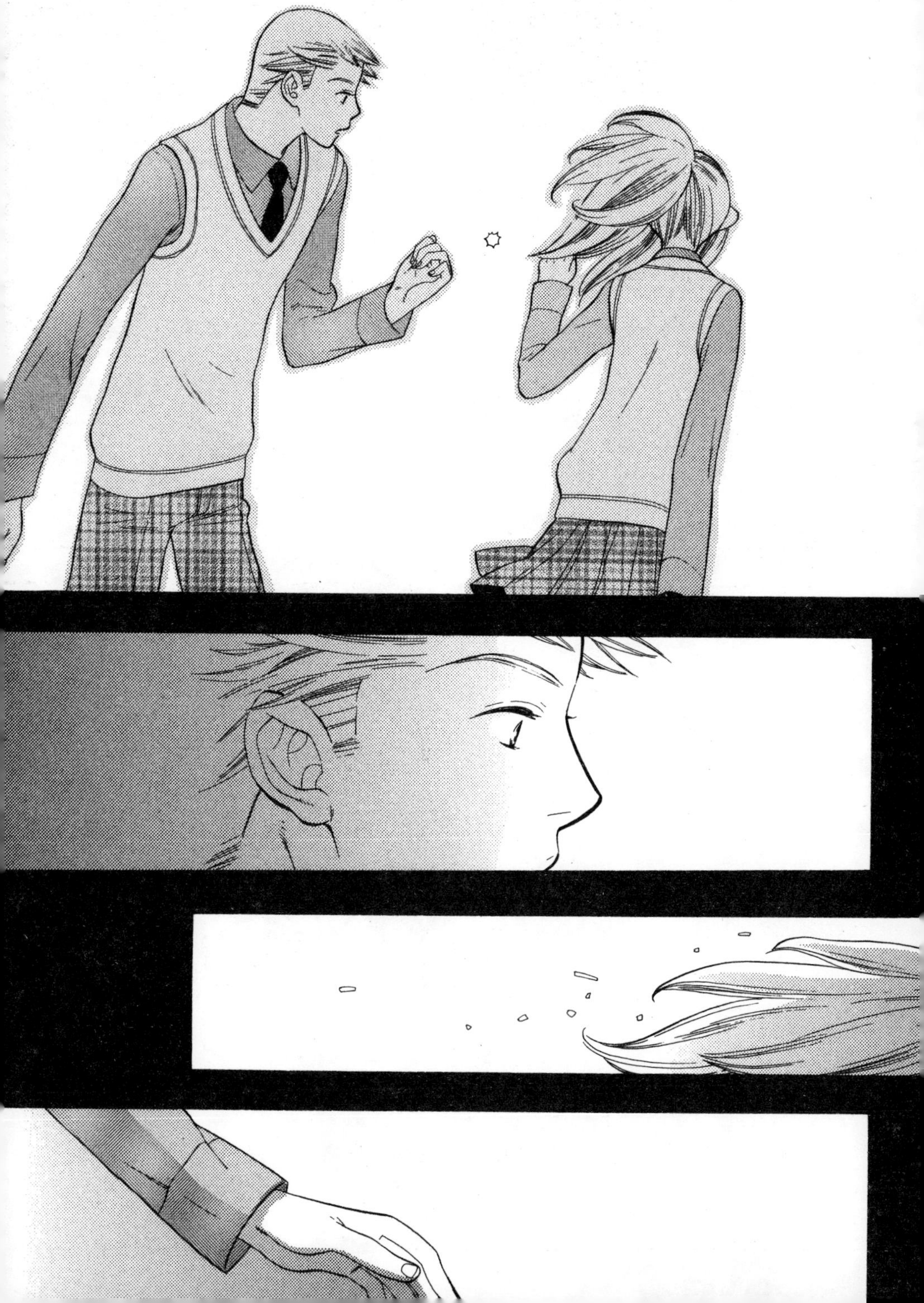

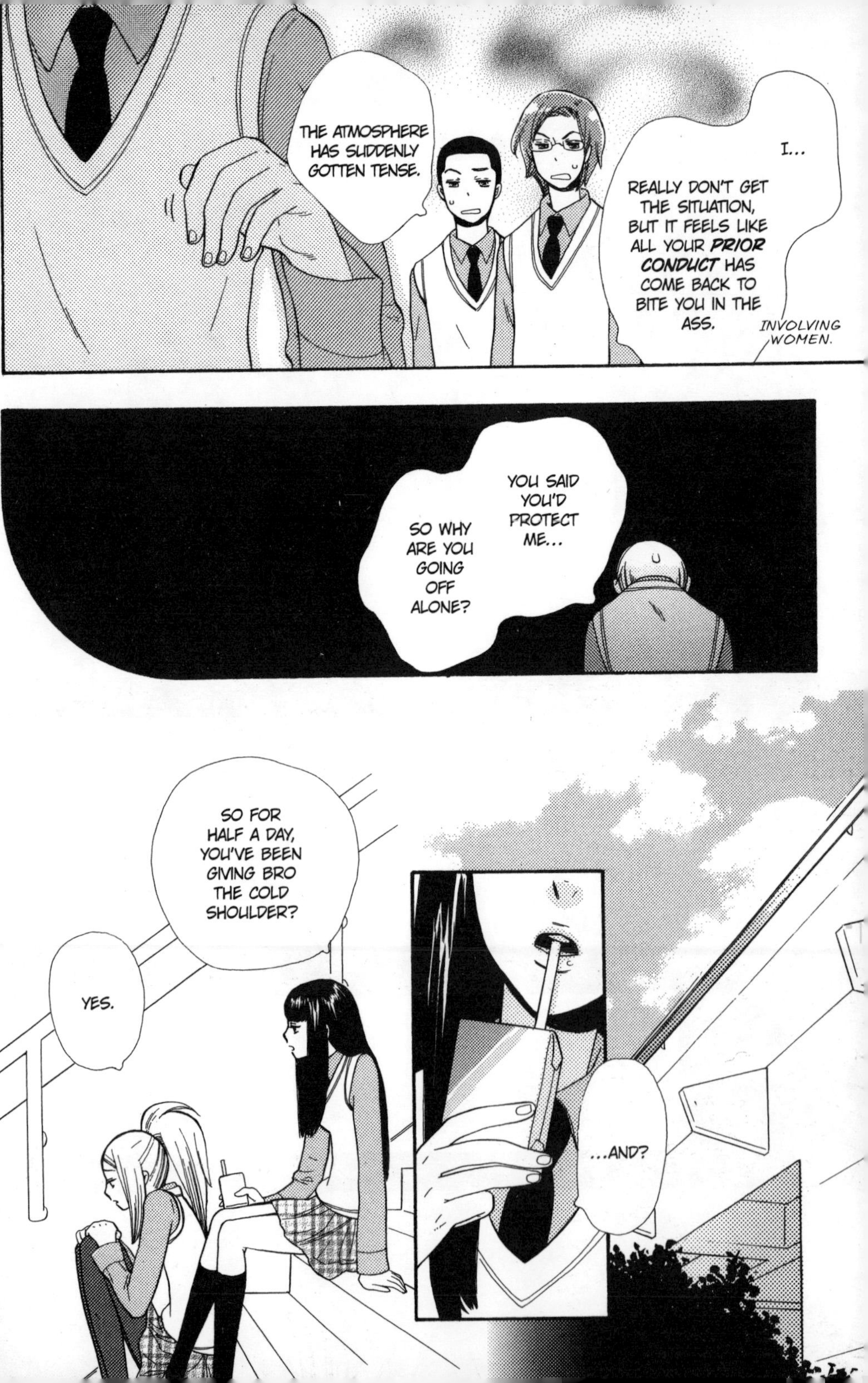
I...
REALLY DON'T GET THE SITUATION, BUT IT FEELS LIKE ALL YOUR **PRIOR CONDUCT** HAS COME BACK TO BITE YOU IN THE ASS.
INVOLVING WOMEN.
THE ATMOSPHERE HAS SUDDENLY GOTTEN TENSE.
YOU SAID YOU'D PROTECT ME...
SO WHY ARE YOU GOING OFF ALONE?
SO FOR HALF A DAY, YOU'VE BEEN GIVING BRO THE COLD SHOULDER?
YES.
...AND?

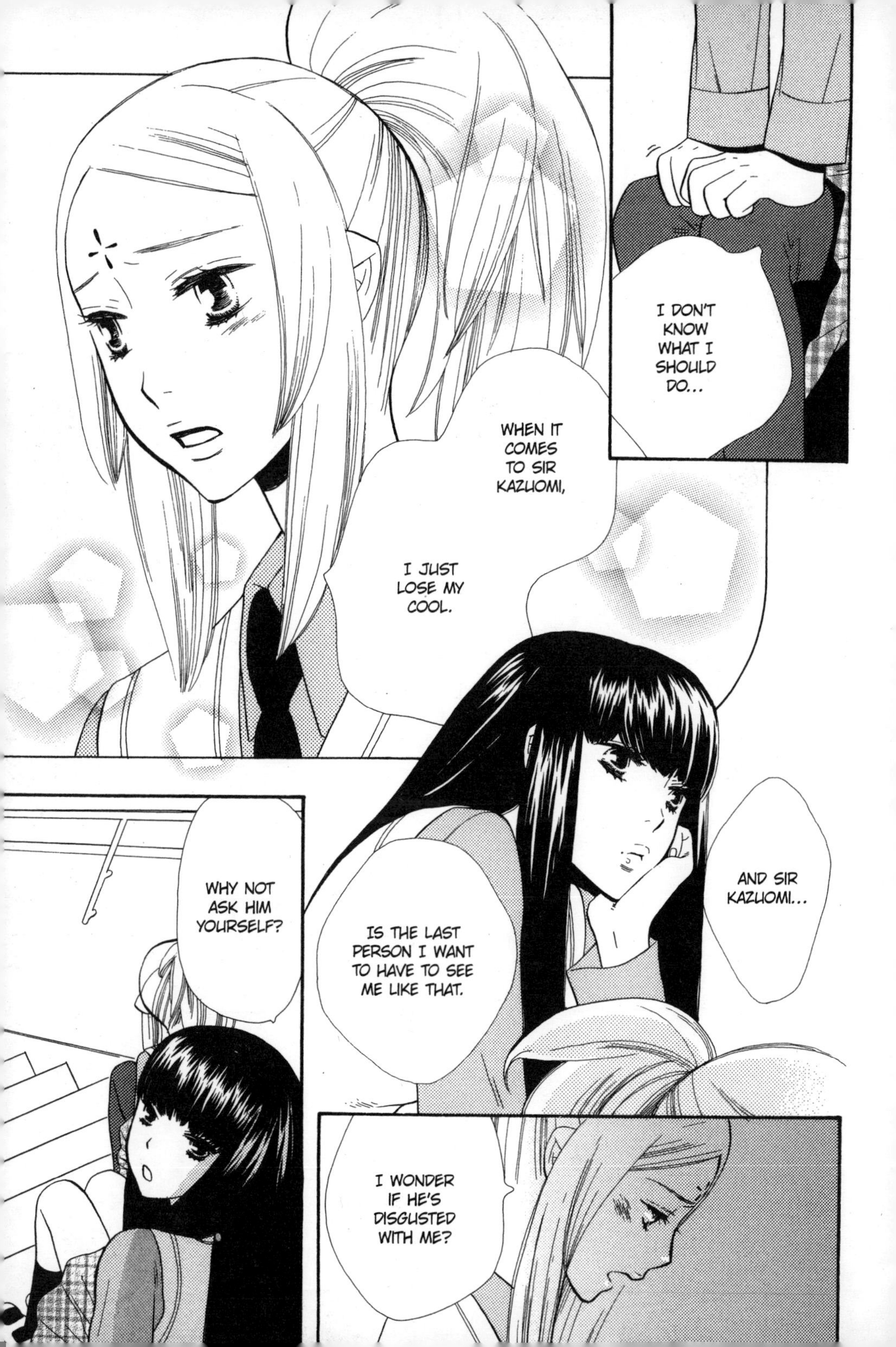
I DON'T KNOW WHAT I SHOULD DO...
WHEN IT COMES TO SIR KAZUOMI,
I JUST LOSE MY COOL.
AND SIR KAZUOMI...
IS THE LAST PERSON I WANT TO HAVE TO SEE ME LIKE THAT.
I WONDER IF HE'S DISGUSTED WITH ME?
WHY NOT ASK HIM YOURSELF?

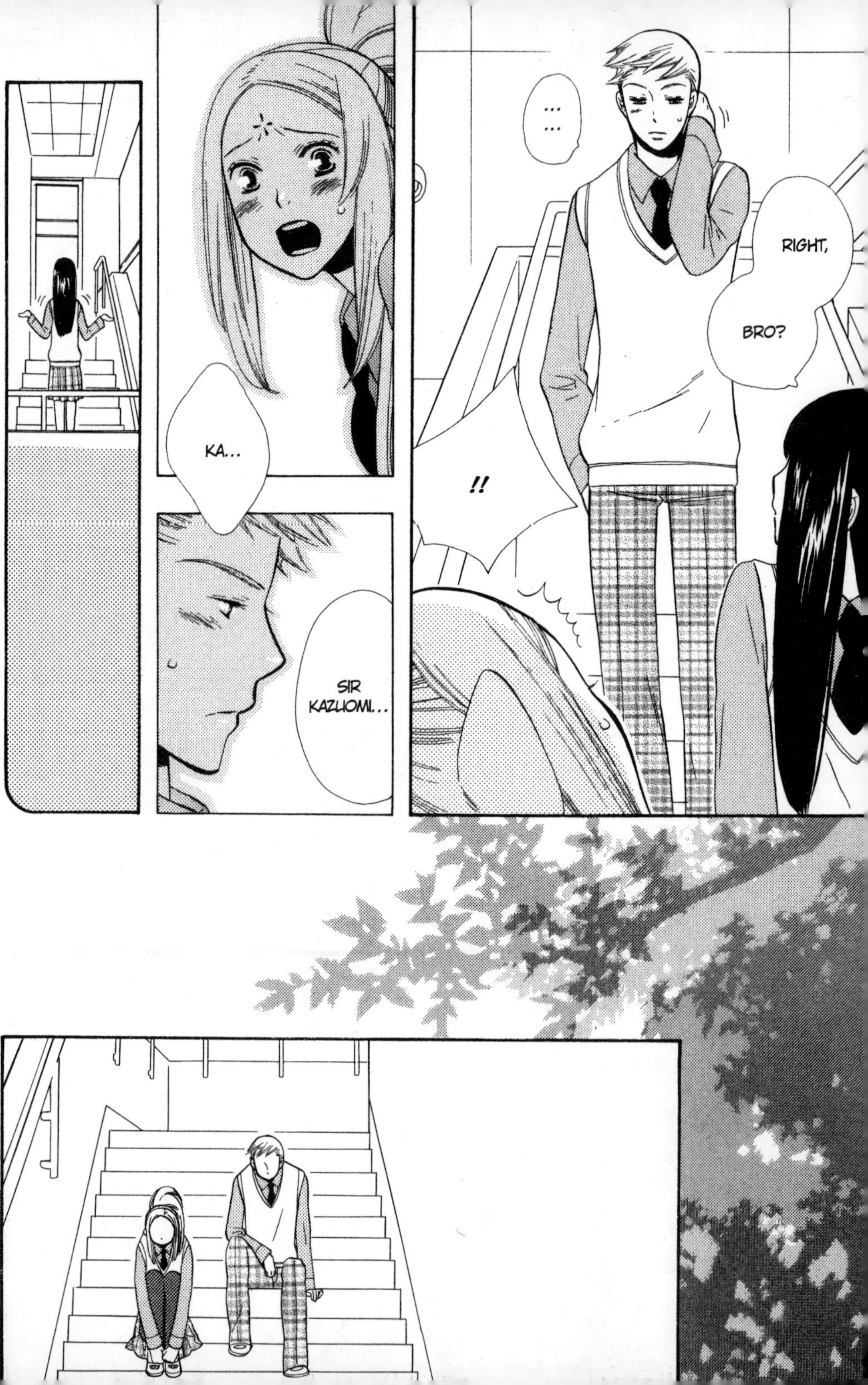
RIGHT, BRO?
... ...
!!
KA...
SIR KAZUOMI...

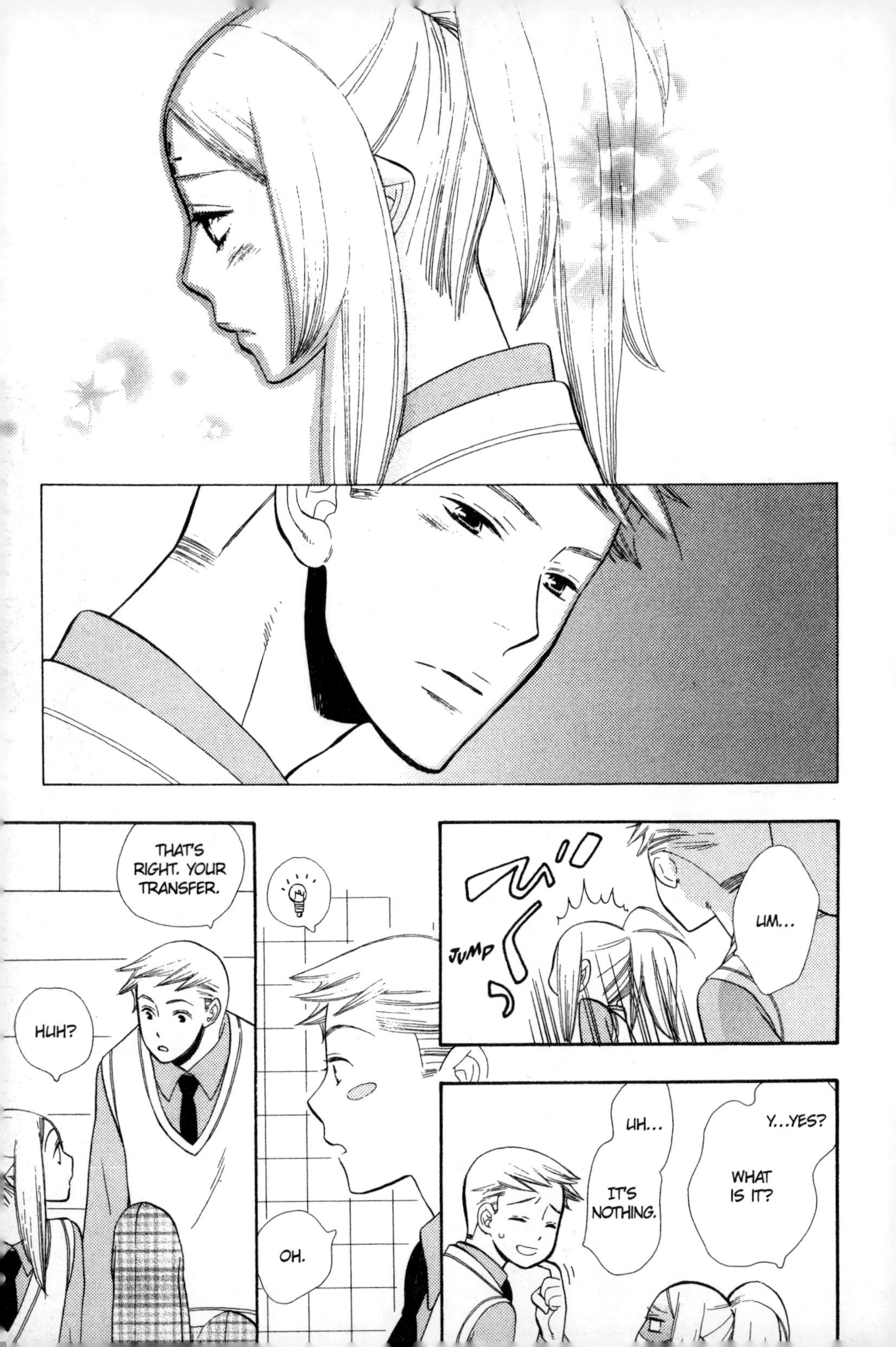

JUMP
UM...
Y...YES? WHAT IS IT?
UH... IT'S NOTHING.
OH.
THAT'S RIGHT. YOUR TRANSFER.
HUH?

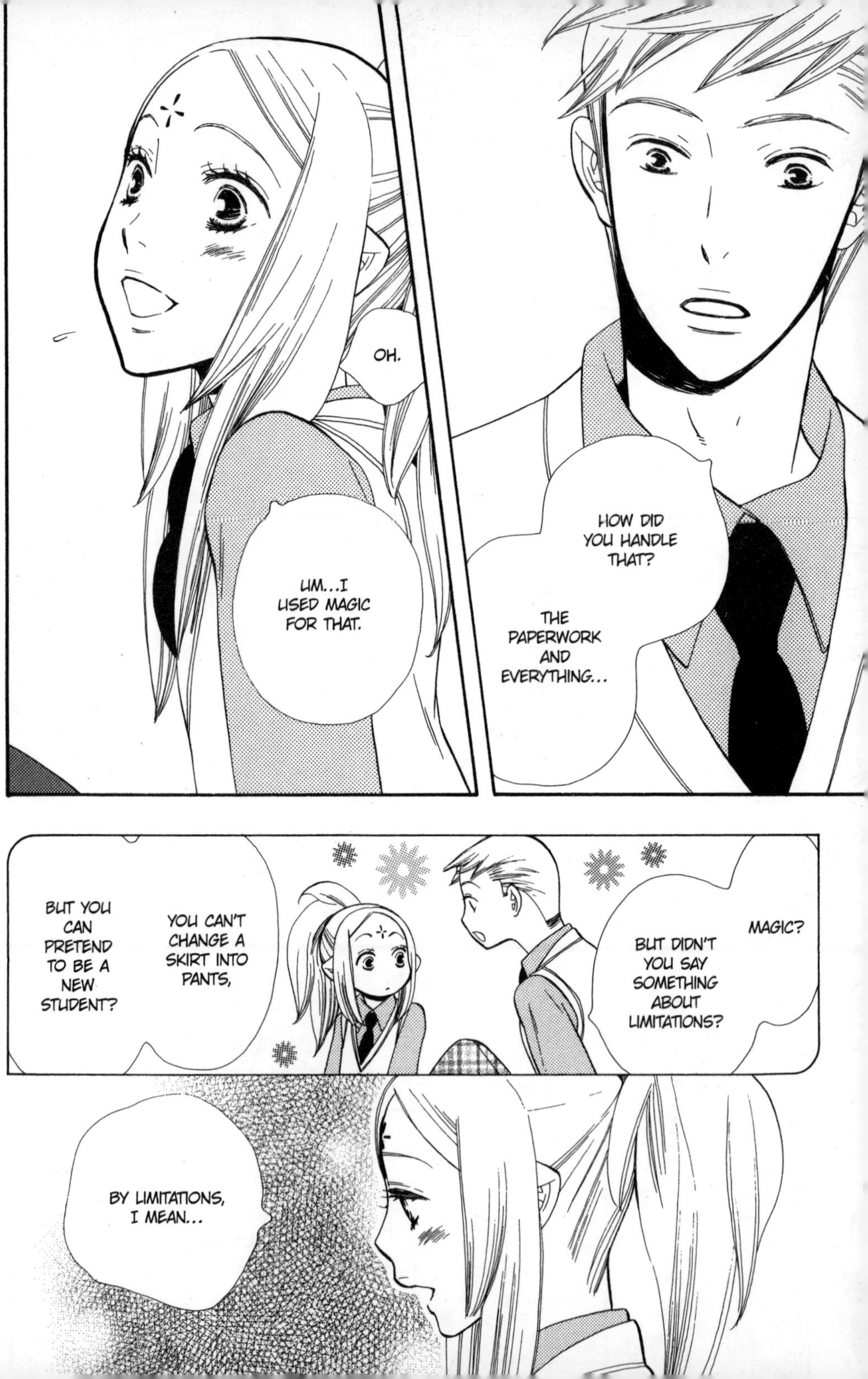
HOW DID YOU HANDLE THAT?
THE PAPERWORK AND EVERYTHING...
OH.
UM...I USED MAGIC FOR THAT.
MAGIC?
BUT DIDN'T YOU SAY SOMETHING ABOUT LIMITATIONS?
YOU CAN'T CHANGE A SKIRT INTO PANTS,
BUT YOU CAN PRETEND TO BE A NEW STUDENT?
BY LIMITATIONS, I MEAN...

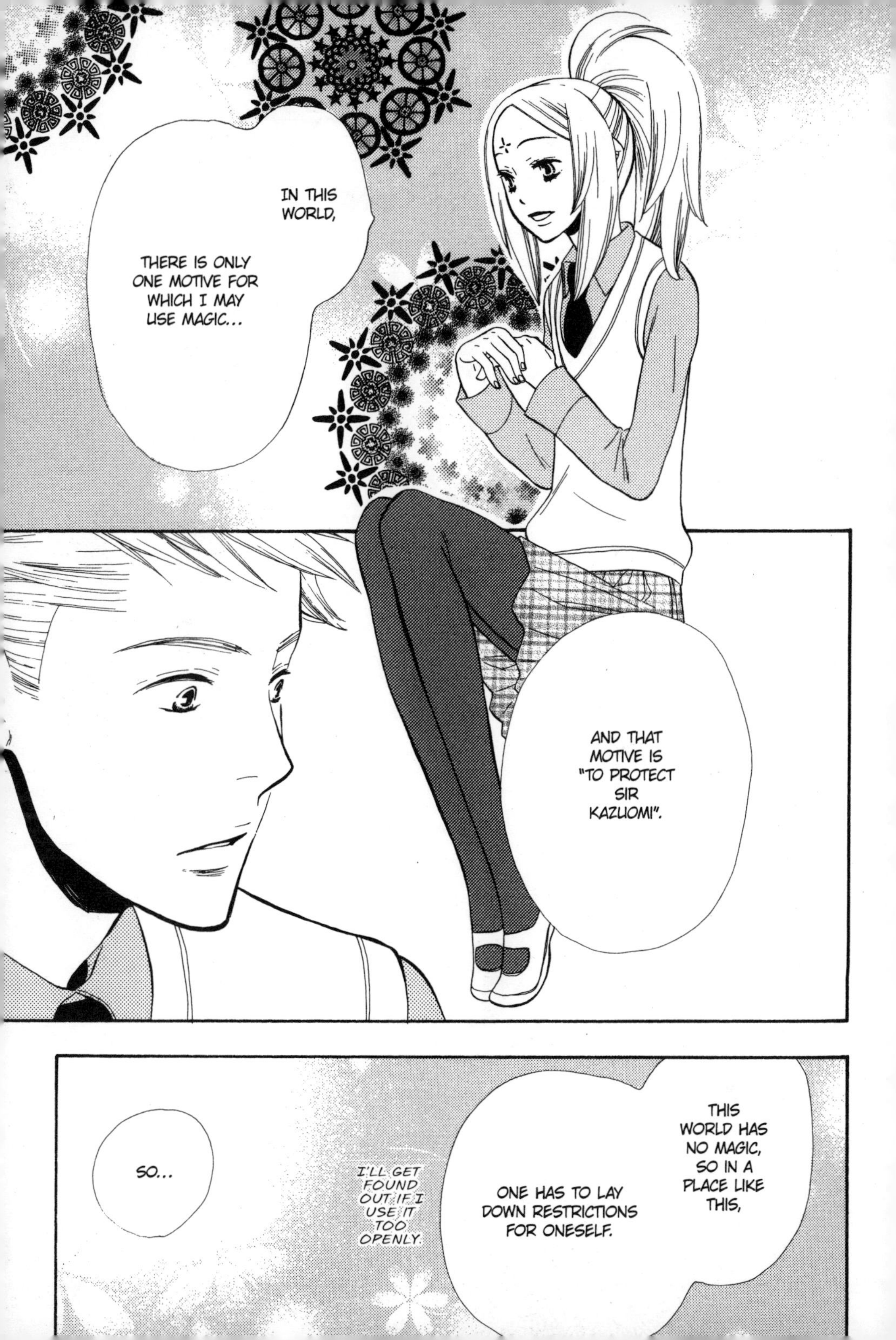
IN THIS WORLD,
THERE IS ONLY ONE MOTIVE FOR WHICH I MAY USE MAGIC...
AND THAT MOTIVE IS "TO PROTECT SIR KAZUOMI".
THIS WORLD HAS NO MAGIC, SO IN A PLACE LIKE THIS,
ONE HAS TO LAY DOWN RESTRICTIONS FOR ONESELF.
I'LL GET FOUND OUT IF I USE IT TOO OPENLY.
SO...

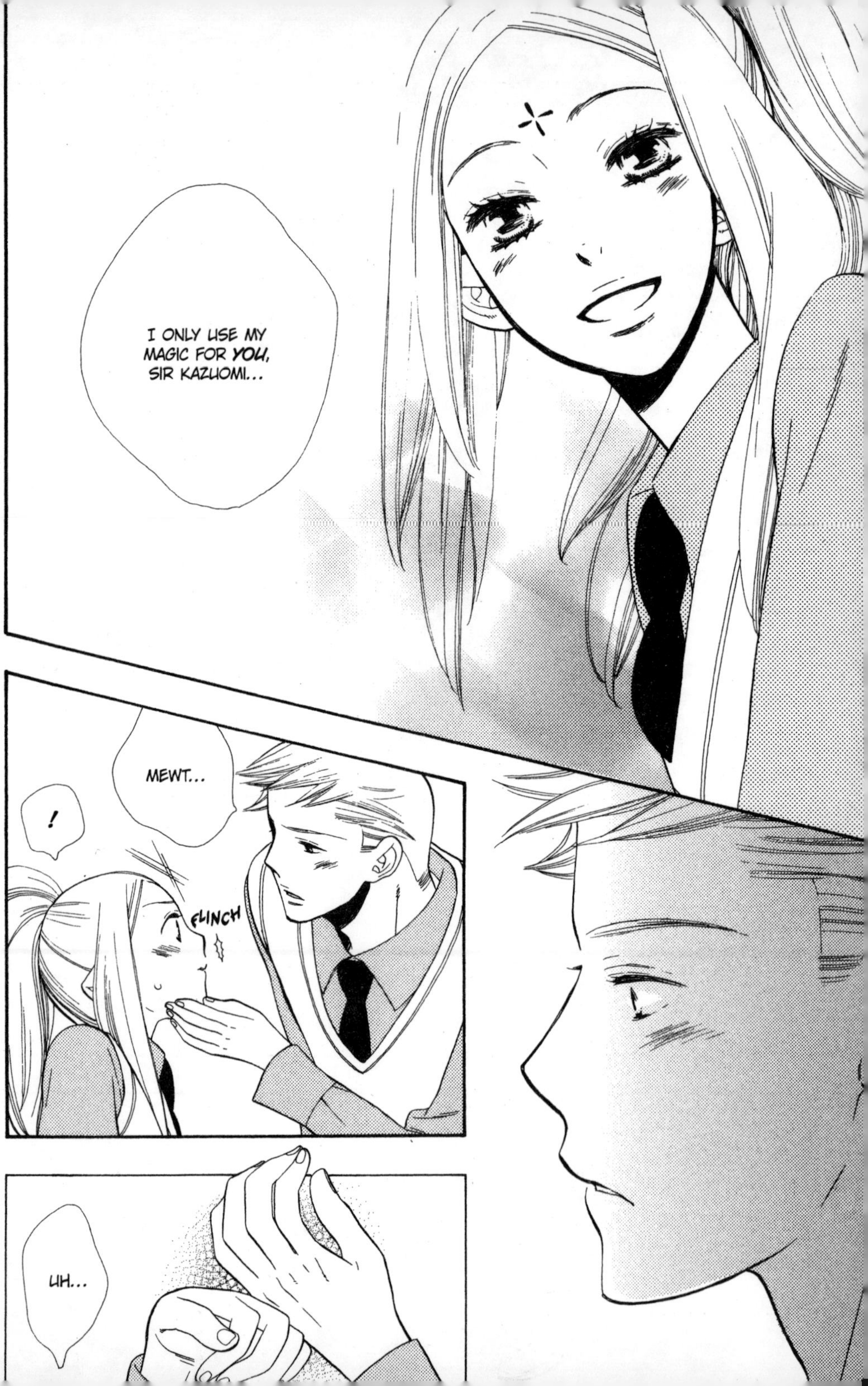
I ONLY USE MY MAGIC FOR YOU, SIR KAZUOMI...
MEWT...
!
FLINCH
UH...

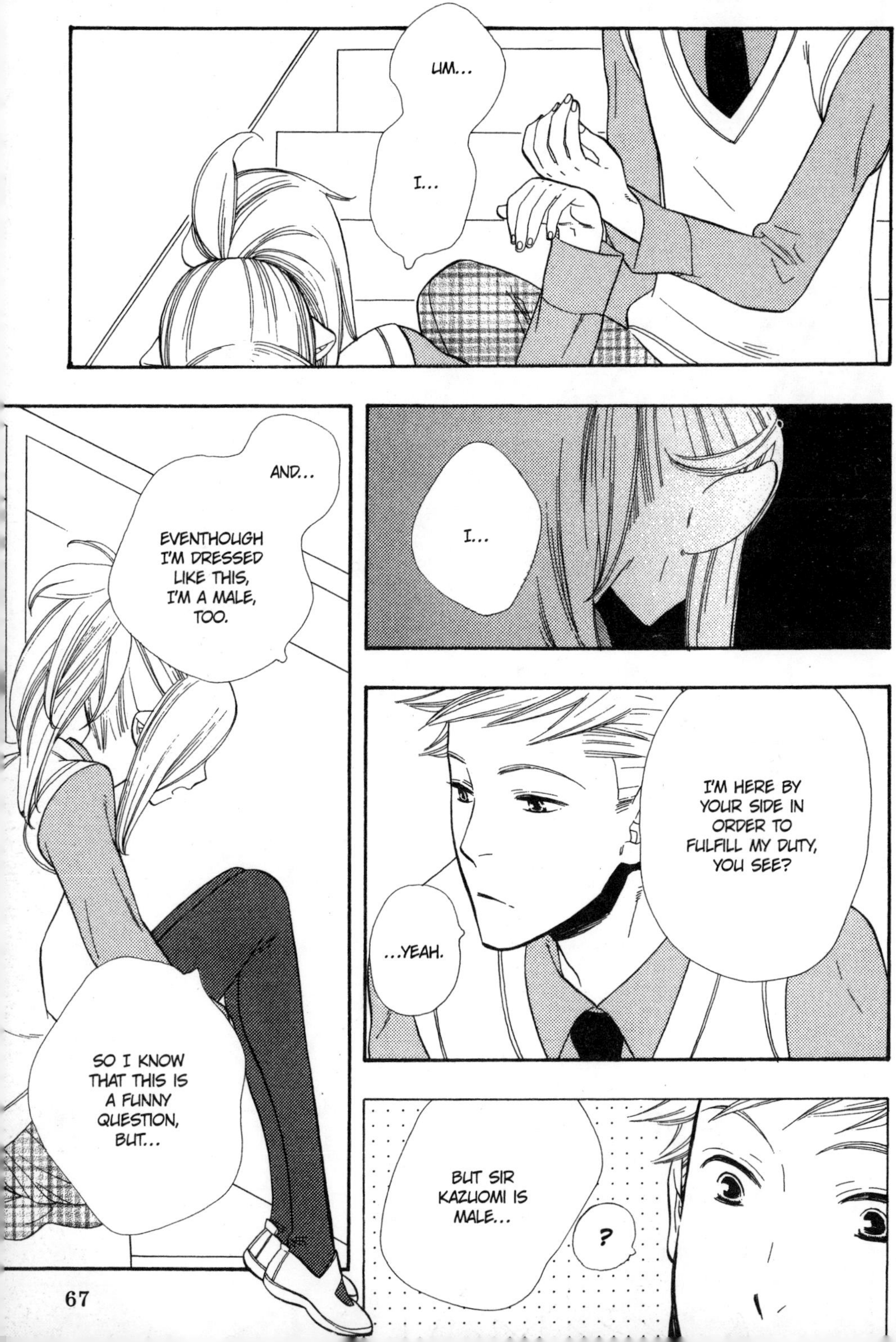
UM...
I...
I...
I'M HERE BY YOUR SIDE IN ORDER TO FULFILL MY DUTY, YOU SEE?
...YEAH.
BUT SIR KAZUOMI IS MALE...
?
AND...
EVENTHOUGH I'M DRESSED LIKE THIS, I'M A MALE, TOO.
SO I KNOW THAT THIS IS A FUNNY QUESTION, BUT...

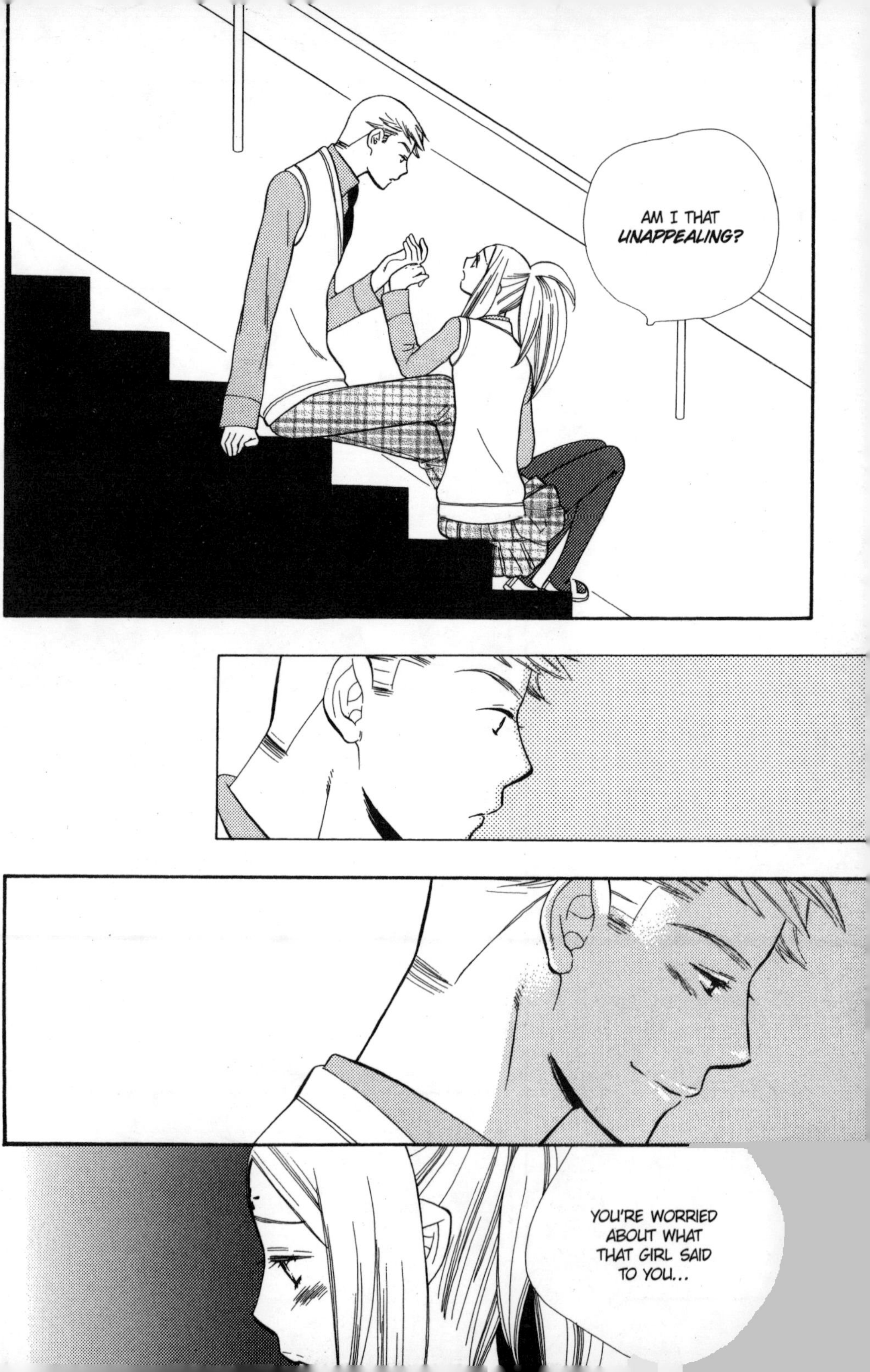
AM I THAT UNAPPEALING?
YOU'RE WORRIED ABOUT WHAT THAT GIRL SAID TO YOU...

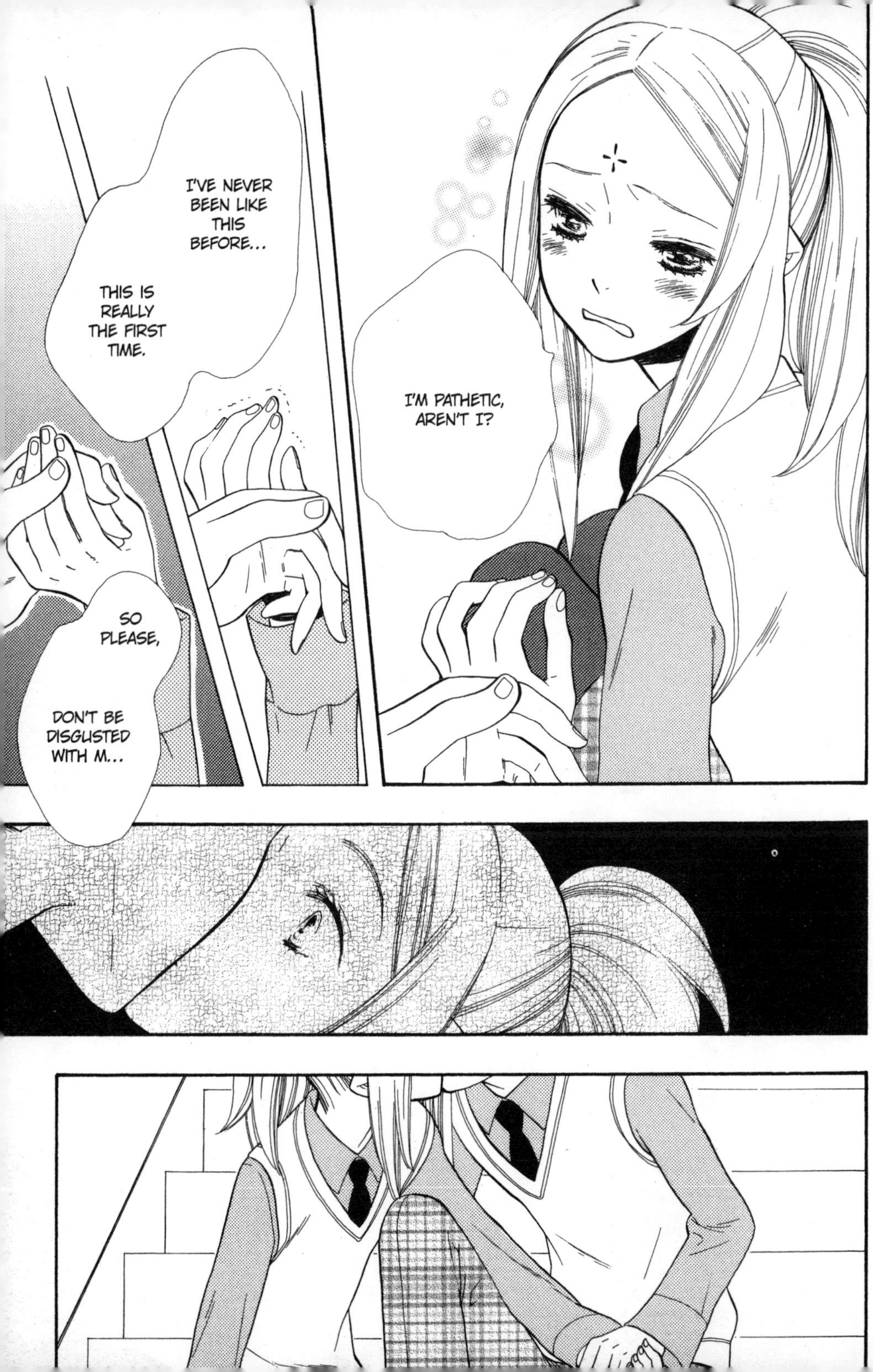
I'M PATHETIC, AREN'T I?
I'VE NEVER BEEN LIKE THIS BEFORE...
THIS IS REALLY THE FIRST TIME.
SO PLEASE,
DON'T BE DISGUSTED WITH M...

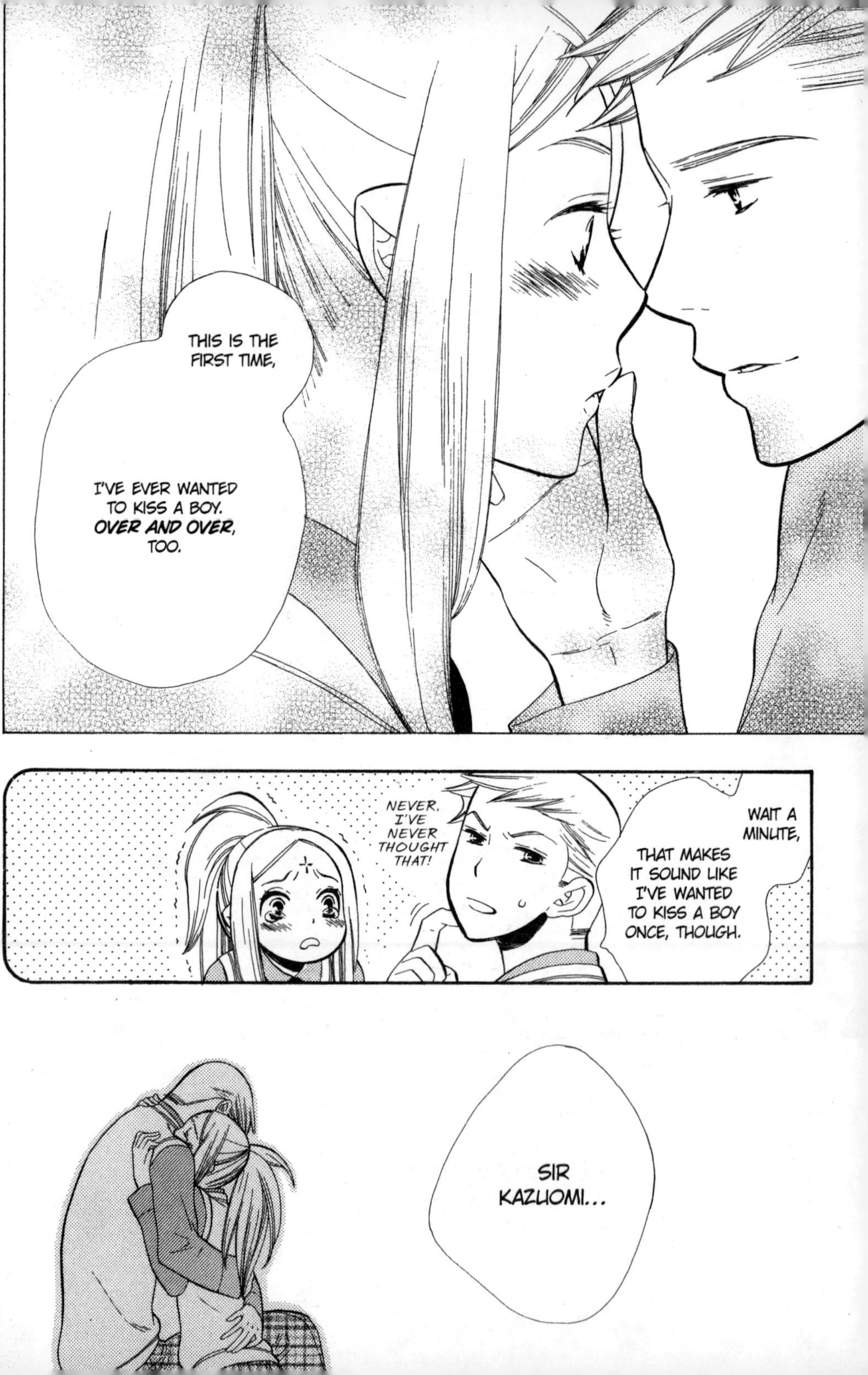
THIS IS THE FIRST TIME,
I'VE EVER WANTED TO KISS A BOY. ***OVER AND OVER***, TOO.
WAIT A MINUTE,
THAT MAKES IT SOUND LIKE I'VE WANTED TO KISS A BOY ONCE, THOUGH.
NEVER, I'VE NEVER THOUGHT THAT!
SIR KAZUOMI...

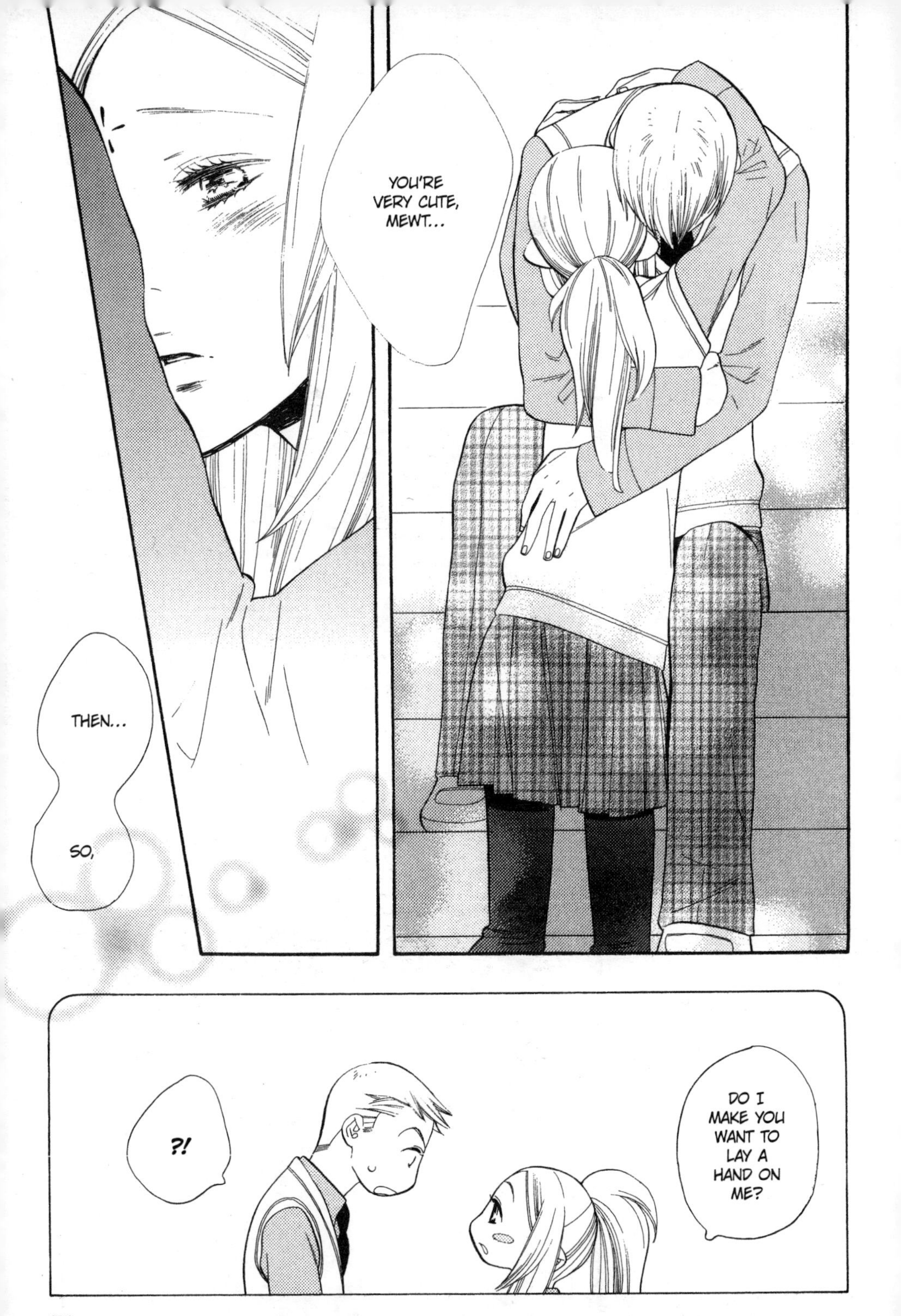
YOU'RE VERY CUTE, MEWT...
THEN...
SO,
DO I MAKE YOU WANT TO LAY A HAND ON ME?
?!

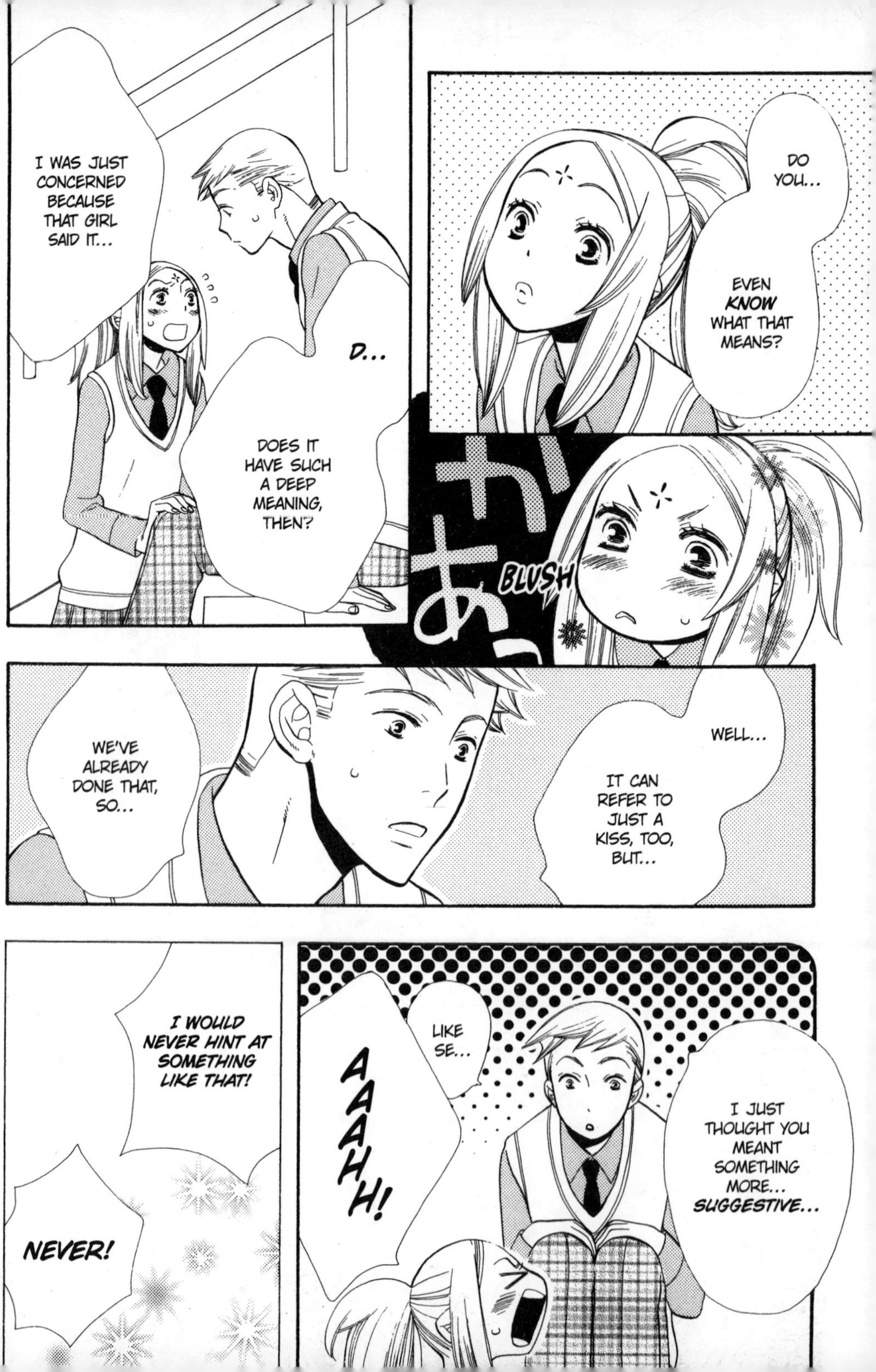
DO YOU...
EVEN KNOW WHAT THAT MEANS?
かぁっ
BLUSH
D...
DOES IT HAVE SUCH A DEEP MEANING, THEN?
I WAS JUST CONCERNED BECAUSE THAT GIRL SAID IT...
WELL...
IT CAN REFER TO JUST A KISS, TOO, BUT...
WE'VE ALREADY DONE THAT, SO...
I JUST THOUGHT YOU MEANT SOMETHING MORE... SUGGESTIVE...
LIKE SE...
AAAAHH!
I WOULD NEVER HINT AT SOMETHING LIKE THAT!
NEVER!

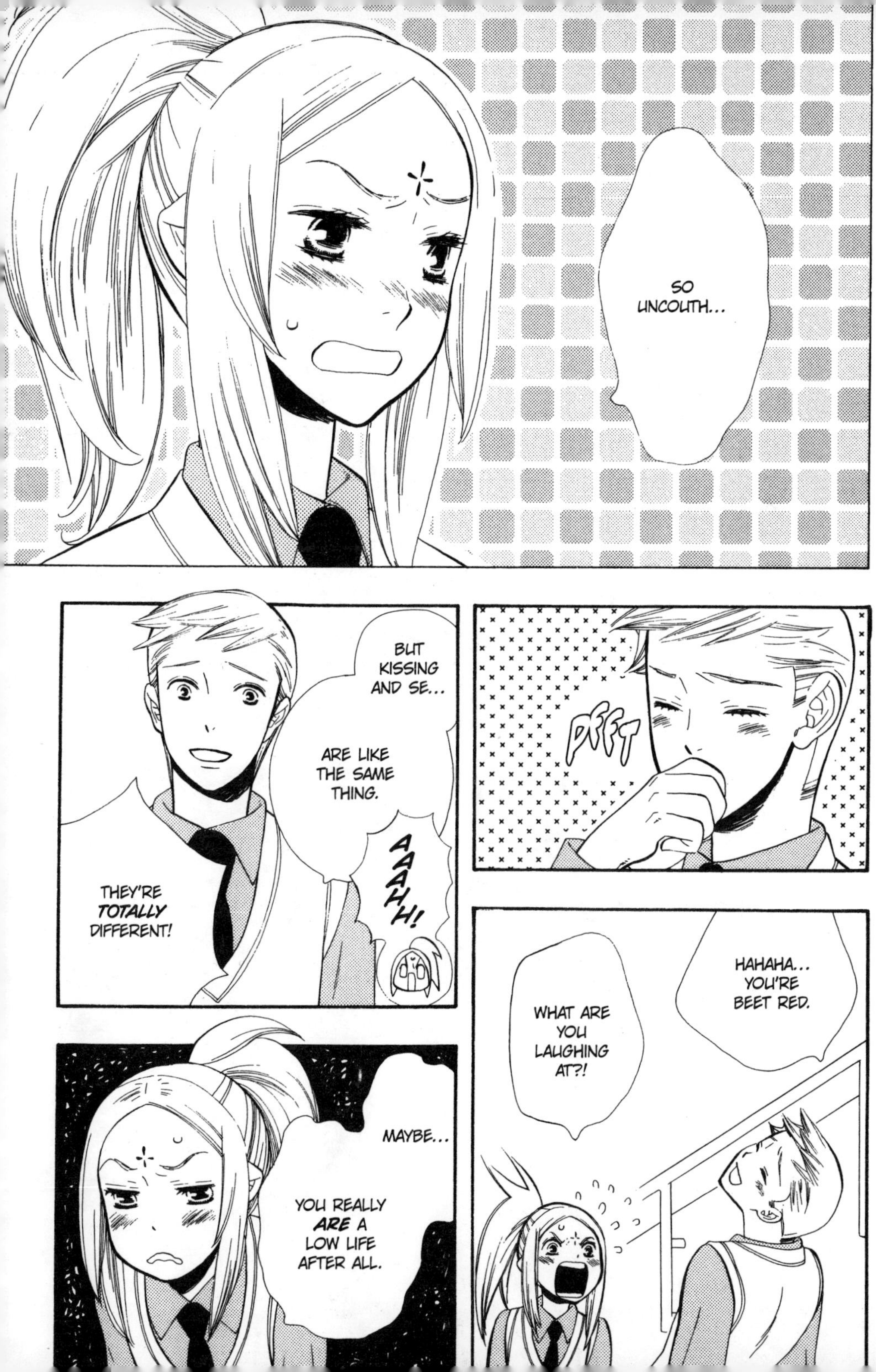
SO UNCOUTH...
BUT KISSING AND SE...
ARE LIKE THE SAME THING.
AAAHH!
THEY'RE *TOTALLY* DIFFERENT!
PFFT
MAYBE...
YOU REALLY *ARE* A LOW LIFE AFTER ALL.
HAHAHA... YOU'RE BEET RED.
WHAT ARE YOU LAUGHING AT?!

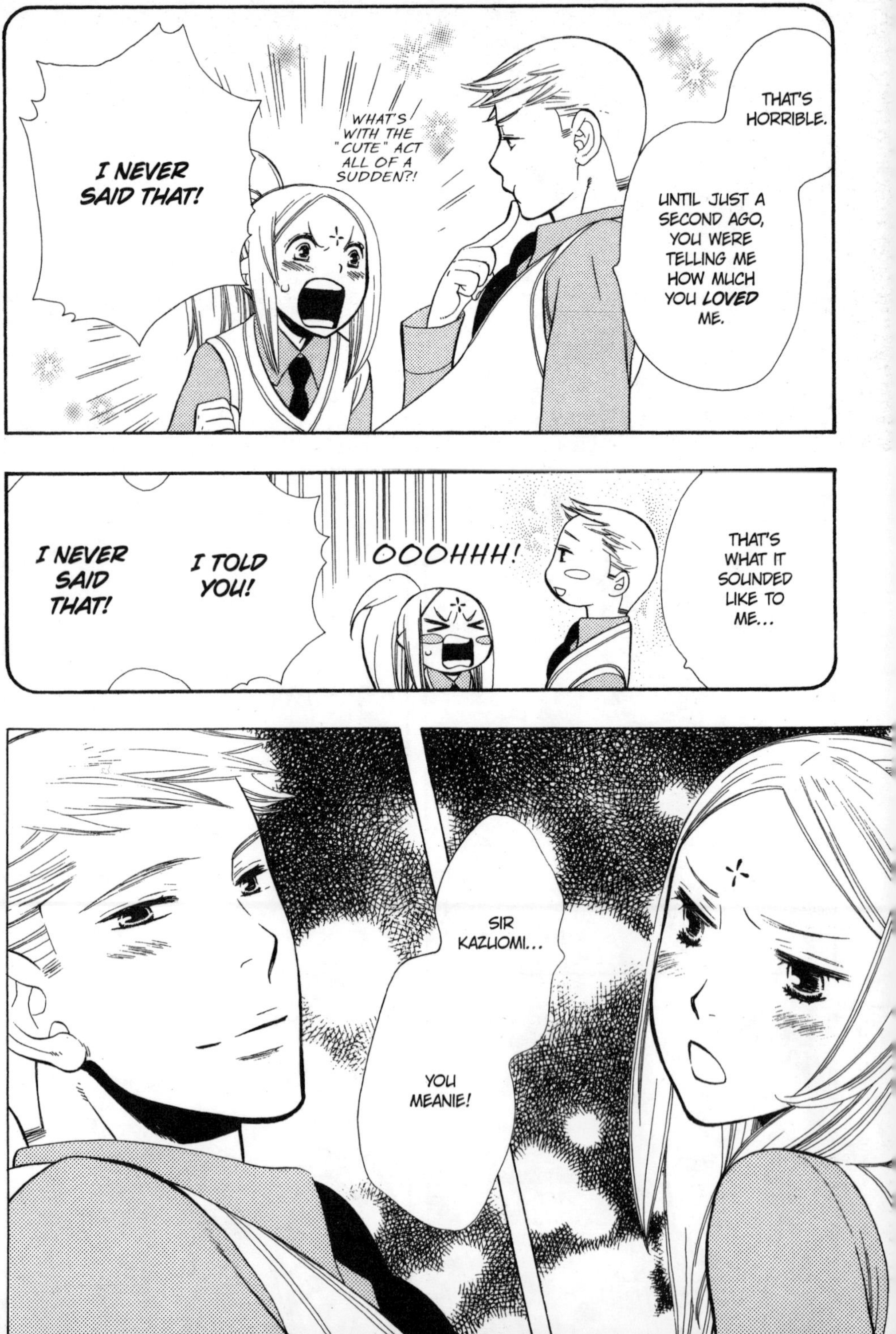
THAT'S HORRIBLE.
UNTIL JUST A SECOND AGO, YOU WERE TELLING ME HOW MUCH YOU LOVED ME.
WHAT'S WITH THE "CUTE" ACT ALL OF A SUDDEN?!
I NEVER SAID THAT!
THAT'S WHAT IT SOUNDED LIKE TO ME...
OOOHHH!
I TOLD YOU!
I NEVER SAID THAT!
SIR KAZUOMI...
YOU MEANIE!

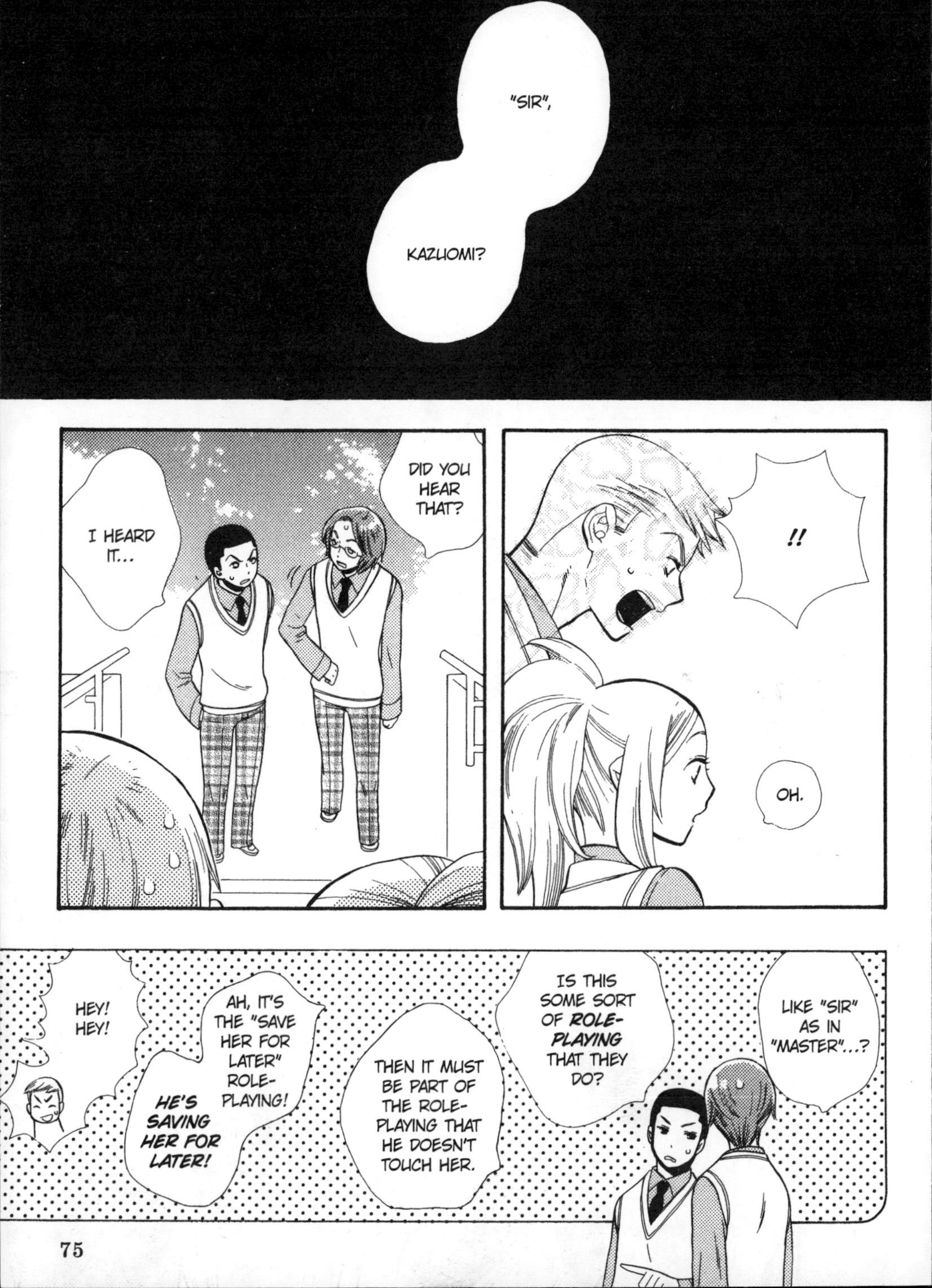
"SIR",
KAZUOMI?
!!
OH.
DID YOU HEAR THAT?
I HEARD IT...
LIKE "SIR" AS IN "MASTER"...?
IS THIS SOME SORT OF ***ROLE-PLAYING*** THAT THEY DO?
THEN IT MUST BE PART OF THE ROLE-PLAYING THAT HE DOESN'T TOUCH HER.
AH, IT'S THE "SAVE HER FOR LATER" ROLE-PLAYING!
HE'S SAVING HER FOR LATER!
HEY! HEY!

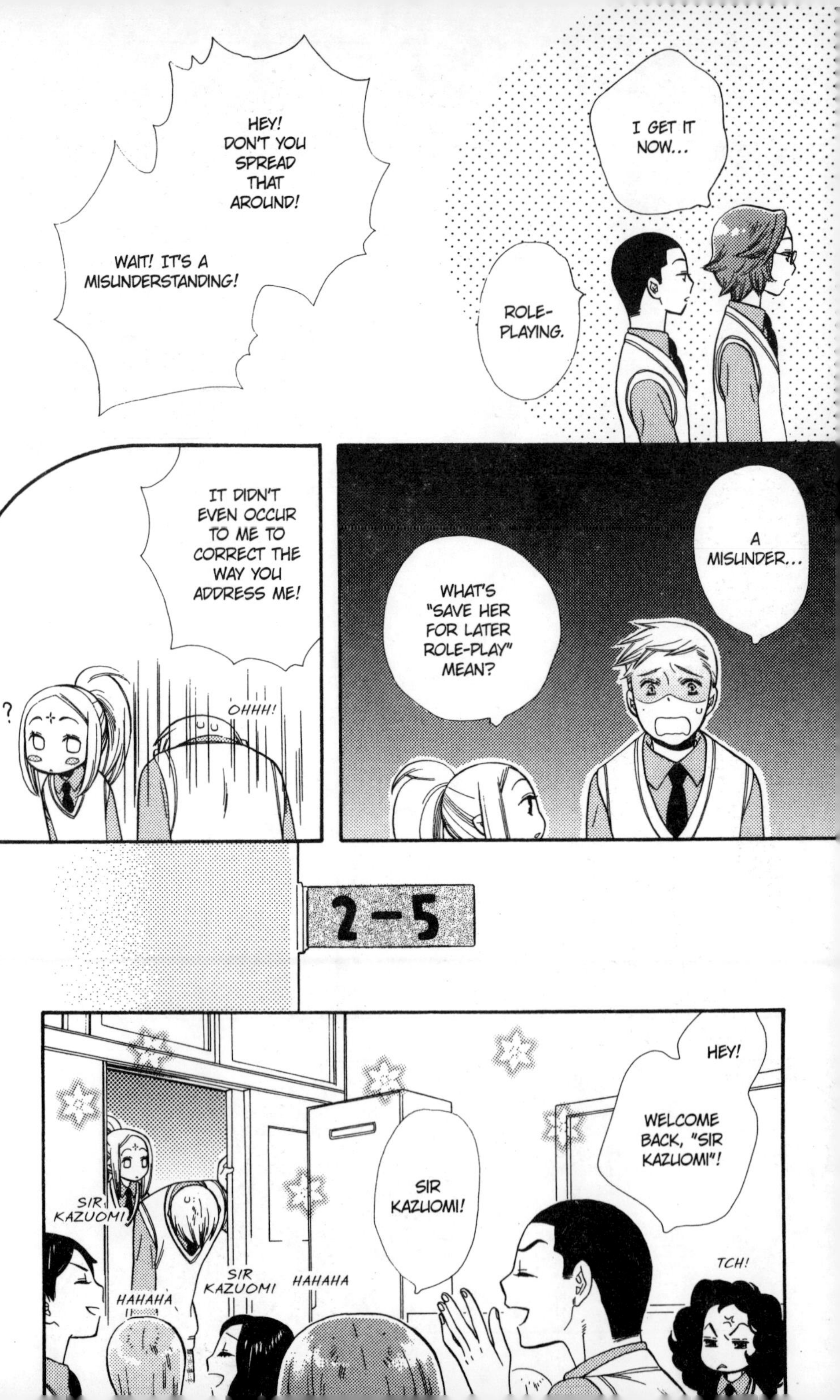
I GET IT NOW...
ROLE-PLAYING.
HEY! DON'T YOU SPREAD THAT AROUND!
WAIT! IT'S A MISUNDERSTANDING!
A MISUNDER...
WHAT'S "SAVE HER FOR LATER ROLE-PLAY" MEAN?
IT DIDN'T EVEN OCCUR TO ME TO CORRECT THE WAY YOU ADDRESS ME!
OHHH!
?
2-5
HEY!
WELCOME BACK, "SIR KAZUOMI"!
SIR KAZUOMI!
TCH!
HAHAHA
SIR KAZUOMI
HAHAHA
SIR KAZUOMI

MY ONLY KING act.3 end

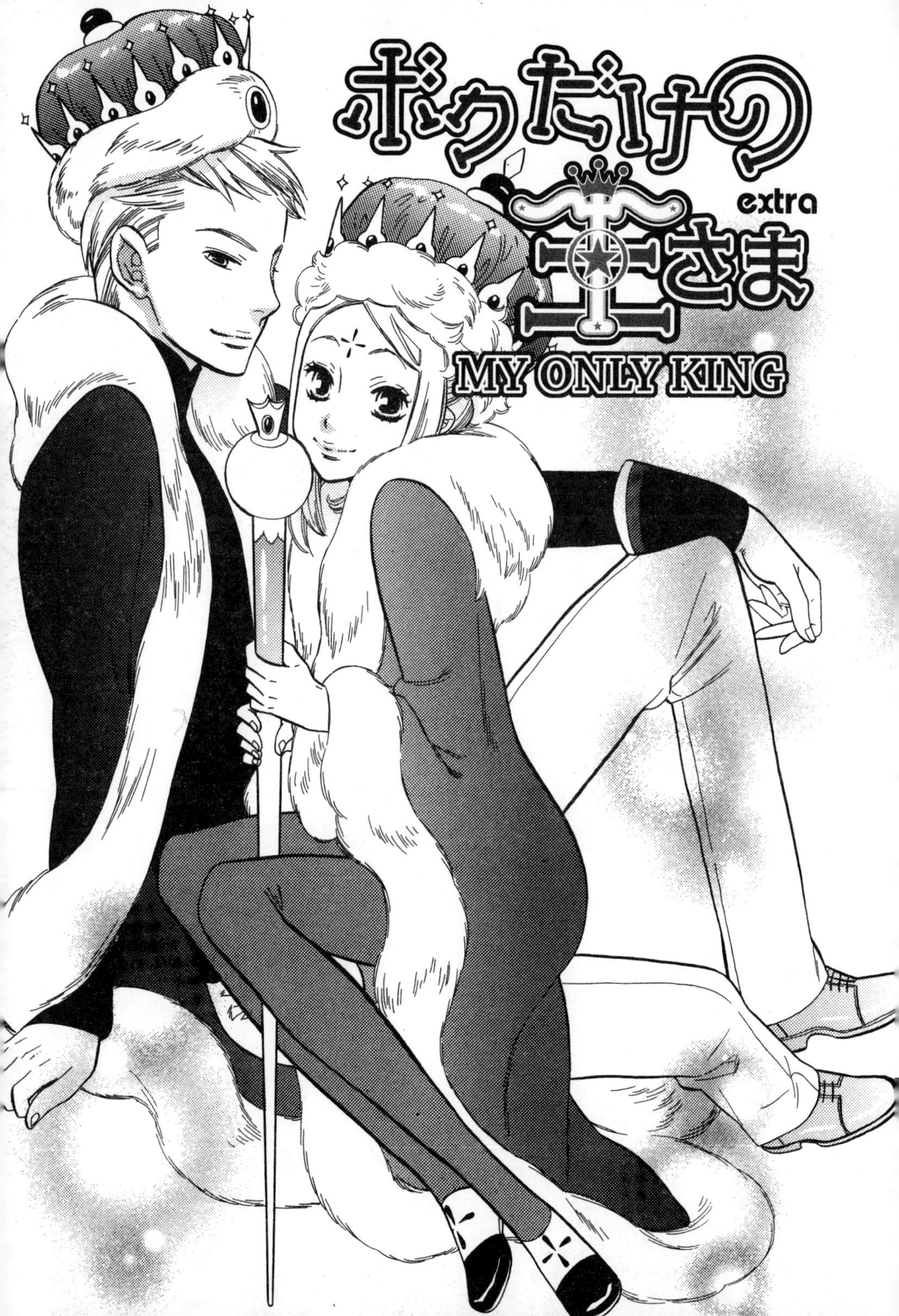
ボクだけの王さま
extra
MY ONLY KING

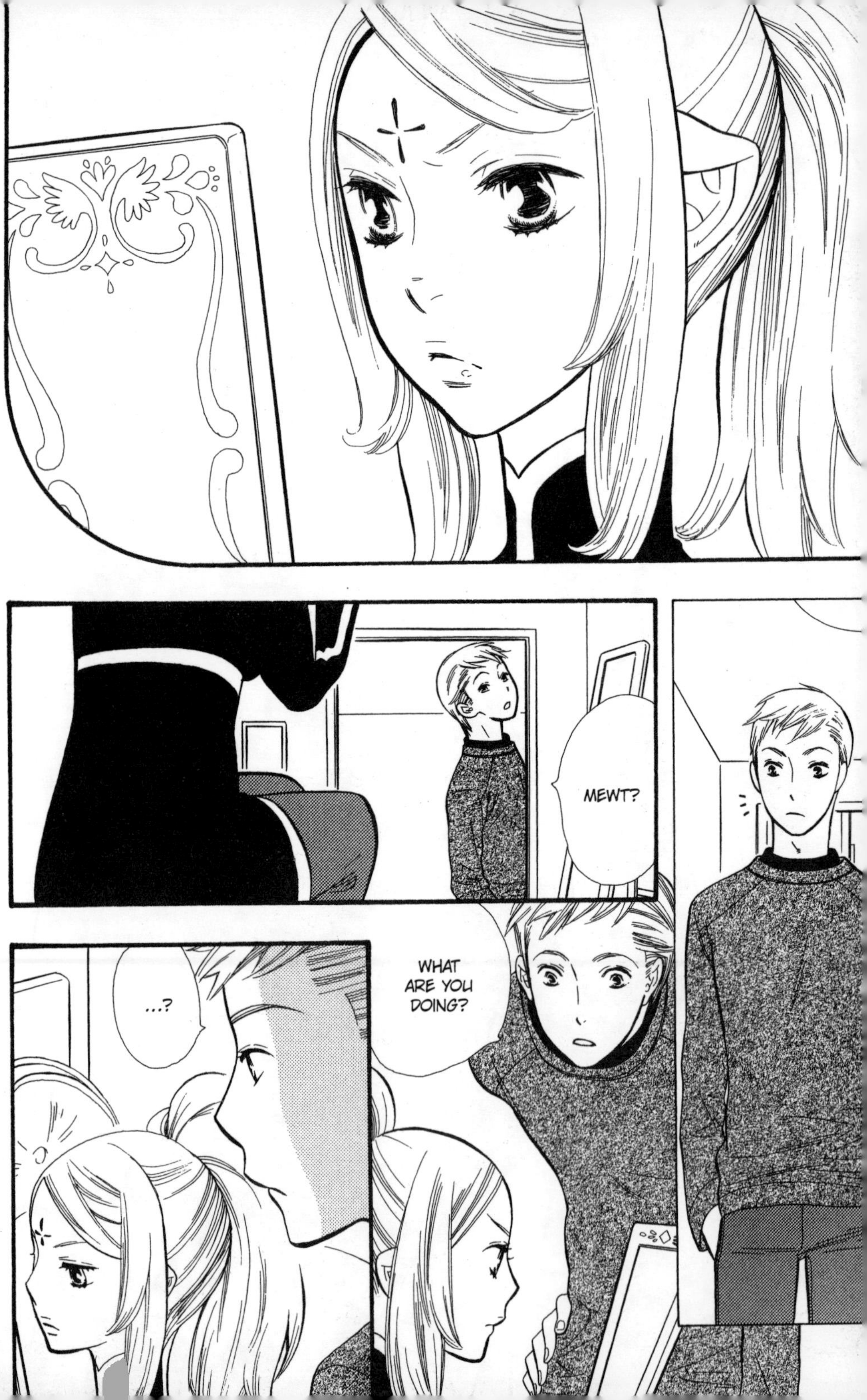
MEWT?
WHAT ARE YOU DOING?
...?

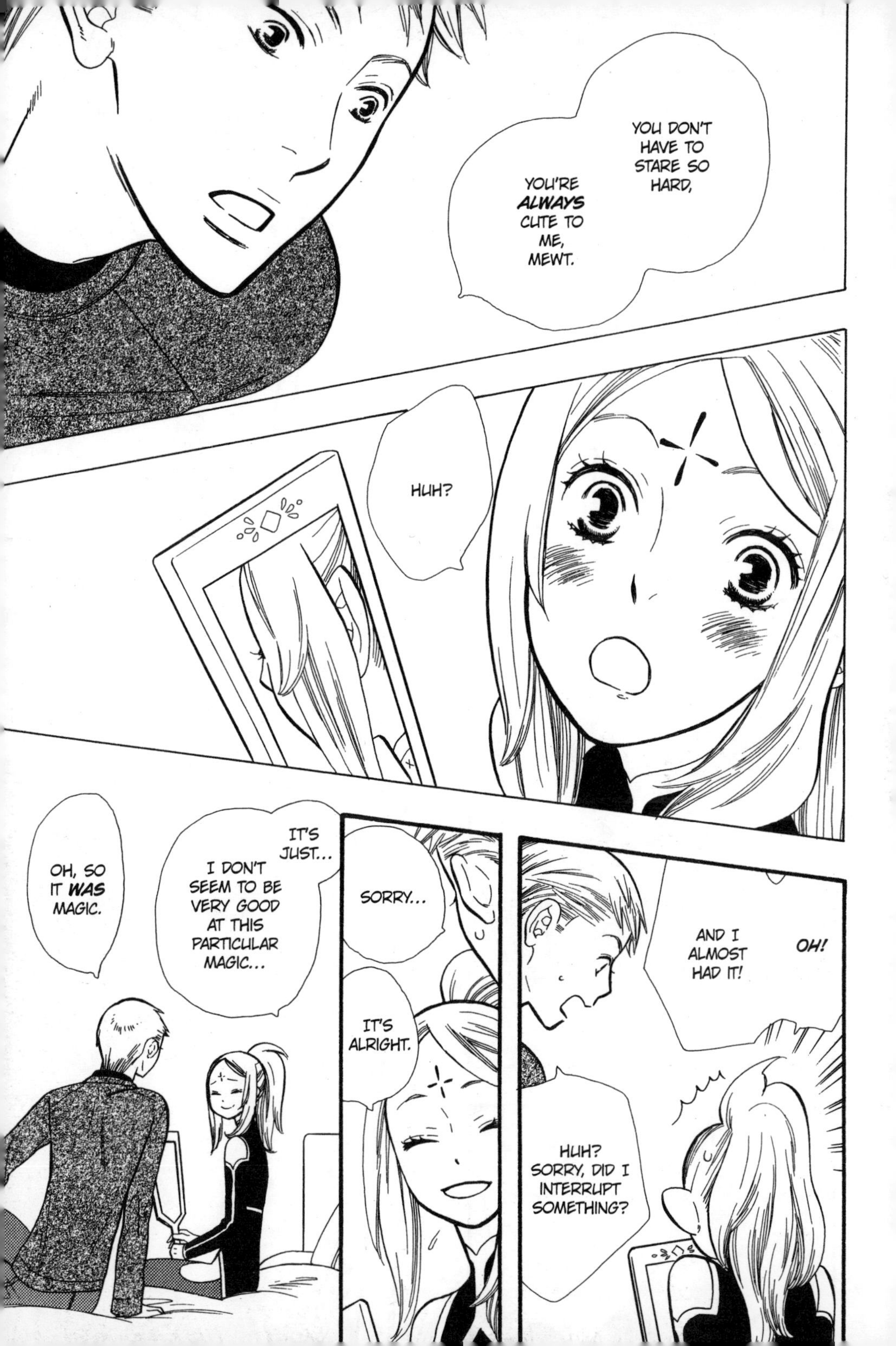
YOU DON'T HAVE TO STARE SO HARD,
YOU'RE **ALWAYS** CUTE TO ME, MEWT.
HUH?
OH!
AND I ALMOST HAD IT!
HUH? SORRY, DID I INTERRUPT SOMETHING?
SORRY...
IT'S ALRIGHT.
IT'S JUST...
I DON'T SEEM TO BE VERY GOOD AT THIS PARTICULAR MAGIC...
OH, SO IT **WAS** MAGIC.

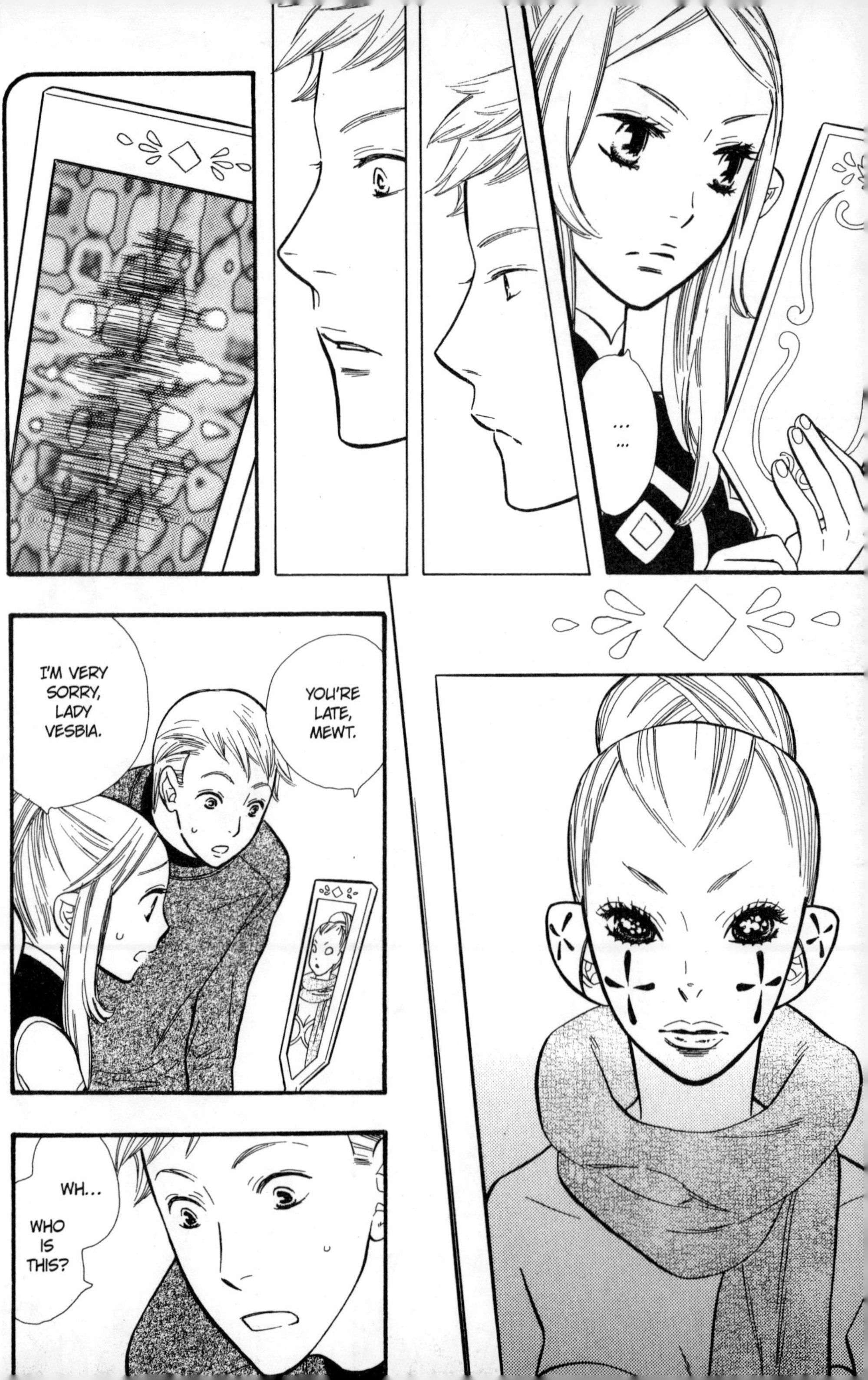
...
...
YOU'RE LATE, MEWT.
I'M VERY SORRY, LADY VESBIA.
WH... WHO IS THIS?

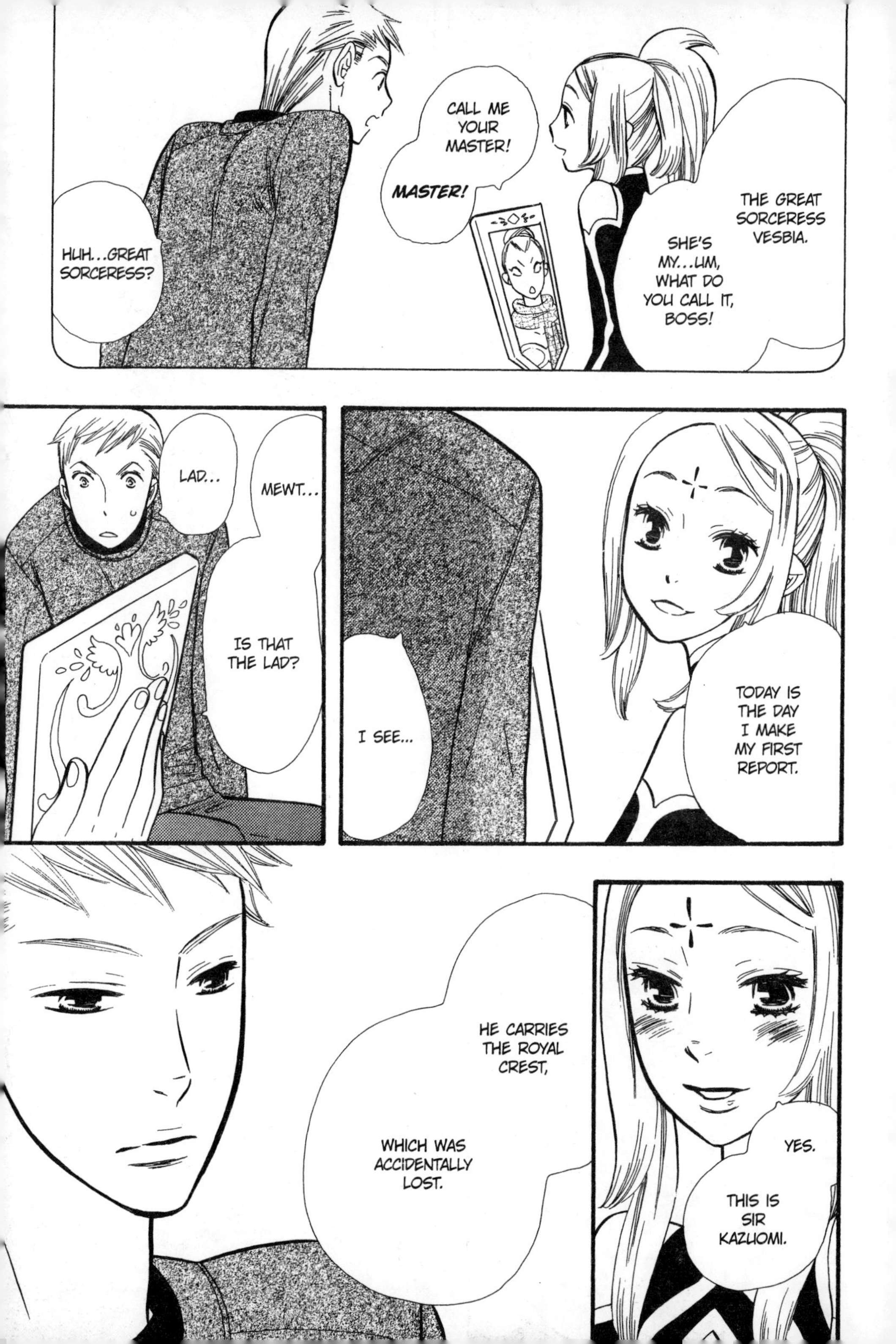
THE GREAT SORCERESS VESBIA.
SHE'S MY...UM, WHAT DO YOU CALL IT, BOSS!
CALL ME YOUR MASTER!
MASTER!
HUH...GREAT SORCERESS?
TODAY IS THE DAY I MAKE MY FIRST REPORT.
I SEE...
MEWT...
LAD...
IS THAT THE LAD?
YES.
THIS IS SIR KAZUOMI.
HE CARRIES THE ROYAL CREST,
WHICH WAS ACCIDENTALLY LOST.

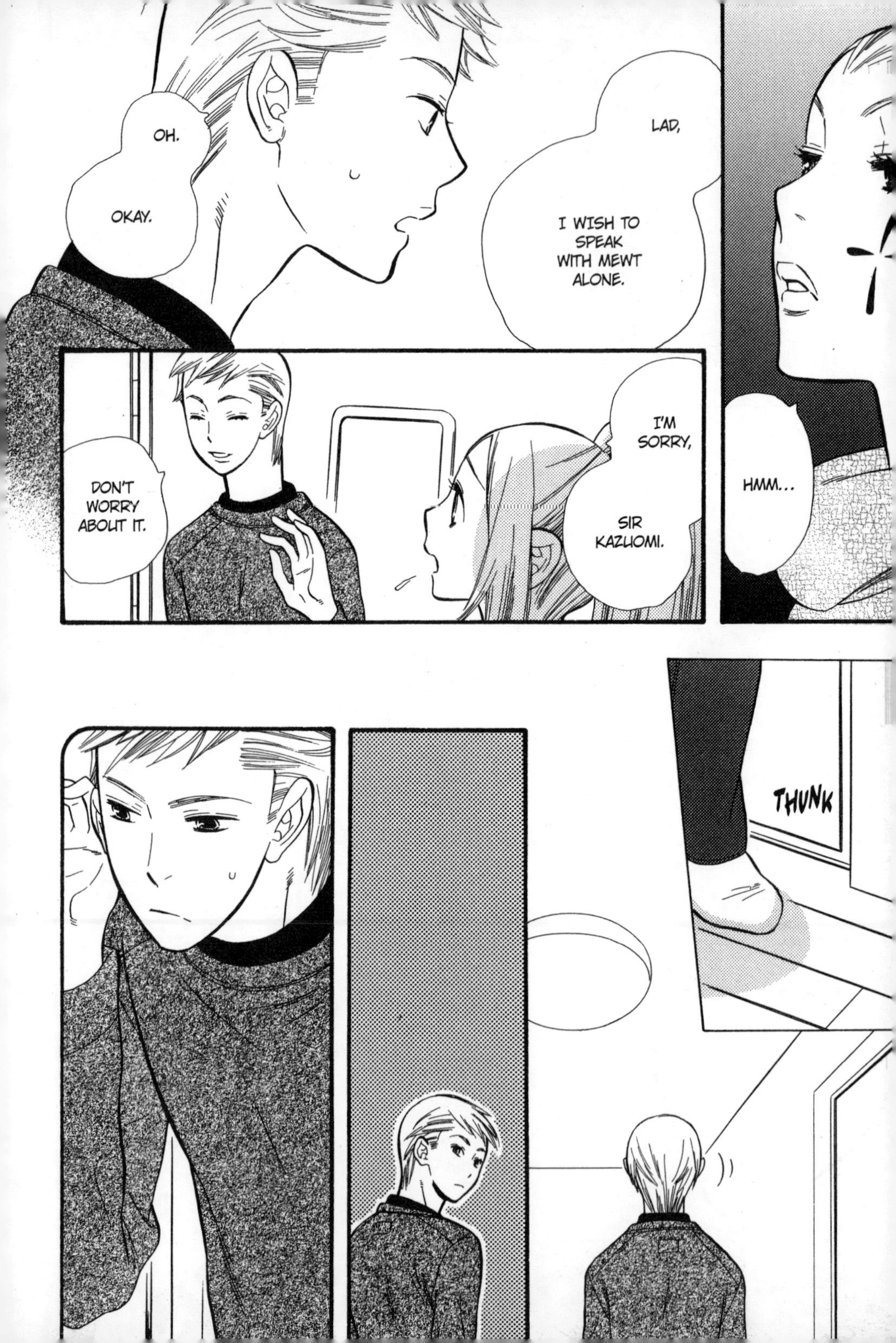
HMM...
LAD, I WISH TO SPEAK WITH MEWT ALONE.
OH. OKAY.
I'M SORRY, SIR KAZUOMI.
DON'T WORRY ABOUT IT.
THUNK

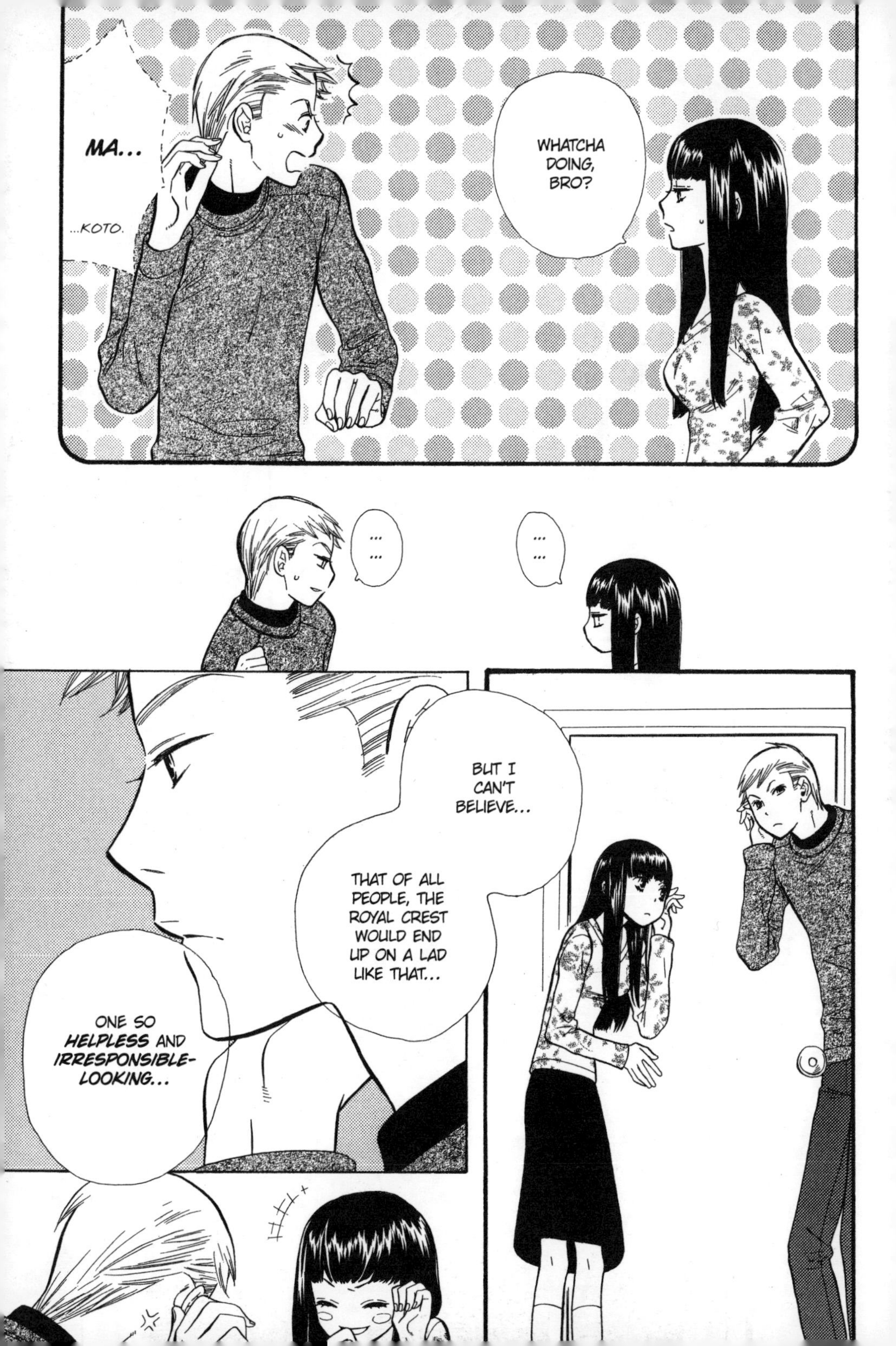
WHATCHA DOING, BRO?
MA...
...KOTO.
......
......
BUT I CAN'T BELIEVE...
THAT OF ALL PEOPLE, THE ROYAL CREST WOULD END UP ON A LAD LIKE THAT...
ONE SO HELPLESS AND IRRESPONSIBLE-LOOKING...

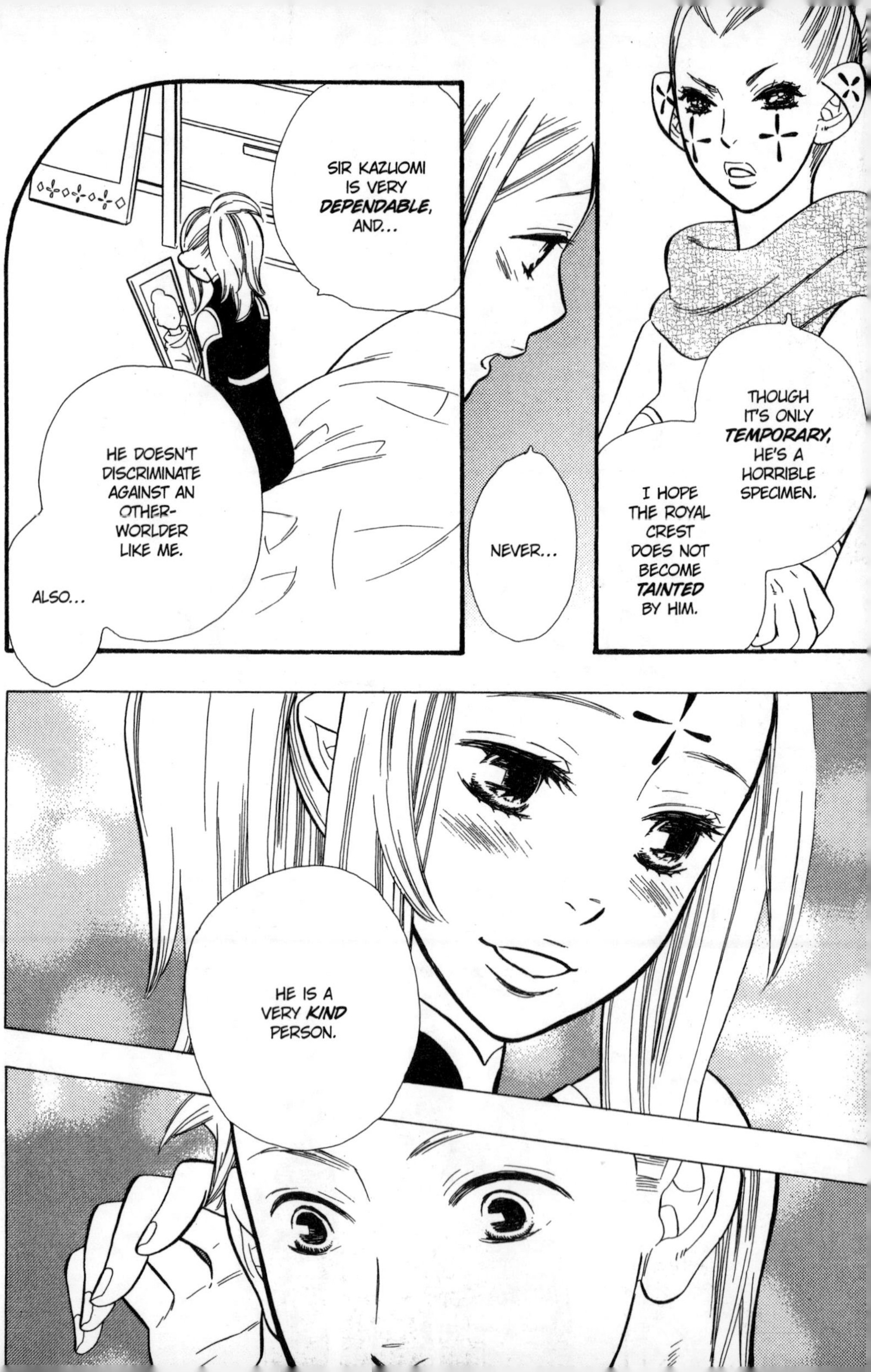
THOUGH IT'S ONLY TEMPORARY, HE'S A HORRIBLE SPECIMEN.
I HOPE THE ROYAL CREST DOES NOT BECOME TAINTED BY HIM.
NEVER...
SIR KAZUOMI IS VERY DEPENDABLE, AND...
HE DOESN'T DISCRIMINATE AGAINST AN OTHER-WORLDER LIKE ME.
ALSO...
HE IS A VERY KIND PERSON.

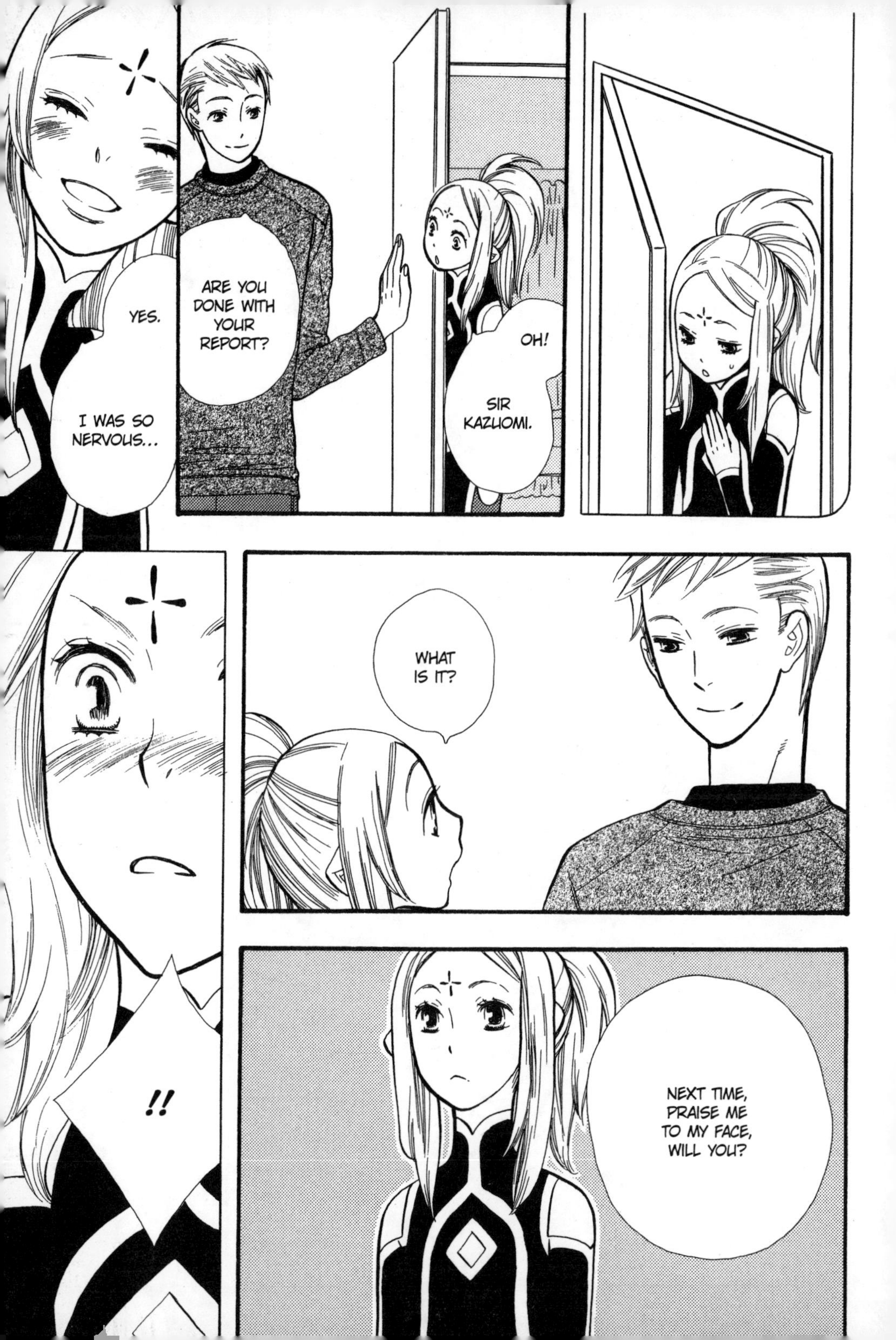
OH!
SIR KAZUOMI.
ARE YOU DONE WITH YOUR REPORT?
YES.
I WAS SO NERVOUS...
WHAT IS IT?
NEXT TIME, PRAISE ME TO MY FACE, WILL YOU?
!!

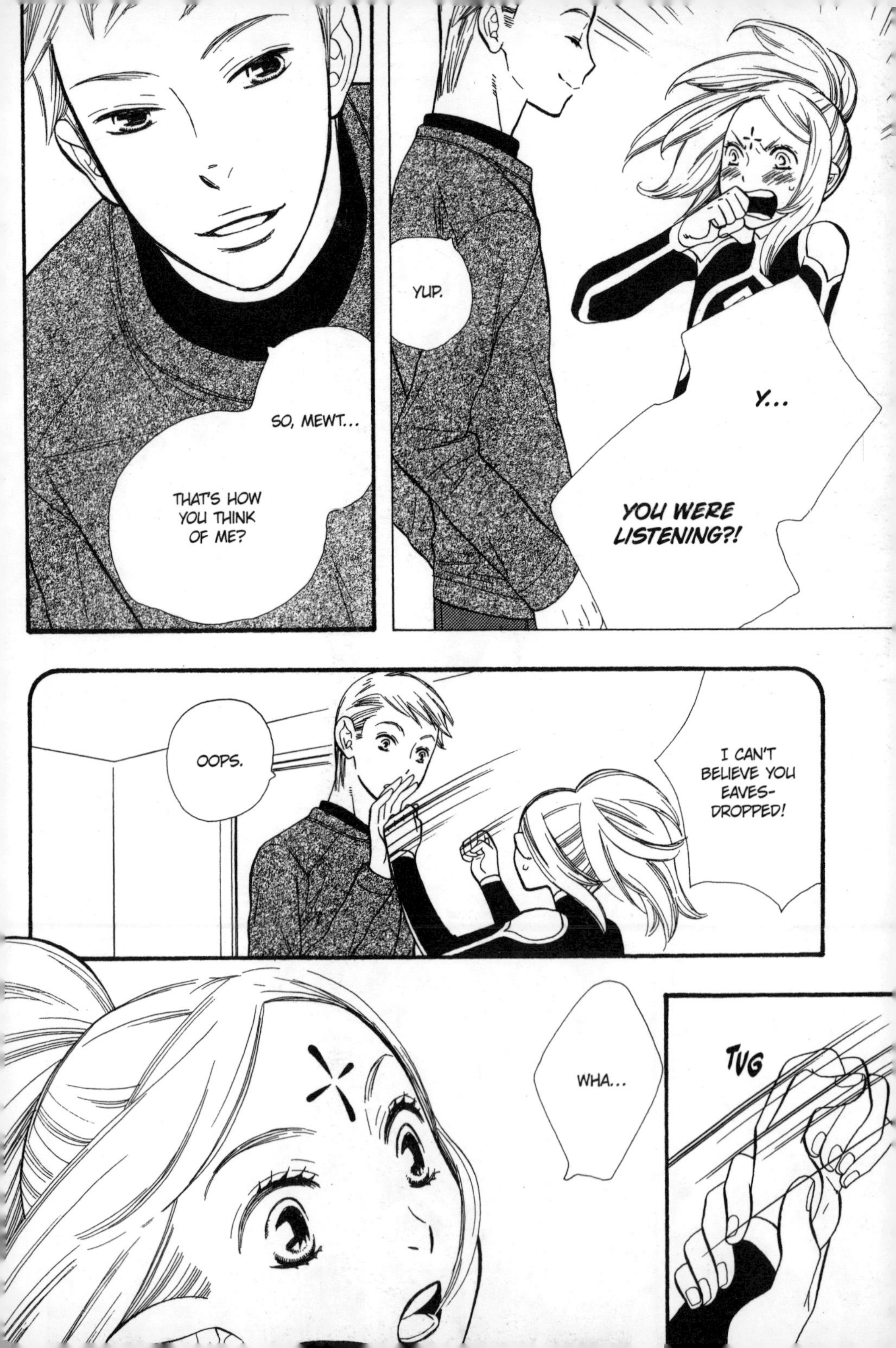
SO, MEWT...
THAT'S HOW YOU THINK OF ME?
YUP.
Y...
YOU WERE LISTENING?!
OOPS.
I CAN'T BELIEVE YOU EAVES-DROPPED!
WHA...
TUG

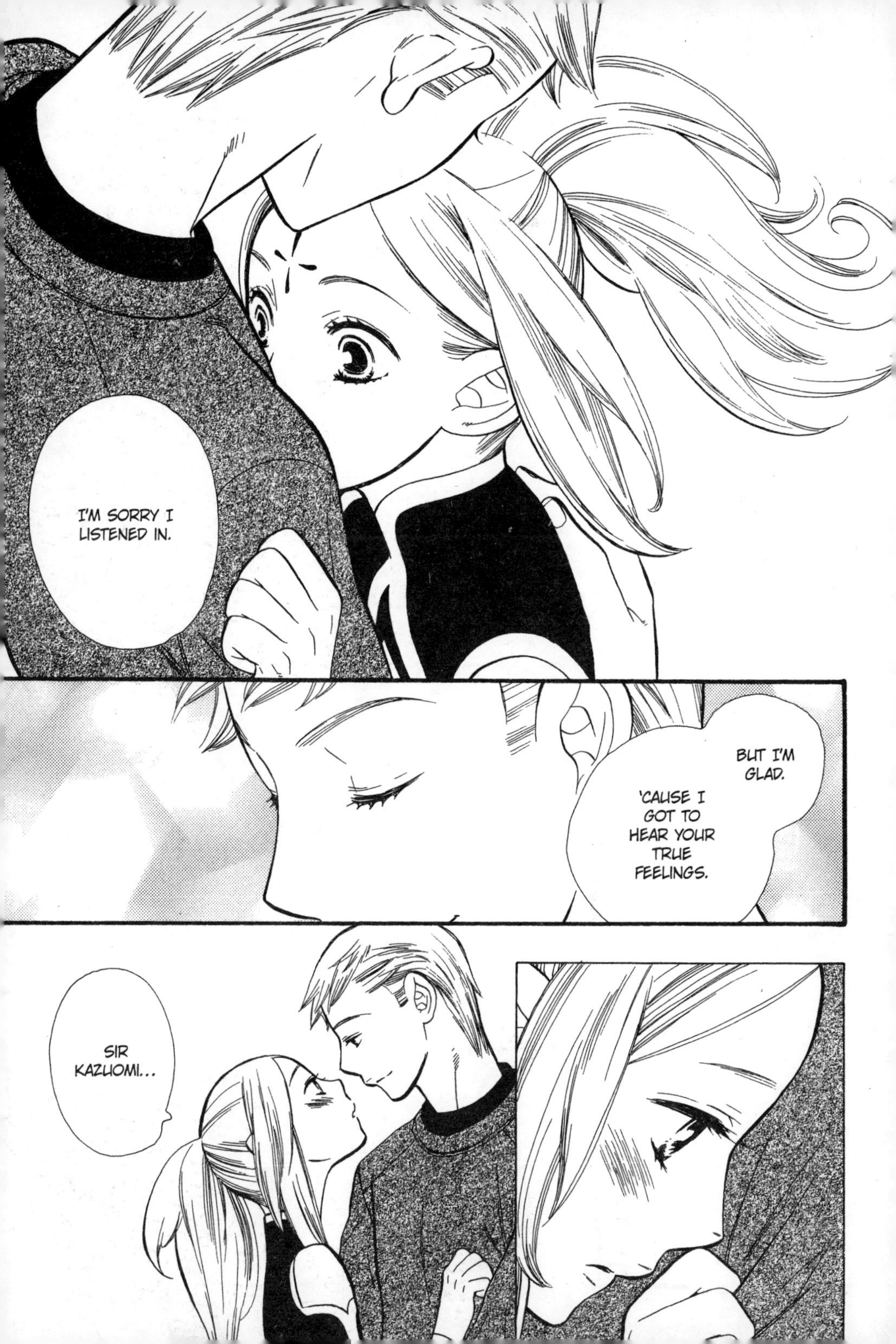
I'M SORRY I LISTENED IN.
BUT I'M GLAD.
'CAUSE I GOT TO HEAR YOUR TRUE FEELINGS.
SIR KAZUOMI...

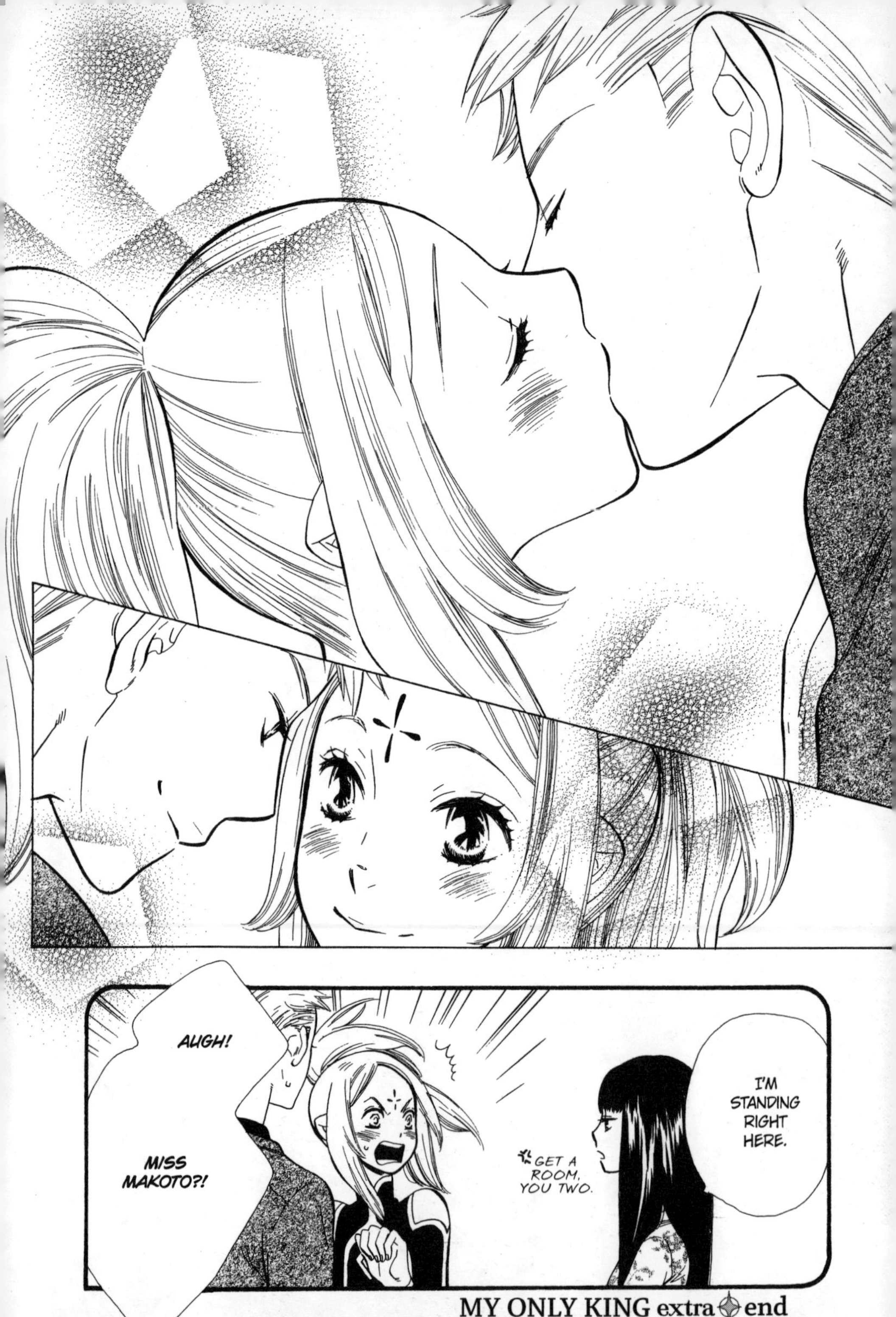
I'M STANDING RIGHT HERE.
GET A ROOM, YOU TWO.
AUGH!
MISS MAKOTO?!

MY ONLY KING extra end

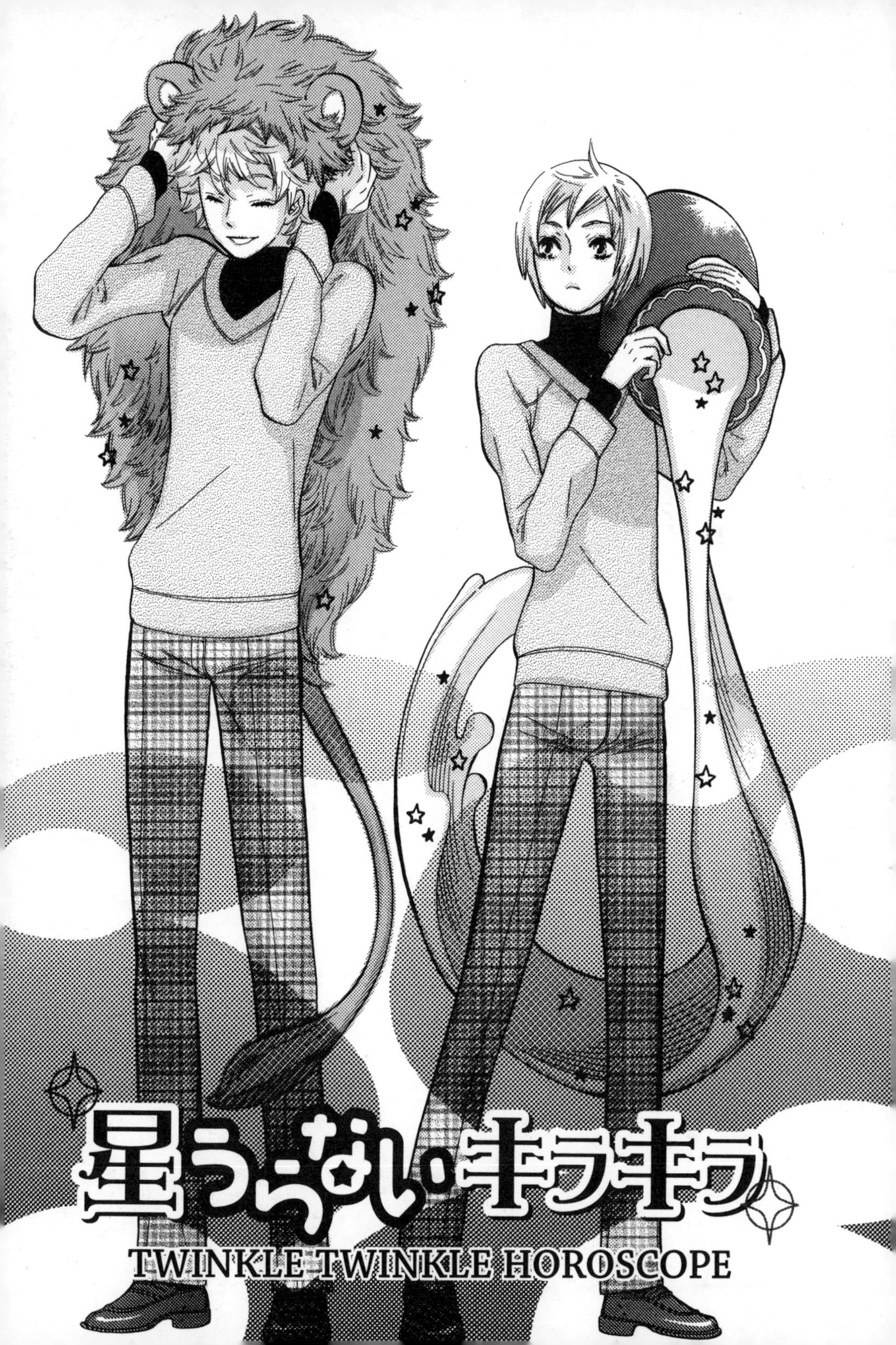

星うらない・キラキラ
TWINKLE TWINKLE HOROSCOPE

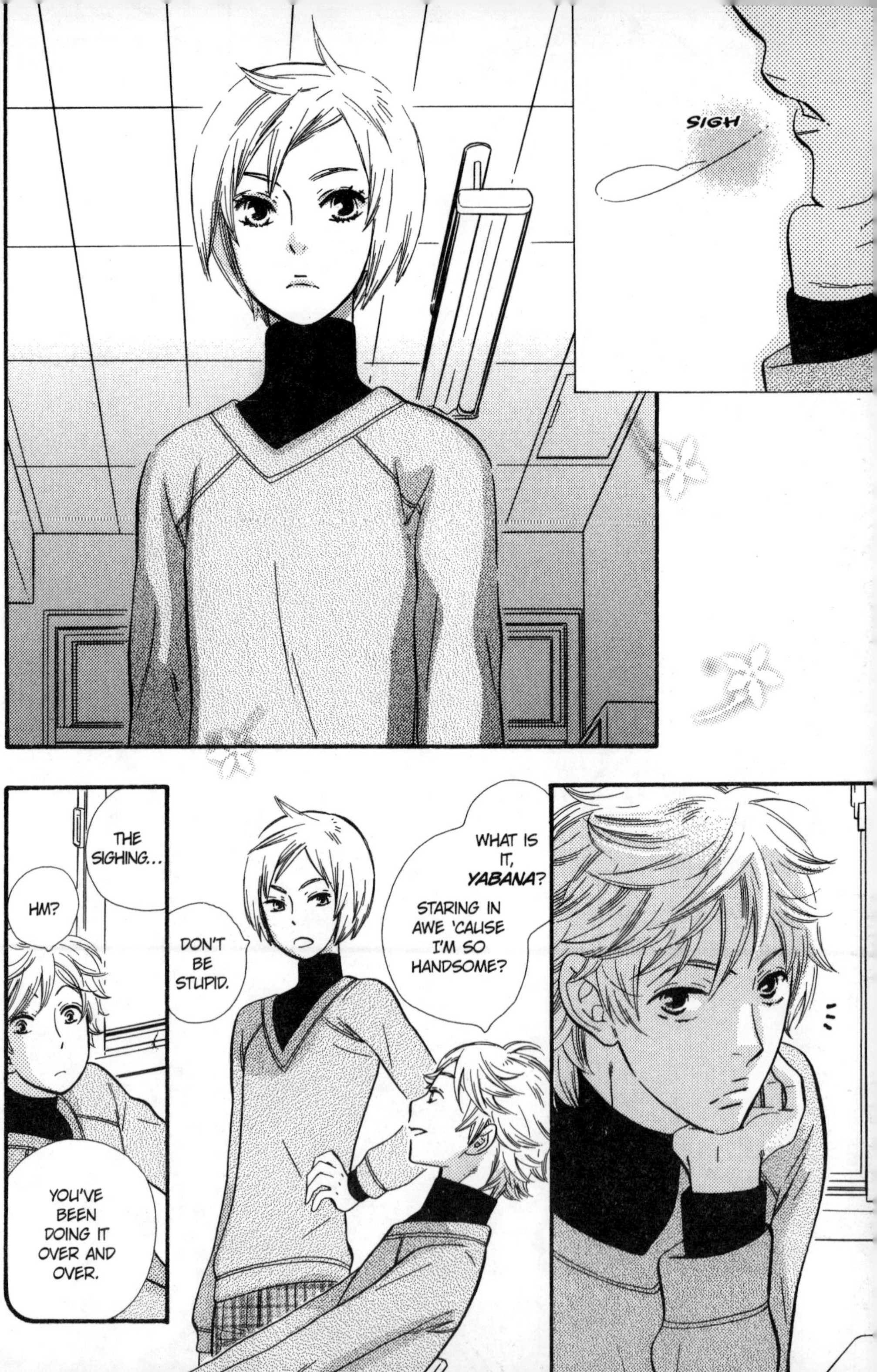
SIGH
WHAT IS IT, YABANA?
STARING IN AWE 'CAUSE I'M SO HANDSOME?
DON'T BE STUPID.
THE SIGHING...
HM?
YOU'VE BEEN DOING IT OVER AND OVER.

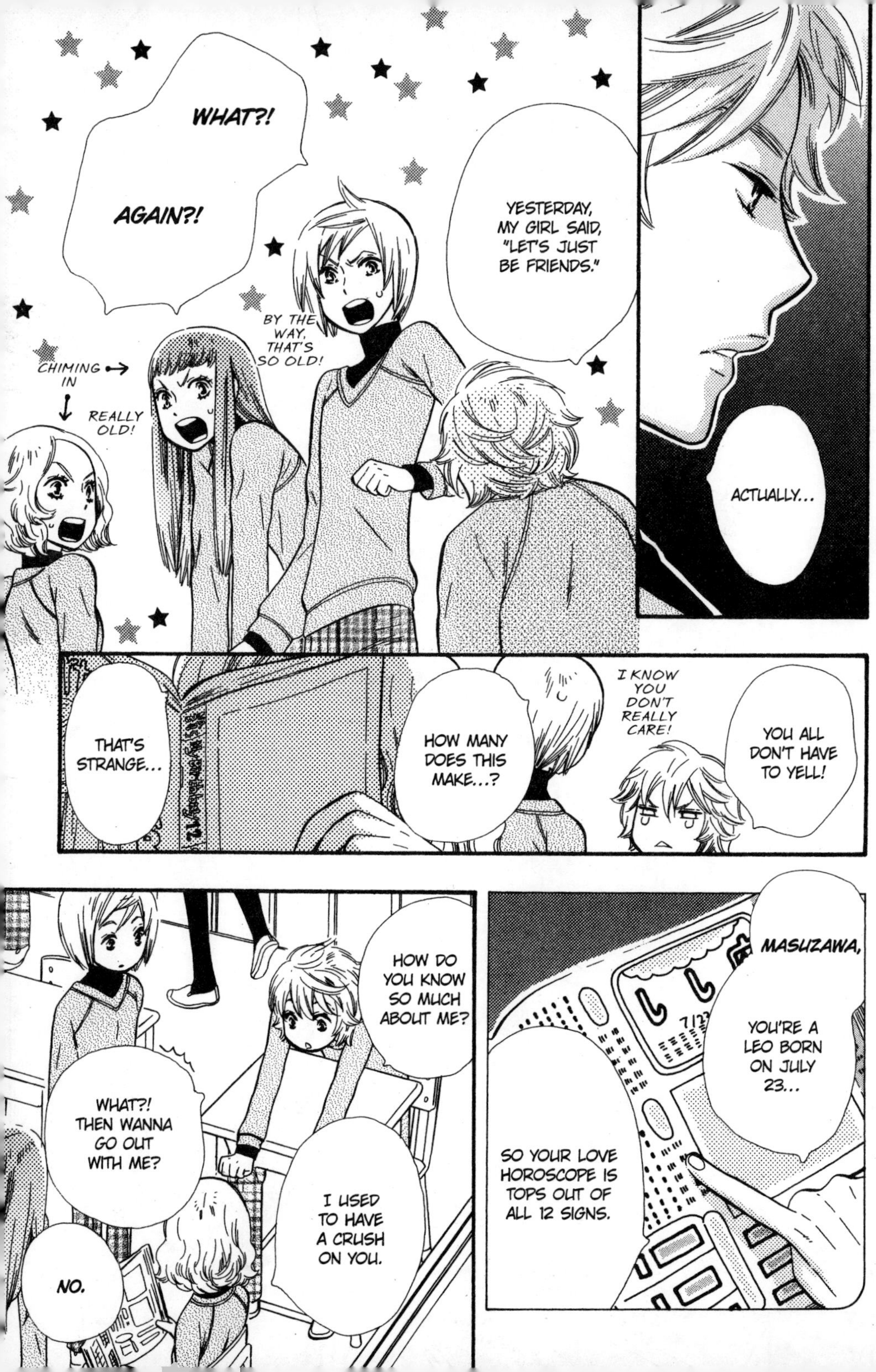
ACTUALLY...
YESTERDAY, MY GIRL SAID, "LET'S JUST BE FRIENDS."
WHAT?!
AGAIN?!
BY THE WAY, THAT'S SO OLD!
CHIMING IN
REALLY OLD!
YOU ALL DON'T HAVE TO YELL!
I KNOW YOU DON'T REALLY CARE!
HOW MANY DOES THIS MAKE...?
THAT'S STRANGE...
MASUZAWA,
YOU'RE A LEO BORN ON JULY 23...
SO YOUR LOVE HOROSCOPE IS TOPS OUT OF ALL 12 SIGNS.
HOW DO YOU KNOW SO MUCH ABOUT ME?
I USED TO HAVE A CRUSH ON YOU.
WHAT?! THEN WANNA GO OUT WITH ME?
NO.

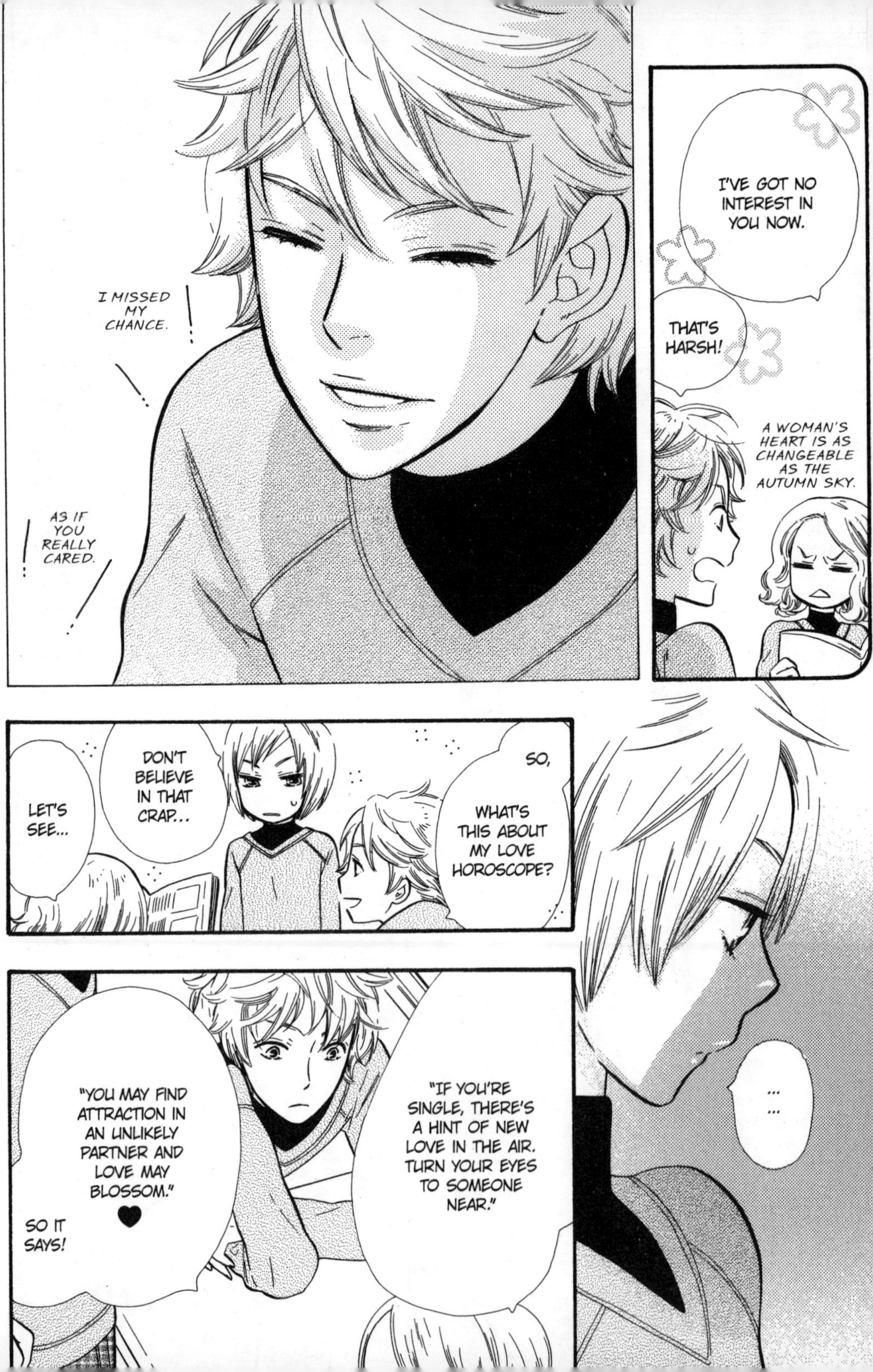
I'VE GOT NO INTEREST IN YOU NOW.
THAT'S HARSH!
A WOMAN'S HEART IS AS CHANGEABLE AS THE AUTUMN SKY.
I MISSED MY CHANCE.
AS IF YOU REALLY CARED.
SO,
WHAT'S THIS ABOUT MY LOVE HOROSCOPE?
DON'T BELIEVE IN THAT CRAP...
LET'S SEE...
"IF YOU'RE SINGLE, THERE'S A HINT OF NEW LOVE IN THE AIR. TURN YOUR EYES TO SOMEONE NEAR."
"YOU MAY FIND ATTRACTION IN AN UNLIKELY PARTNER AND LOVE MAY BLOSSOM."
SO IT SAYS!
......

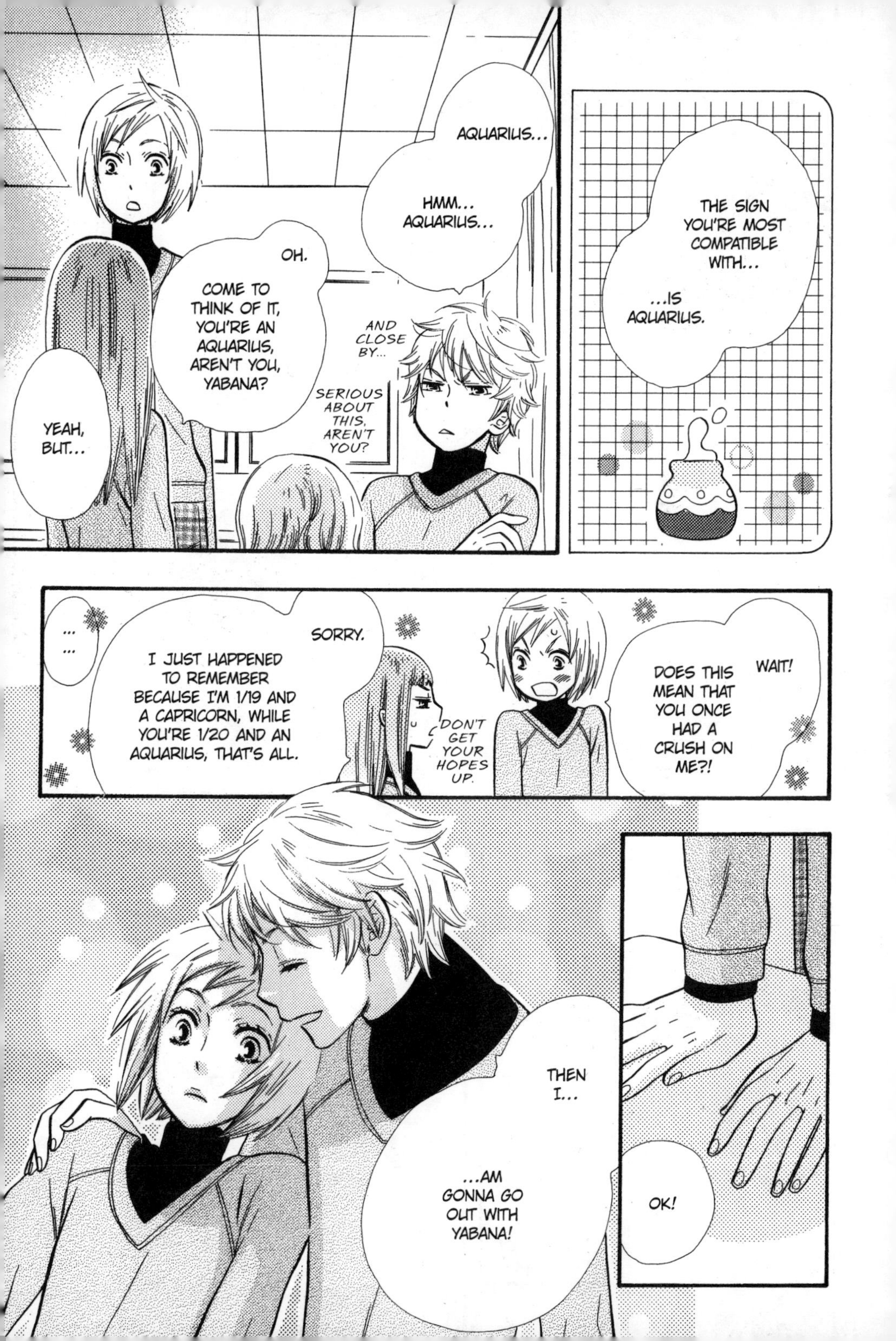
THE SIGN YOU'RE MOST COMPATIBLE WITH...
...IS AQUARIUS.
AQUARIUS...
HMM... AQUARIUS...
OH.
COME TO THINK OF IT, YOU'RE AN AQUARIUS, AREN'T YOU, YABANA?
AND CLOSE BY...
SERIOUS ABOUT THIS, AREN'T YOU?
YEAH, BUT...
WAIT!
DOES THIS MEAN THAT YOU ONCE HAD A CRUSH ON ME?!
DON'T GET YOUR HOPES UP.
SORRY.
I JUST HAPPENED TO REMEMBER BECAUSE I'M 1/19 AND A CAPRICORN, WHILE YOU'RE 1/20 AND AN AQUARIUS, THAT'S ALL.
... ...
THEN I...
...AM GONNA GO OUT WITH YABANA!
OK!

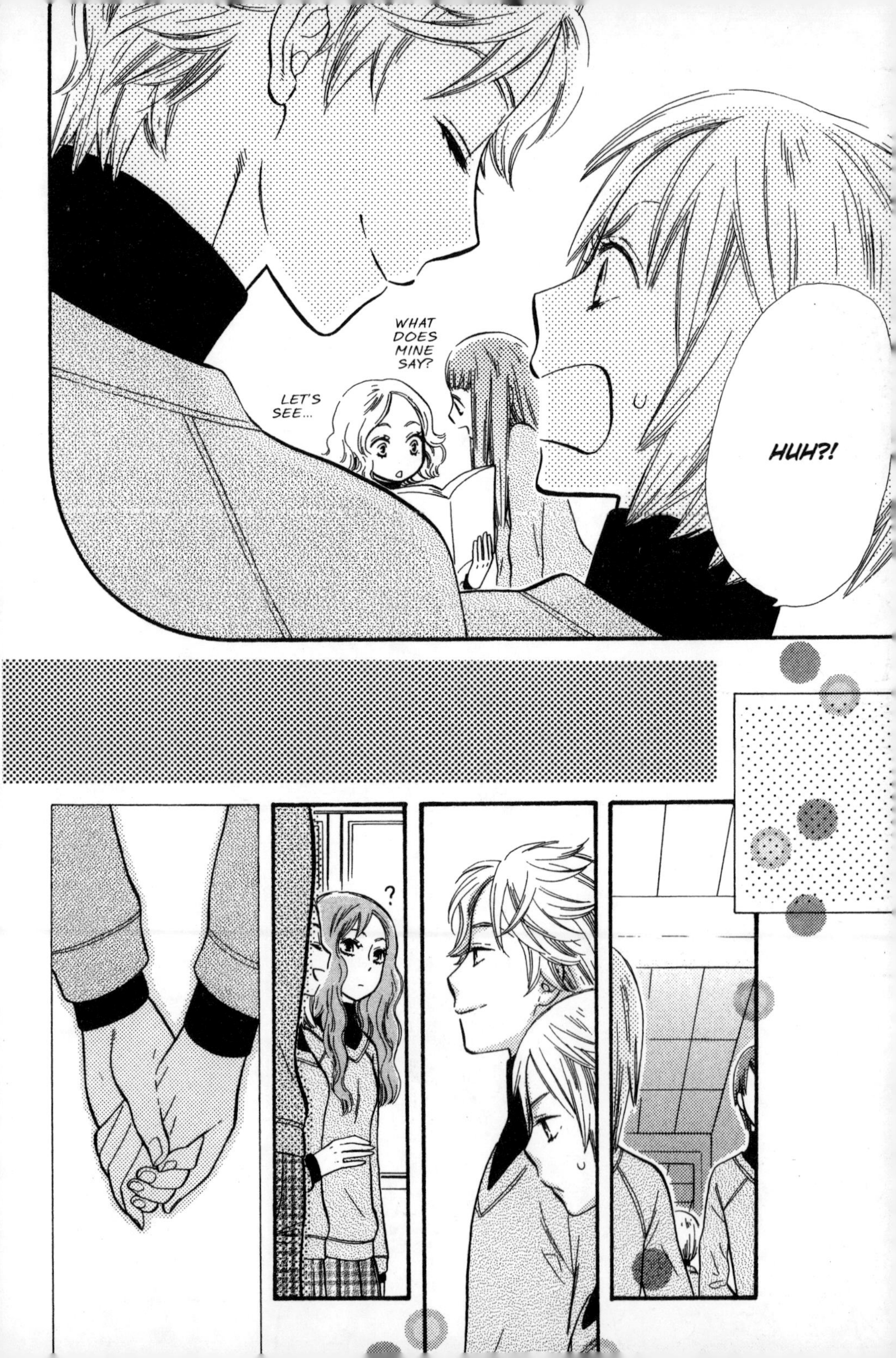
HUH?!
WHAT DOES MINE SAY?
LET'S SEE...
?

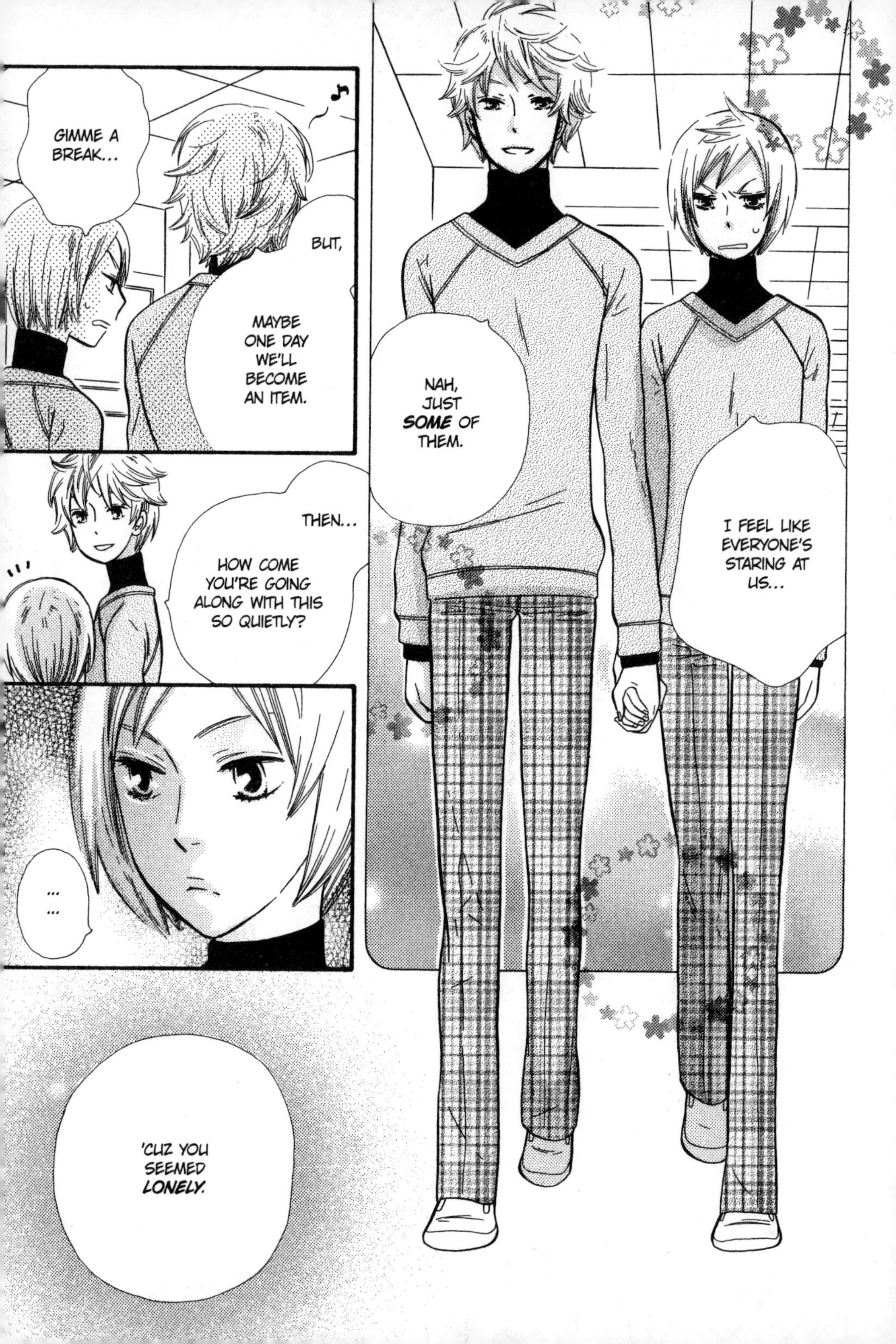
I FEEL LIKE EVERYONE'S STARING AT US...
NAH, JUST SOME OF THEM.
GIMME A BREAK...
BUT,
MAYBE ONE DAY WE'LL BECOME AN ITEM.
THEN...
HOW COME YOU'RE GOING ALONG WITH THIS SO QUIETLY?
......
'CUZ YOU SEEMED LONELY.

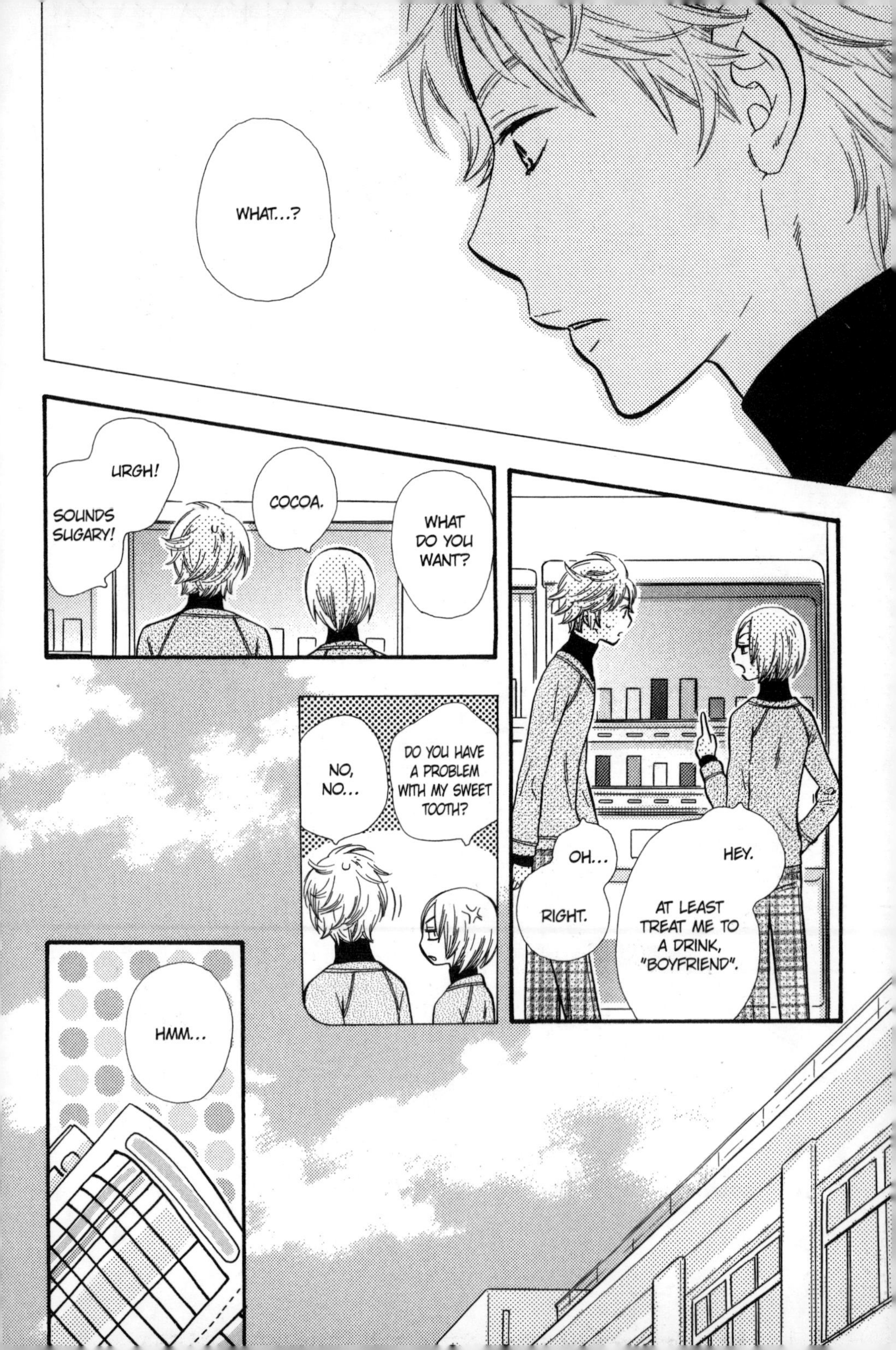
WHAT...?
HEY.
AT LEAST TREAT ME TO A DRINK, "BOYFRIEND".
OH... RIGHT.
WHAT DO YOU WANT?
COCOA.
URGH! SOUNDS SUGARY!
DO YOU HAVE A PROBLEM WITH MY SWEET TOOTH?
NO, NO...
HMM...

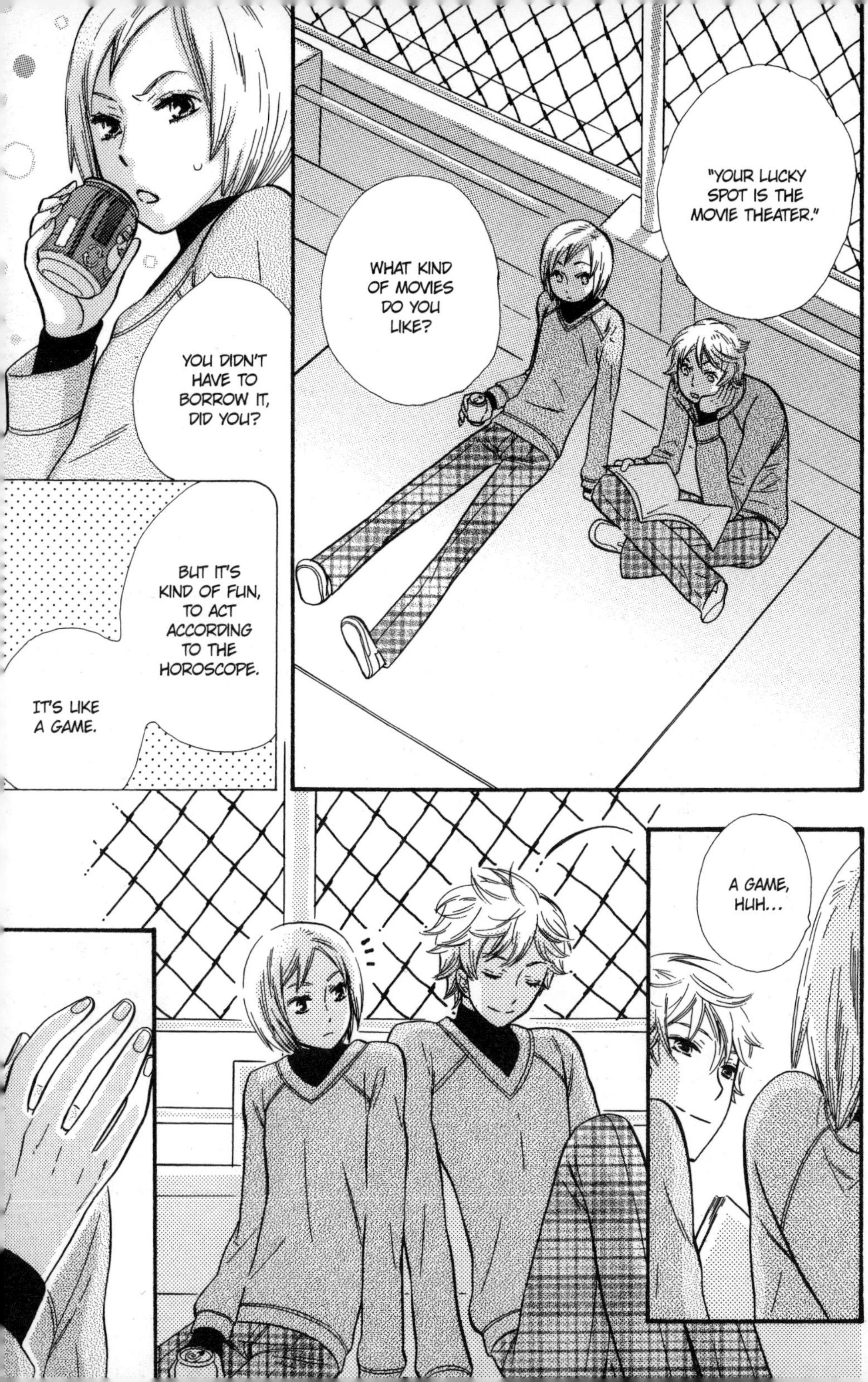
"YOUR LUCKY SPOT IS THE MOVIE THEATER."
WHAT KIND OF MOVIES DO YOU LIKE?
YOU DIDN'T HAVE TO BORROW IT, DID YOU?
BUT IT'S KIND OF FUN, TO ACT ACCORDING TO THE HOROSCOPE.
IT'S LIKE A GAME.
A GAME, HUH...

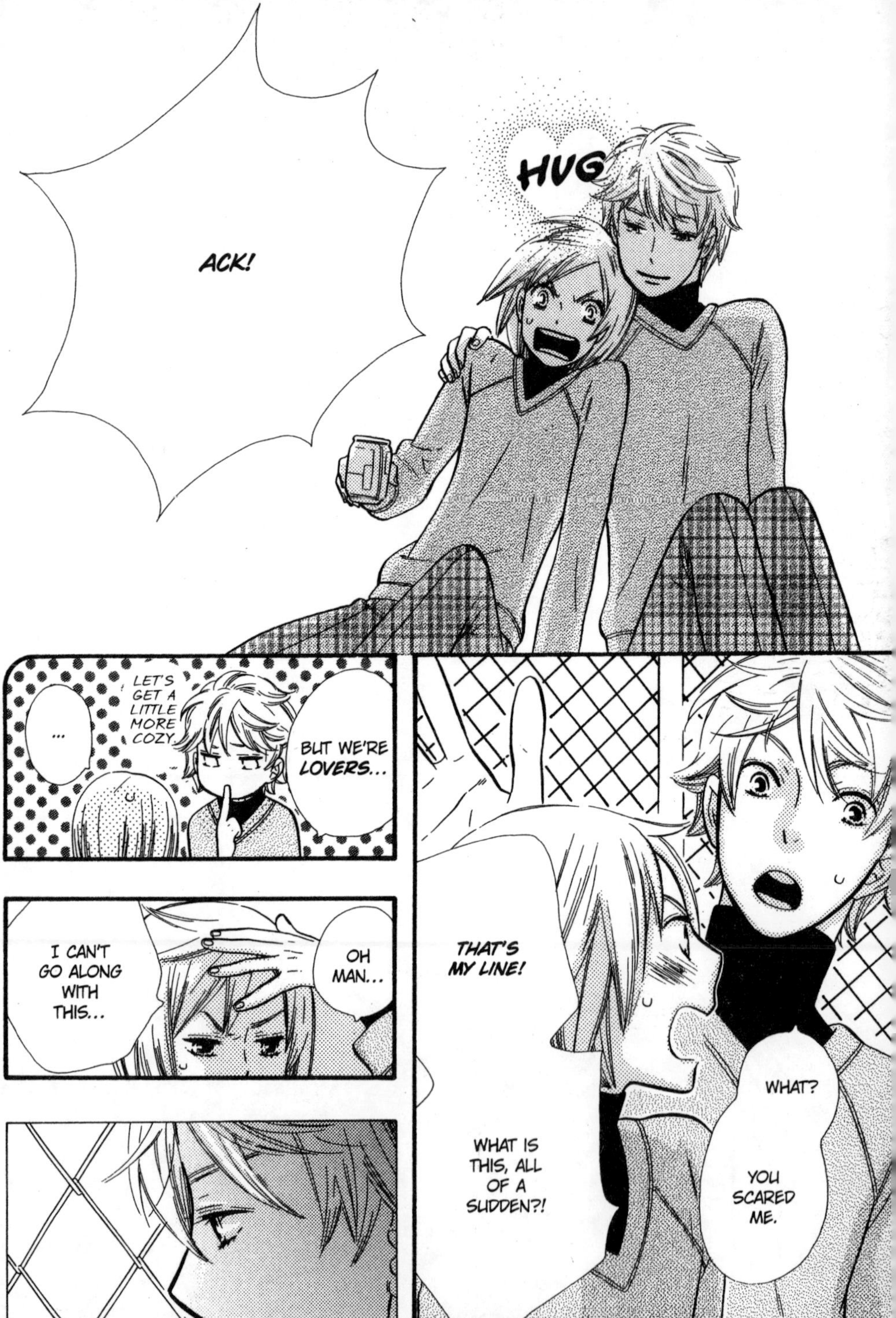
HUG
ACK!
WHAT?
YOU SCARED ME.
THAT'S MY LINE!
WHAT IS THIS, ALL OF A SUDDEN?!
BUT WE'RE LOVERS...
LET'S GET A LITTLE MORE COZY.
...
OH MAN...
I CAN'T GO ALONG WITH THIS...

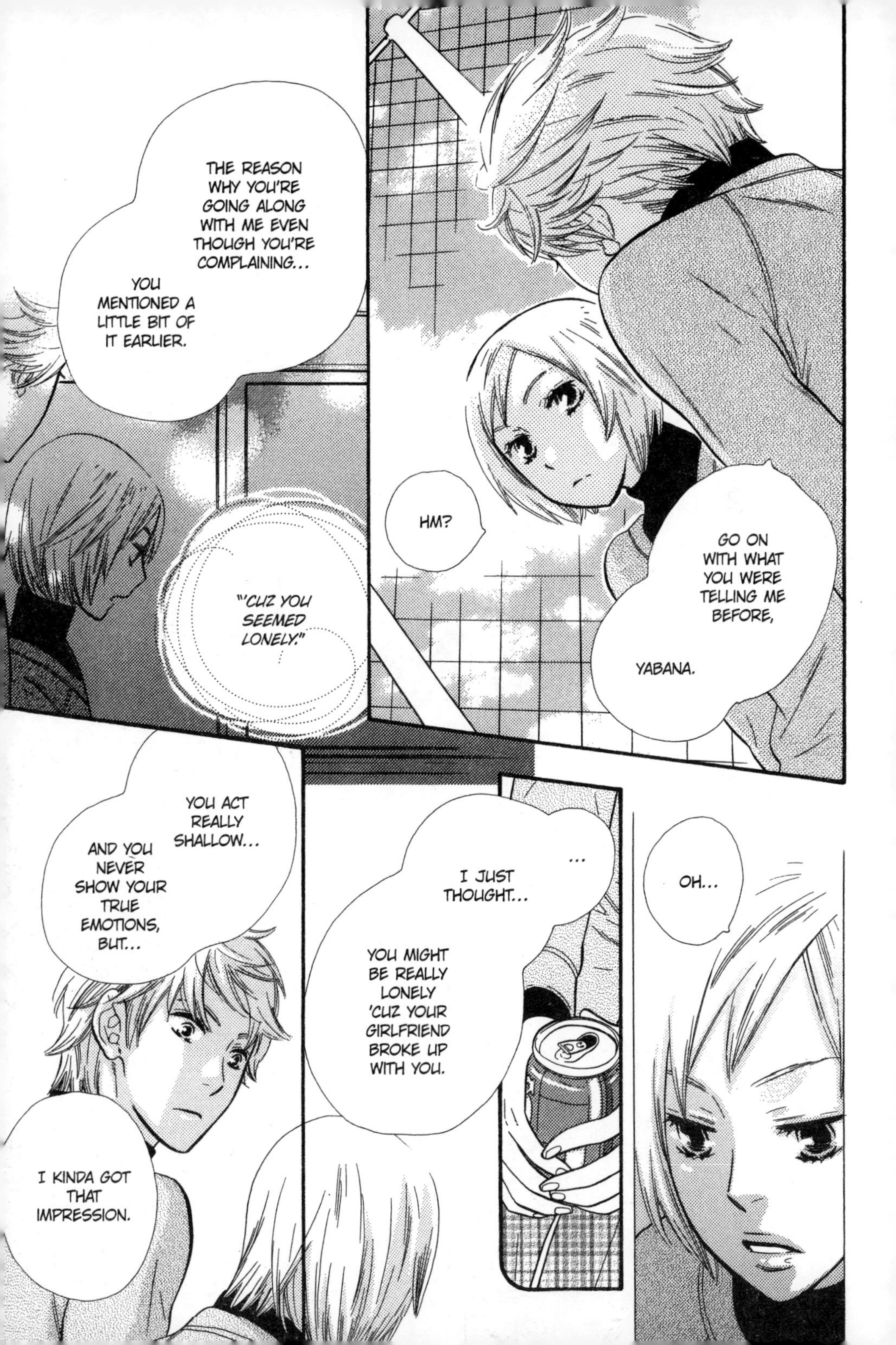
GO ON WITH WHAT YOU WERE TELLING ME BEFORE,
YABANA.
HM?
THE REASON WHY YOU'RE GOING ALONG WITH ME EVEN THOUGH YOU'RE COMPLAINING...
YOU MENTIONED A LITTLE BIT OF IT EARLIER.
"'CUZ YOU SEEMED LONELY."
OH...
...
I JUST THOUGHT...
YOU MIGHT BE REALLY LONELY 'CUZ YOUR GIRLFRIEND BROKE UP WITH YOU.
YOU ACT REALLY SHALLOW...
AND YOU NEVER SHOW YOUR TRUE EMOTIONS, BUT...
I KINDA GOT THAT IMPRESSION.

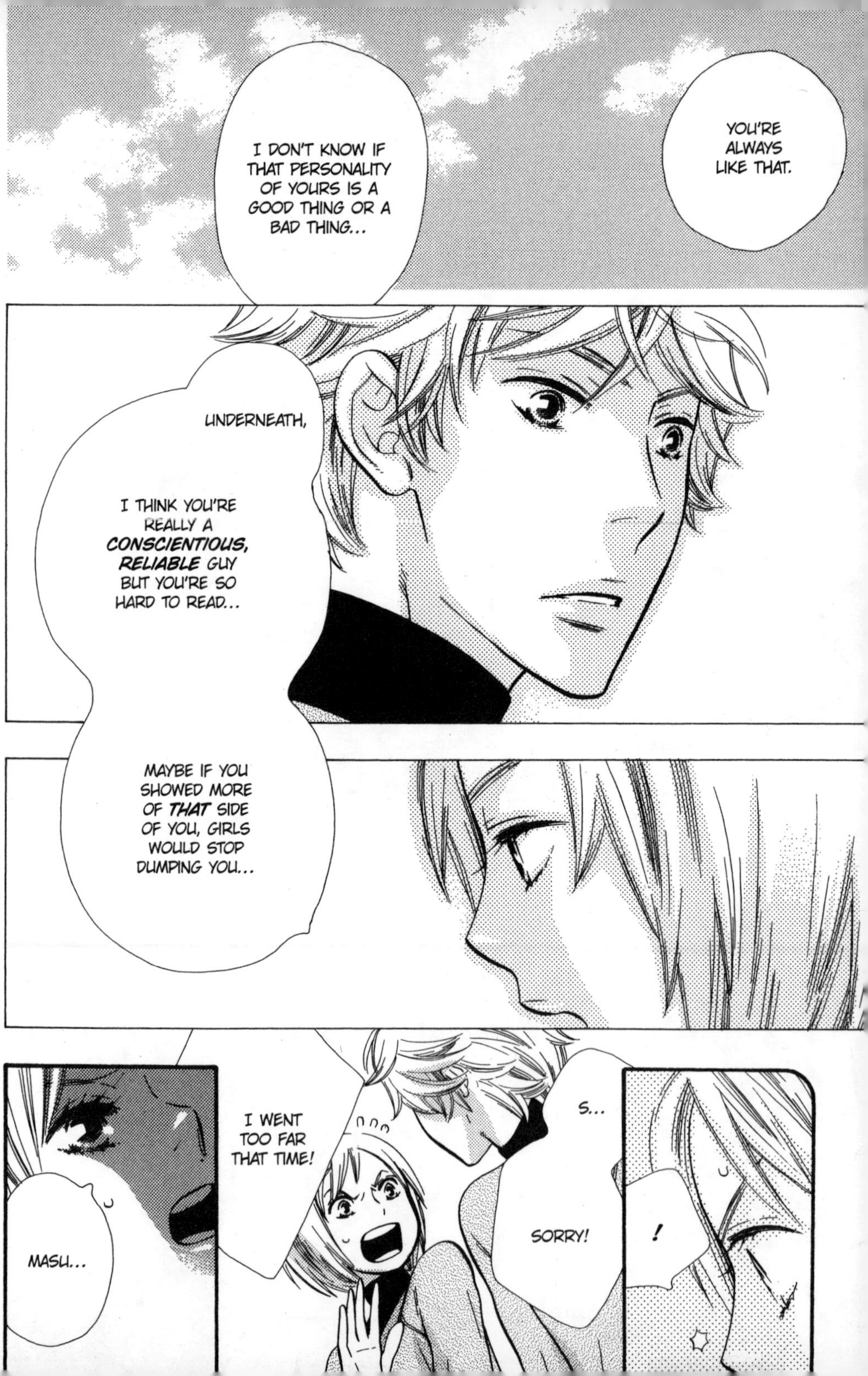
YOU'RE ALWAYS LIKE THAT.
I DON'T KNOW IF THAT PERSONALITY OF YOURS IS A GOOD THING OR A BAD THING...
UNDERNEATH,
I THINK YOU'RE REALLY A CONSCIENTIOUS, RELIABLE GUY BUT YOU'RE SO HARD TO READ...
MAYBE IF YOU SHOWED MORE OF THAT SIDE OF YOU, GIRLS WOULD STOP DUMPING YOU...
!
S...
SORRY!
I WENT TOO FAR THAT TIME!
MASU...

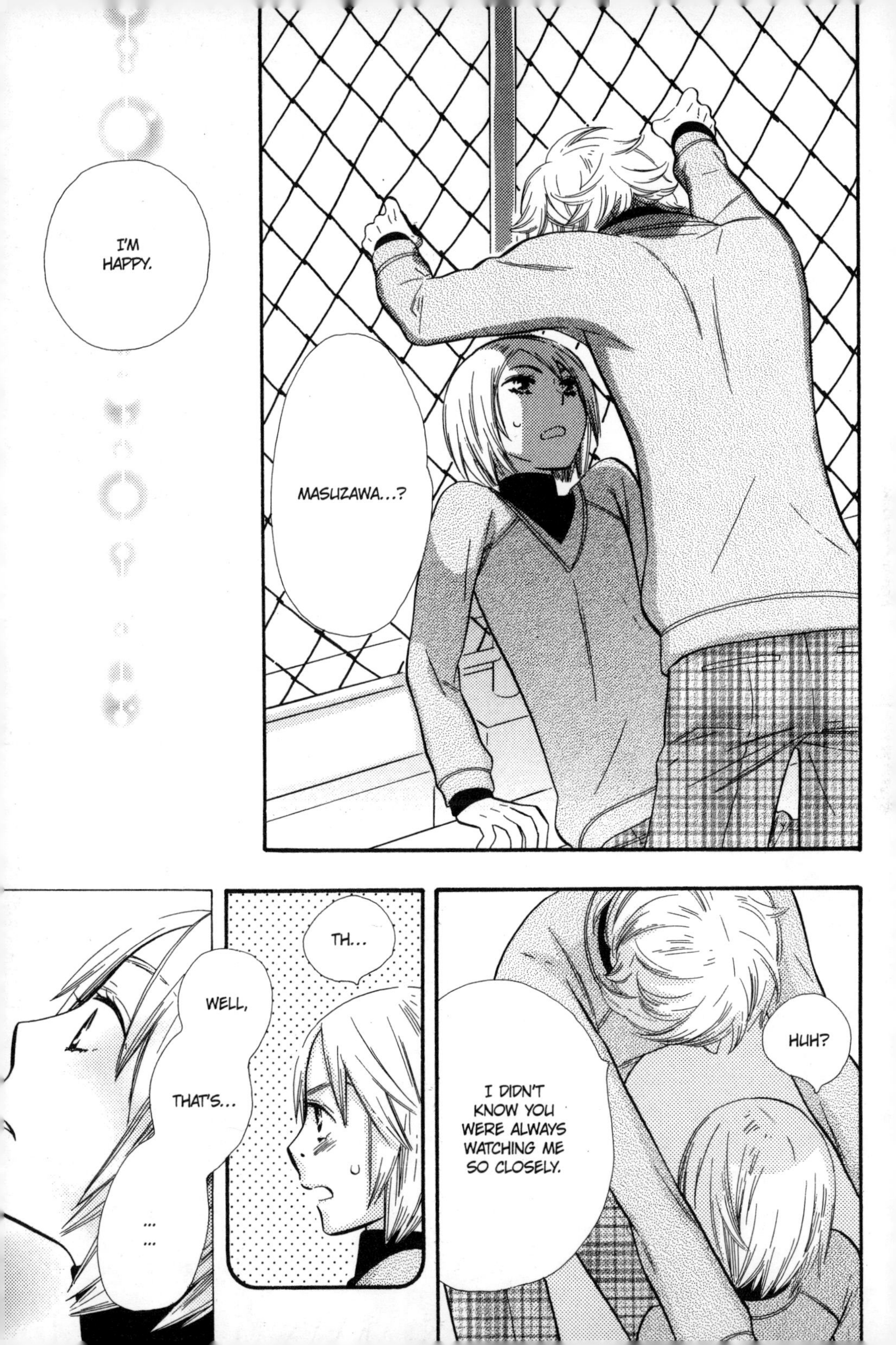

I'M HAPPY.
MASUZAWA...?
HUH?
I DIDN'T KNOW YOU WERE ALWAYS WATCHING ME SO CLOSELY.
TH...
WELL, THAT'S...
... ...

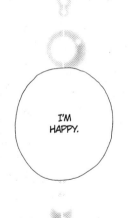

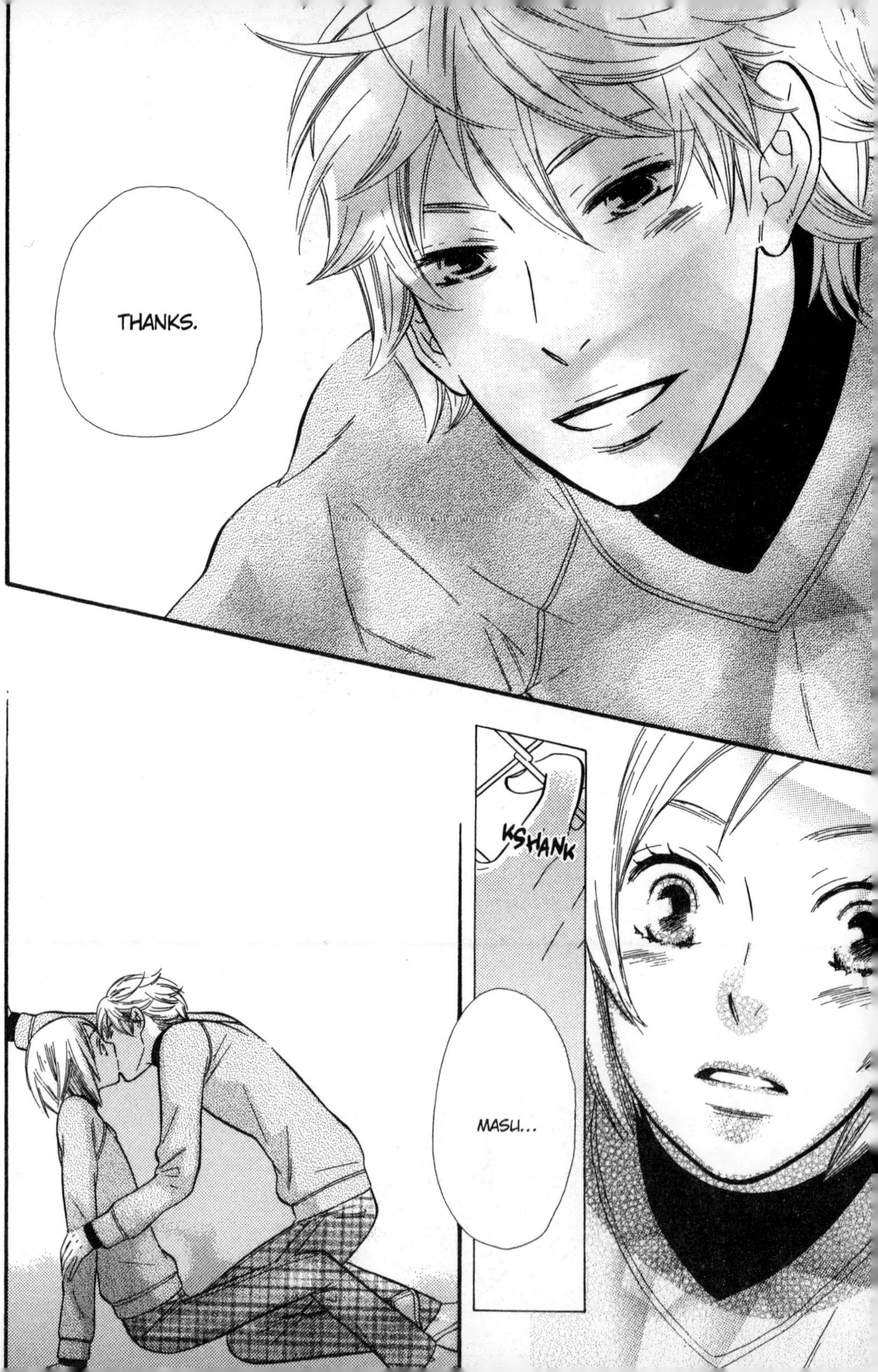
THANKS.
KSHANK
MASU...

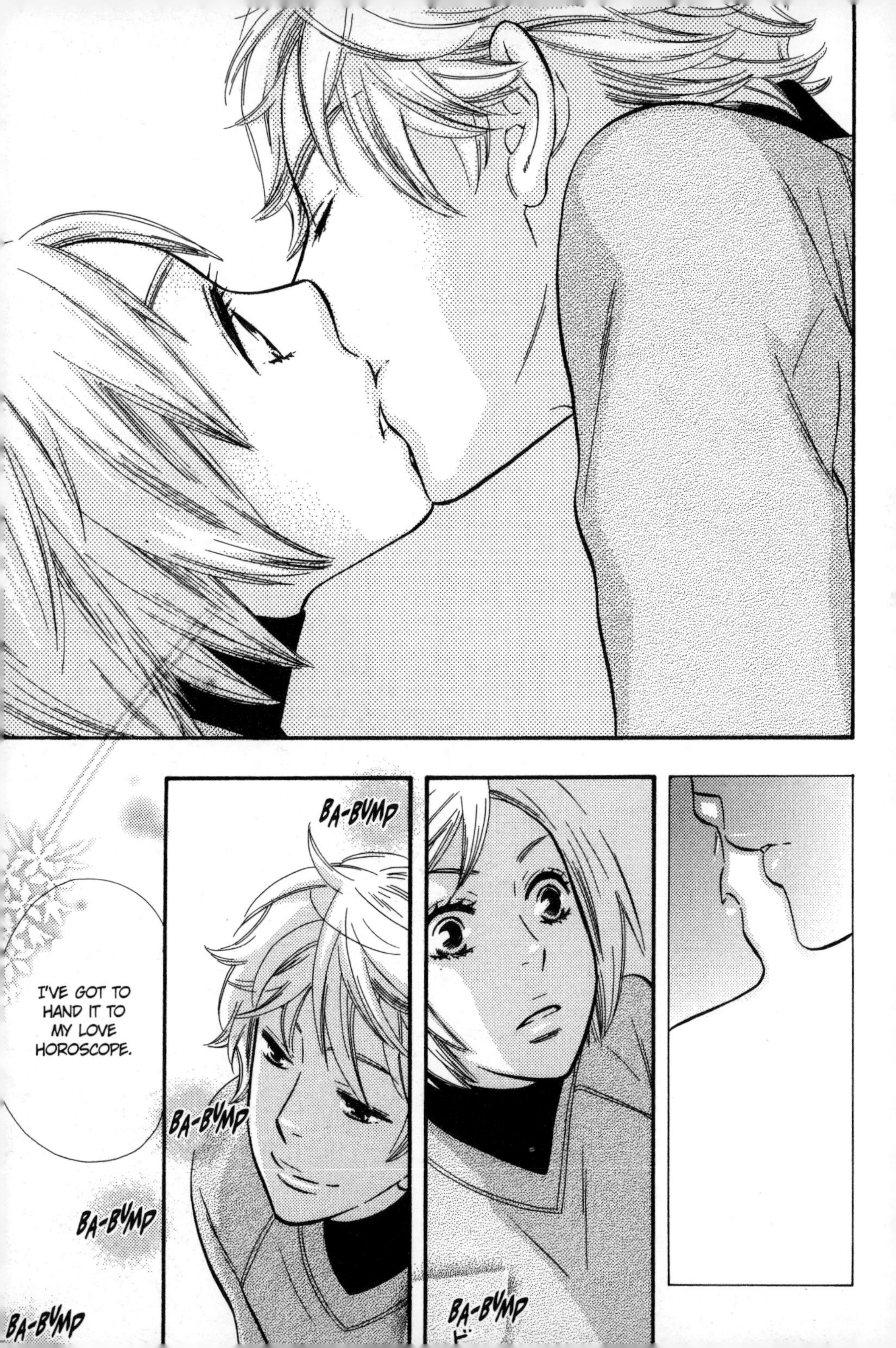
BA-BUMP
BA-BUMP
BA-BUMP
I'VE GOT TO HAND IT TO MY LOVE HOROSCOPE.
BA-BUMP
BA-BUMP

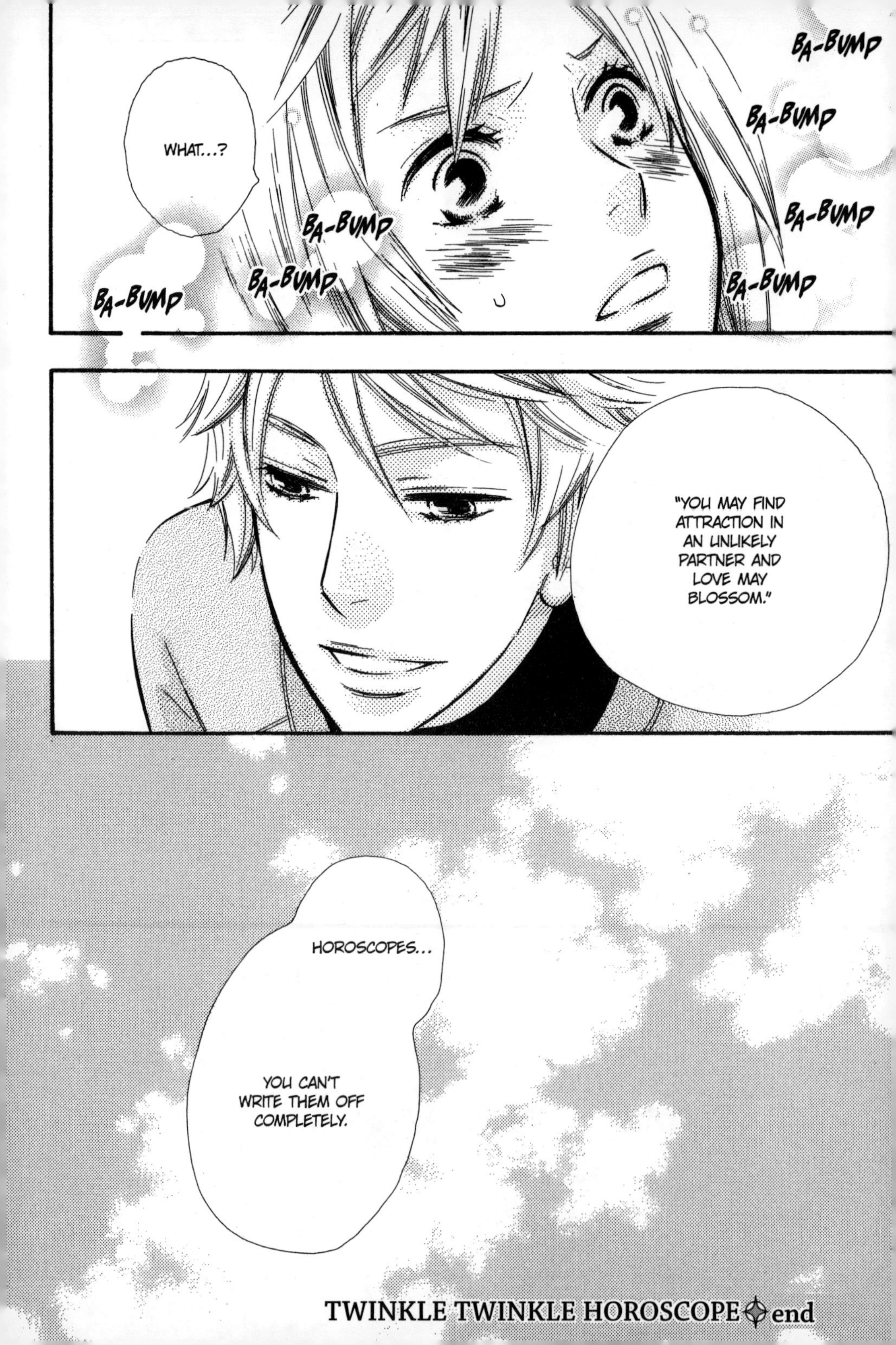
BA-BUMP
BA-BUMP
BA-BUMP
BA-BUMP
WHAT...?
BA-BUMP
BA-BUMP
BA-BUMP
"YOU MAY FIND ATTRACTION IN AN UNLIKELY PARTNER AND LOVE MAY BLOSSOM."
HOROSCOPES...
YOU CAN'T WRITE THEM OFF COMPLETELY.
TWINKLE TWINKLE HOROSCOPE end

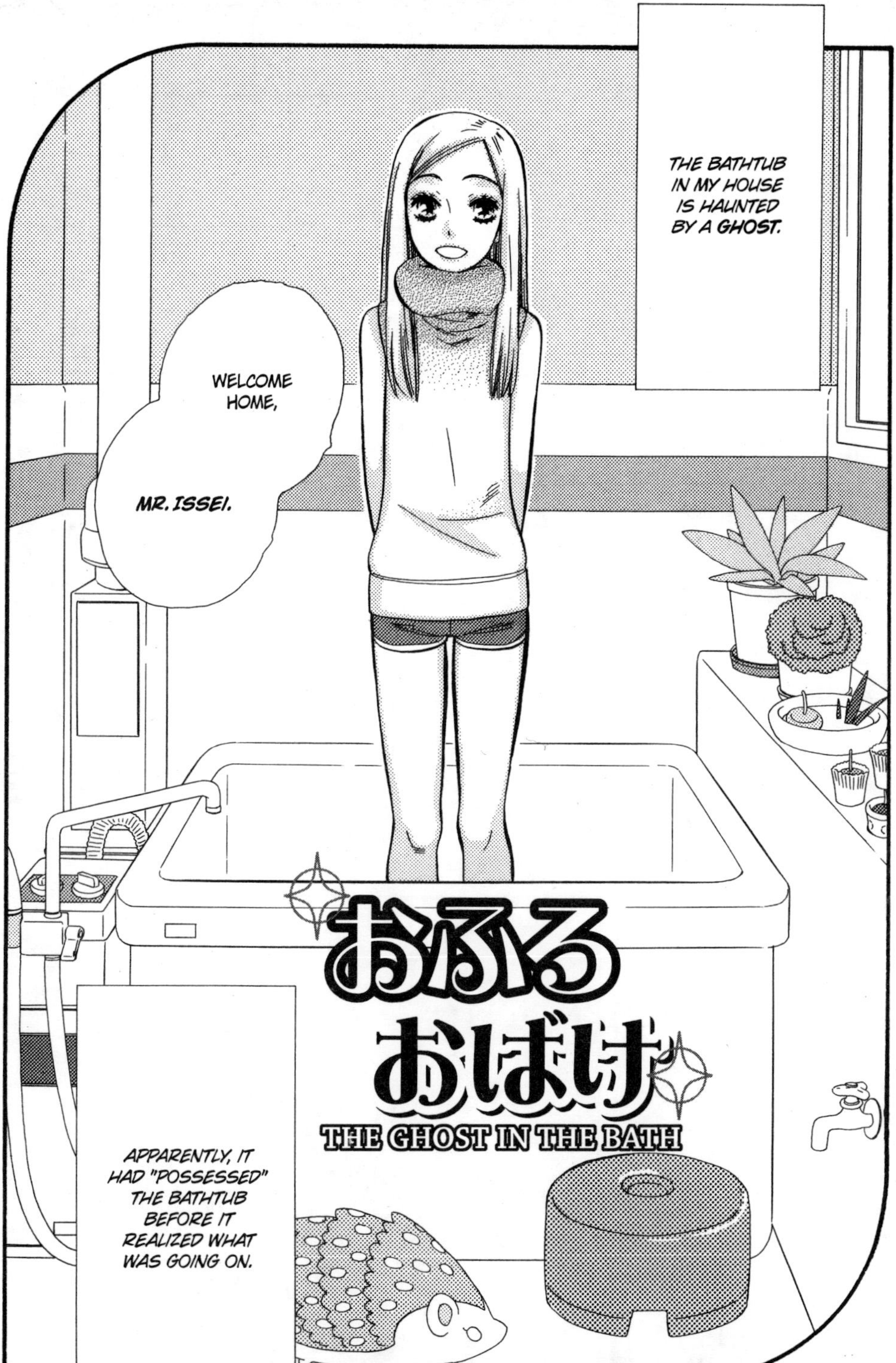
THE BATHTUB IN MY HOUSE IS HAUNTED BY A GHOST.
WELCOME HOME,
MR. ISSEI.
おふろおばけ
THE GHOST IN THE BATH
APPARENTLY, IT HAD "POSSESSED" THE BATHTUB BEFORE IT REALIZED WHAT WAS GOING ON.

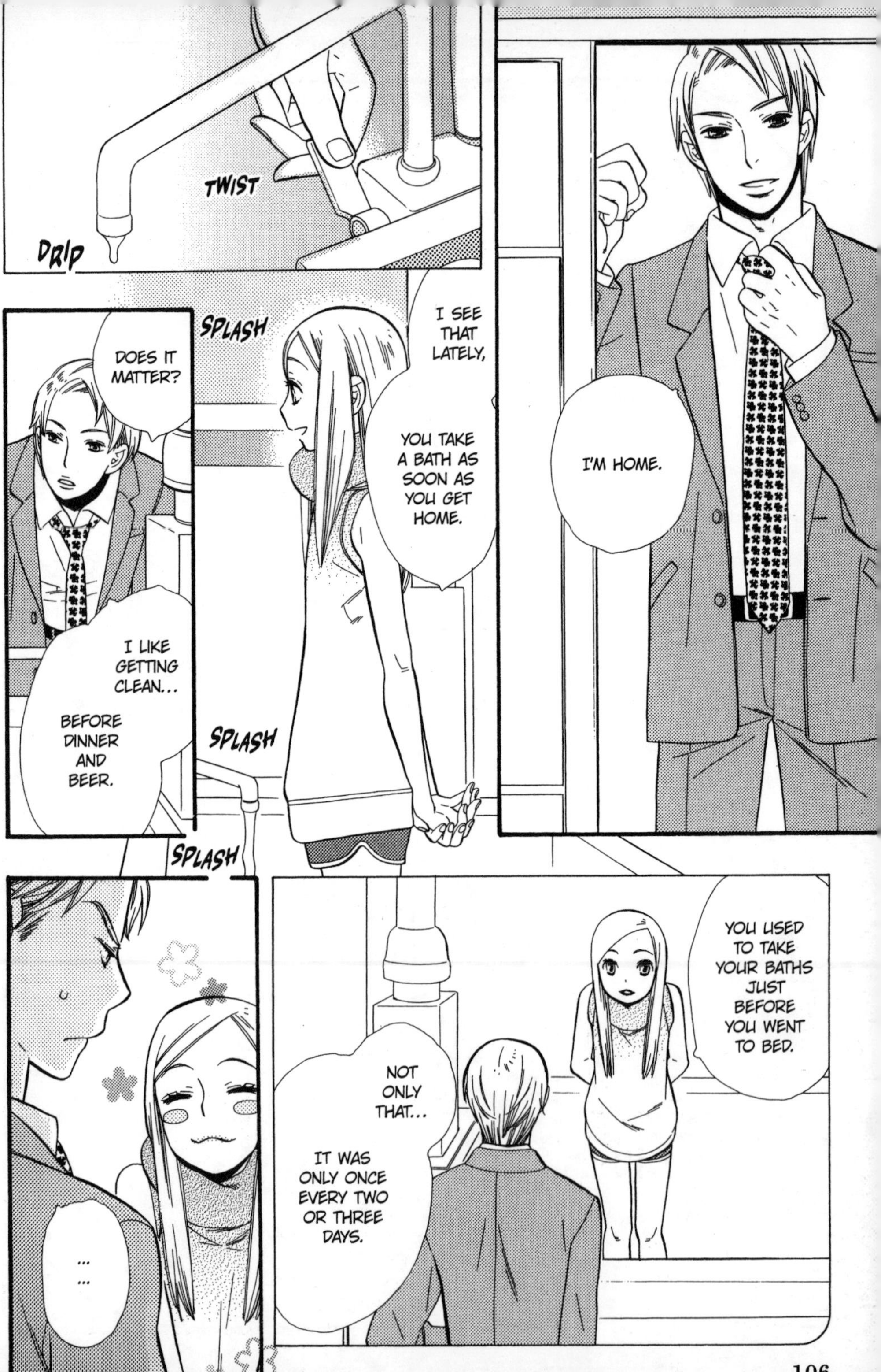
I'M HOME.
TWIST
DRIP
I SEE THAT LATELY,
YOU TAKE A BATH AS SOON AS YOU GET HOME.
SPLASH
DOES IT MATTER?
I LIKE GETTING CLEAN...
BEFORE DINNER AND BEER.
SPLASH
SPLASH
YOU USED TO TAKE YOUR BATHS JUST BEFORE YOU WENT TO BED.
NOT ONLY THAT...
IT WAS ONLY ONCE EVERY TWO OR THREE DAYS.
...
...

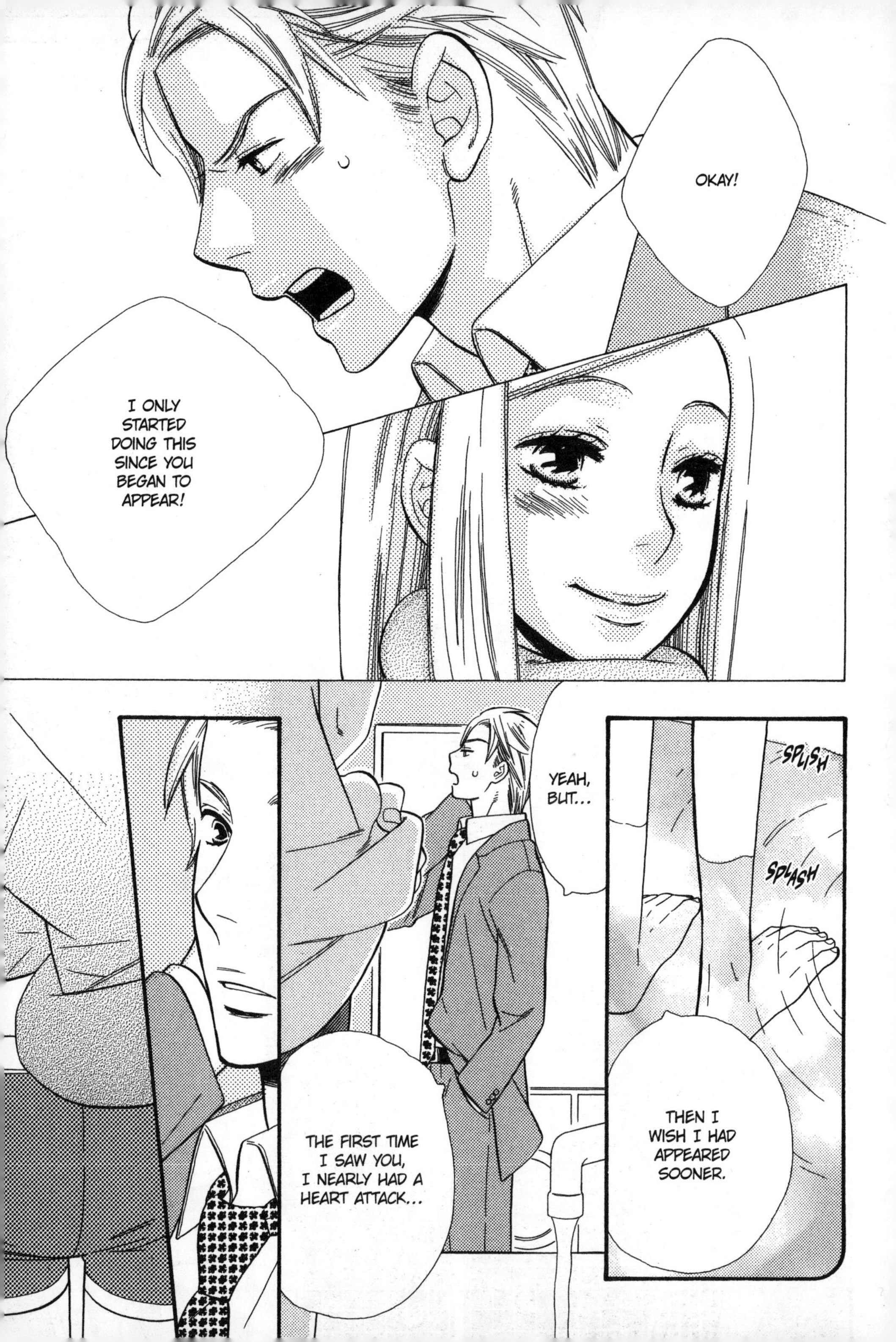
OKAY!
I ONLY STARTED DOING THIS SINCE YOU BEGAN TO APPEAR!
SPLISH
SPLASH
THEN I WISH I HAD APPEARED SOONER.
YEAH, BUT...
THE FIRST TIME I SAW YOU, I NEARLY HAD A HEART ATTACK...

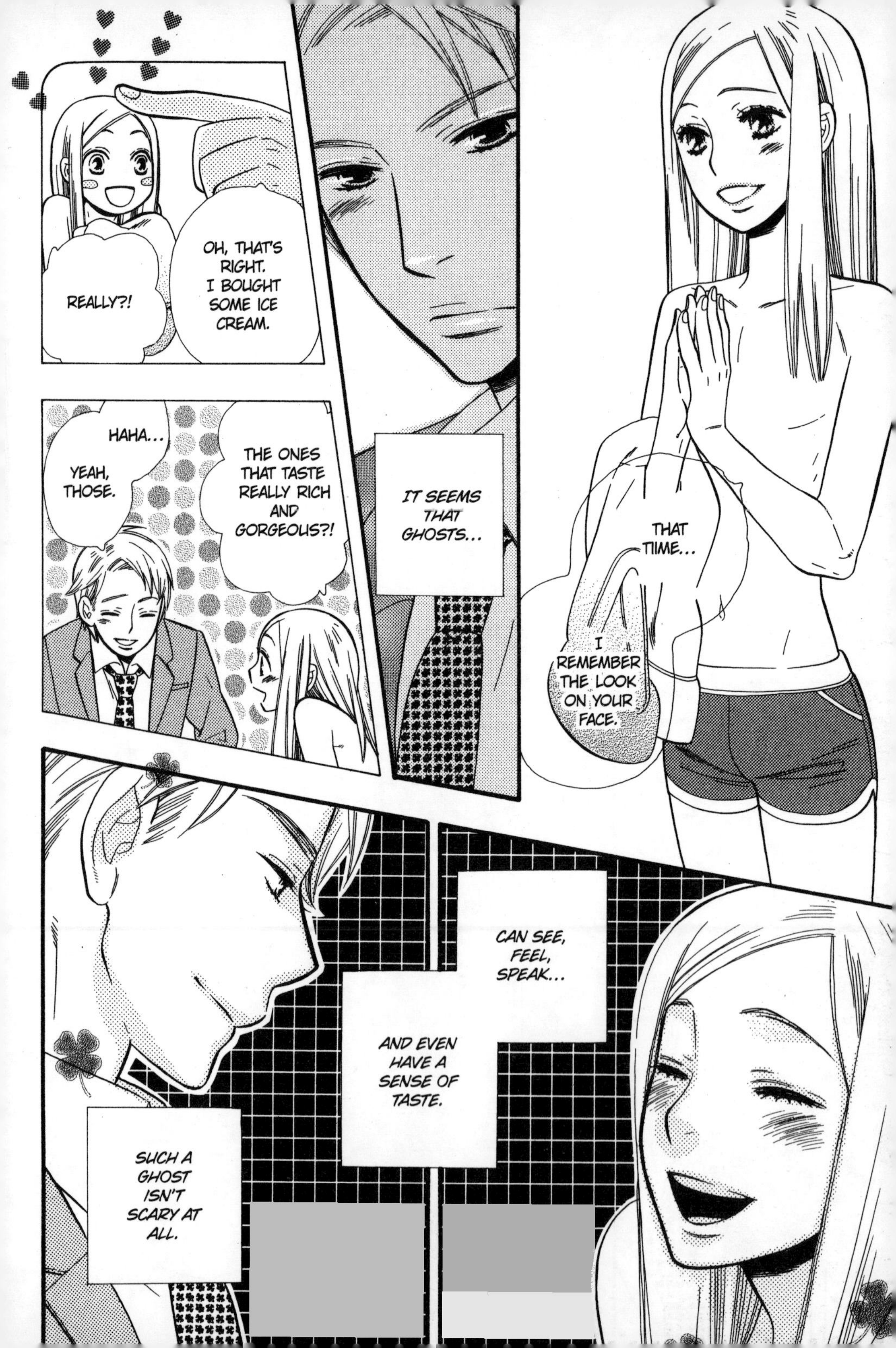
THAT TIIME...
I REMEMBER THE LOOK ON YOUR FACE.
IT SEEMS THAT GHOSTS...
OH, THAT'S RIGHT. I BOUGHT SOME ICE CREAM.
REALLY?!
THE ONES THAT TASTE REALLY RICH AND GORGEOUS?!
HAHA...
YEAH, THOSE.
CAN SEE, FEEL, SPEAK...
AND EVEN HAVE A SENSE OF TASTE.
SUCH A GHOST ISN'T SCARY AT ALL.

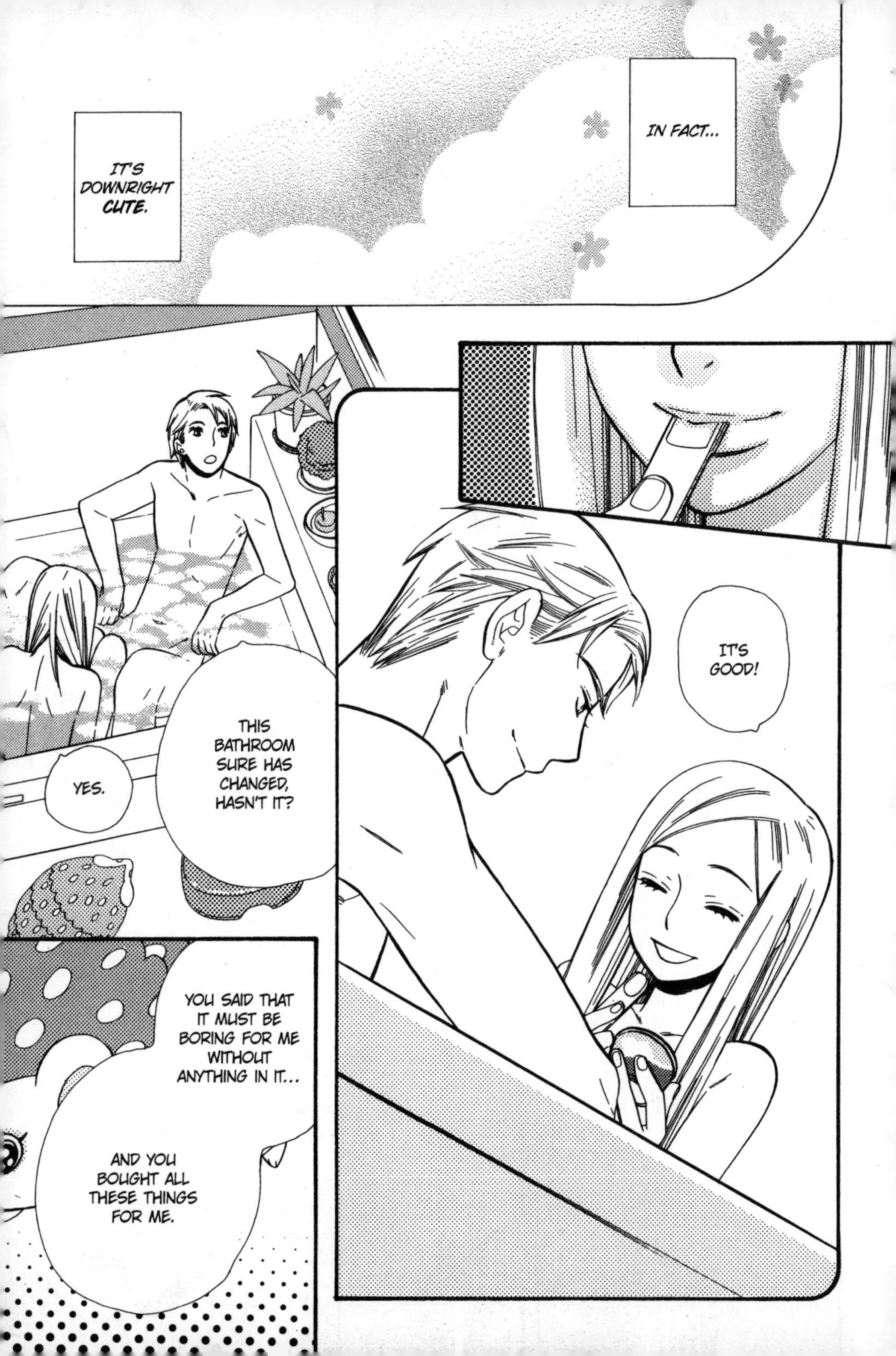
IN FACT...
IT'S DOWNRIGHT CUTE.
IT'S GOOD!
THIS BATHROOM SURE HAS CHANGED, HASN'T IT?
YES.
YOU SAID THAT IT MUST BE BORING FOR ME WITHOUT ANYTHING IN IT...
AND YOU BOUGHT ALL THESE THINGS FOR ME.

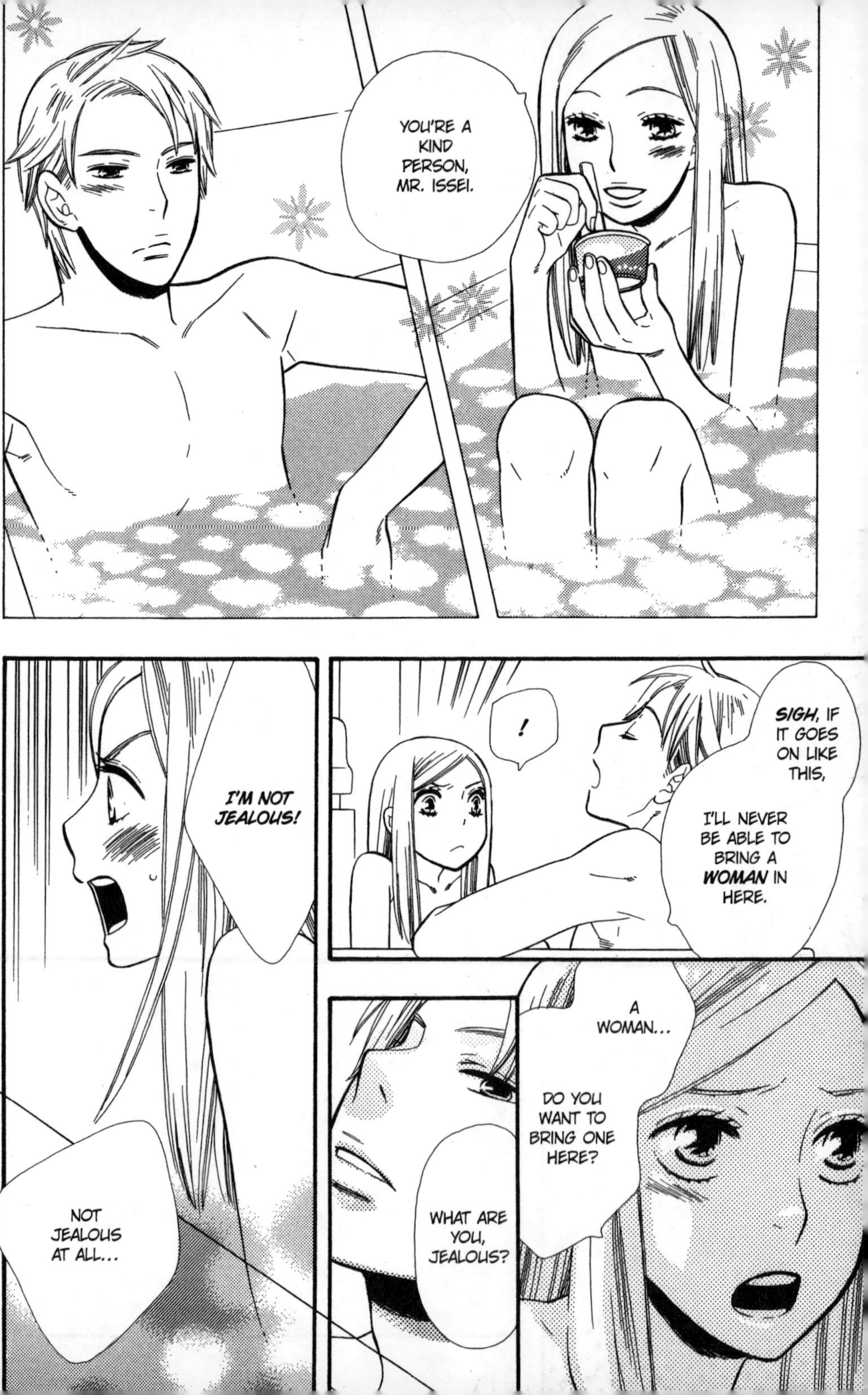
YOU'RE A KIND PERSON, MR. ISSEI.
SIGH, IF IT GOES ON LIKE THIS,
I'LL NEVER BE ABLE TO BRING A *WOMAN* IN HERE.
!
A WOMAN...
DO YOU WANT TO BRING ONE HERE?
WHAT ARE YOU, JEALOUS?
I'M NOT JEALOUS!
NOT JEALOUS AT ALL...

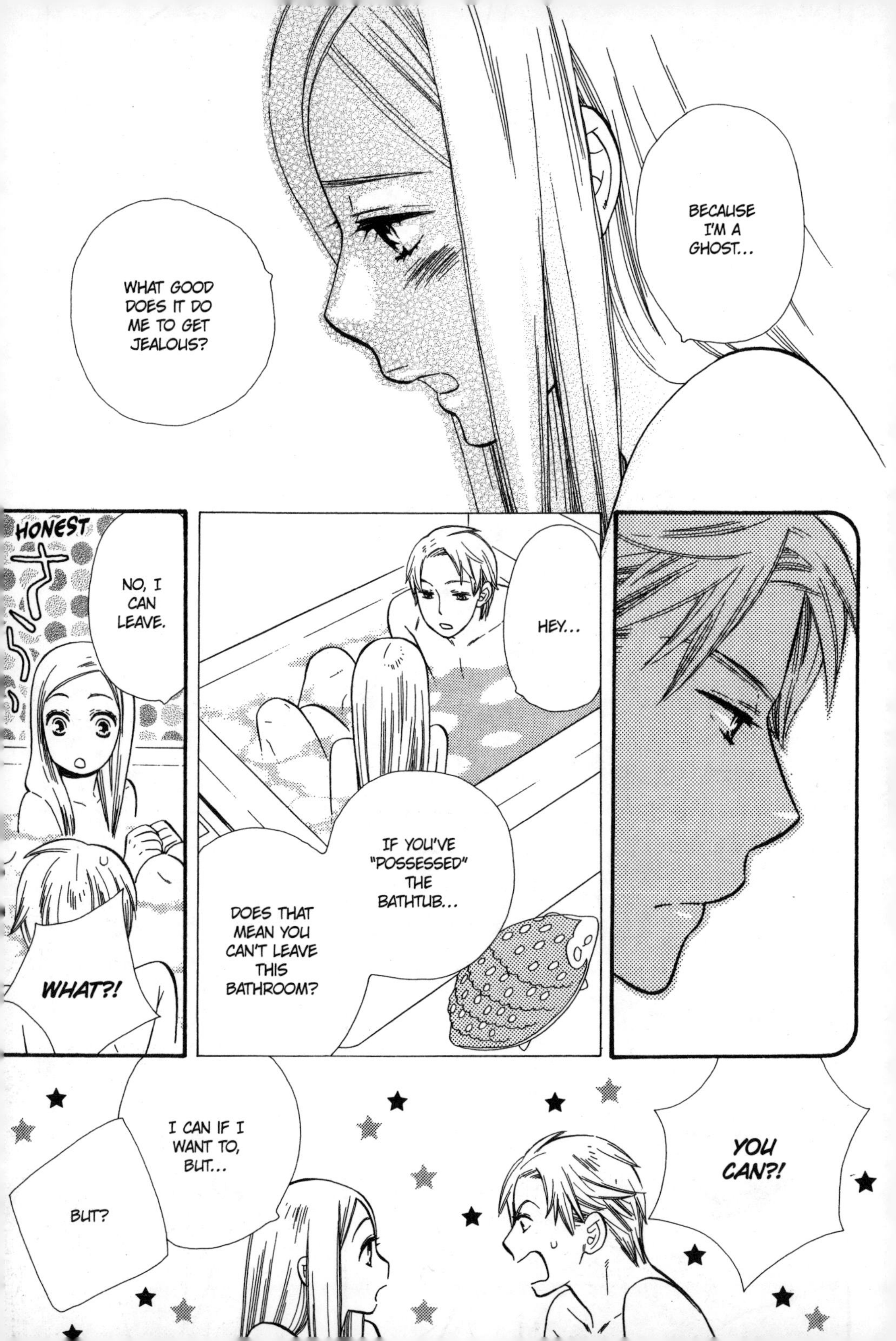
BECAUSE I'M A GHOST...
WHAT GOOD DOES IT DO ME TO GET JEALOUS?
HEY...
IF YOU'VE "POSSESSED" THE BATHTUB...
DOES THAT MEAN YOU CAN'T LEAVE THIS BATHROOM?
HONEST
NO, I CAN LEAVE.
WHAT?!
YOU CAN?!
I CAN IF I WANT TO, BUT...
BUT?

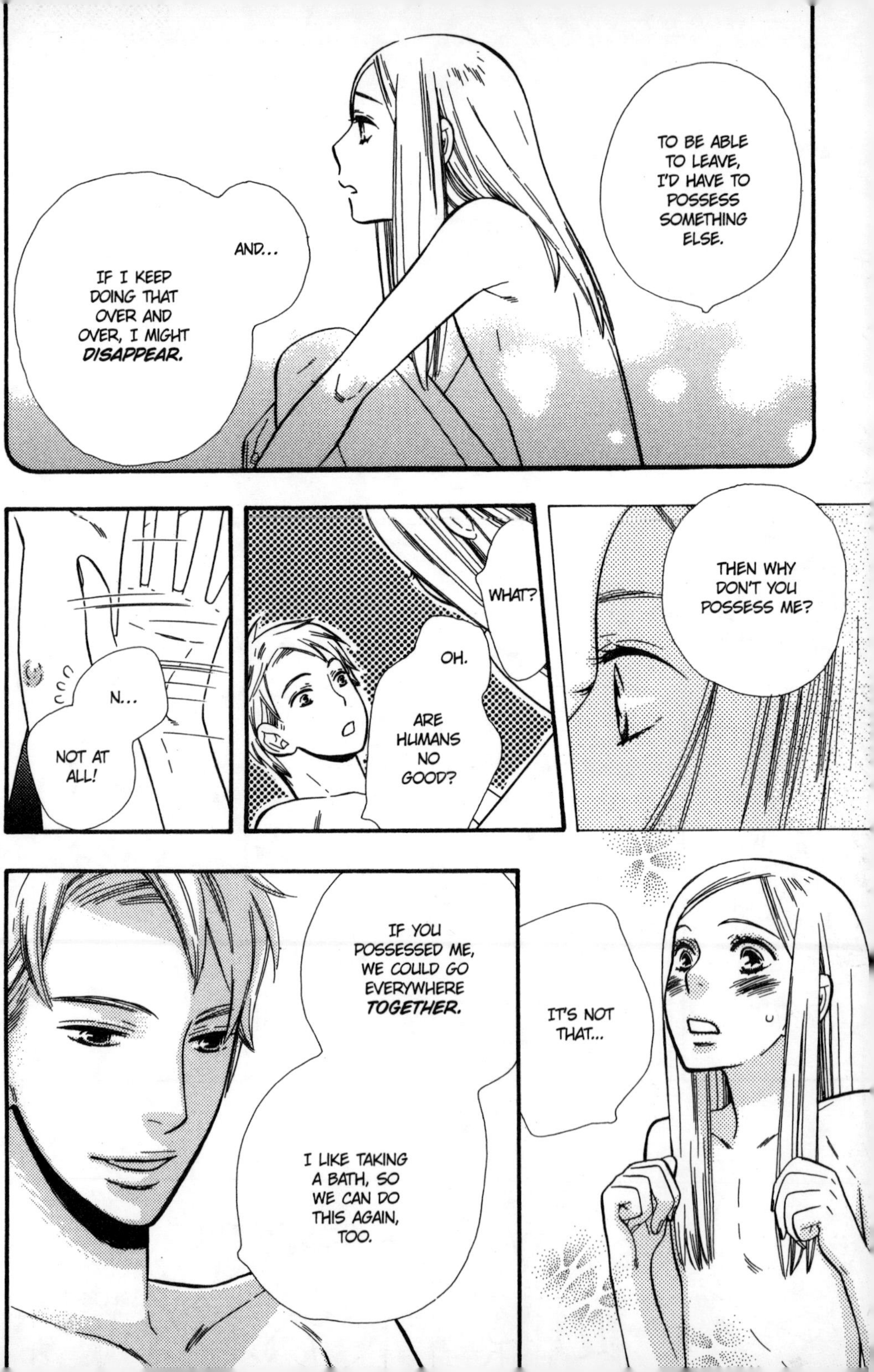
TO BE ABLE TO LEAVE, I'D HAVE TO POSSESS SOMETHING ELSE.
AND...
IF I KEEP DOING THAT OVER AND OVER, I MIGHT **DISAPPEAR.**
THEN WHY DON'T YOU POSSESS ME?
WHAT?
OH.
ARE HUMANS NO GOOD?
N...
NOT AT ALL!
IT'S NOT THAT...
IF YOU POSSESSED ME, WE COULD GO EVERYWHERE **TOGETHER.**
I LIKE TAKING A BATH, SO WE CAN DO THIS AGAIN, TOO.

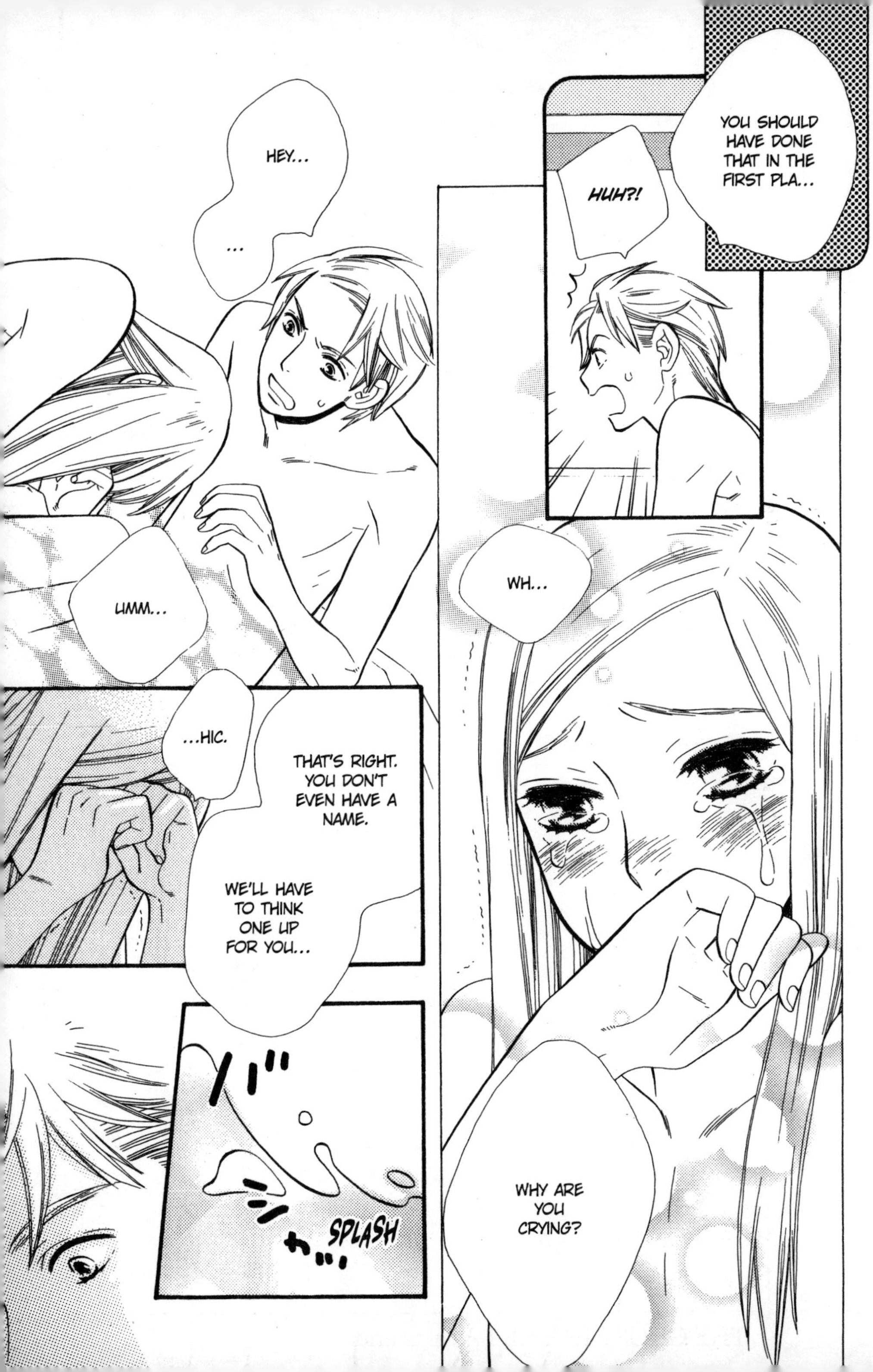
HEY...
...
UMM...
...HIC.
THAT'S RIGHT. YOU DON'T EVEN HAVE A NAME.
WE'LL HAVE TO THINK ONE UP FOR YOU...
SPLASH
YOU SHOULD HAVE DONE THAT IN THE FIRST PLA...
HUH?!
WH...
WHY ARE YOU CRYING?

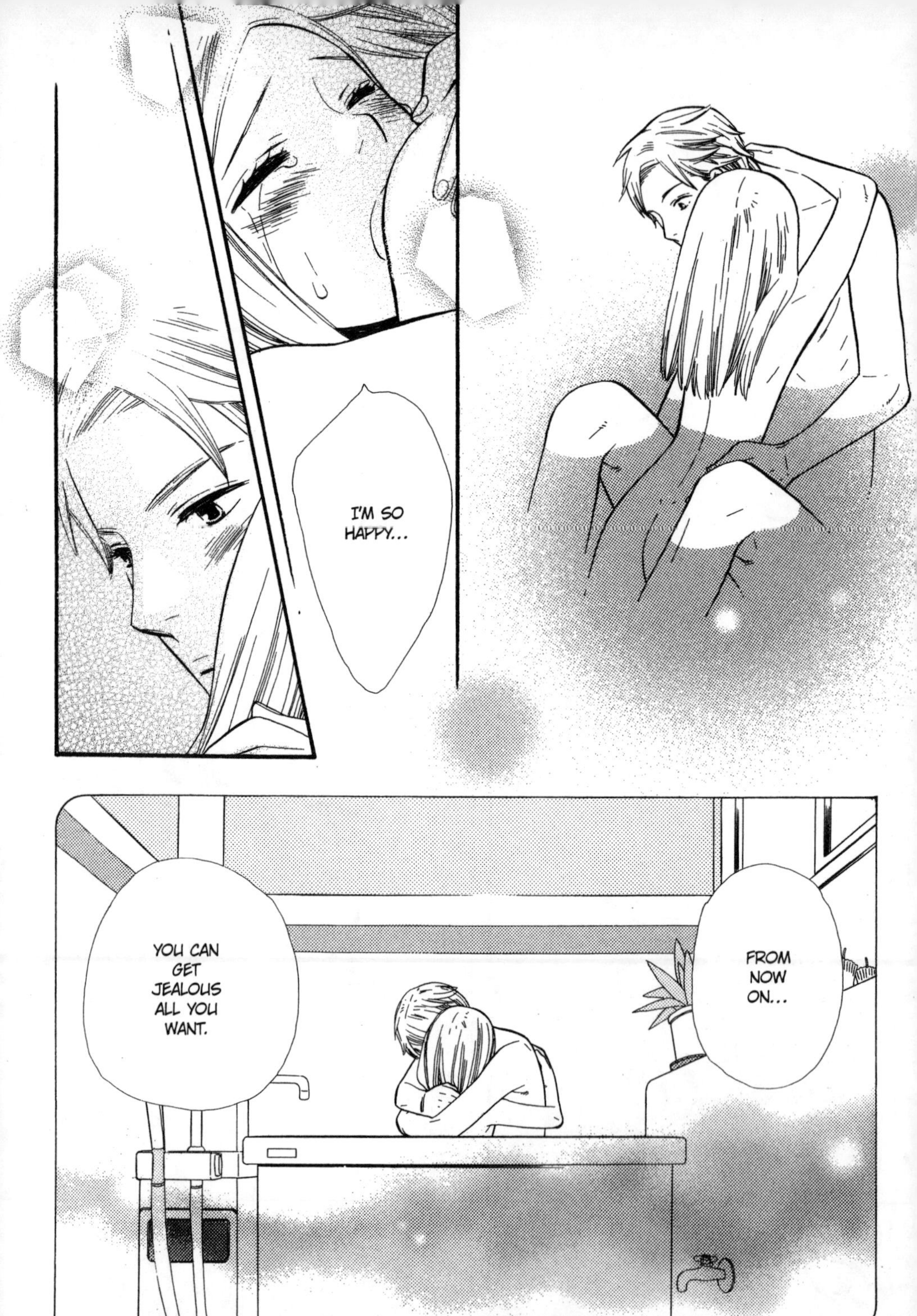
I'M SO HAPPY...
FROM NOW ON...
YOU CAN GET JEALOUS ALL YOU WANT.

THE GHOST IN THE BATH ◈ end

*JUST A LITTLE
EXPLANATION...*

*THE STORY "MIXED CHOCOLATE",
WHICH STARTS ON THE NEXT PAGE,
IS AN EXTRA EPISODE OF TWO
OTHER STORIES, "AISHICHATTANO
(I FELL IN LOVE WITH YOU)" AND
"MIX MIX CHOCOLATE", WHICH
HAVE ALREADY BEEN PUBLISHED
IN ANOTHER VOLUME. FOR THOSE
OF YOU WHO ARE INTERESTED
(AND EVEN IF YOU AREN'T),
PLEASE TRY READING THOSE
OTHER ONES, TOO.*

*I WONDER WHAT
HE WAS FINALLY
NAMED...*

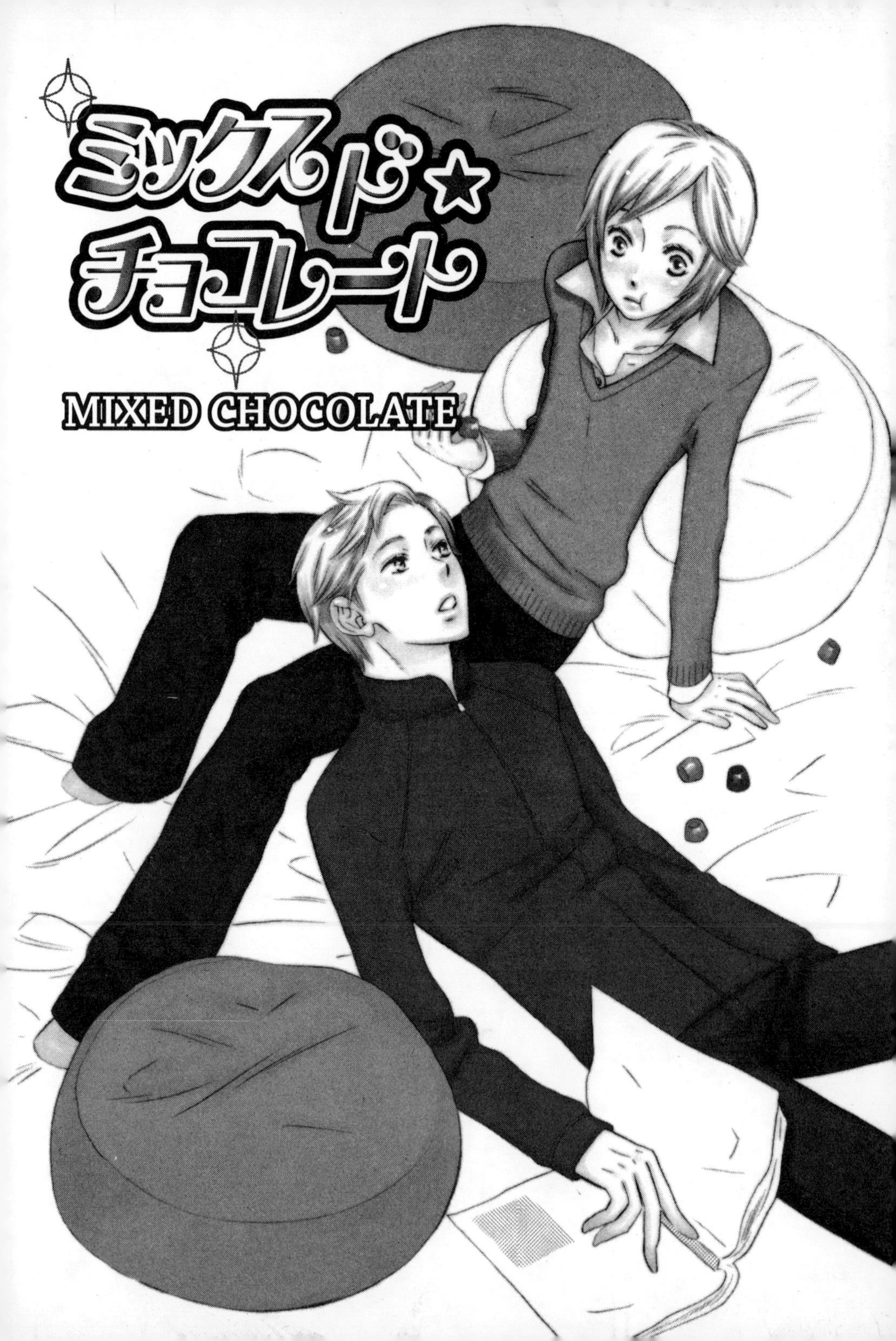
ミックスド☆チョコレート
MIXED CHOCOLATE

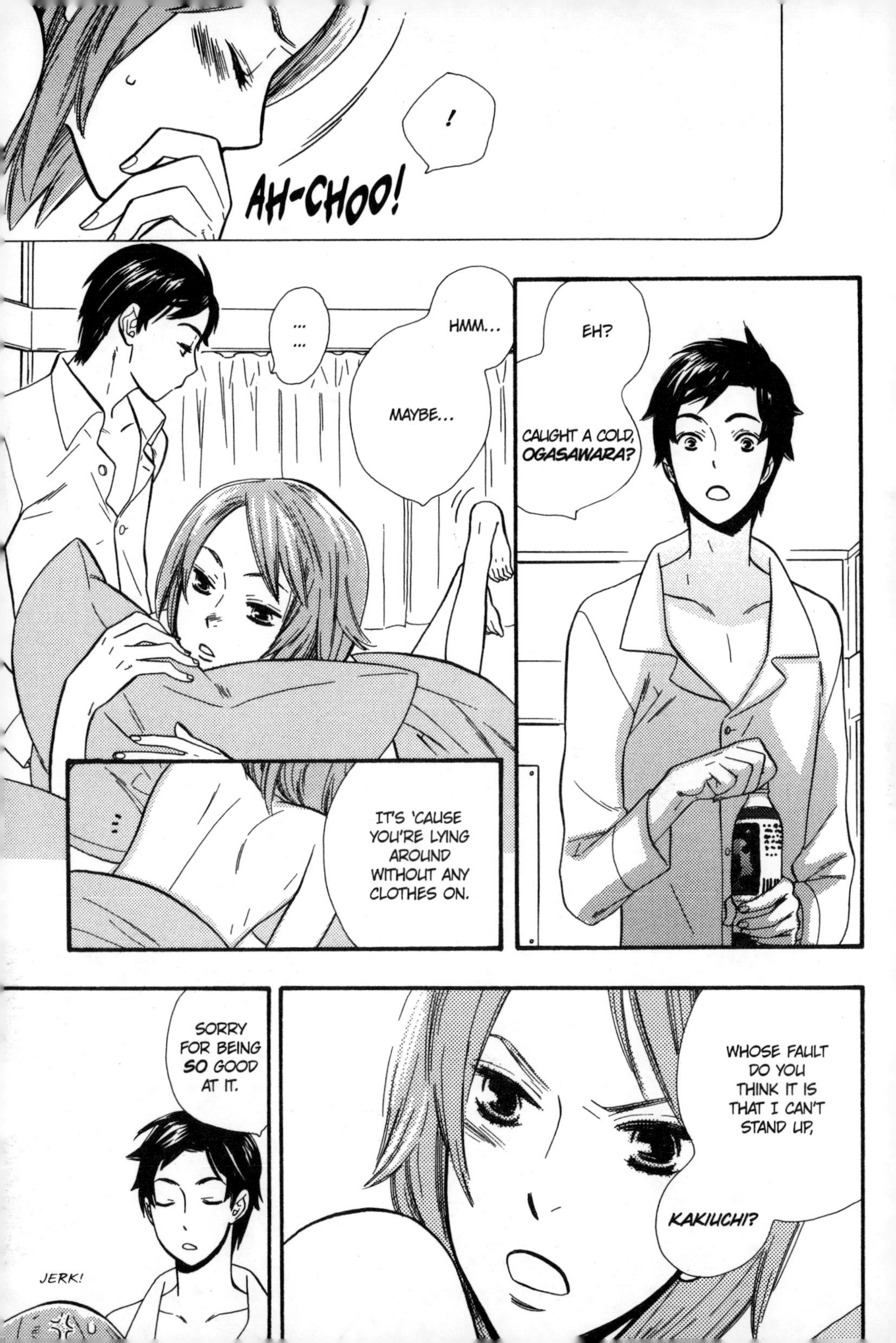
!
AH-CHOO!
EH?
CAUGHT A COLD, OGASAWARA?
HMM... MAYBE...
... ...
IT'S 'CAUSE YOU'RE LYING AROUND WITHOUT ANY CLOTHES ON.
WHOSE FAULT DO YOU THINK IT IS THAT I CAN'T STAND UP, KAKIUCHI?
SORRY FOR BEING SO GOOD AT IT.
JERK!

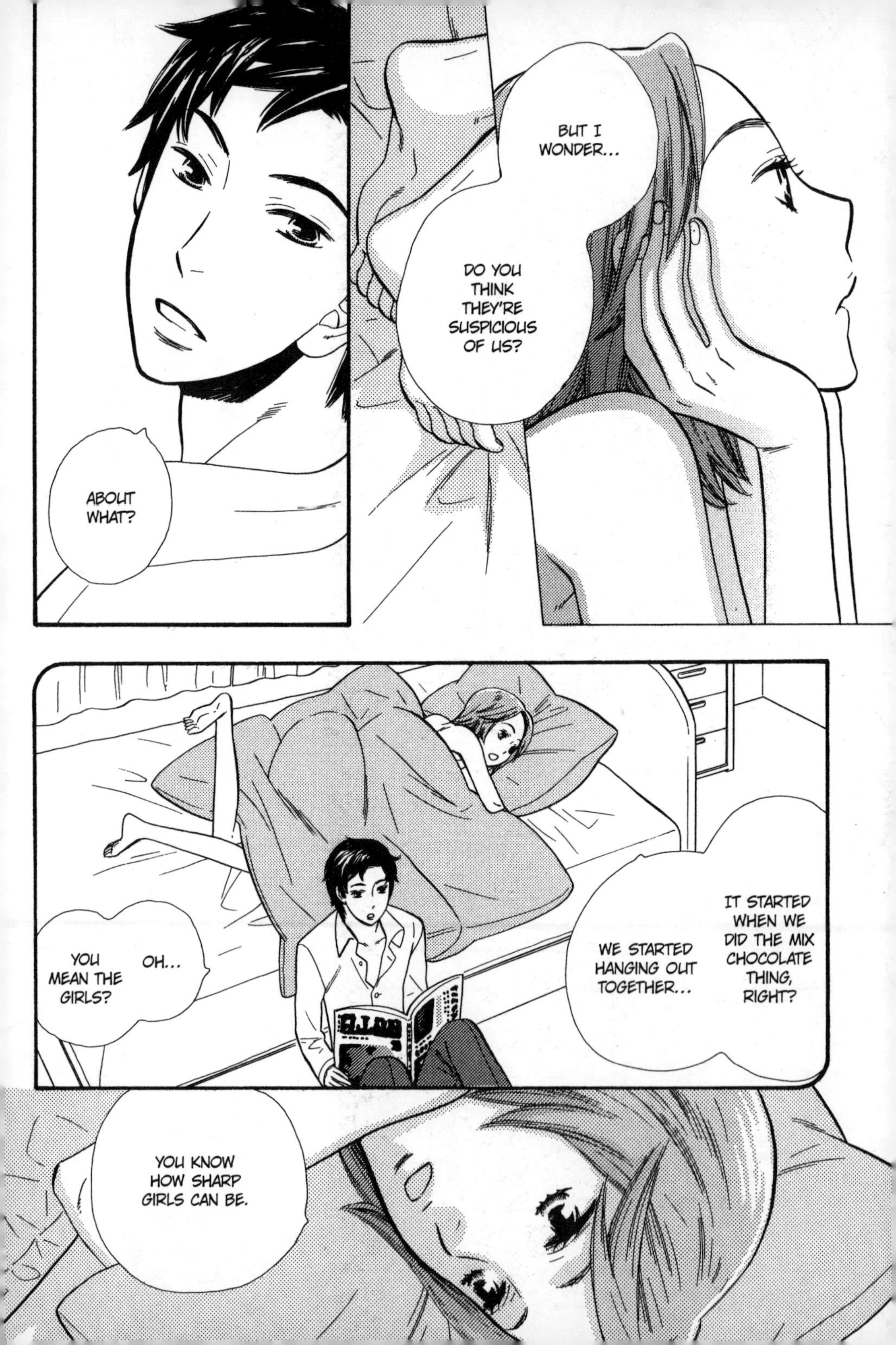
BUT I WONDER...
DO YOU THINK THEY'RE SUSPICIOUS OF US?
ABOUT WHAT?
IT STARTED WHEN WE DID THE MIX CHOCOLATE THING, RIGHT?
WE STARTED HANGING OUT TOGETHER...
OH...
YOU MEAN THE GIRLS?
YOU KNOW HOW SHARP GIRLS CAN BE.

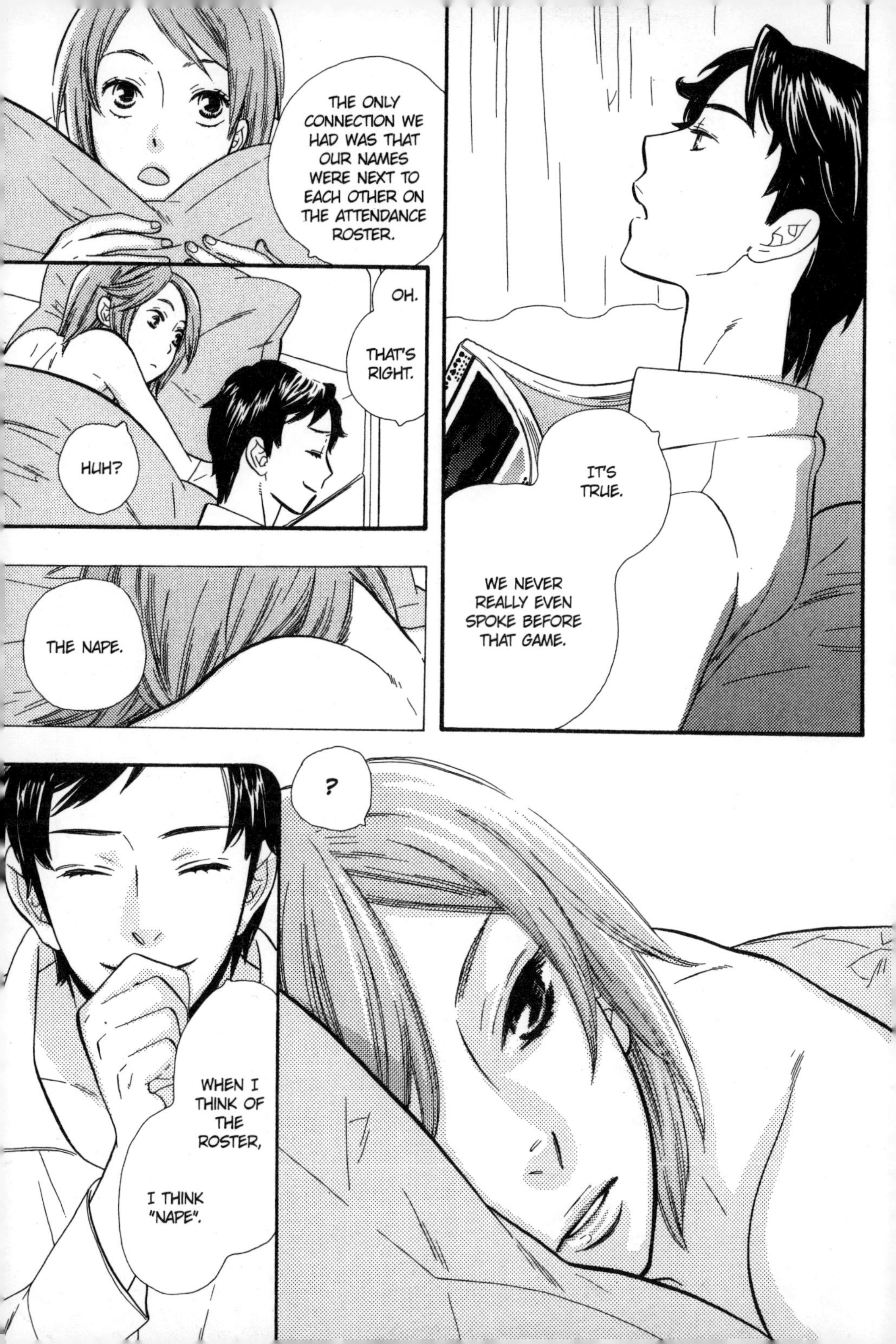
IT'S TRUE.
WE NEVER REALLY EVEN SPOKE BEFORE THAT GAME.
THE ONLY CONNECTION WE HAD WAS THAT OUR NAMES WERE NEXT TO EACH OTHER ON THE ATTENDANCE ROSTER.
OH.
THAT'S RIGHT.
HUH?
THE NAPE.
?
WHEN I THINK OF THE ROSTER,
I THINK "NAPE".

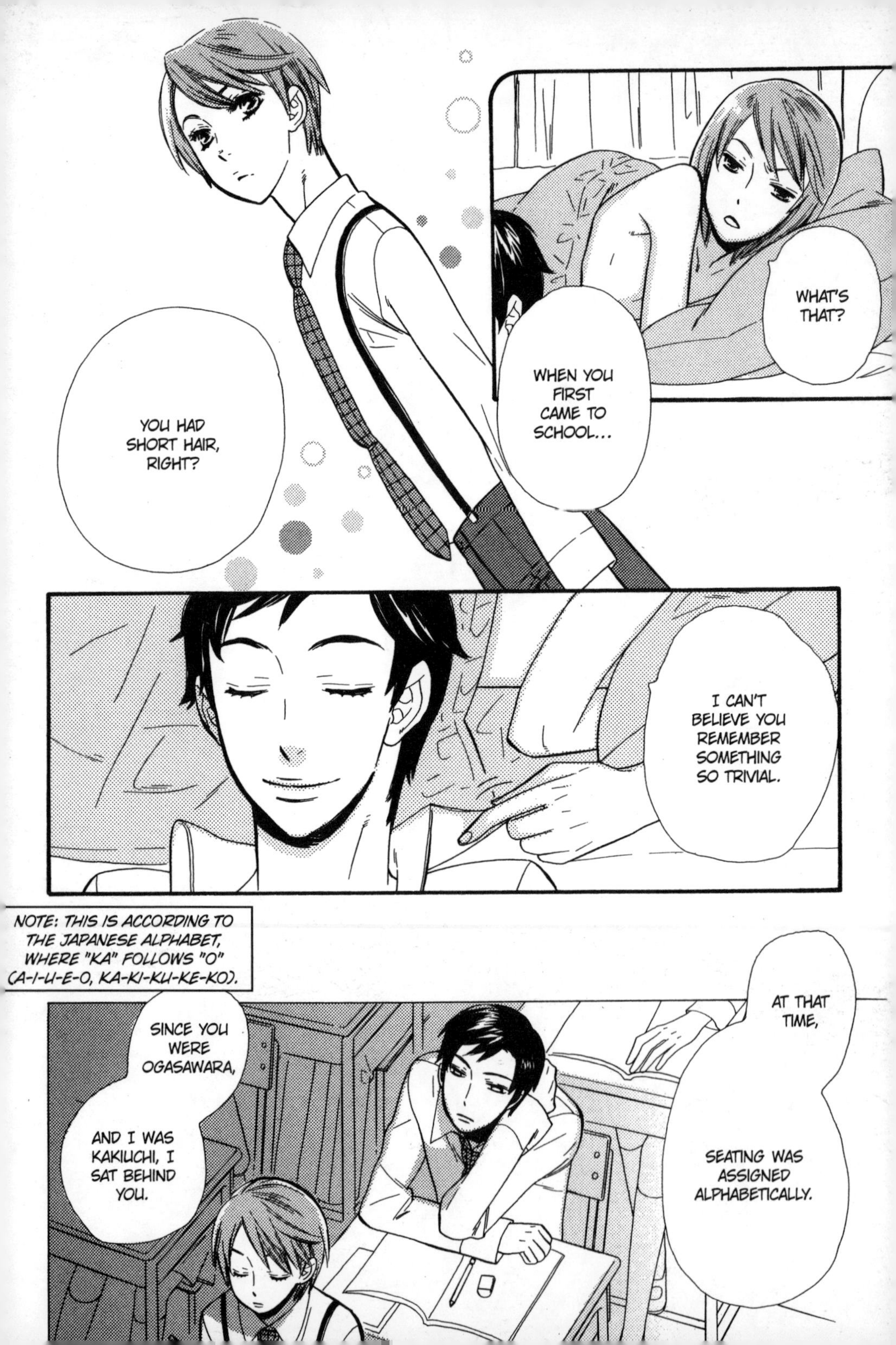
WHAT'S THAT?
WHEN YOU FIRST CAME TO SCHOOL...
YOU HAD SHORT HAIR, RIGHT?
I CAN'T BELIEVE YOU REMEMBER SOMETHING SO TRIVIAL.
NOTE: THIS IS ACCORDING TO THE JAPANESE ALPHABET, WHERE "KA" FOLLOWS "O" (A-I-U-E-O, KA-KI-KU-KE-KO).
AT THAT TIME,
SEATING WAS ASSIGNED ALPHABETICALLY.
SINCE YOU WERE OGASAWARA,
AND I WAS KAKIUCHI, I SAT BEHIND YOU.

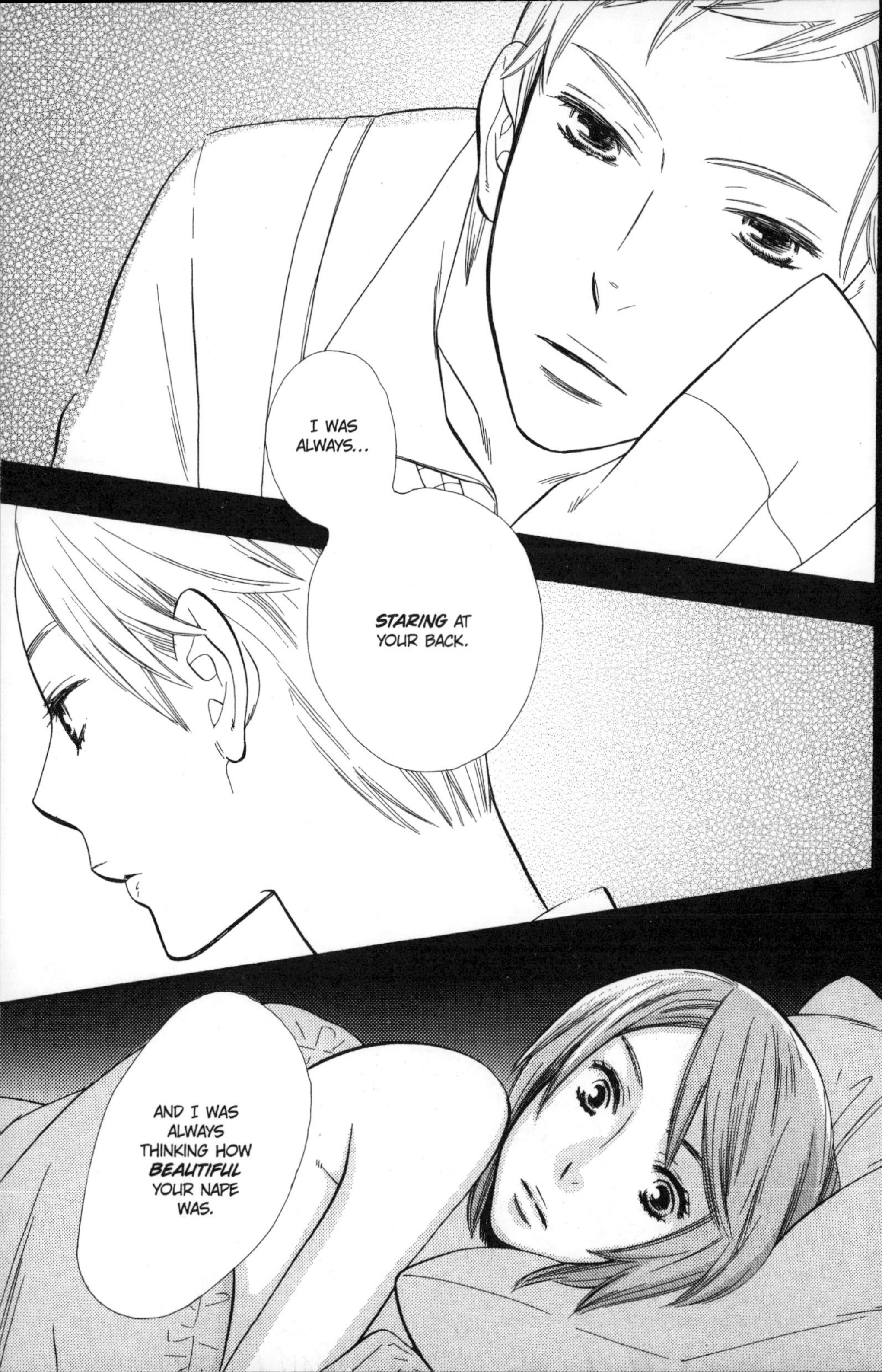
I WAS ALWAYS...
STARING AT YOUR BACK.
AND I WAS ALWAYS THINKING HOW BEAUTIFUL YOUR NAPE WAS.

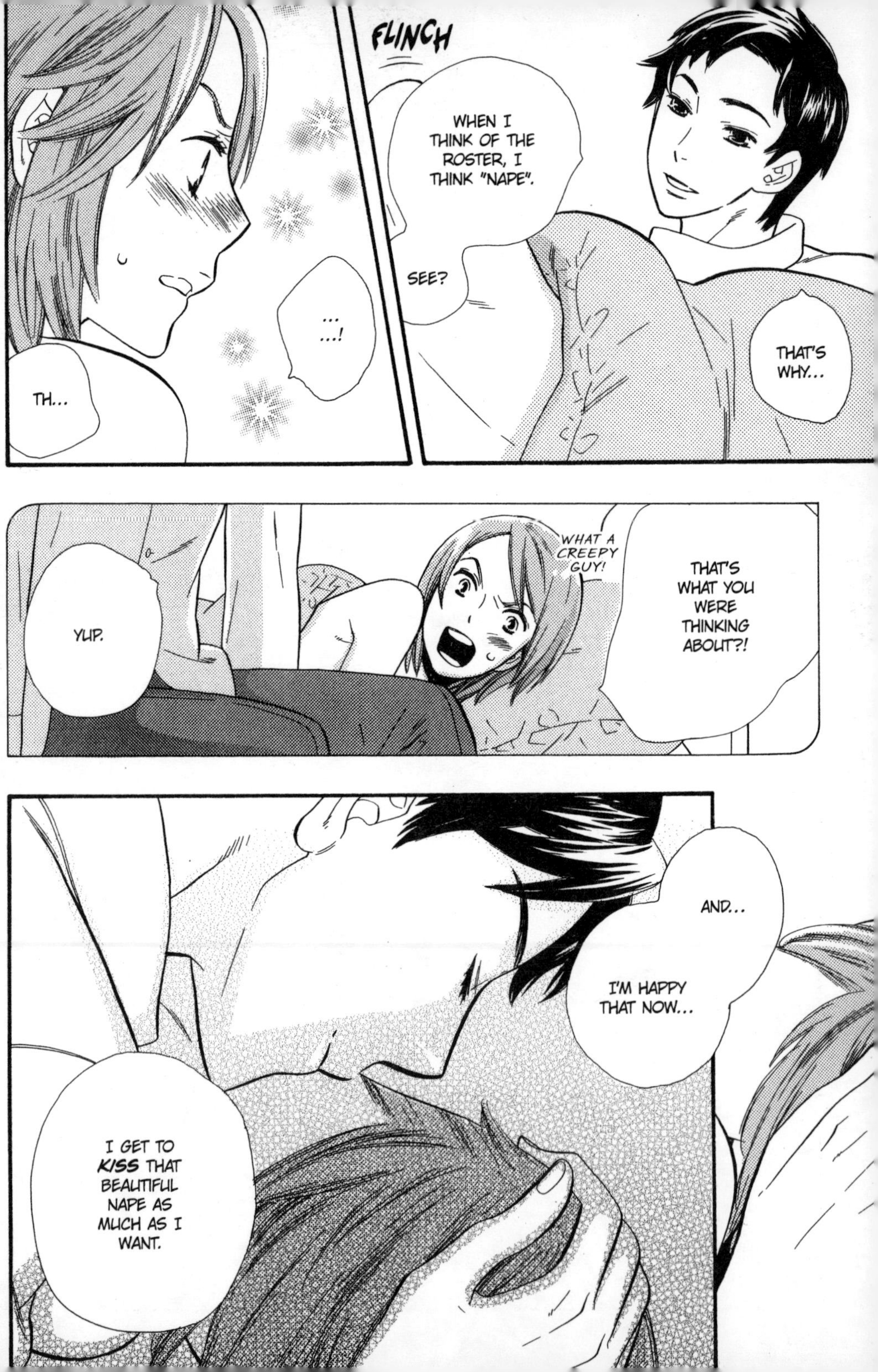
FLINCH
WHEN I THINK OF THE ROSTER, I THINK "NAPE".
SEE?
THAT'S WHY...
... ...!
TH...
THAT'S WHAT YOU WERE THINKING ABOUT?!
WHAT A CREEPY GUY!
YUP.
AND...
I'M HAPPY THAT NOW...
I GET TO **KISS** THAT BEAUTIFUL NAPE AS MUCH AS I WANT.

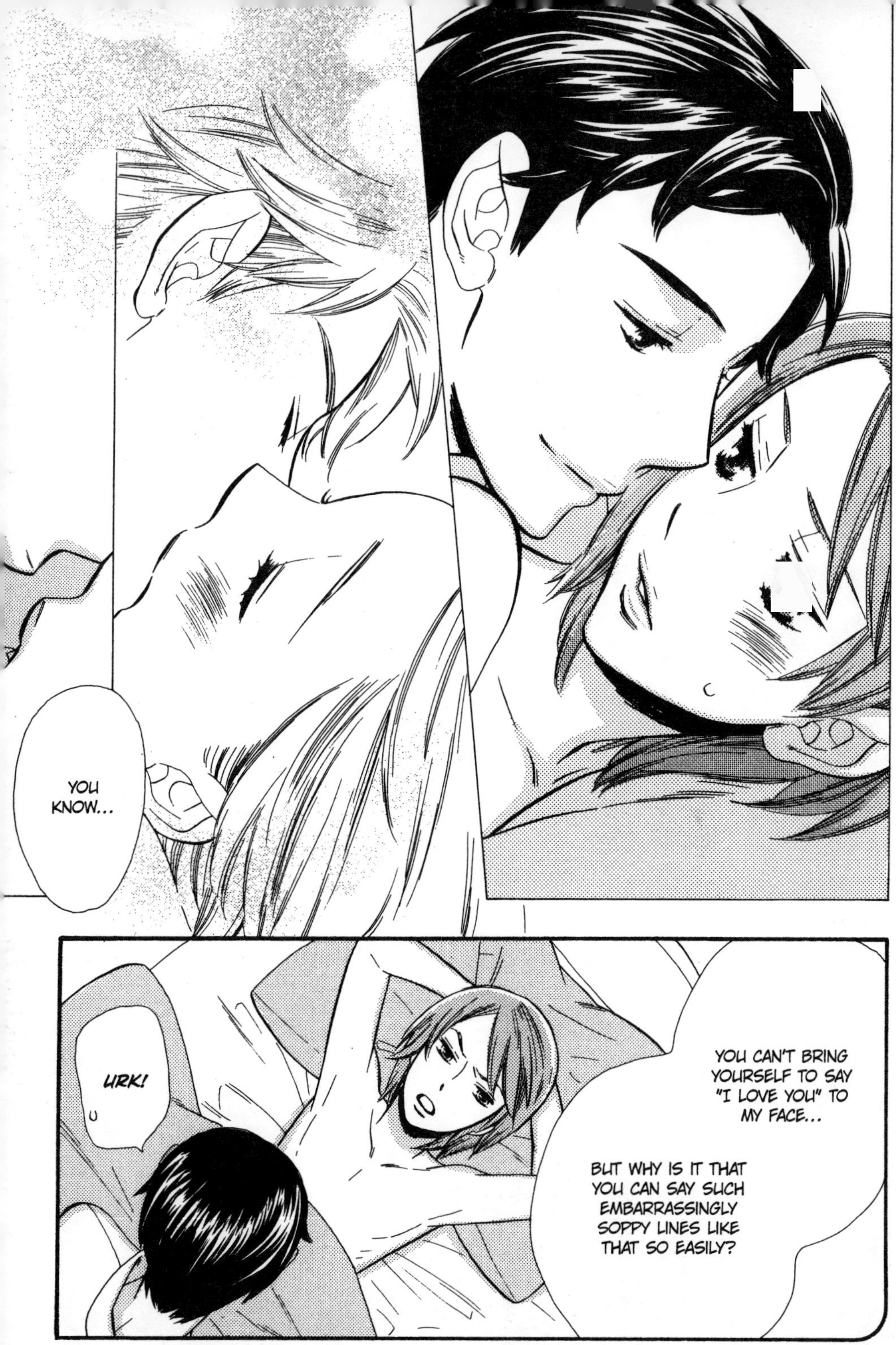
YOU KNOW...
YOU CAN'T BRING YOURSELF TO SAY "I LOVE YOU" TO MY FACE...
BUT WHY IS IT THAT YOU CAN SAY SUCH EMBARRASSINGLY SOPPY LINES LIKE THAT SO EASILY?
URK!

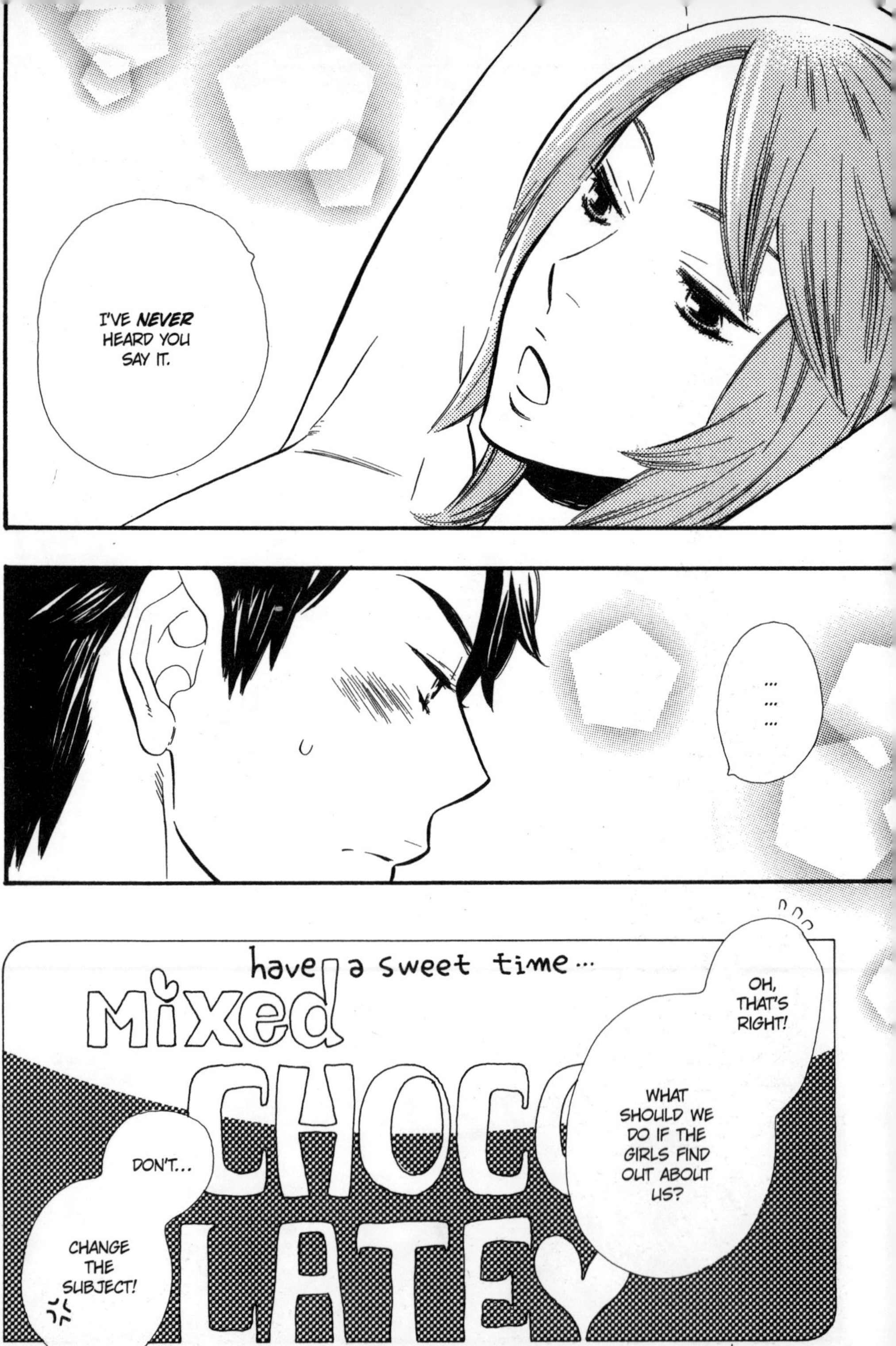
I'VE **NEVER** HEARD YOU SAY IT.
... ...
OH, THAT'S RIGHT!
WHAT SHOULD WE DO IF THE GIRLS FIND OUT ABOUT US?
have a sweet time...
Mixed CHOCOLATE
DON'T...
CHANGE THE SUBJECT!

MIXED CHOCOLATE end

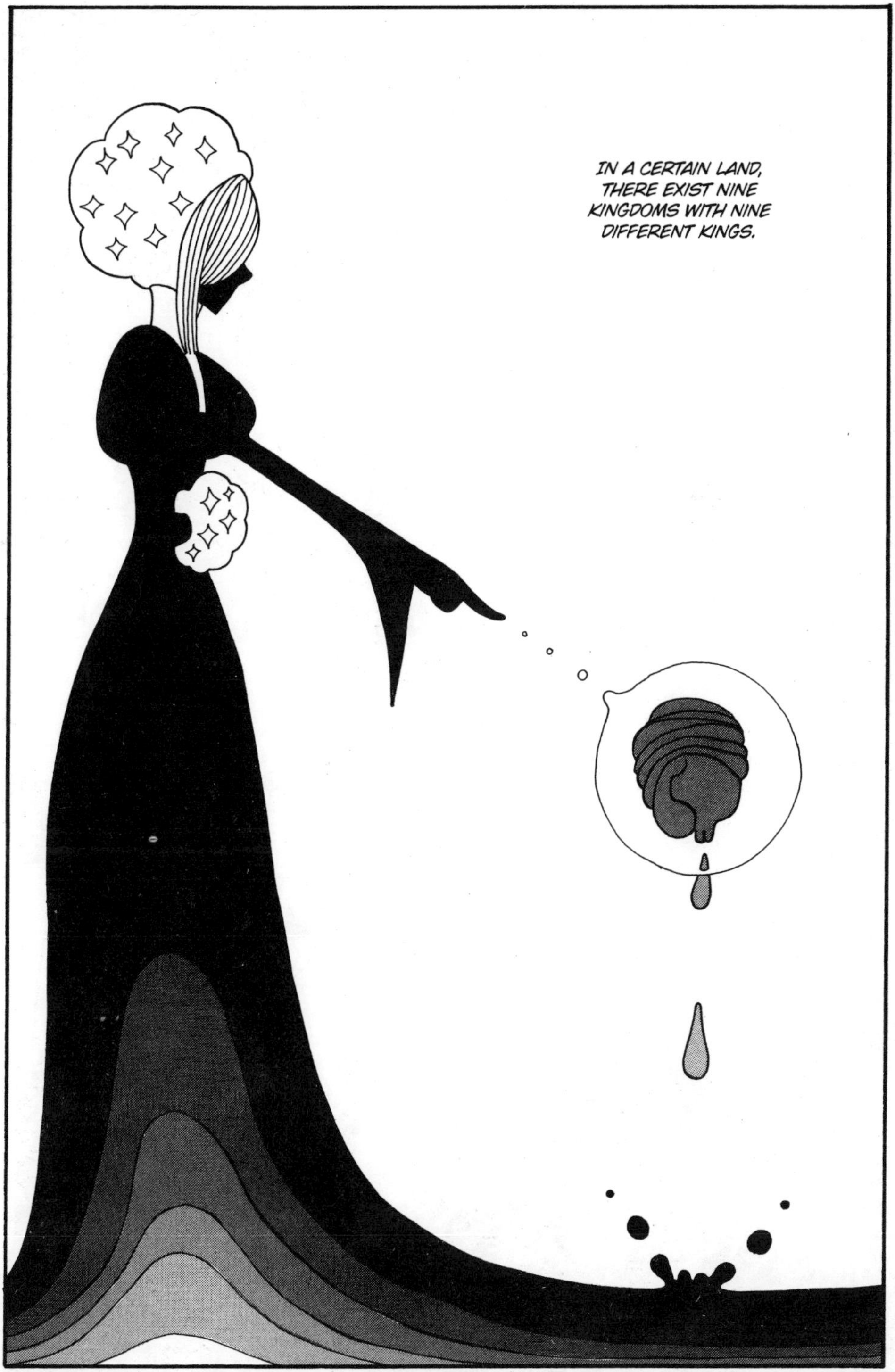
IN A CERTAIN LAND, THERE EXIST NINE KINGDOMS WITH NINE DIFFERENT KINGS.

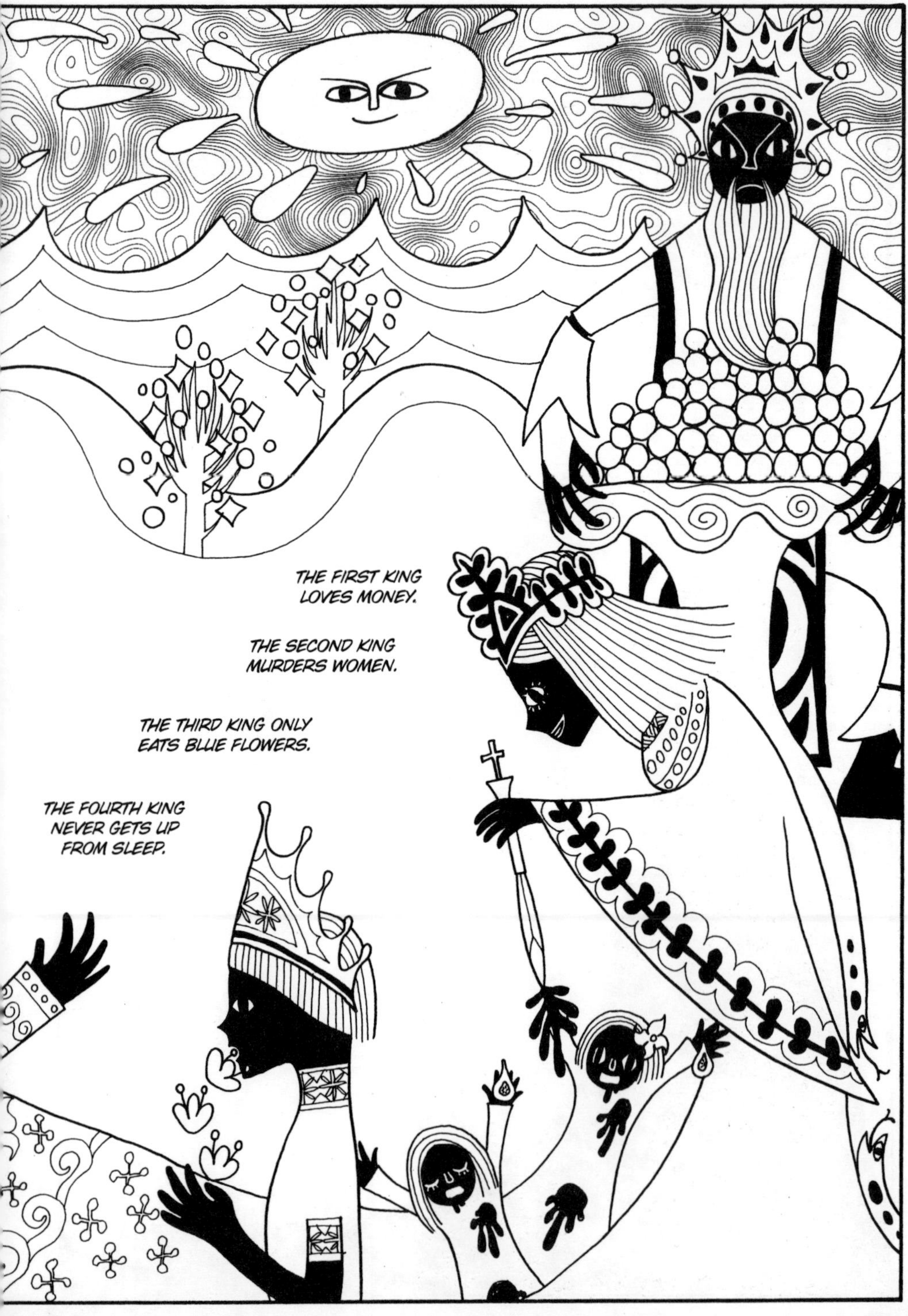
THE FIRST KING
LOVES MONEY.
THE SECOND KING
MURDERS WOMEN.
THE THIRD KING ONLY
EATS BLUE FLOWERS.
THE FOURTH KING
NEVER GETS UP
FROM SLEEP.

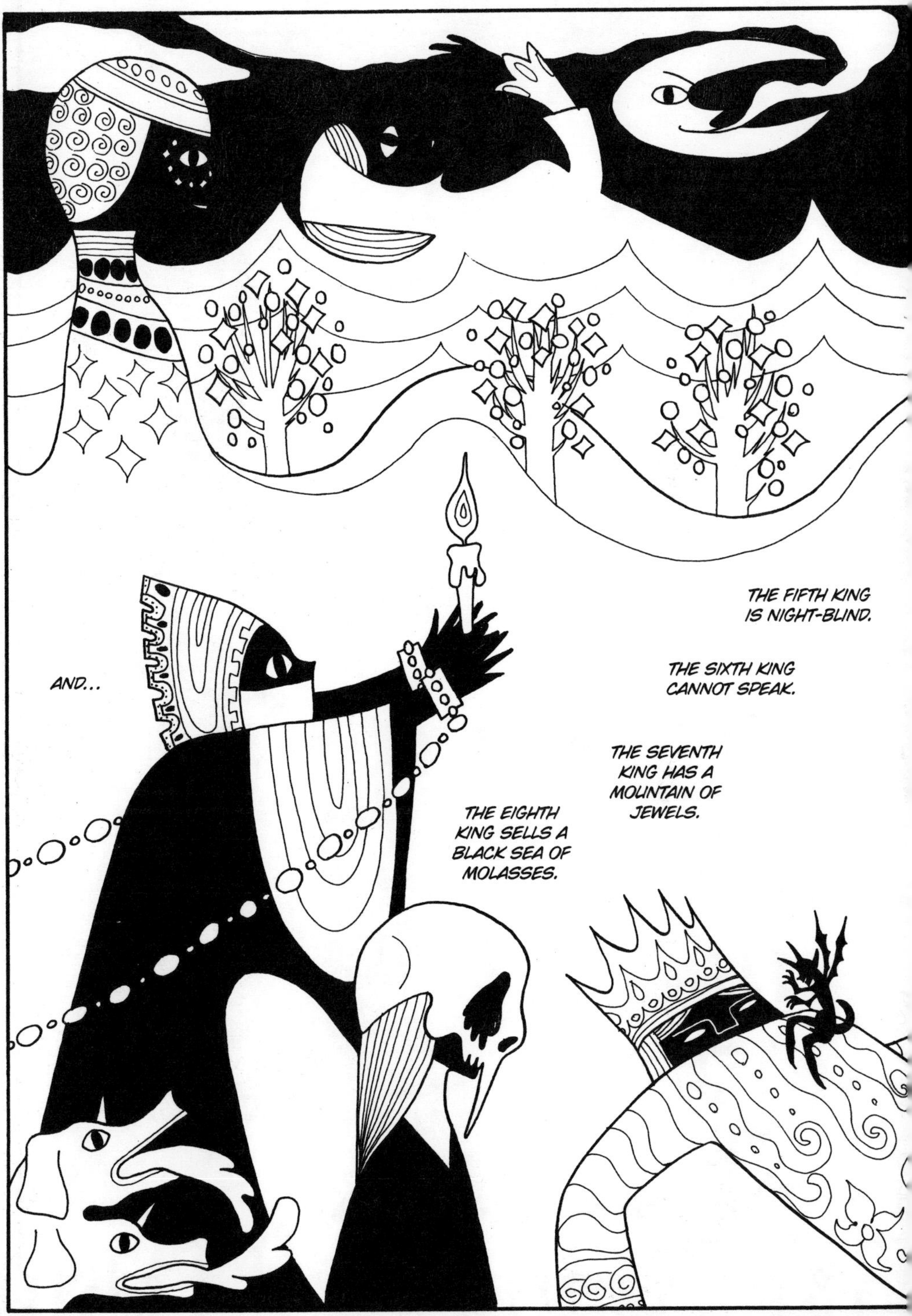
THE FIFTH KING IS NIGHT-BLIND.
THE SIXTH KING CANNOT SPEAK.
THE SEVENTH KING HAS A MOUNTAIN OF JEWELS.
THE EIGHTH KING SELLS A BLACK SEA OF MOLASSES.
AND...

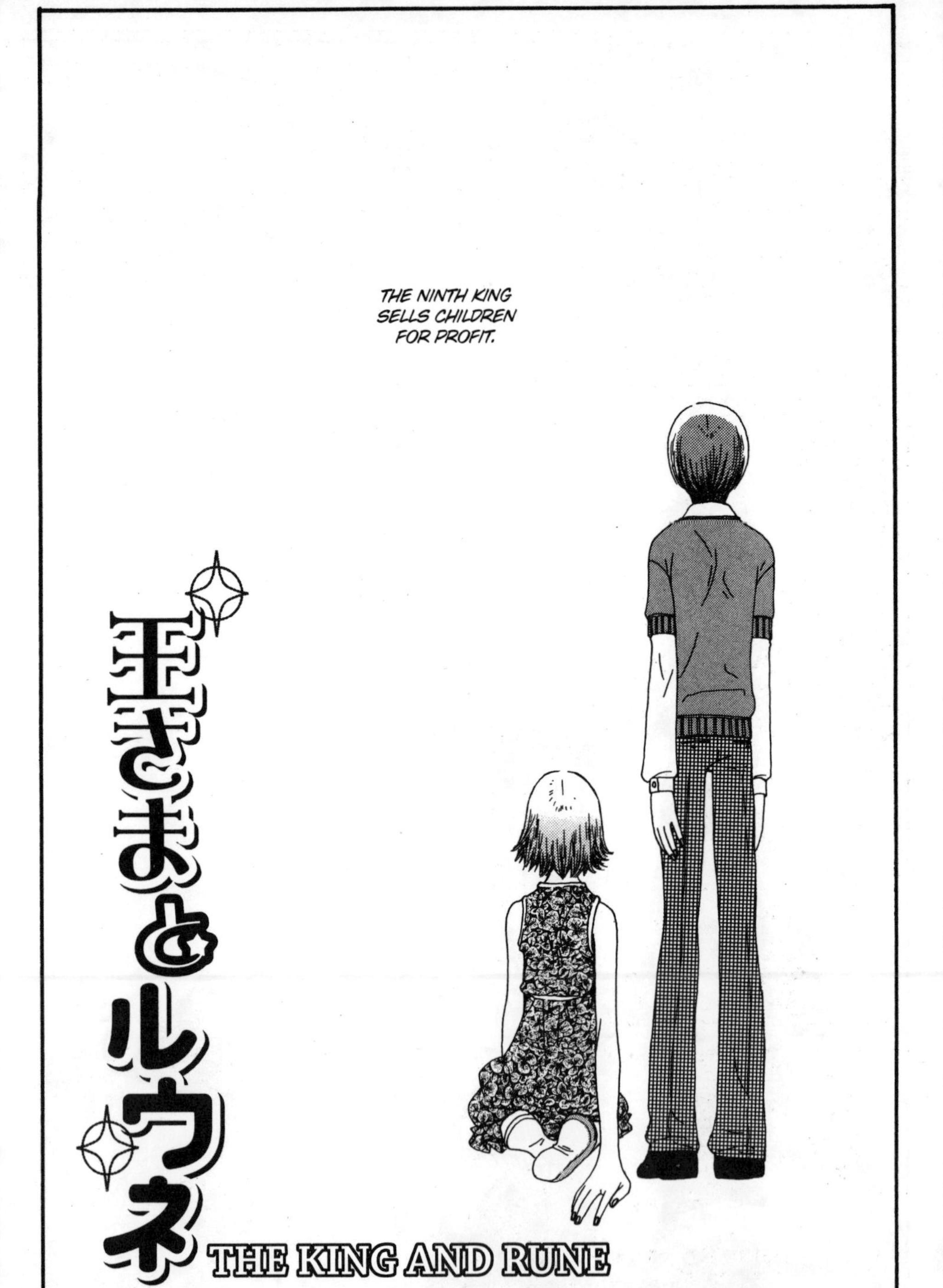
THE NINTH KING SELLS CHILDREN FOR PROFIT.
王さまとルウネ
THE KING AND RUNE
der König und Rune

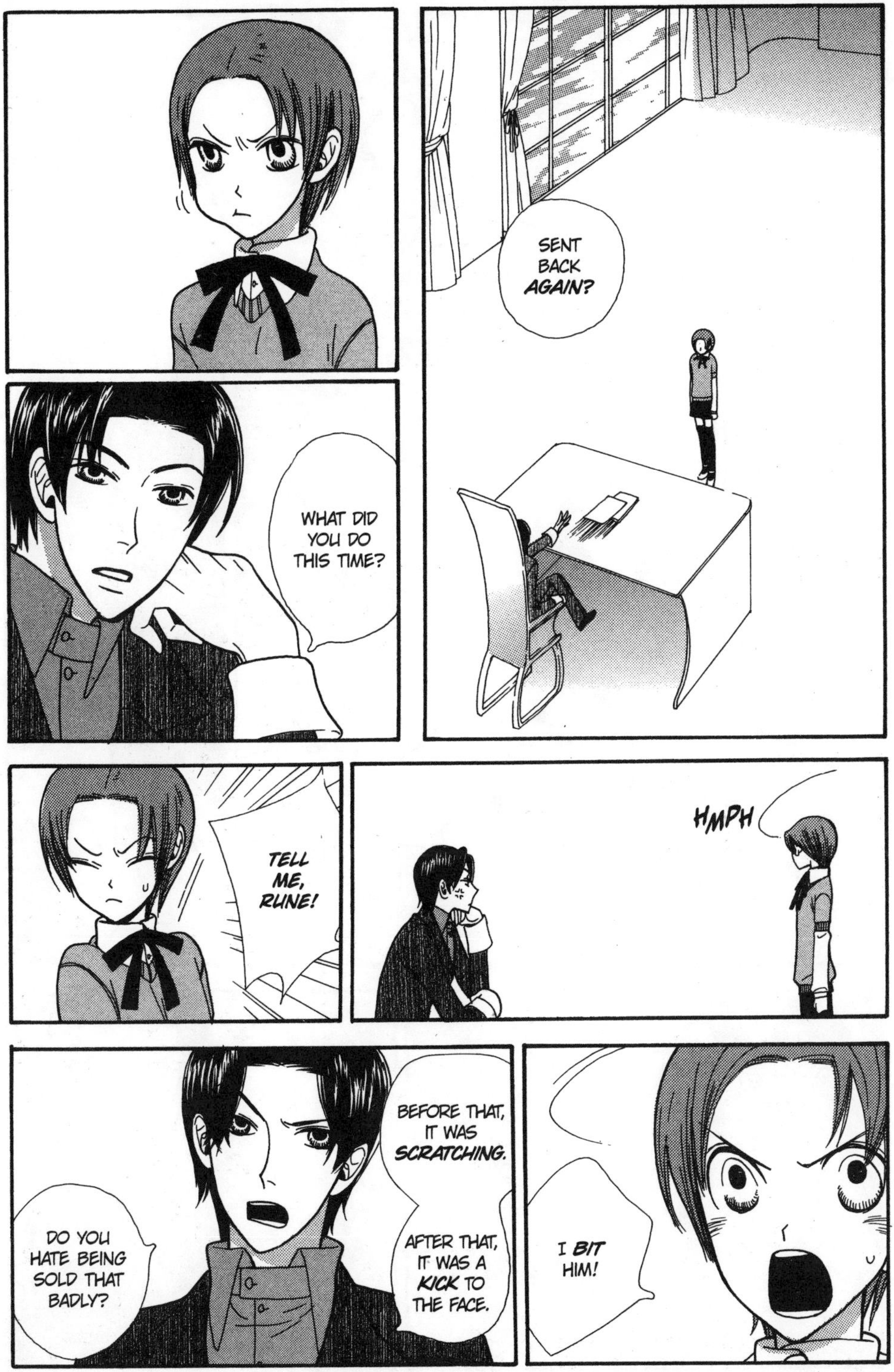
SENT BACK AGAIN?
WHAT DID YOU DO THIS TIME?
HMPH
TELL ME, RUNE!
I BIT HIM!
BEFORE THAT, IT WAS SCRATCHING.
AFTER THAT, IT WAS A KICK TO THE FACE.
DO YOU HATE BEING SOLD THAT BADLY?

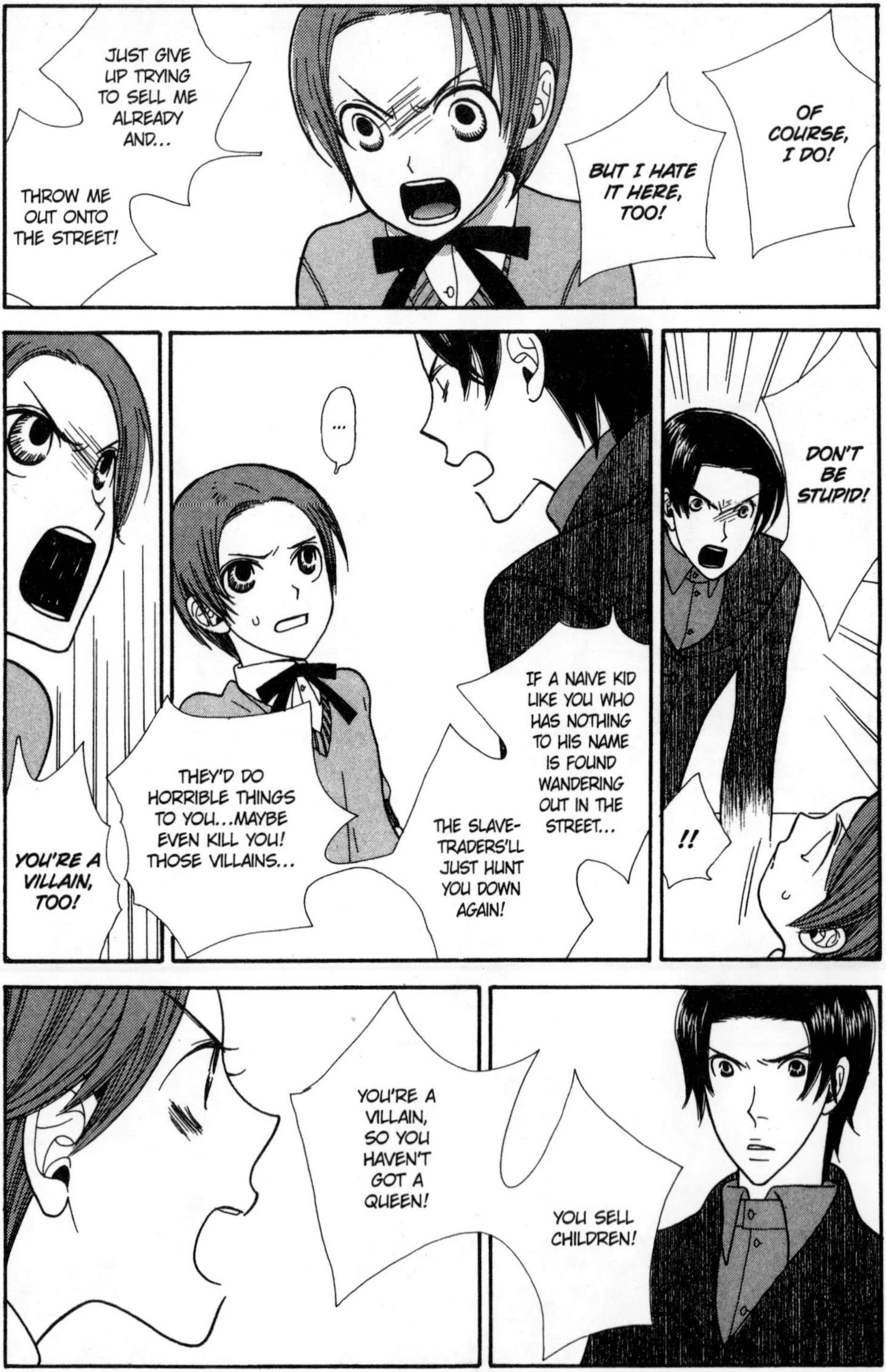
OF COURSE, I DO!
BUT I HATE IT HERE, TOO!
JUST GIVE UP TRYING TO SELL ME ALREADY AND...
THROW ME OUT ONTO THE STREET!
DON'T BE STUPID!
!!
IF A NAIVE KID LIKE YOU WHO HAS NOTHING TO HIS NAME IS FOUND WANDERING OUT IN THE STREET...
THE SLAVE-TRADERS'LL JUST HUNT YOU DOWN AGAIN!
THEY'D DO HORRIBLE THINGS TO YOU...MAYBE EVEN KILL YOU! THOSE VILLAINS...
...
YOU'RE A VILLAIN, TOO!
YOU SELL CHILDREN!
YOU'RE A VILLAIN, SO YOU HAVEN'T GOT A QUEEN!

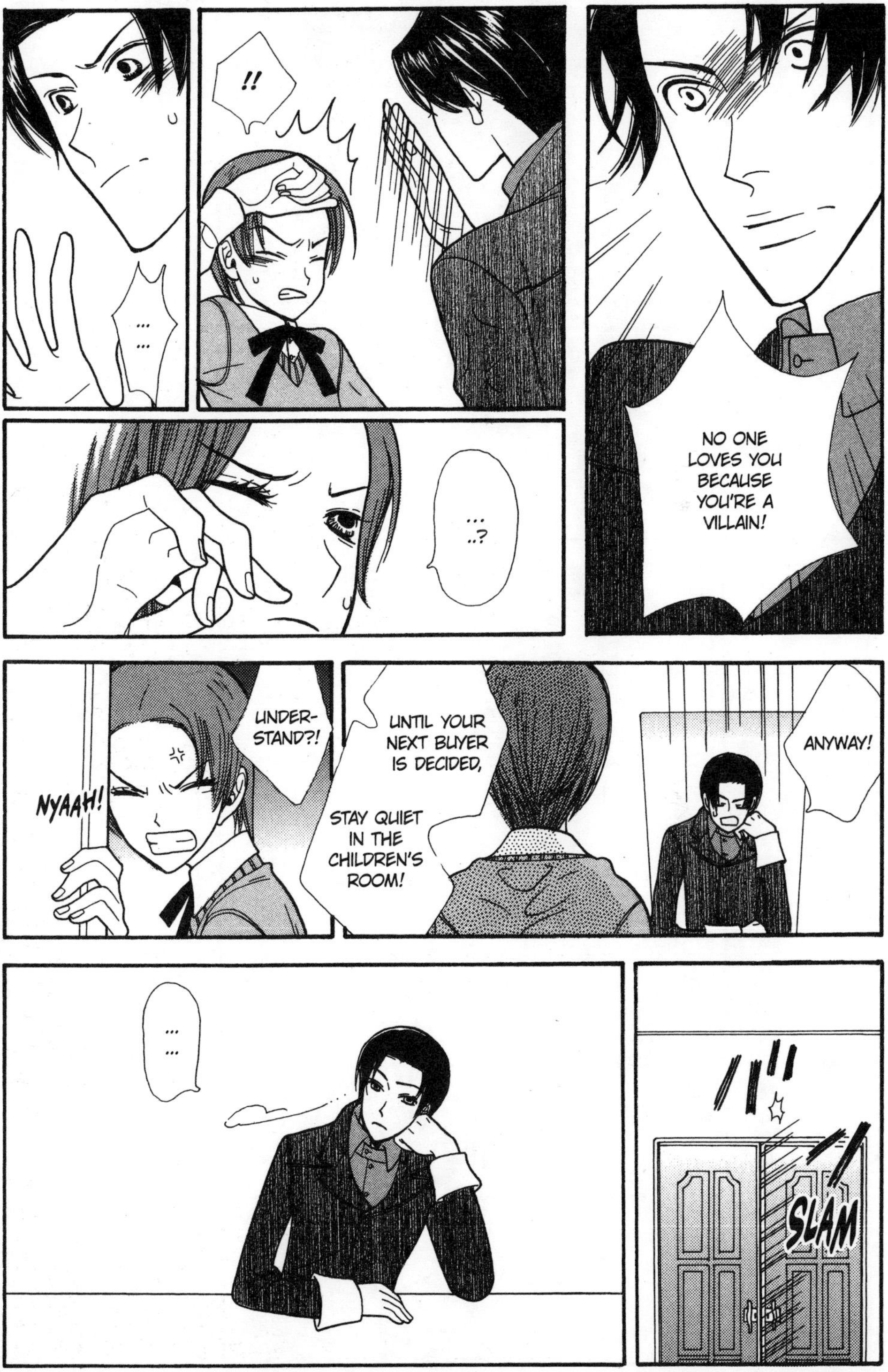
NO ONE LOVES YOU BECAUSE YOU'RE A VILLAIN!
!!
......
.....?
ANYWAY!
UNTIL YOUR NEXT BUYER IS DECIDED,
STAY QUIET IN THE CHILDREN'S ROOM!
UNDER-STAND?!
NYAAH!
SLAM
......

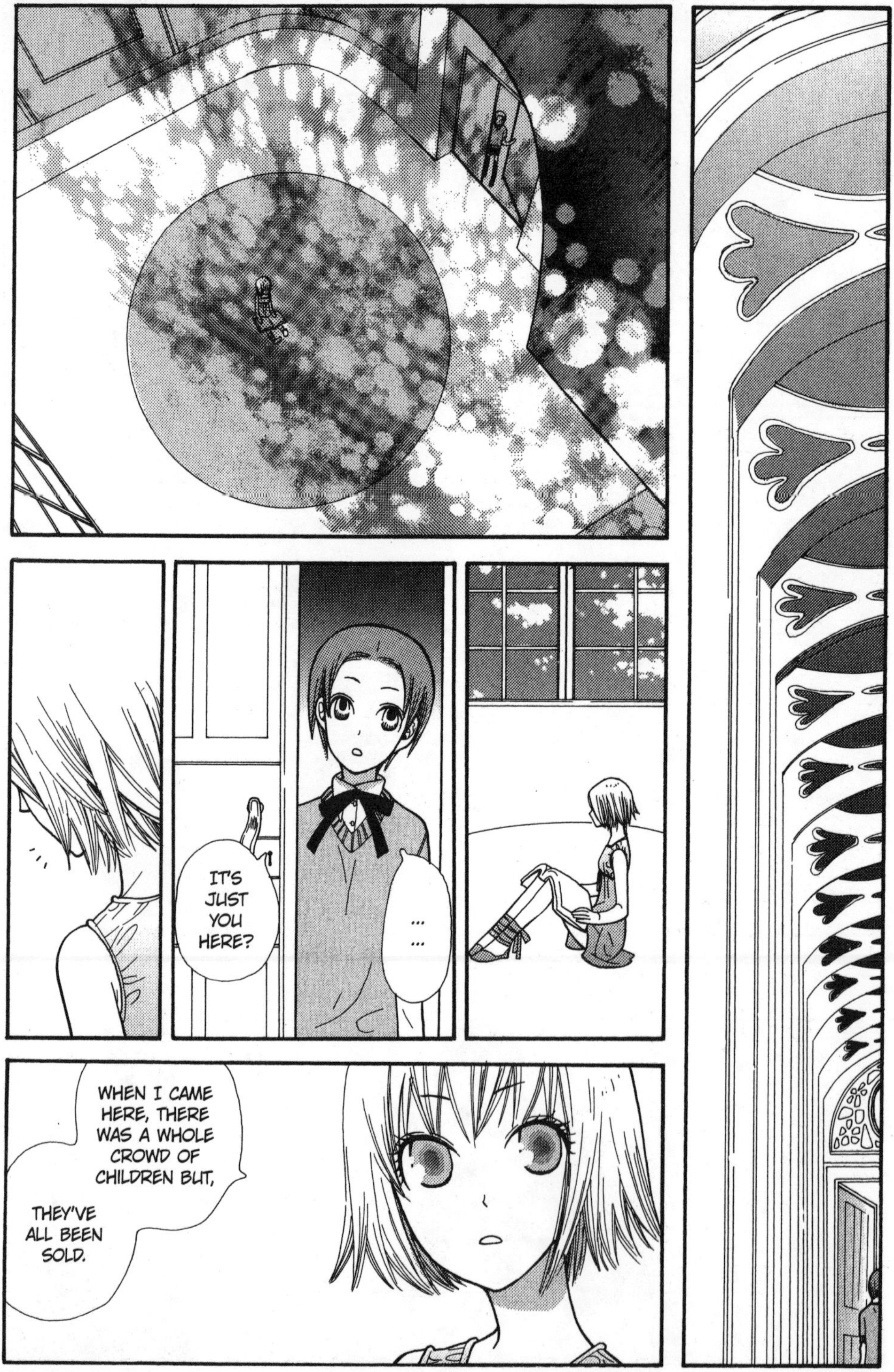
IT'S JUST YOU HERE?
...
...
WHEN I CAME HERE, THERE WAS A WHOLE CROWD OF CHILDREN BUT,
THEY'VE ALL BEEN SOLD.

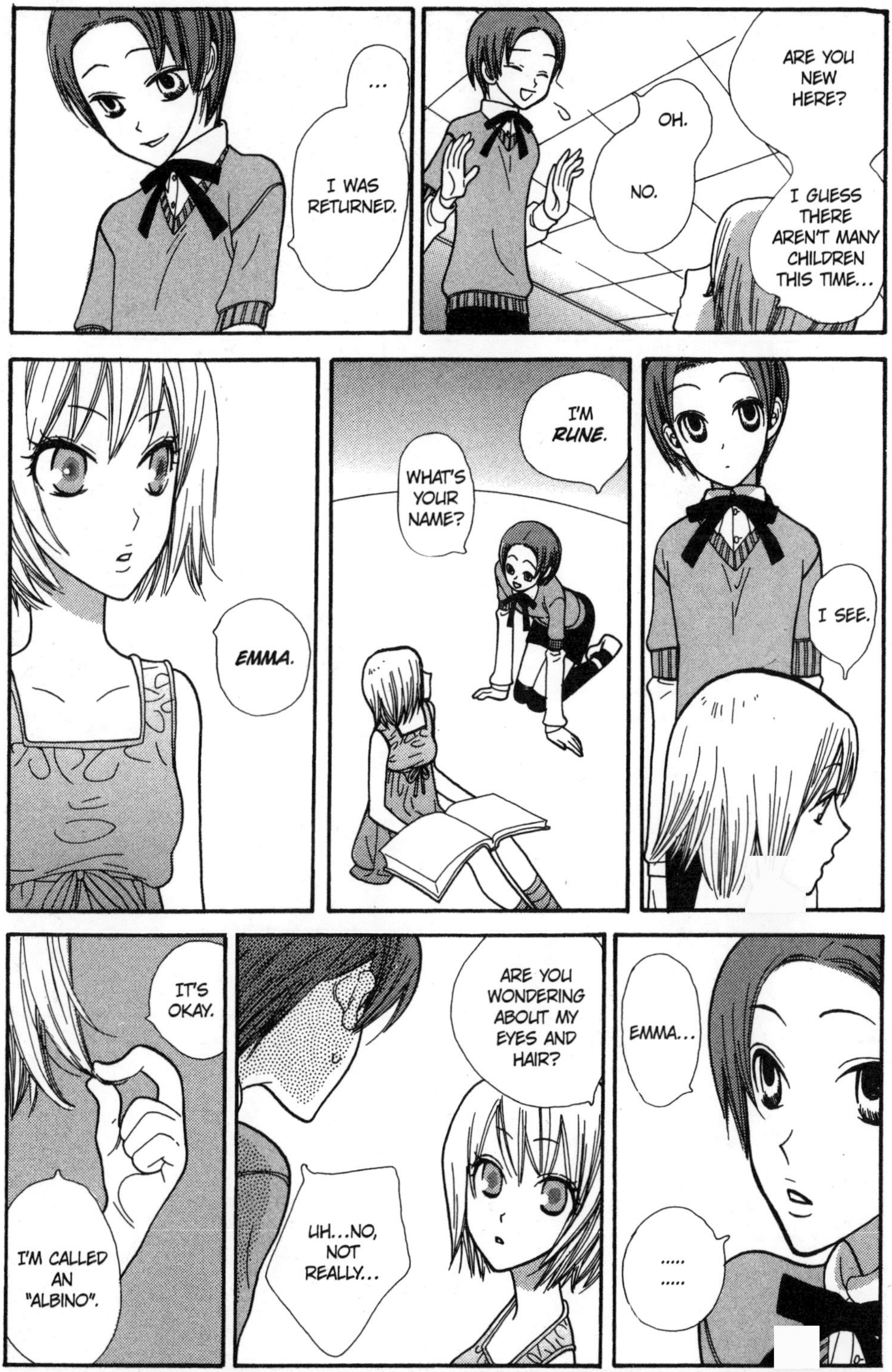
ARE YOU NEW HERE?
OH.
NO.
I GUESS THERE AREN'T MANY CHILDREN THIS TIME...
...
I WAS RETURNED.
I SEE.
I'M RUNE.
WHAT'S YOUR NAME?
EMMA.
EMMA...
.....
.....
ARE YOU WONDERING ABOUT MY EYES AND HAIR?
UH...NO, NOT REALLY...
IT'S OKAY.
I'M CALLED AN "ALBINO".

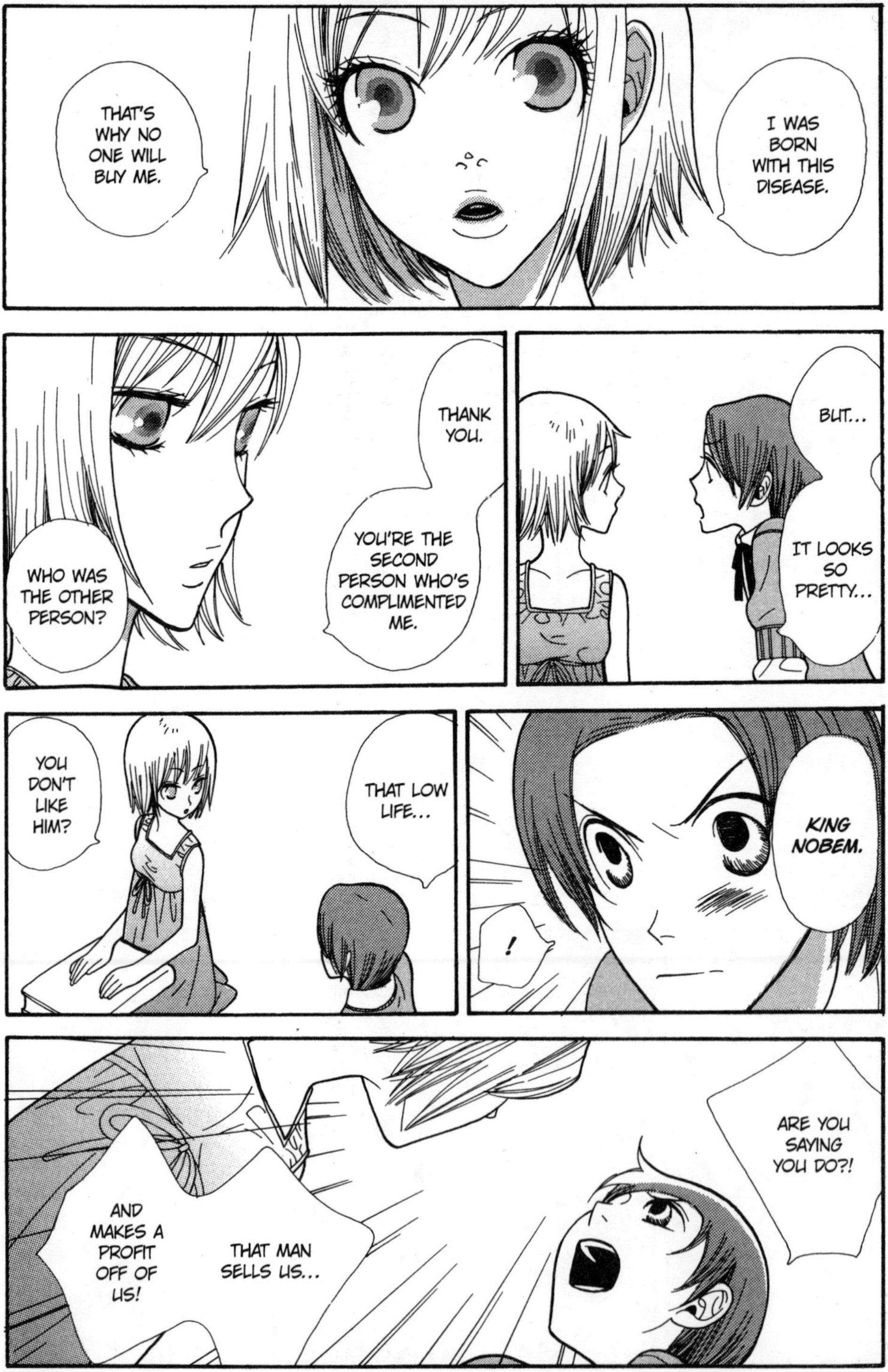
I WAS BORN WITH THIS DISEASE.
THAT'S WHY NO ONE WILL BUY ME.
BUT...
IT LOOKS SO PRETTY...
THANK YOU.
YOU'RE THE SECOND PERSON WHO'S COMPLIMENTED ME.
WHO WAS THE OTHER PERSON?
KING NOBEM.
!
THAT LOW LIFE...
YOU DON'T LIKE HIM?
ARE YOU SAYING YOU DO?!
THAT MAN SELLS US...
AND MAKES A PROFIT OFF OF US!

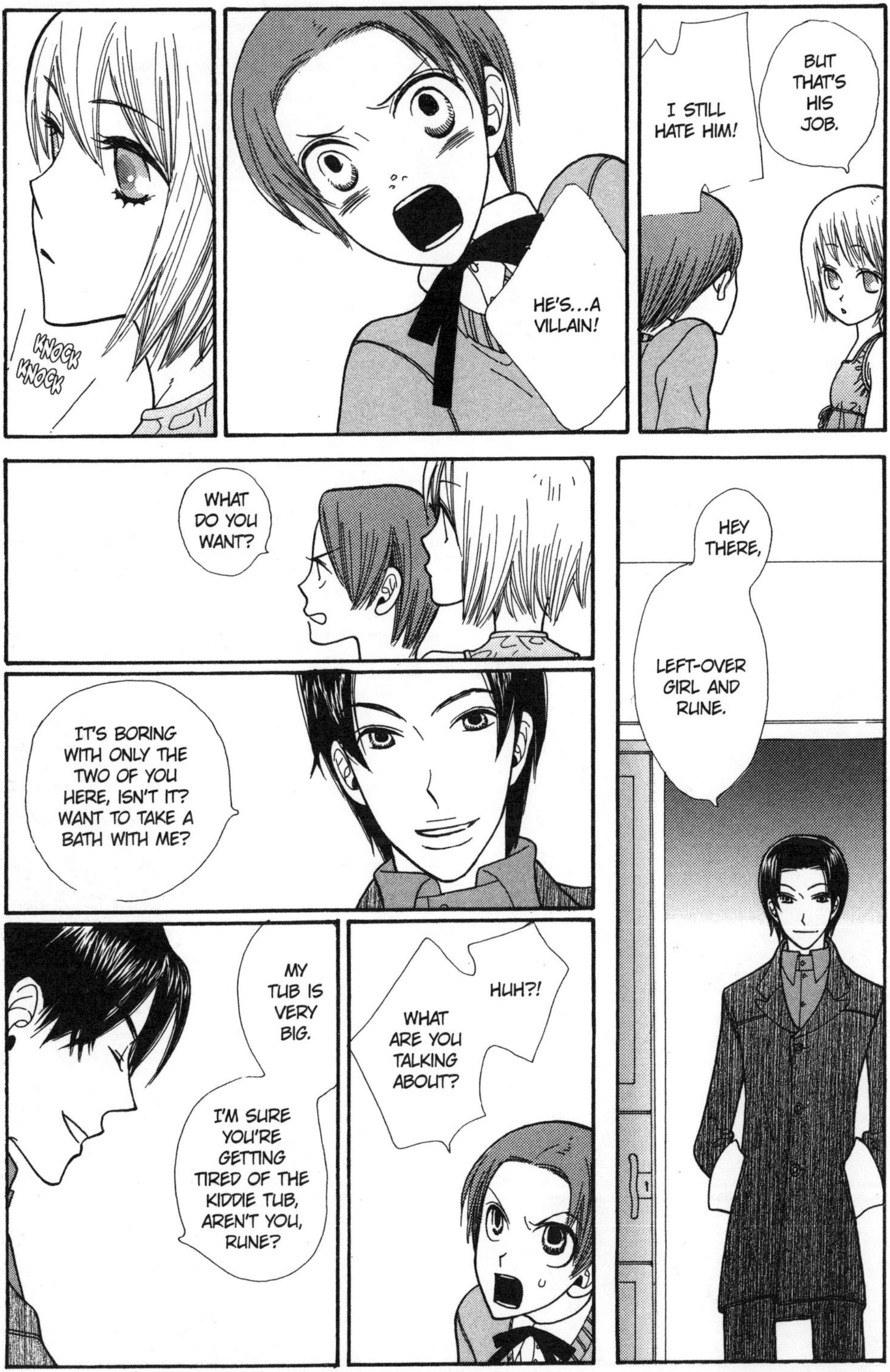
BUT THAT'S HIS JOB.
I STILL HATE HIM!
HE'S...A VILLAIN!
KNOCK KNOCK
HEY THERE,
LEFT-OVER GIRL AND RUNE.
WHAT DO YOU WANT?
IT'S BORING WITH ONLY THE TWO OF YOU HERE, ISN'T IT? WANT TO TAKE A BATH WITH ME?
HUH?!
WHAT ARE YOU TALKING ABOUT?
MY TUB IS VERY BIG.
I'M SURE YOU'RE GETTING TIRED OF THE KIDDIE TUB, AREN'T YOU, RUNE?

STAND

THAT'S NOT...!

AREN'T YOU COMING?

...

EMMA?

SEE?

ISN'T IT PRETTY?

...
...

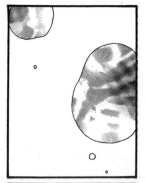

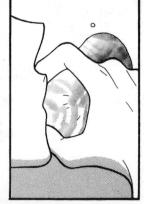

OH, THAT'S RIGHT, YOU TWO.

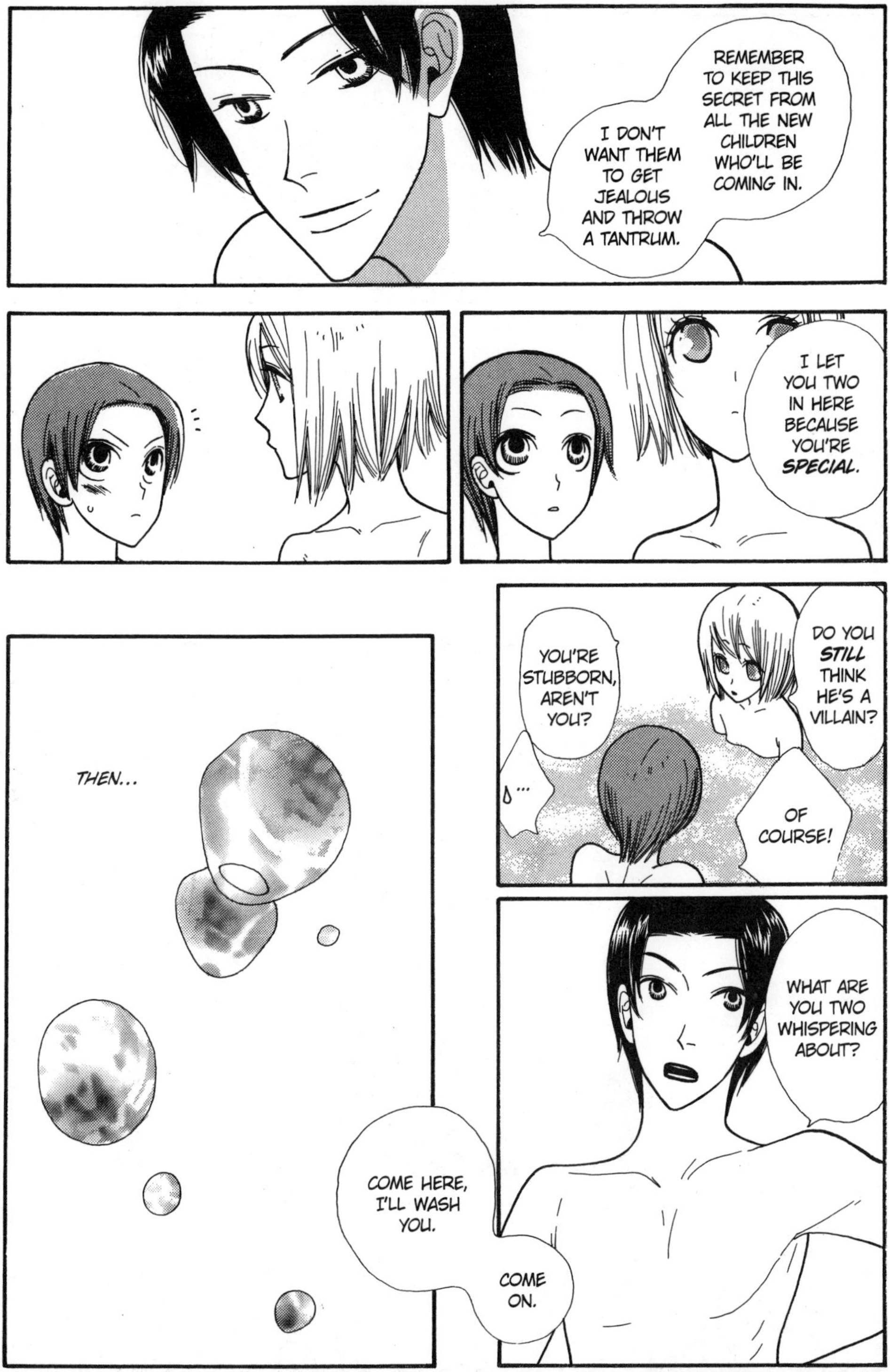
REMEMBER TO KEEP THIS SECRET FROM ALL THE NEW CHILDREN WHO'LL BE COMING IN.
I DON'T WANT THEM TO GET JEALOUS AND THROW A TANTRUM.
I LET YOU TWO IN HERE BECAUSE YOU'RE ***SPECIAL***.
DO YOU ***STILL*** THINK HE'S A VILLAIN?
OF COURSE!
YOU'RE STUBBORN, AREN'T YOU?
...
WHAT ARE YOU TWO WHISPERING ABOUT?
COME HERE, I'LL WASH YOU.
COME ON.
THEN...

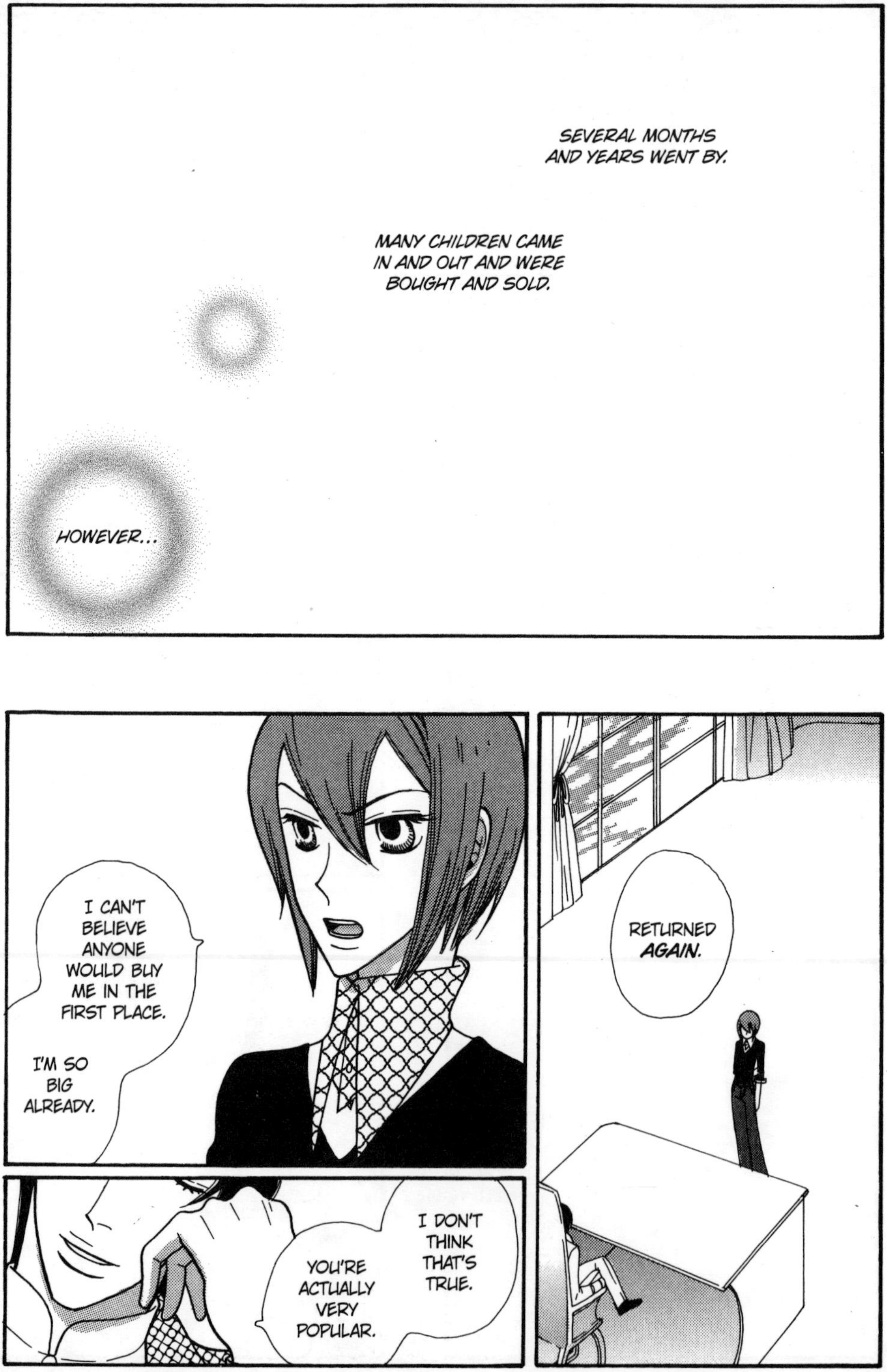
SEVERAL MONTHS AND YEARS WENT BY.
MANY CHILDREN CAME IN AND OUT AND WERE BOUGHT AND SOLD.
HOWEVER...
RETURNED AGAIN.
I CAN'T BELIEVE ANYONE WOULD BUY ME IN THE FIRST PLACE.
I'M SO BIG ALREADY.
I DON'T THINK THAT'S TRUE.
YOU'RE ACTUALLY VERY POPULAR.

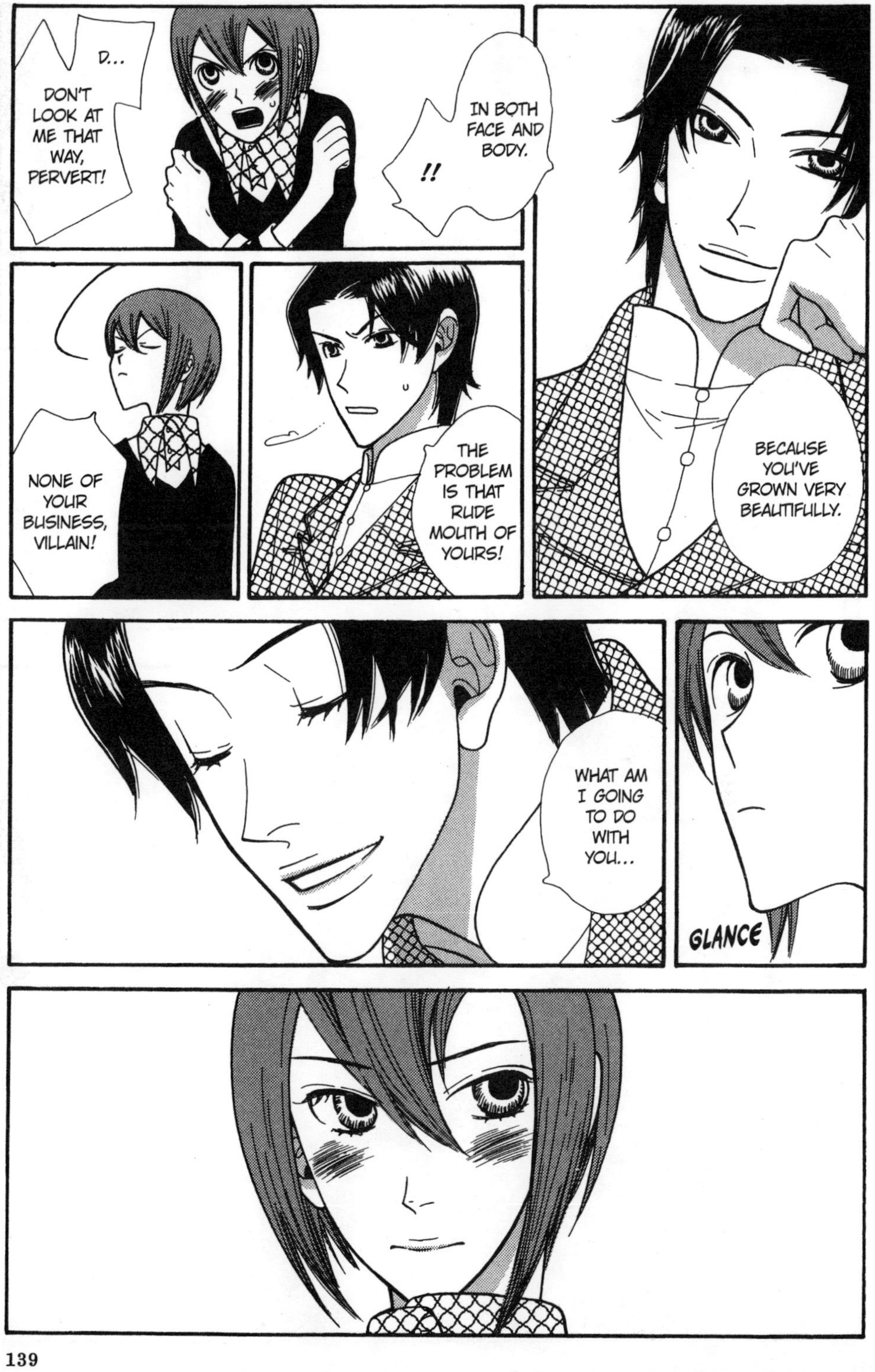
BECAUSE YOU'VE GROWN VERY BEAUTIFULLY.
IN BOTH FACE AND BODY.
!!
D...
DON'T LOOK AT ME THAT WAY, PERVERT!
THE PROBLEM IS THAT RUDE MOUTH OF YOURS!
NONE OF YOUR BUSINESS, VILLAIN!
GLANCE
WHAT AM I GOING TO DO WITH YOU...

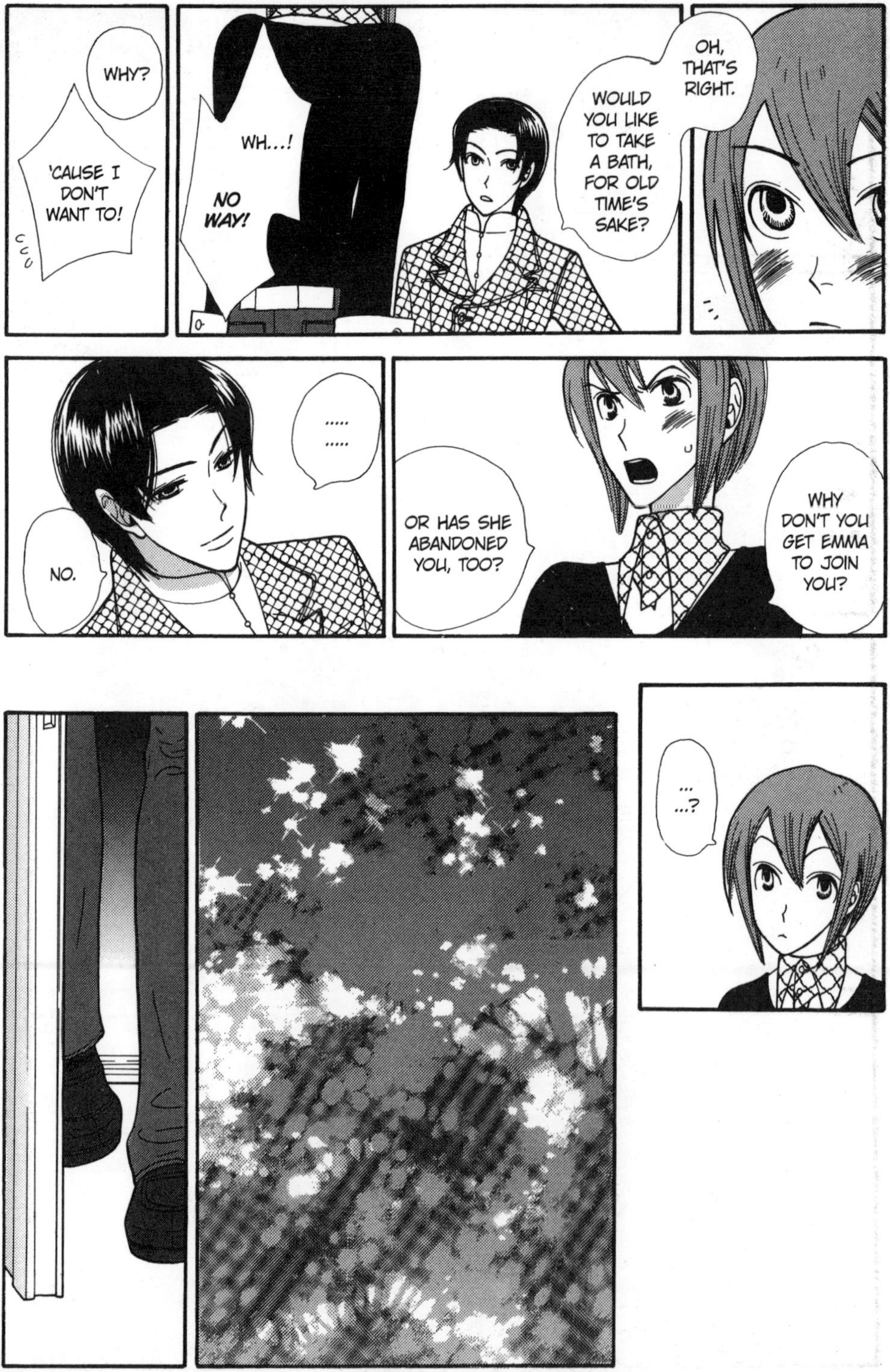
OH, THAT'S RIGHT.
WOULD YOU LIKE TO TAKE A BATH, FOR OLD TIME'S SAKE?
WH...!
NO WAY!
WHY?
'CAUSE I DON'T WANT TO!
WHY DON'T YOU GET EMMA TO JOIN YOU?
OR HAS SHE ABANDONED YOU, TOO?
....
NO.
... ...?

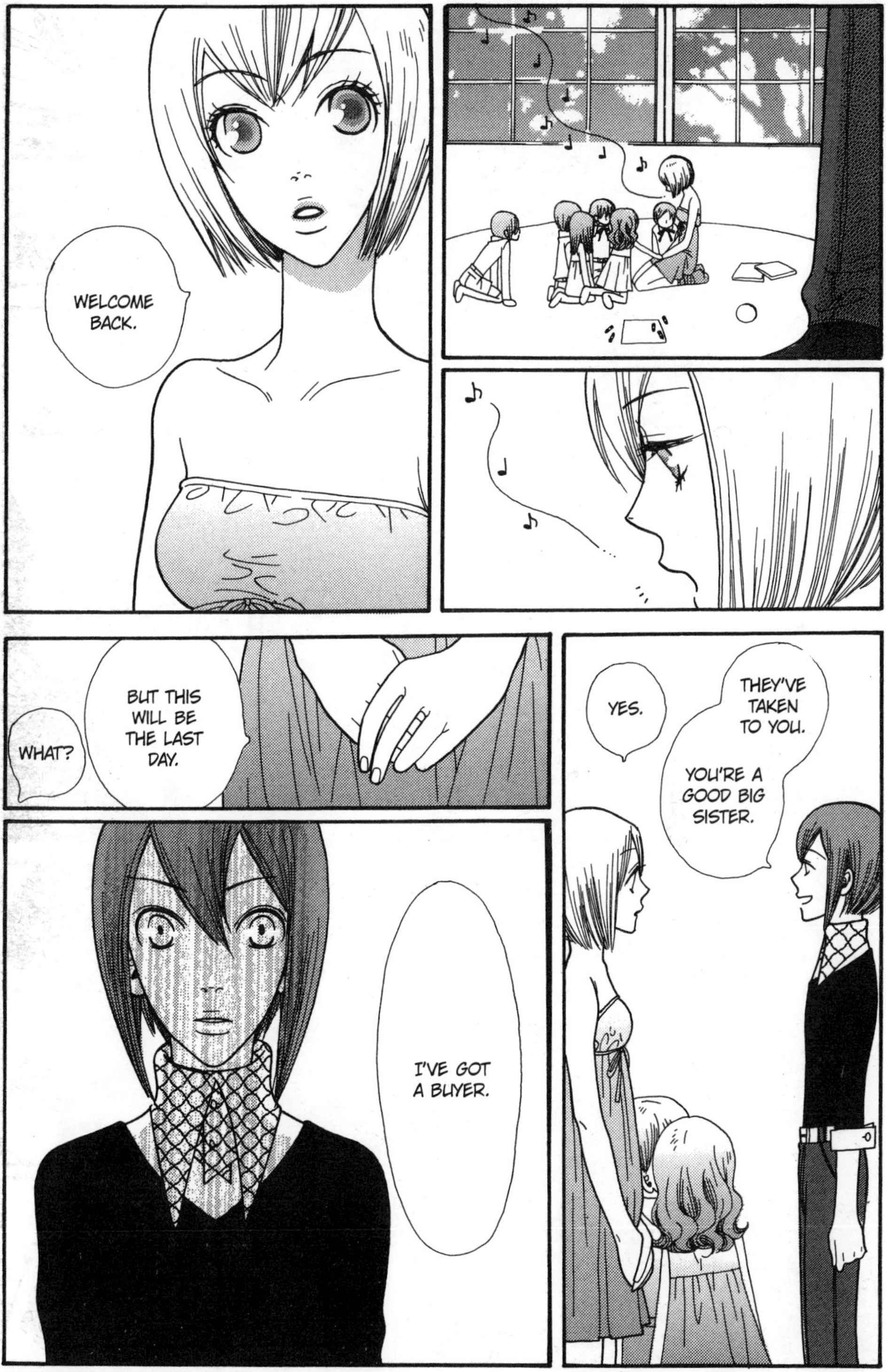
WELCOME BACK.
THEY'VE TAKEN TO YOU.
YOU'RE A GOOD BIG SISTER.
YES.
BUT THIS WILL BE THE LAST DAY.
WHAT?
I'VE GOT A BUYER.

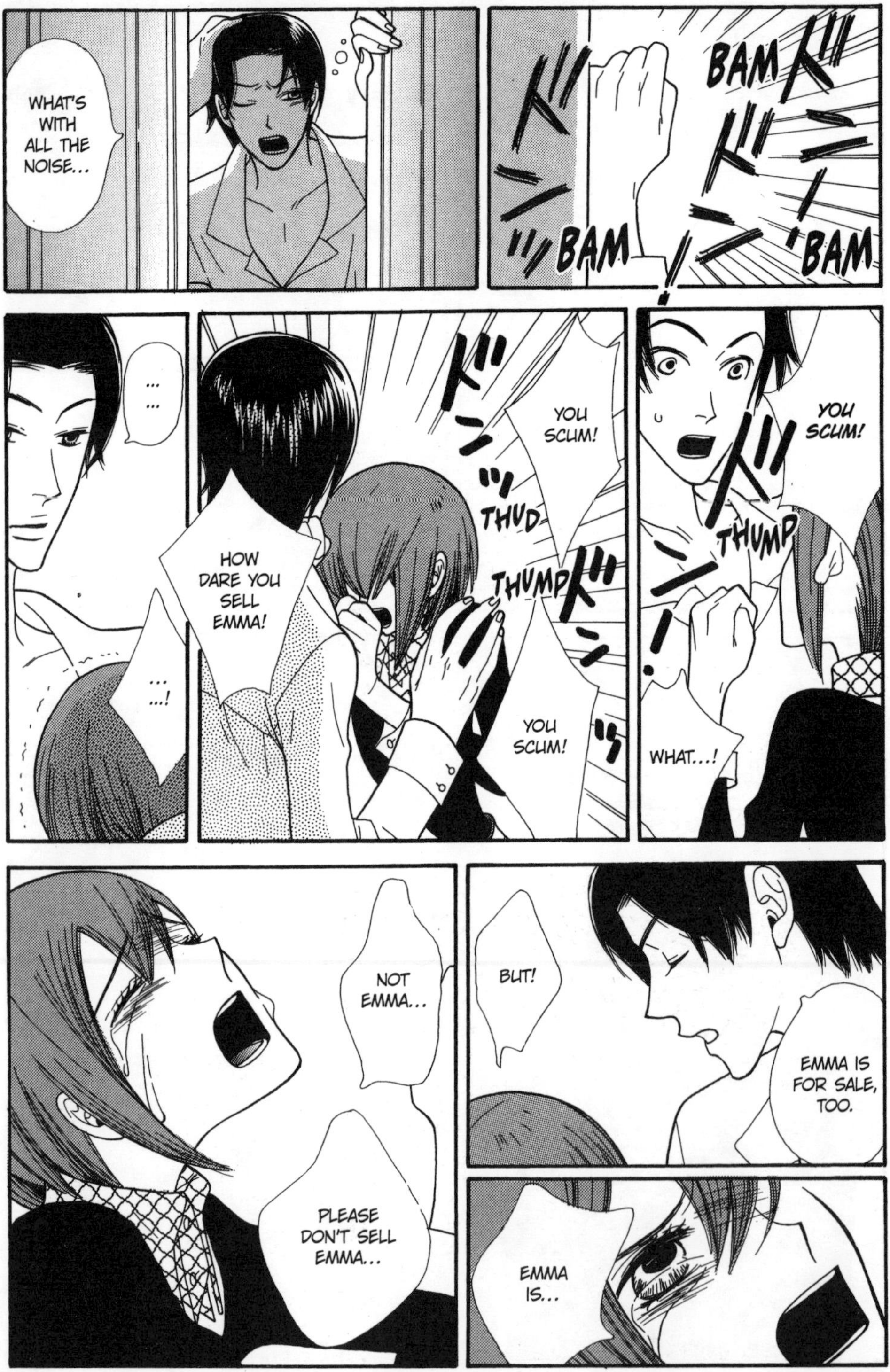
BAM
BAM
BAM
WHAT'S WITH ALL THE NOISE...
YOU SCUM!
THUMP
WHAT...!
YOU SCUM!
THUD
THUMP
HOW DARE YOU SELL EMMA!
YOU SCUM!
... ...
... ...!
BUT!
EMMA IS FOR SALE, TOO.
EMMA IS...
NOT EMMA...
PLEASE DON'T SELL EMMA...

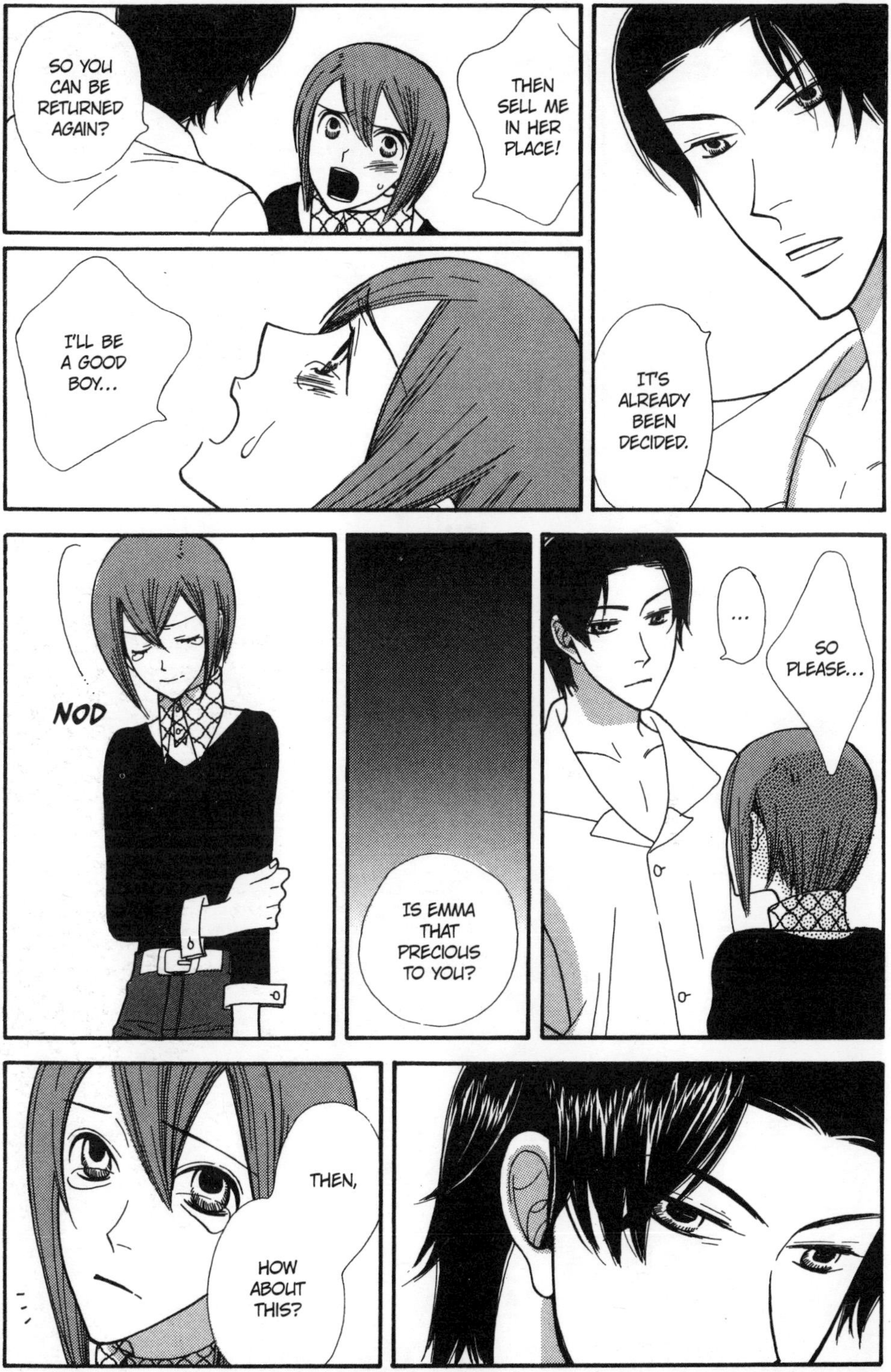
IT'S ALREADY BEEN DECIDED.
THEN SELL ME IN HER PLACE!
SO YOU CAN BE RETURNED AGAIN?
I'LL BE A GOOD BOY...
...
SO PLEASE...
IS EMMA THAT PRECIOUS TO YOU?
NOD
THEN,
HOW ABOUT THIS?

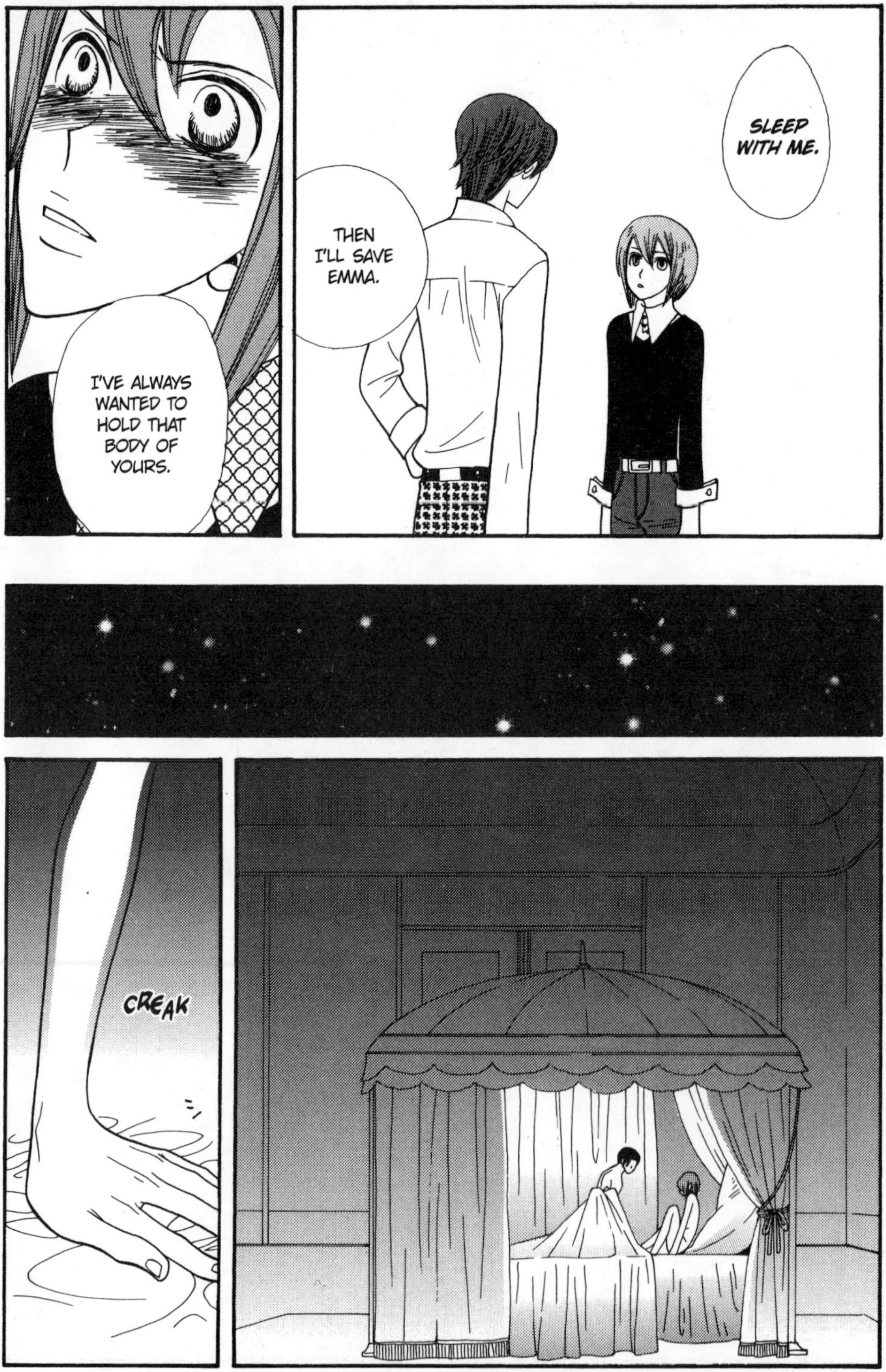
SLEEP WITH ME.
THEN I'LL SAVE EMMA.
I'VE ALWAYS WANTED TO HOLD THAT BODY OF YOURS.
CREAK

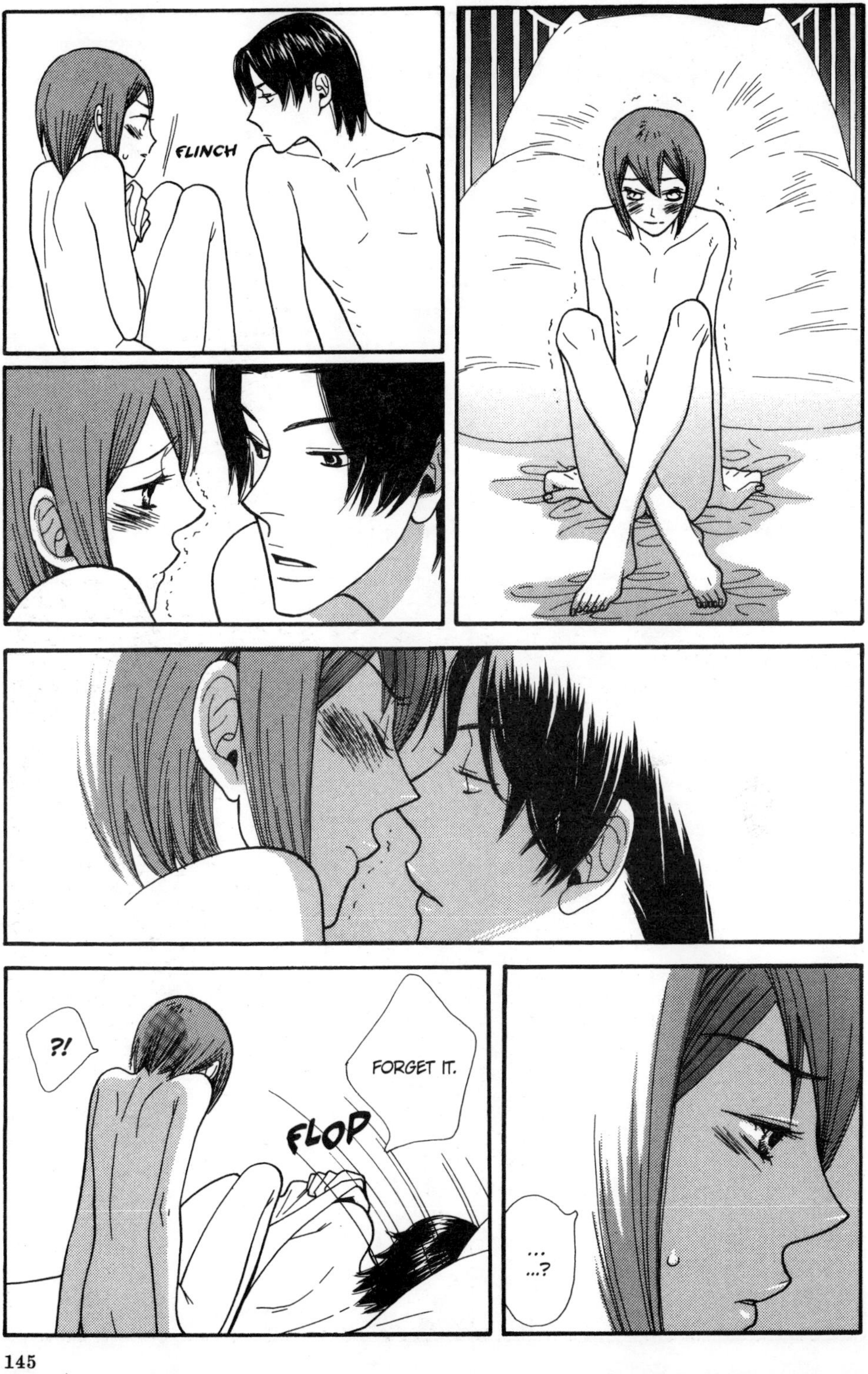
FLINCH
...
...?
FORGET IT.
FLOP
?!

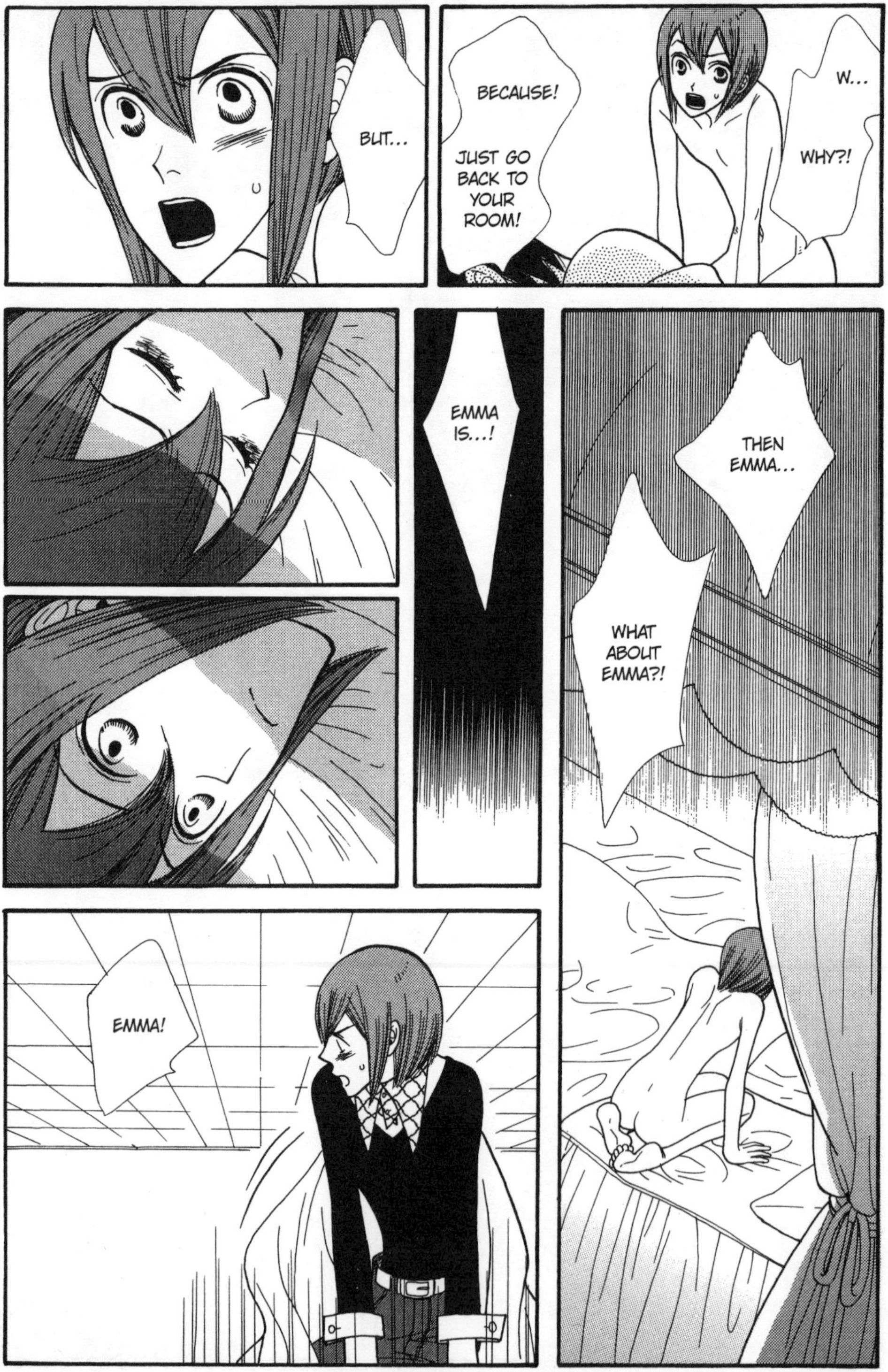
W...
WHY?!
BECAUSE!
JUST GO BACK TO YOUR ROOM!
BUT...
THEN EMMA...
WHAT ABOUT EMMA?!
EMMA IS...!
EMMA!

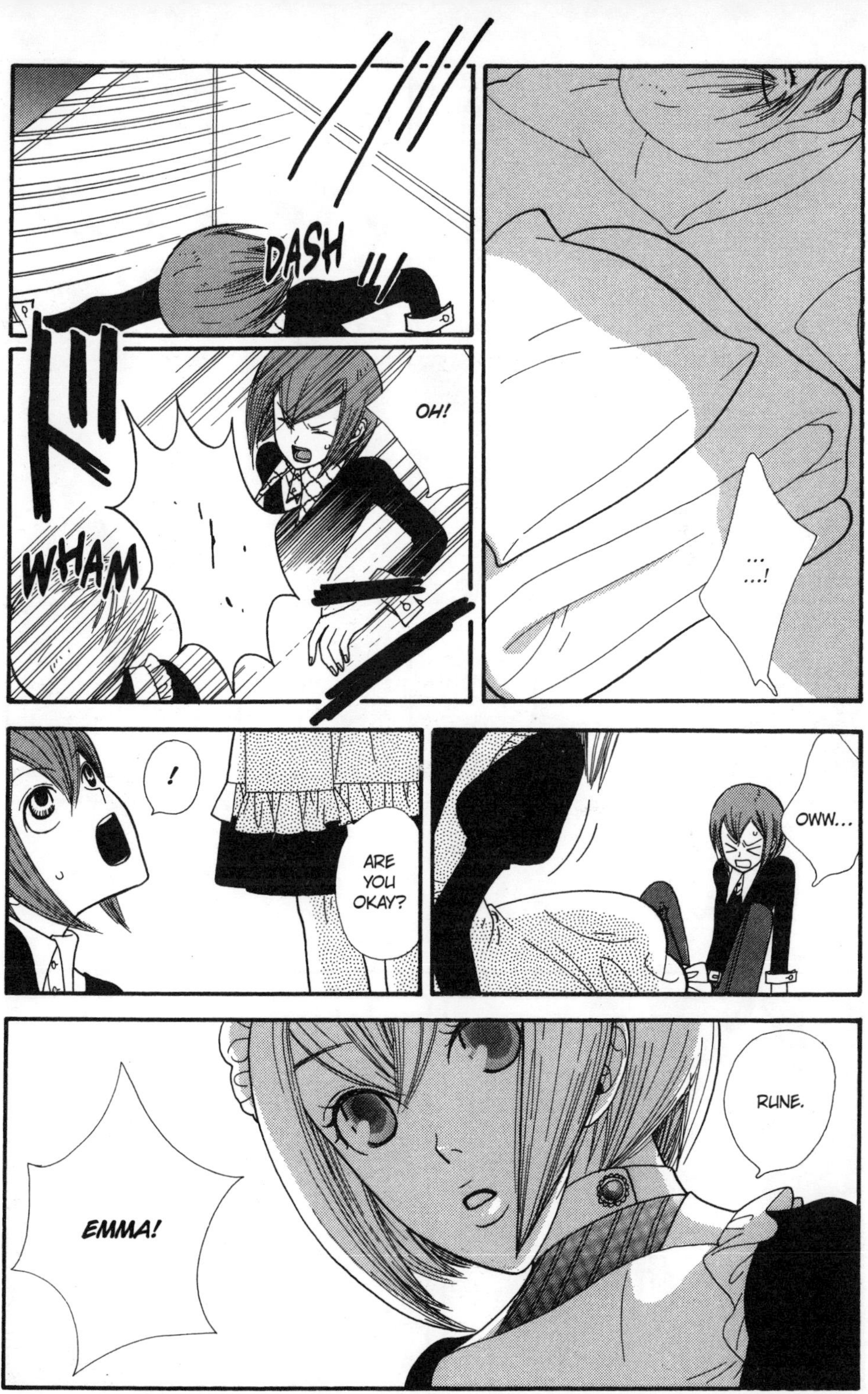
...
...!
DASH
OH!
WHAM
OWW...
ARE YOU OKAY?
!
RUNE.
EMMA!

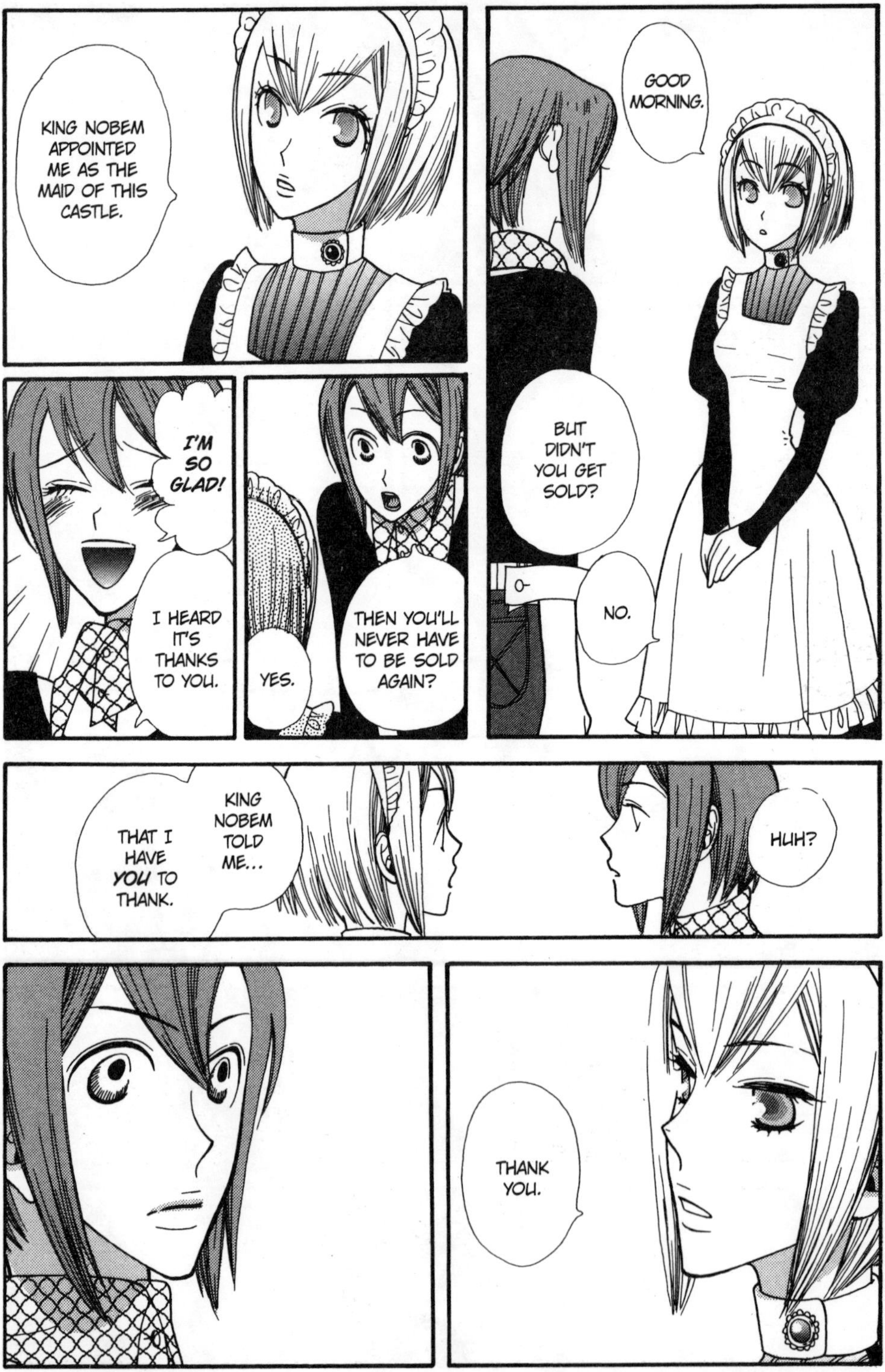
GOOD MORNING.
BUT DIDN'T YOU GET SOLD?
NO.
KING NOBEM APPOINTED ME AS THE MAID OF THIS CASTLE.
THEN YOU'LL NEVER HAVE TO BE SOLD AGAIN?
YES.
I'M SO GLAD!
I HEARD IT'S THANKS TO YOU.
HUH?
KING NOBEM TOLD ME...
THAT I HAVE YOU TO THANK.
THANK YOU.

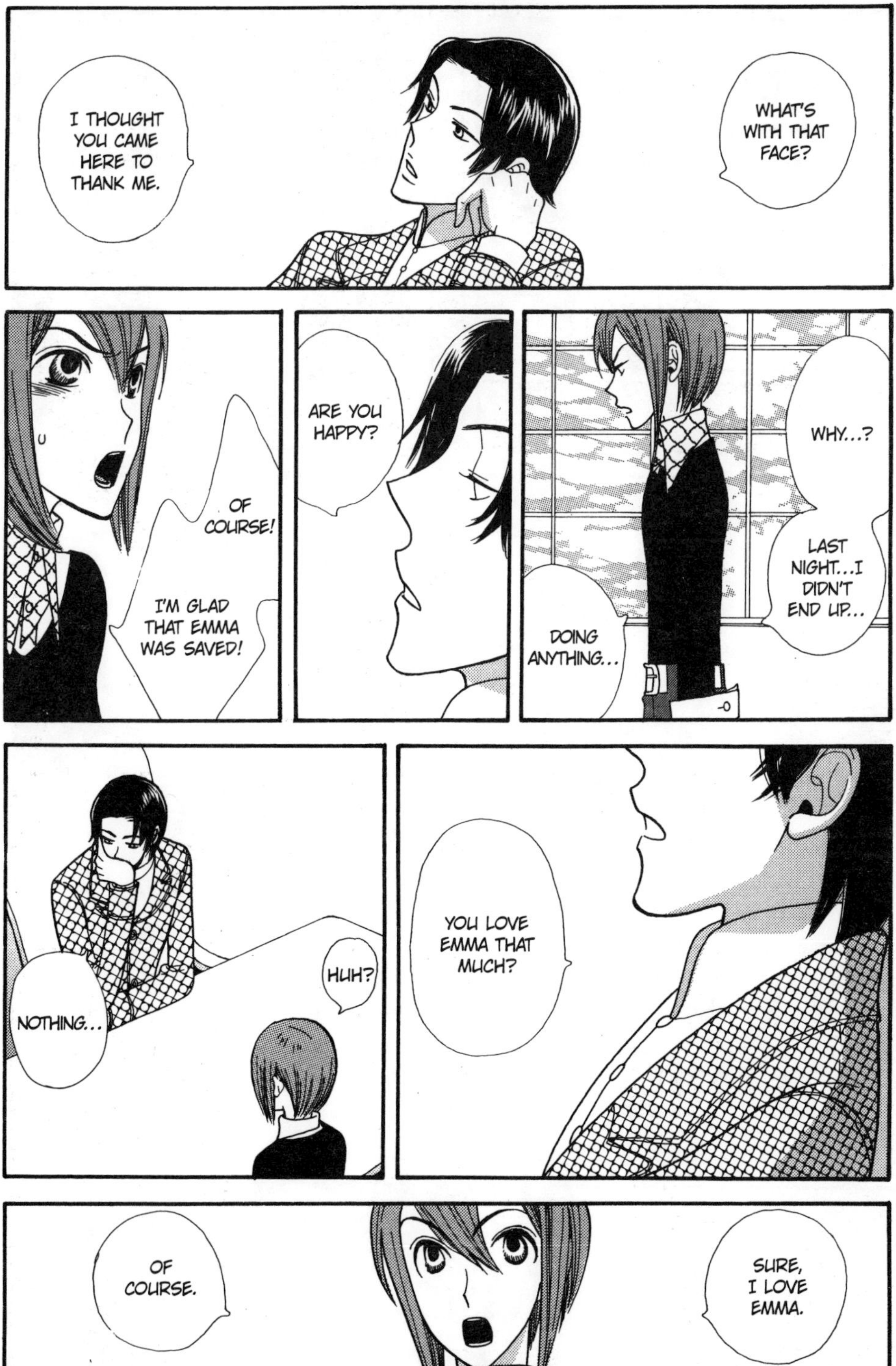
WHAT'S WITH THAT FACE?
I THOUGHT YOU CAME HERE TO THANK ME.
WHY...?
LAST NIGHT...I DIDN'T END UP...
DOING ANYTHING...
ARE YOU HAPPY?
OF COURSE!
I'M GLAD THAT EMMA WAS SAVED!
YOU LOVE EMMA THAT MUCH?
HUH?
NOTHING...
SURE, I LOVE EMMA.
OF COURSE.

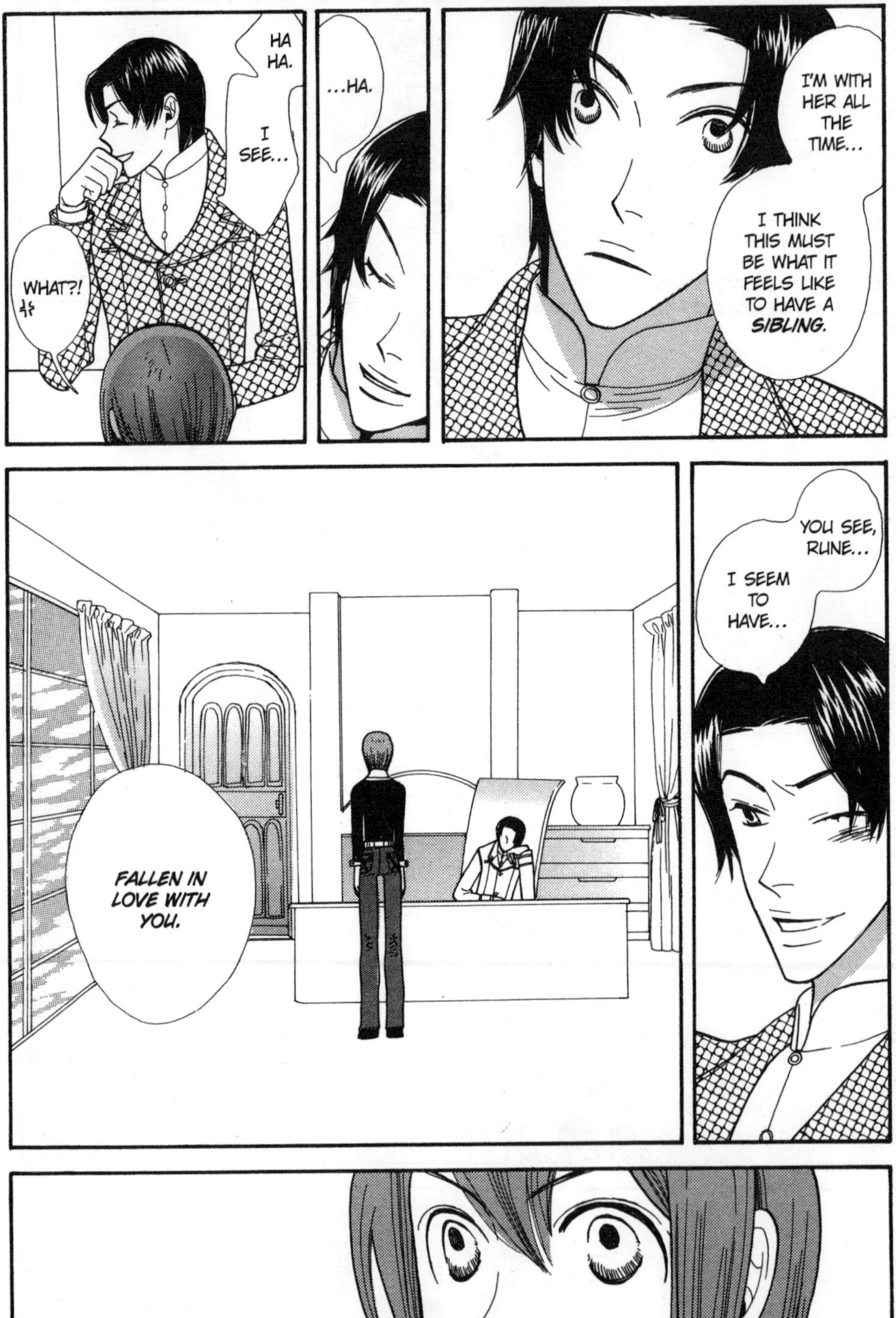
I'M WITH HER ALL THE TIME...
I THINK THIS MUST BE WHAT IT FEELS LIKE TO HAVE A *SIBLING*.
...HA.
HA HA.
I SEE...
WHAT?!
YOU SEE, RUNE...
I SEEM TO HAVE...
FALLEN IN LOVE WITH YOU.

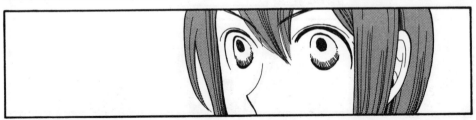

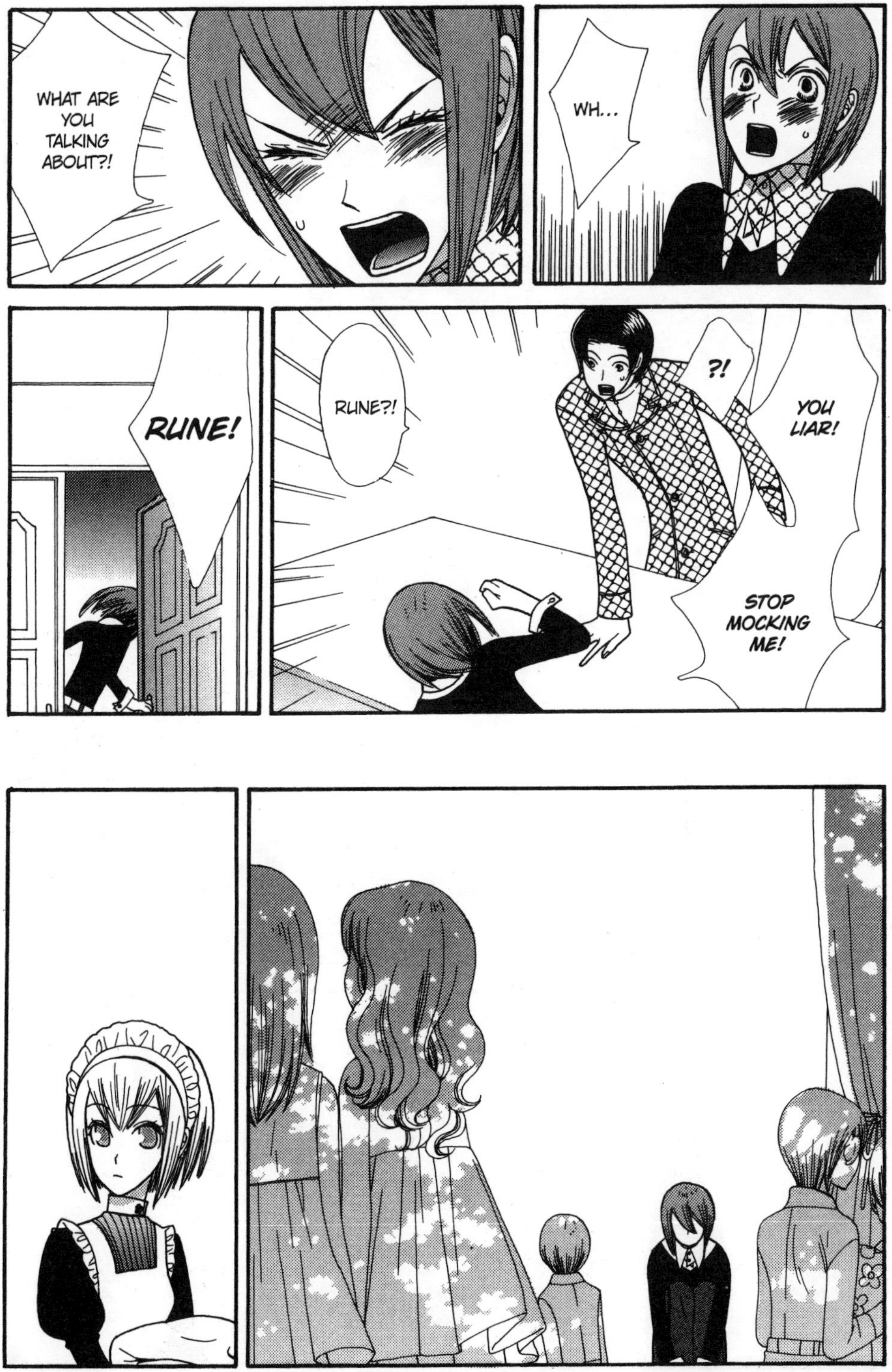
WH...
WHAT ARE YOU TALKING ABOUT?!
YOU LIAR!
STOP MOCKING ME!
?!
RUNE?!
RUNE!

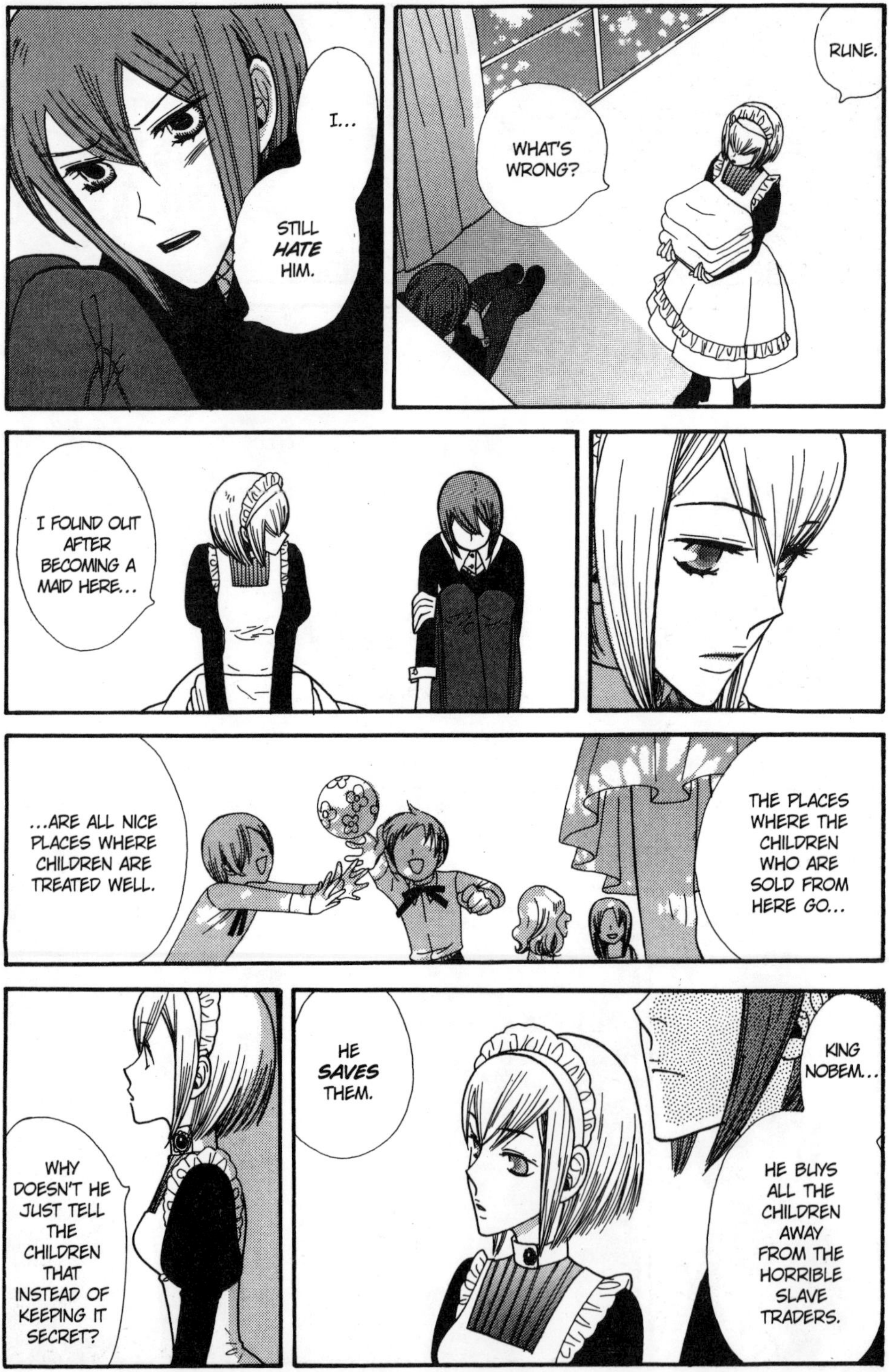
RUNE.
WHAT'S WRONG?
I...
STILL *HATE* HIM.
I FOUND OUT AFTER BECOMING A MAID HERE...
THE PLACES WHERE THE CHILDREN WHO ARE SOLD FROM HERE GO...
...ARE ALL NICE PLACES WHERE CHILDREN ARE TREATED WELL.
KING NOBEM...
HE BUYS ALL THE CHILDREN AWAY FROM THE HORRIBLE SLAVE TRADERS.
HE *SAVES* THEM.
WHY DOESN'T HE JUST TELL THE CHILDREN THAT INSTEAD OF KEEPING IT SECRET?

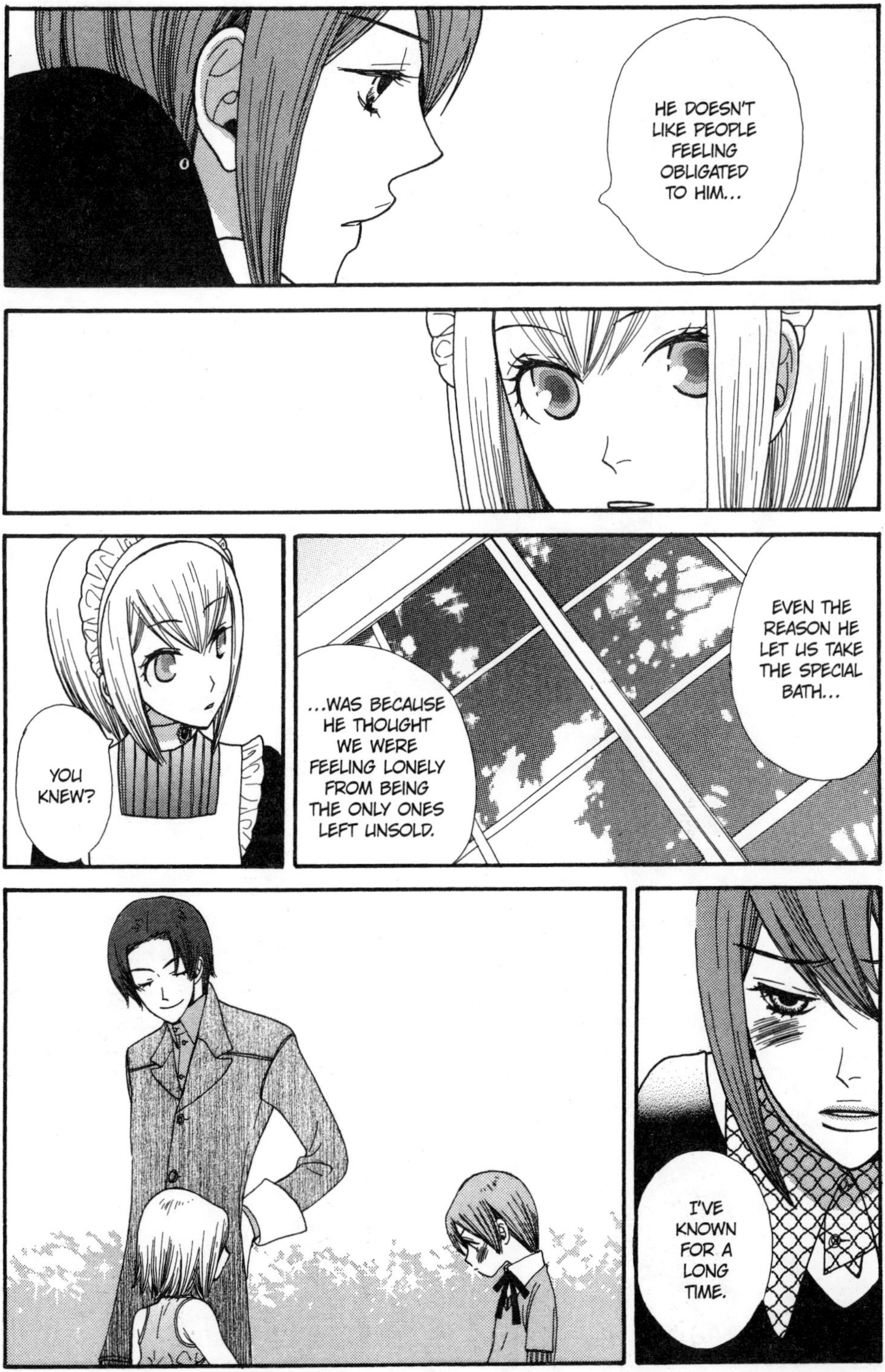
HE DOESN'T LIKE PEOPLE FEELING OBLIGATED TO HIM...
EVEN THE REASON HE LET US TAKE THE SPECIAL BATH...
...WAS BECAUSE HE THOUGHT WE WERE FEELING LONELY FROM BEING THE ONLY ONES LEFT UNSOLD.
YOU KNEW?
I'VE KNOWN FOR A LONG TIME.

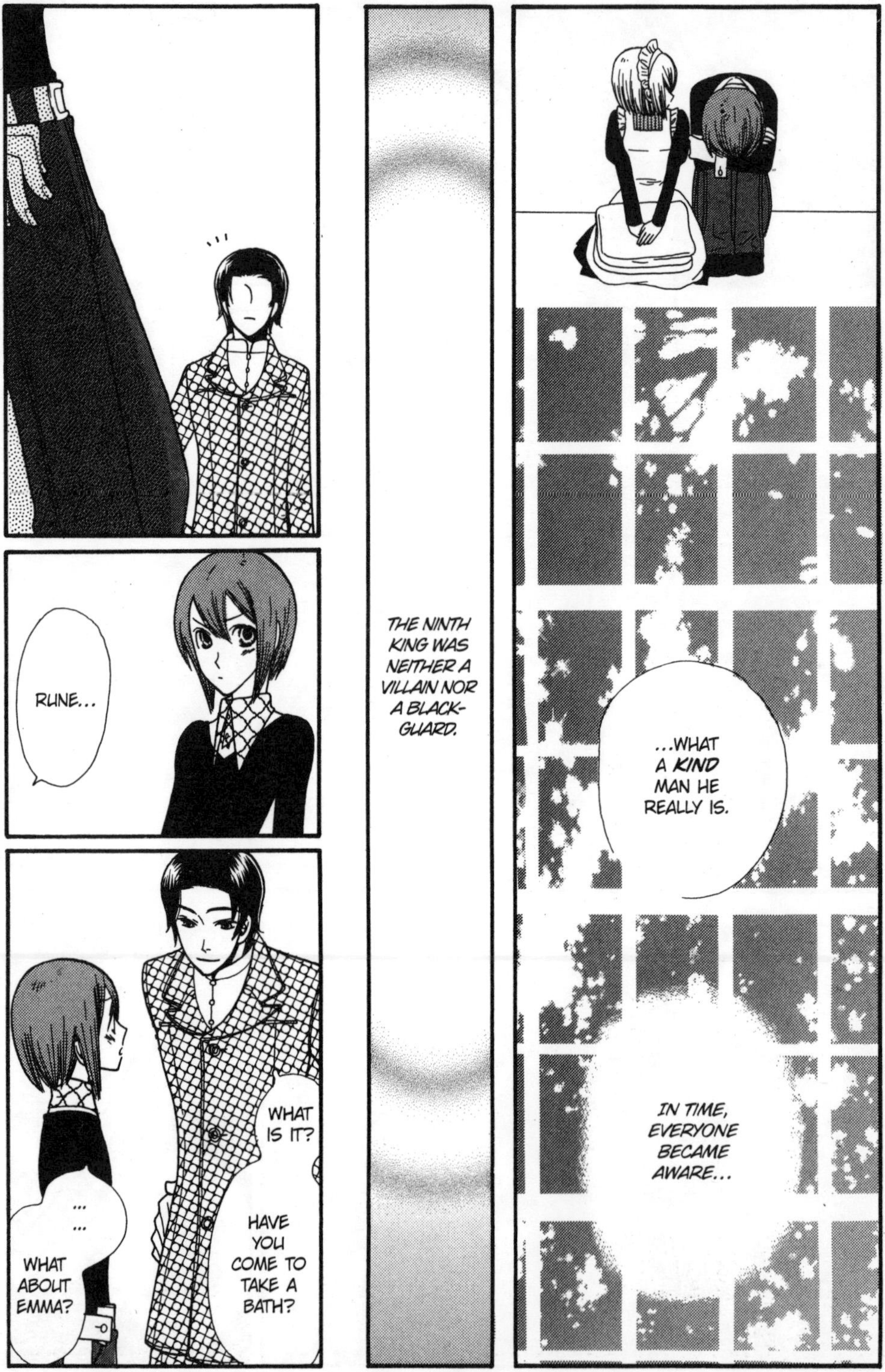
...WHAT A KIND MAN HE REALLY IS.
IN TIME, EVERYONE BECAME AWARE...
THE NINTH KING WAS NEITHER A VILLAIN NOR A BLACK-GUARD.
RUNE...
WHAT IS IT?
HAVE YOU COME TO TAKE A BATH?
... ...
WHAT ABOUT EMMA?

OKAY...

YOU DON'T WANT IT TO BE *JUST* US TWO?

I'M STILL MAD!

YOU'RE NOT MAD ANYMORE?

L...

LOTS OF THINGS!

GET WHAT?

BUT...

I DON'T GET IT...

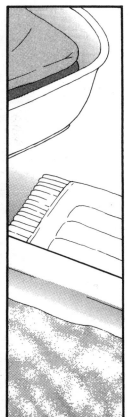

155

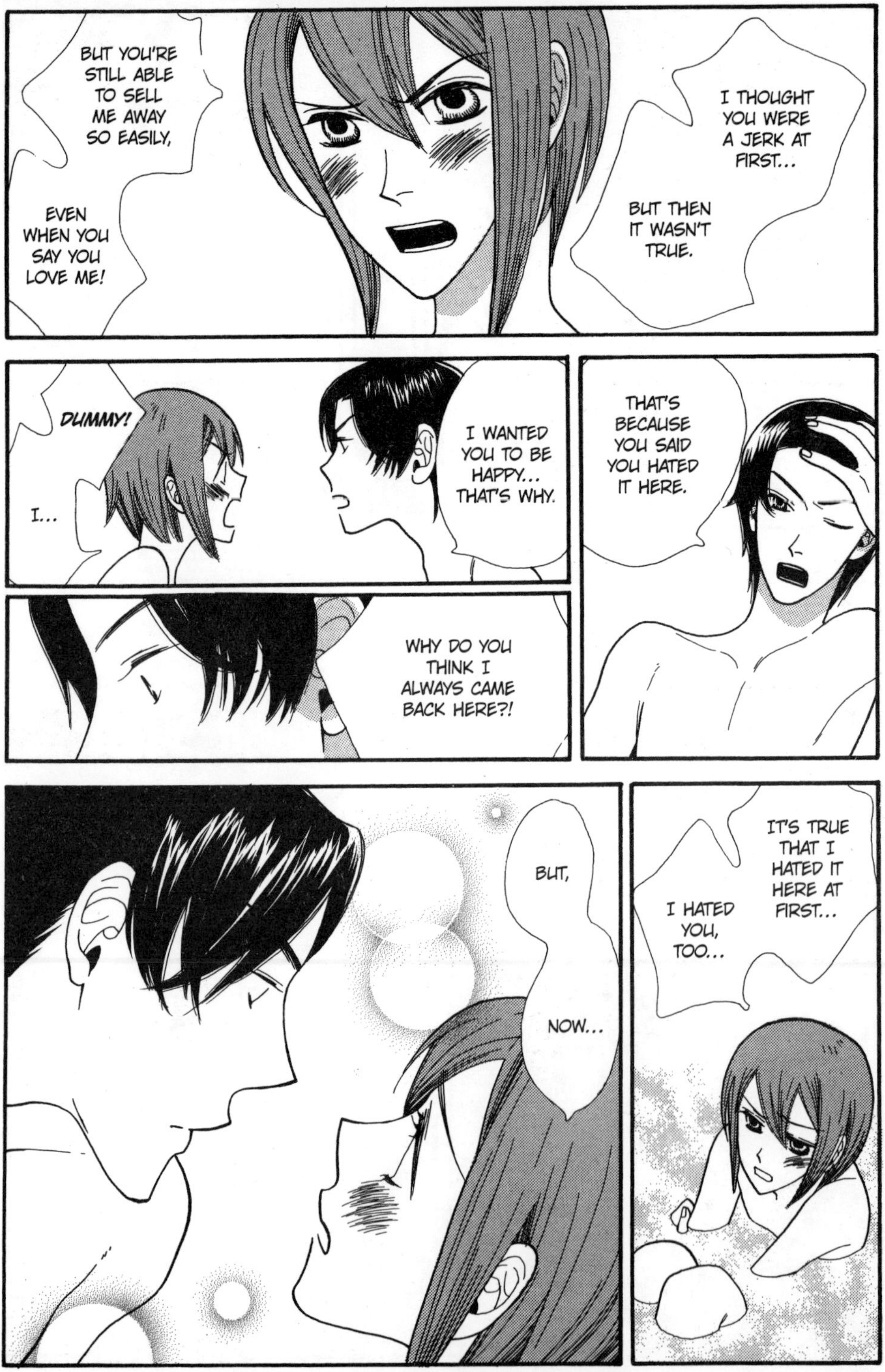
I THOUGHT YOU WERE A JERK AT FIRST...
BUT THEN IT WASN'T TRUE.
BUT YOU'RE STILL ABLE TO SELL ME AWAY SO EASILY,
EVEN WHEN YOU SAY YOU LOVE ME!
THAT'S BECAUSE YOU SAID YOU HATED IT HERE.
I WANTED YOU TO BE HAPPY... THAT'S WHY.
DUMMY!
I...
WHY DO YOU THINK I ALWAYS CAME BACK HERE?!
IT'S TRUE THAT I HATED IT HERE AT FIRST...
I HATED YOU, TOO...
BUT,
NOW...

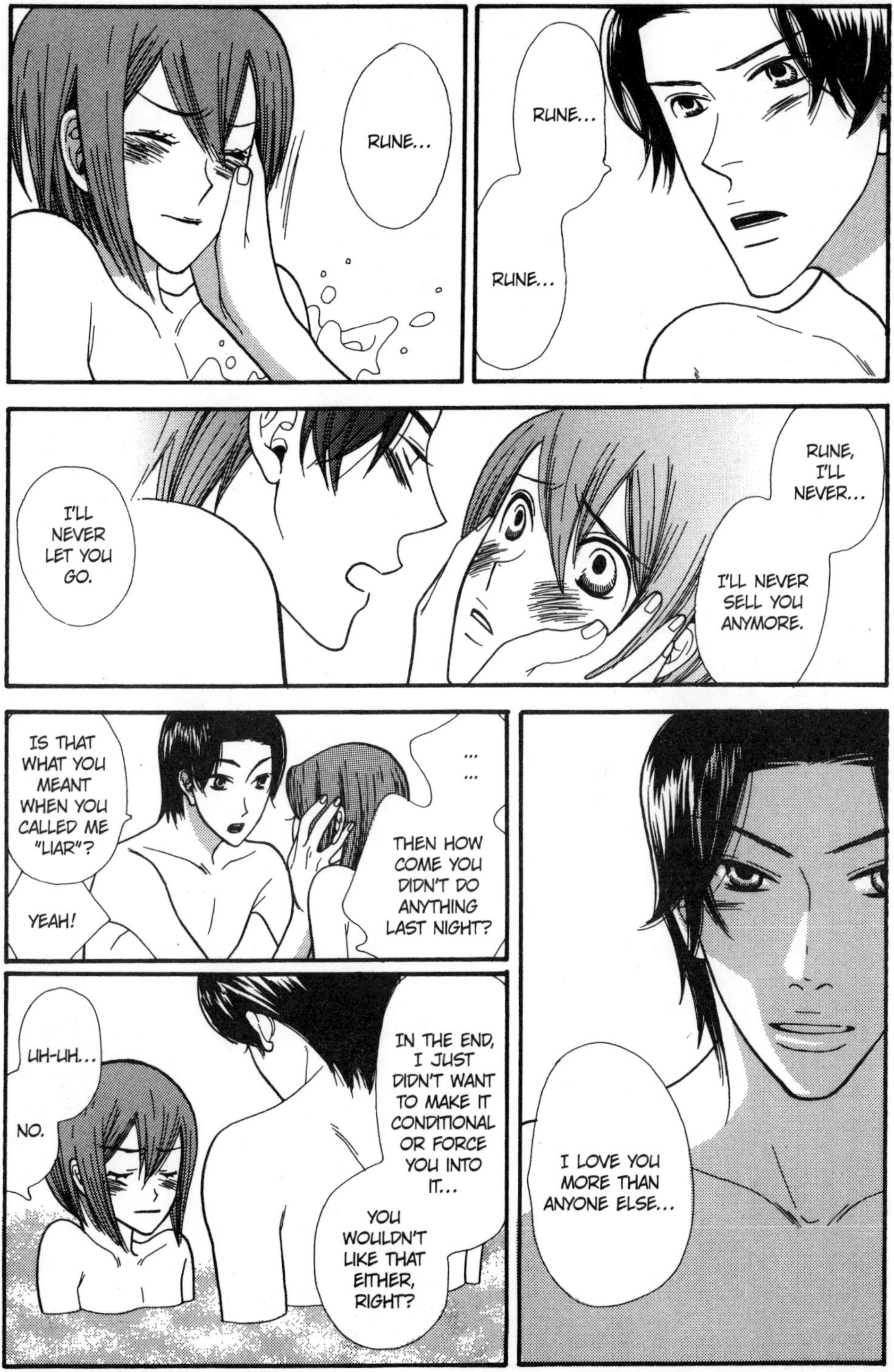
RUNE...
RUNE...
RUNE...
RUNE, I'LL NEVER...
I'LL NEVER SELL YOU ANYMORE.
I'LL NEVER LET YOU GO.
... ...
THEN HOW COME YOU DIDN'T DO ANYTHING LAST NIGHT?
IS THAT WHAT YOU MEANT WHEN YOU CALLED ME "LIAR"?
YEAH!
IN THE END, I JUST DIDN'T WANT TO MAKE IT CONDITIONAL OR FORCE YOU INTO IT...
YOU WOULDN'T LIKE THAT EITHER, RIGHT?
UH-UH...
NO.
I LOVE YOU MORE THAN ANYONE ELSE...

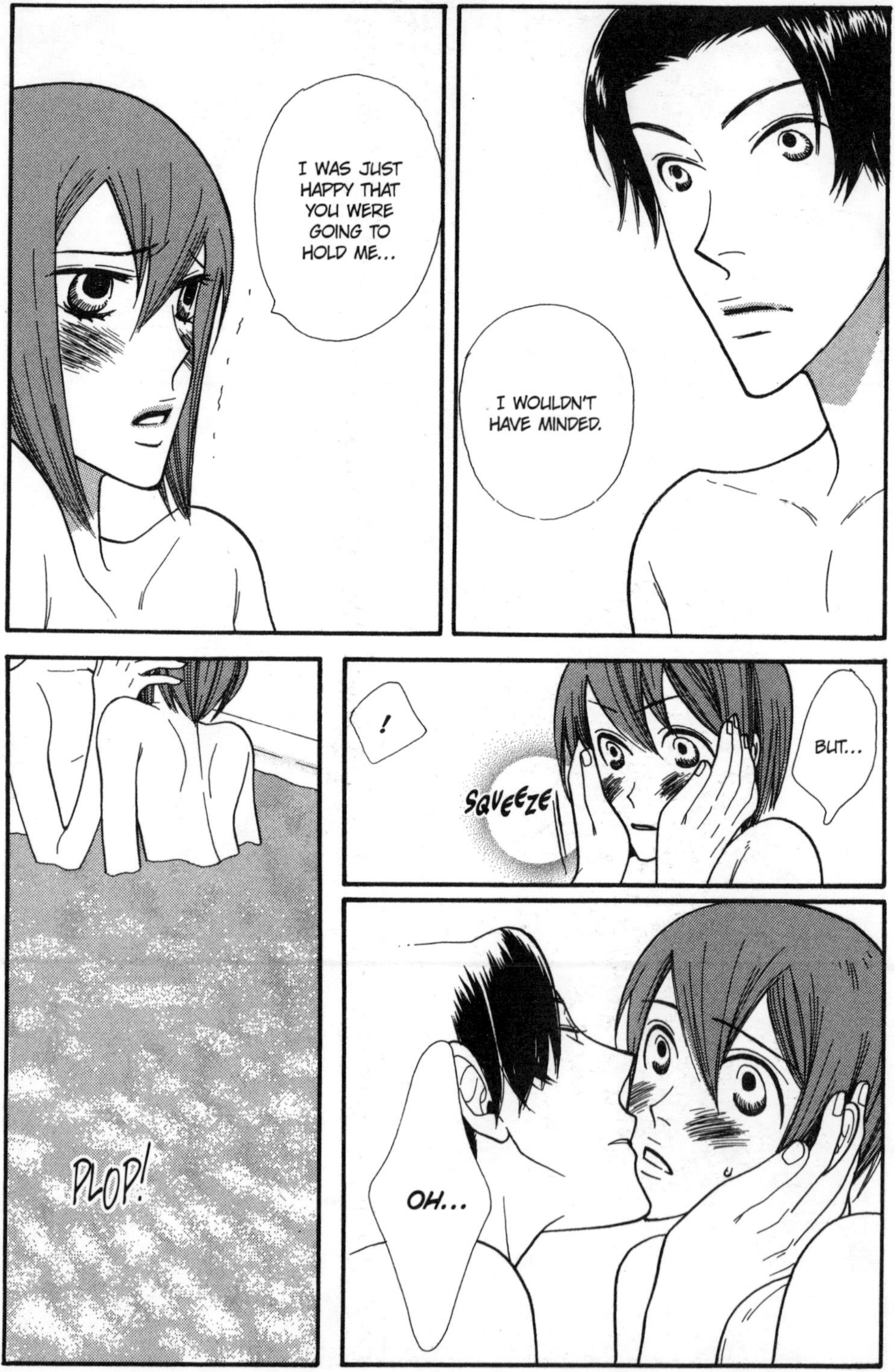
I WOULDN'T HAVE MINDED.
I WAS JUST HAPPY THAT YOU WERE GOING TO HOLD ME...
BUT...
!
SQUEEZE
OH...
PLOP!

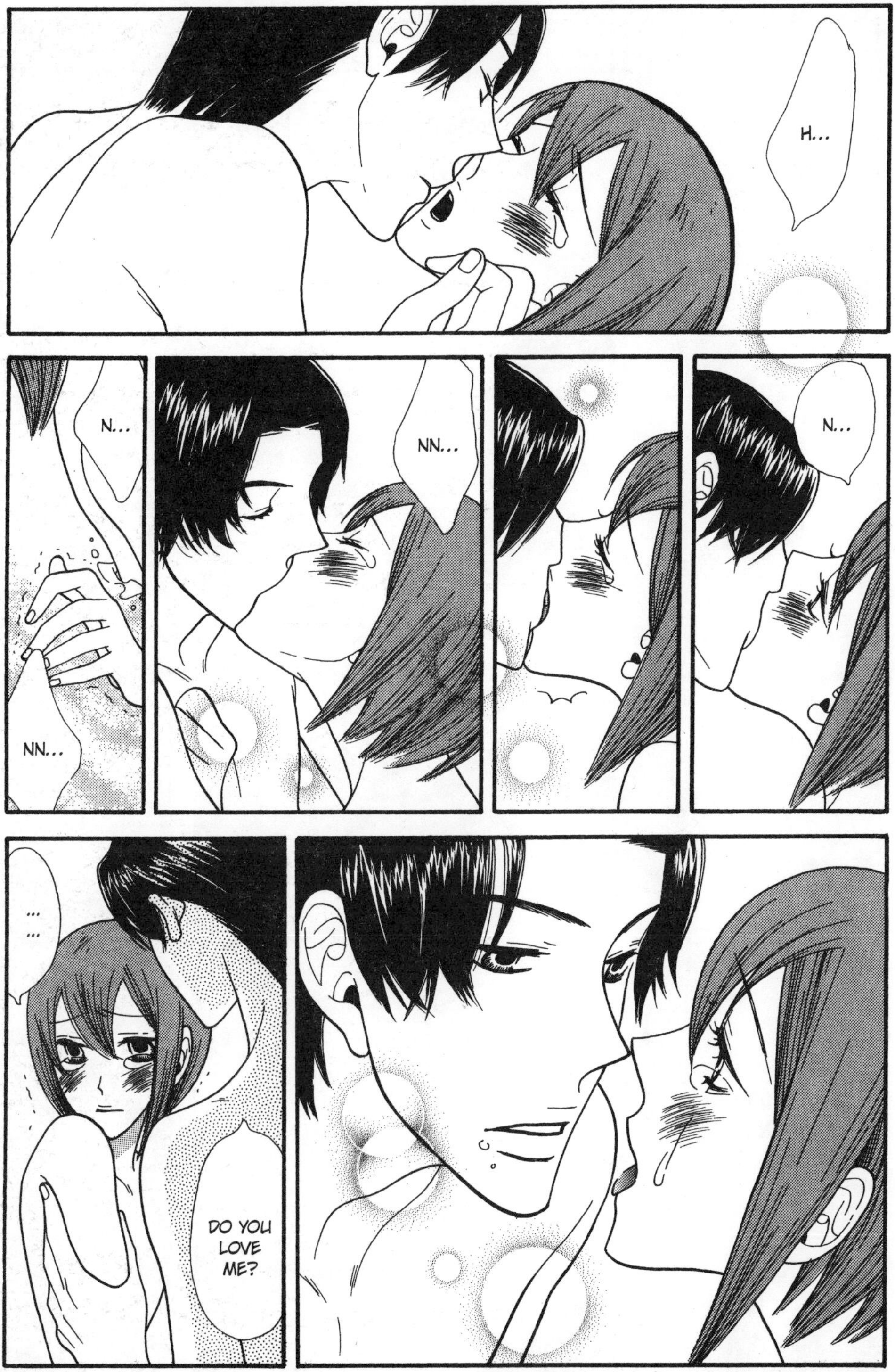
H...
N...
NN...
N...
NN...
... ...
DO YOU LOVE ME?

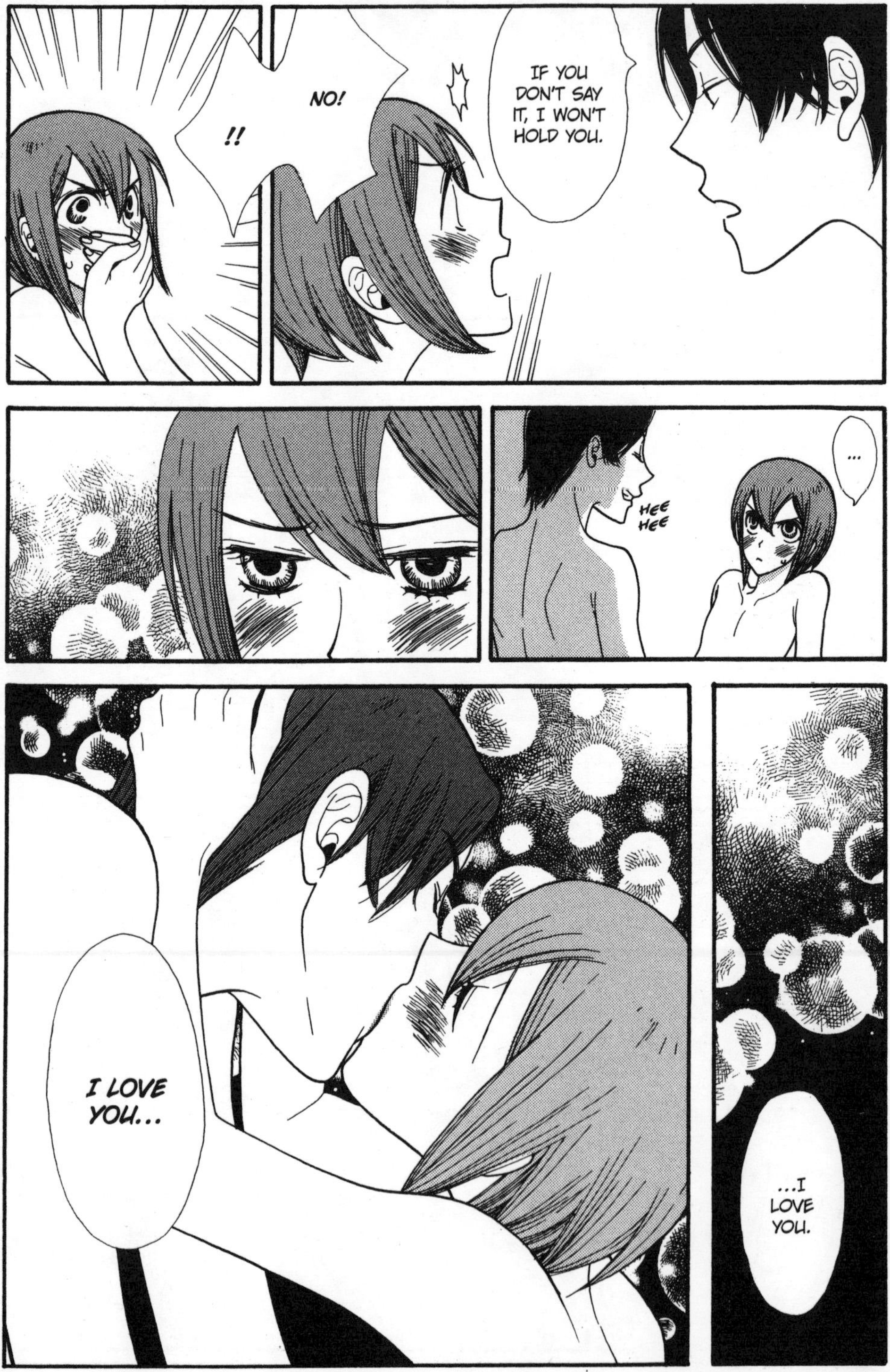
IF YOU DON'T SAY IT, I WON'T HOLD YOU.
NO!
!!
...
HEE HEE
...I LOVE YOU.
I LOVE YOU...

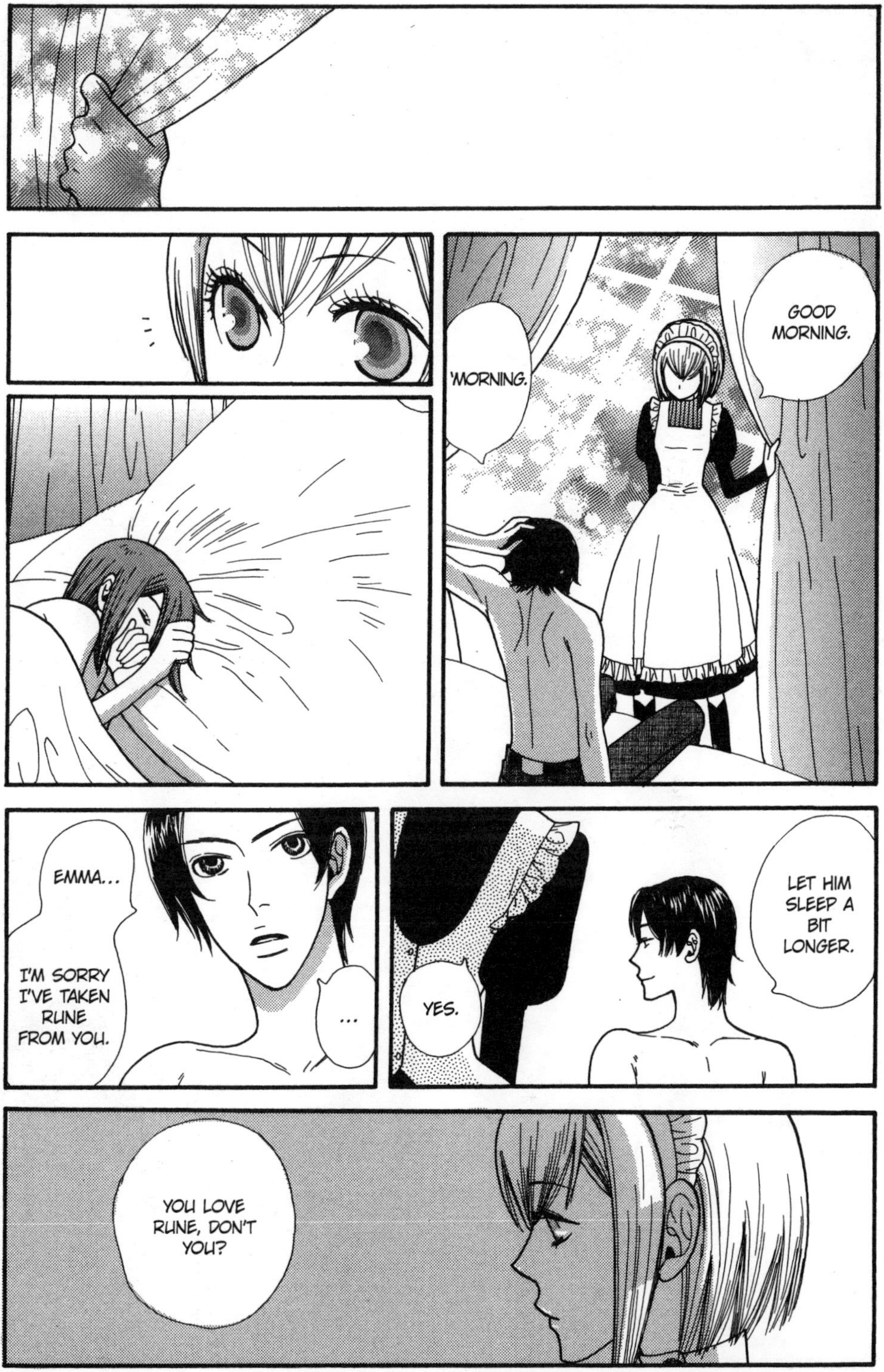
GOOD MORNING.
'MORNING.
LET HIM SLEEP A BIT LONGER.
YES.
EMMA...
I'M SORRY I'VE TAKEN RUNE FROM YOU.
...
YOU LOVE RUNE, DON'T YOU?

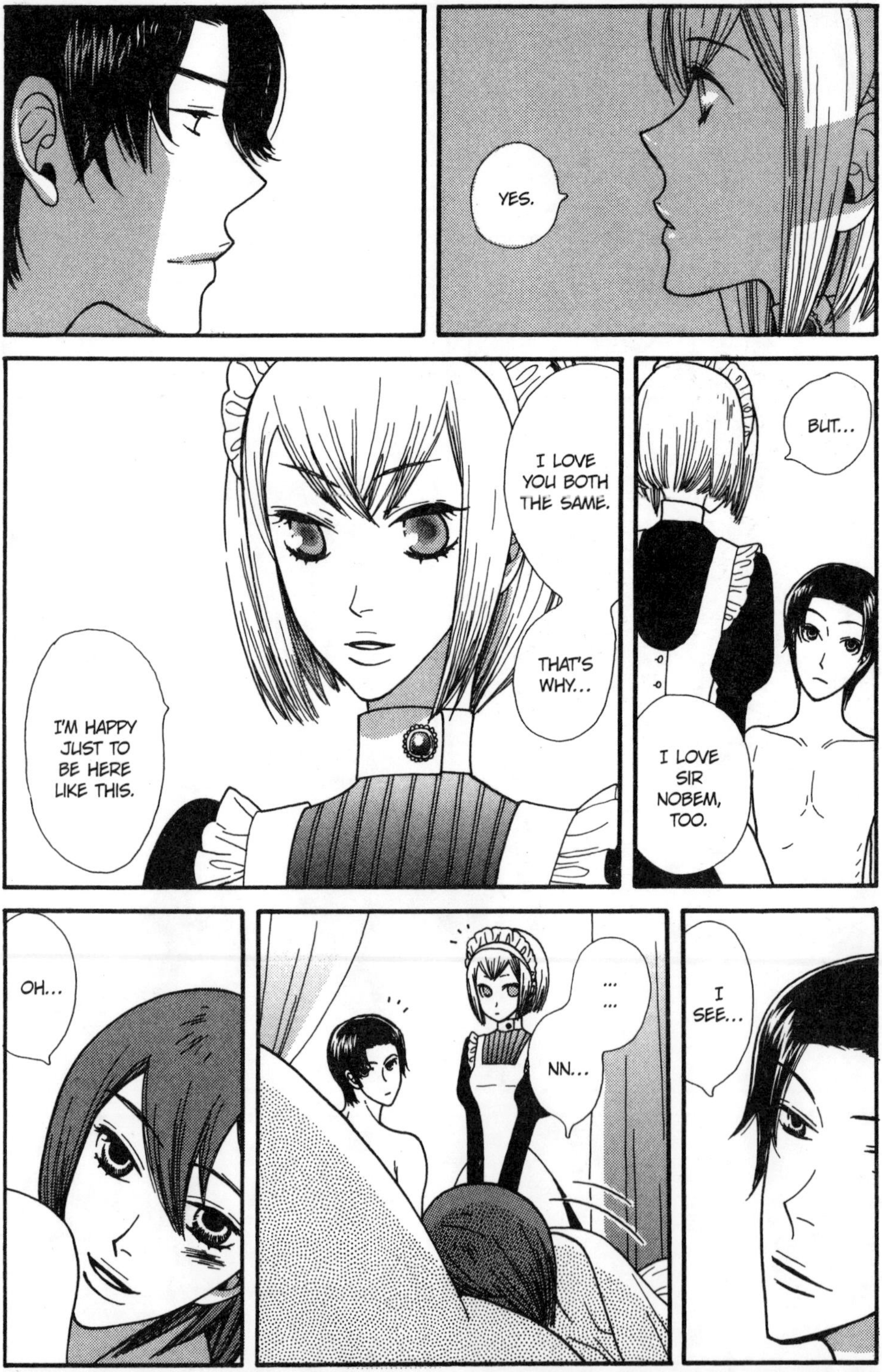
YES.
BUT...
I LOVE SIR NOBEM, TOO.
I LOVE YOU BOTH THE SAME.
THAT'S WHY...
I'M HAPPY JUST TO BE HERE LIKE THIS.
I SEE...
......
NN...
OH...

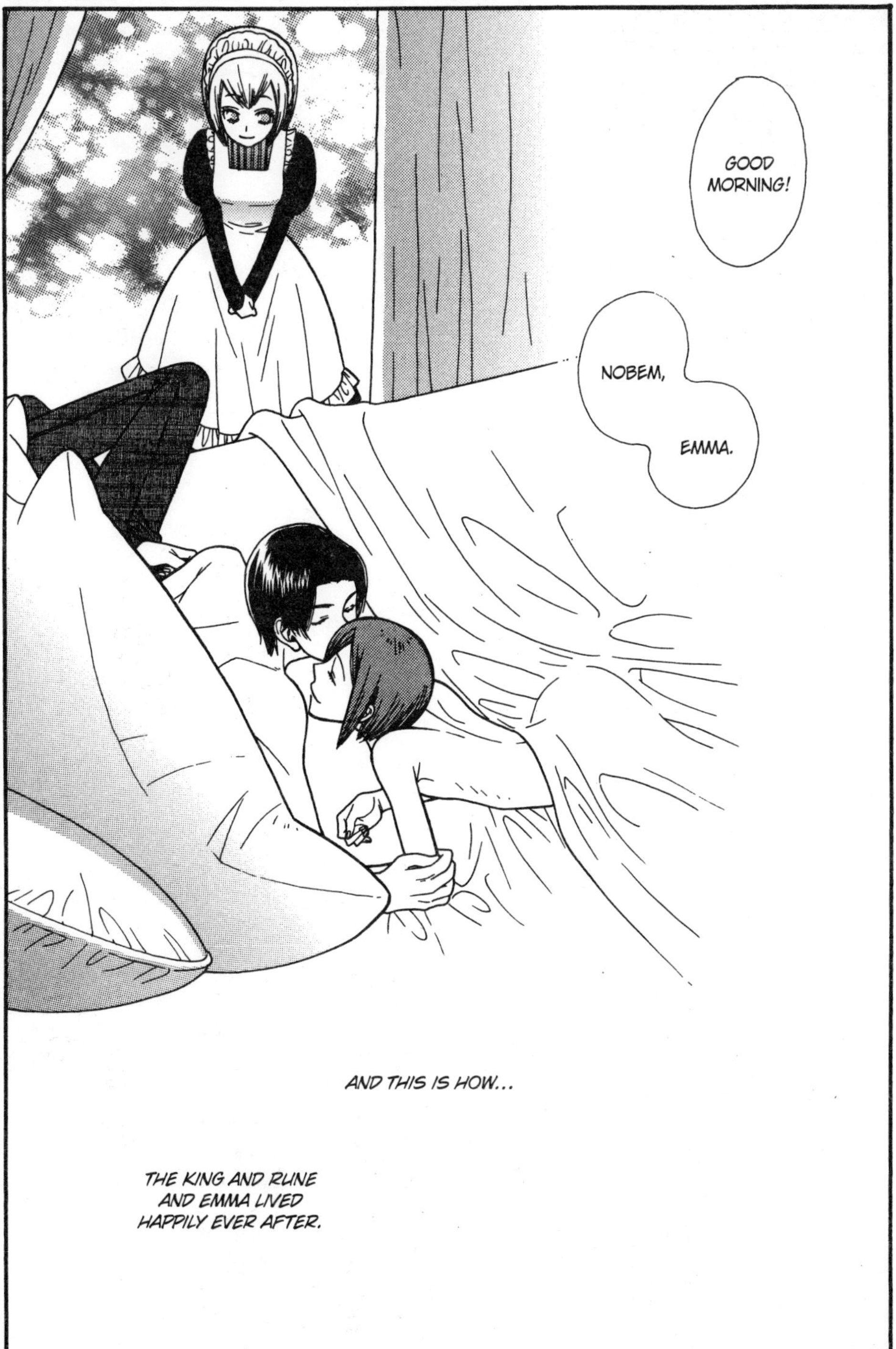
GOOD MORNING!
NOBEM, EMMA.
AND THIS IS HOW...
THE KING AND RUNE AND EMMA LIVED HAPPILY EVER AFTER.

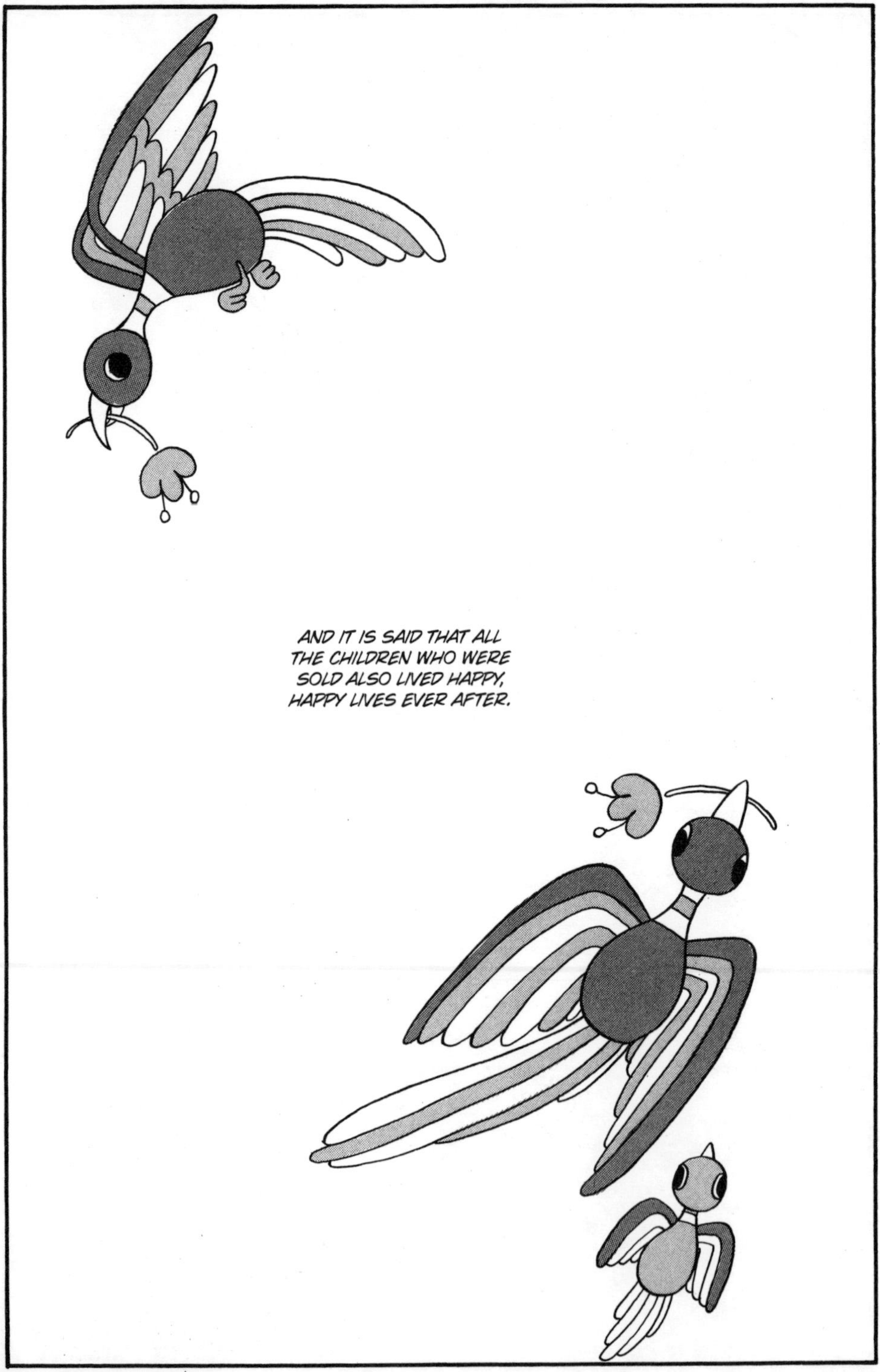
AND IT IS SAID THAT ALL
THE CHILDREN WHO WERE
SOLD ALSO LIVED HAPPY,
HAPPY LIVES EVER AFTER.

THE KING AND RUNE end

AFTERWORD

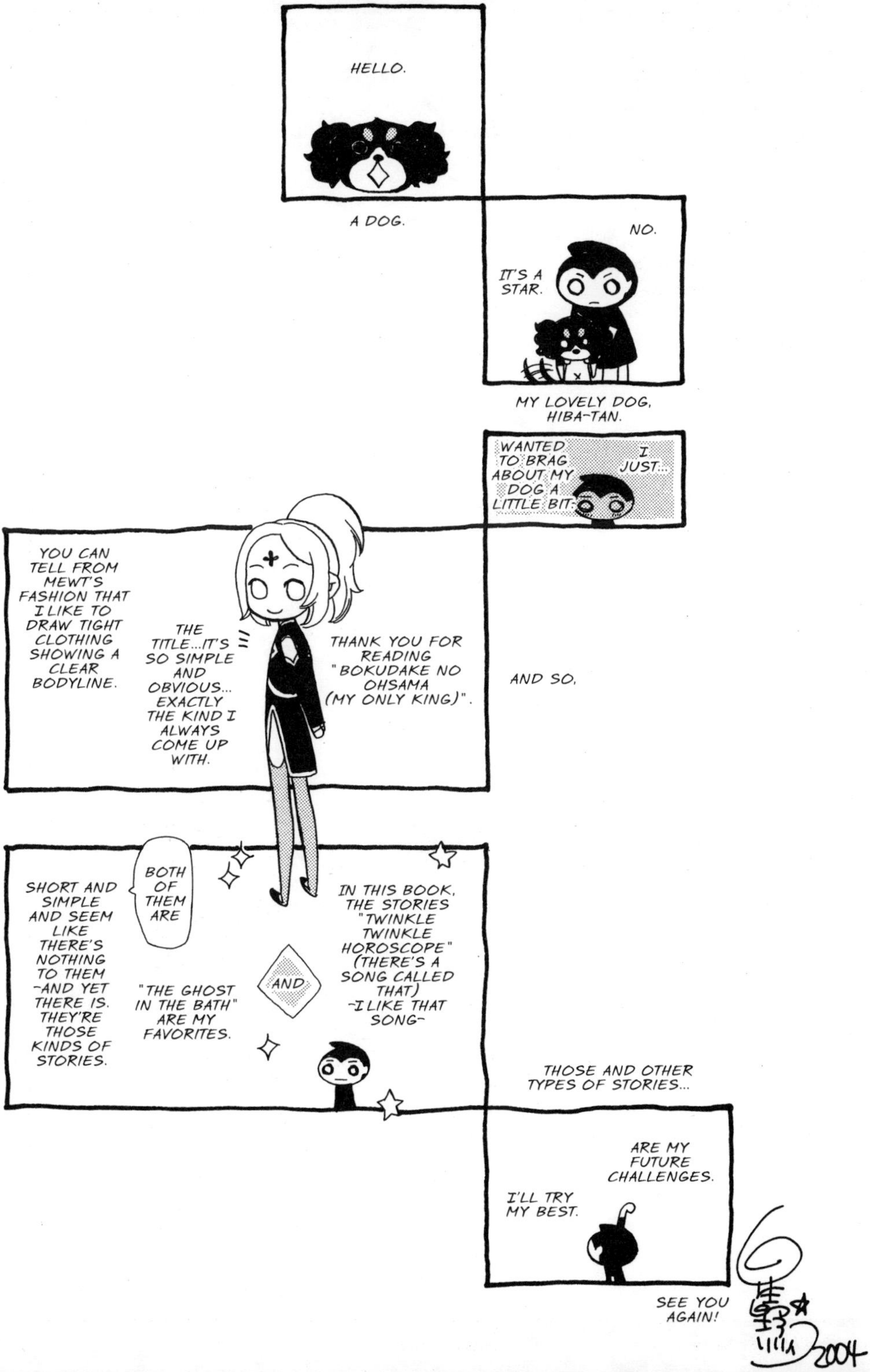
HELLO.
A DOG.
NO.
IT'S A STAR.
MY LOVELY DOG, HIBA-TAN.
I JUST...
WANTED TO BRAG ABOUT MY DOG A LITTLE BIT.
AND SO,
THANK YOU FOR READING "BOKUDAKE NO OHSAMA (MY ONLY KING)".
THE TITLE...IT'S SO SIMPLE AND OBVIOUS... EXACTLY THE KIND I ALWAYS COME UP WITH.
YOU CAN TELL FROM MEWT'S FASHION THAT I LIKE TO DRAW TIGHT CLOTHING SHOWING A CLEAR BODYLINE.
IN THIS BOOK, THE STORIES "TWINKLE TWINKLE HOROSCOPE" (THERE'S A SONG CALLED THAT) ~I LIKE THAT SONG~
AND
"THE GHOST IN THE BATH" ARE MY FAVORITES.
BOTH OF THEM ARE
SHORT AND SIMPLE AND SEEM LIKE THERE'S NOTHING TO THEM ~AND YET THERE IS. THEY'RE THOSE KINDS OF STORIES.
THOSE AND OTHER TYPES OF STORIES...
ARE MY FUTURE CHALLENGES.
I'LL TRY MY BEST.
SEE YOU AGAIN!
2004

MY ONLY KING

Translation	Sachiko Sato
Lettering	Replibooks
Graphic Design	Wendy Lee
Editing	Bambi Eloriaga
Editor in Chief	Fred Lui
Publisher	Hikaru Sasahara

English Edition Published by
DIGITAL MANGA PUBLISHING
A division of DIGITAL MANGA, Inc.
1487 W 178th Street, Suite 300
Gardena, CA 90248

www.dmpbooks.com

First Edition: February 2006
ISBN: 1-56970-911-4

1 3 5 7 9 10 8 6 4 2

Printed in China

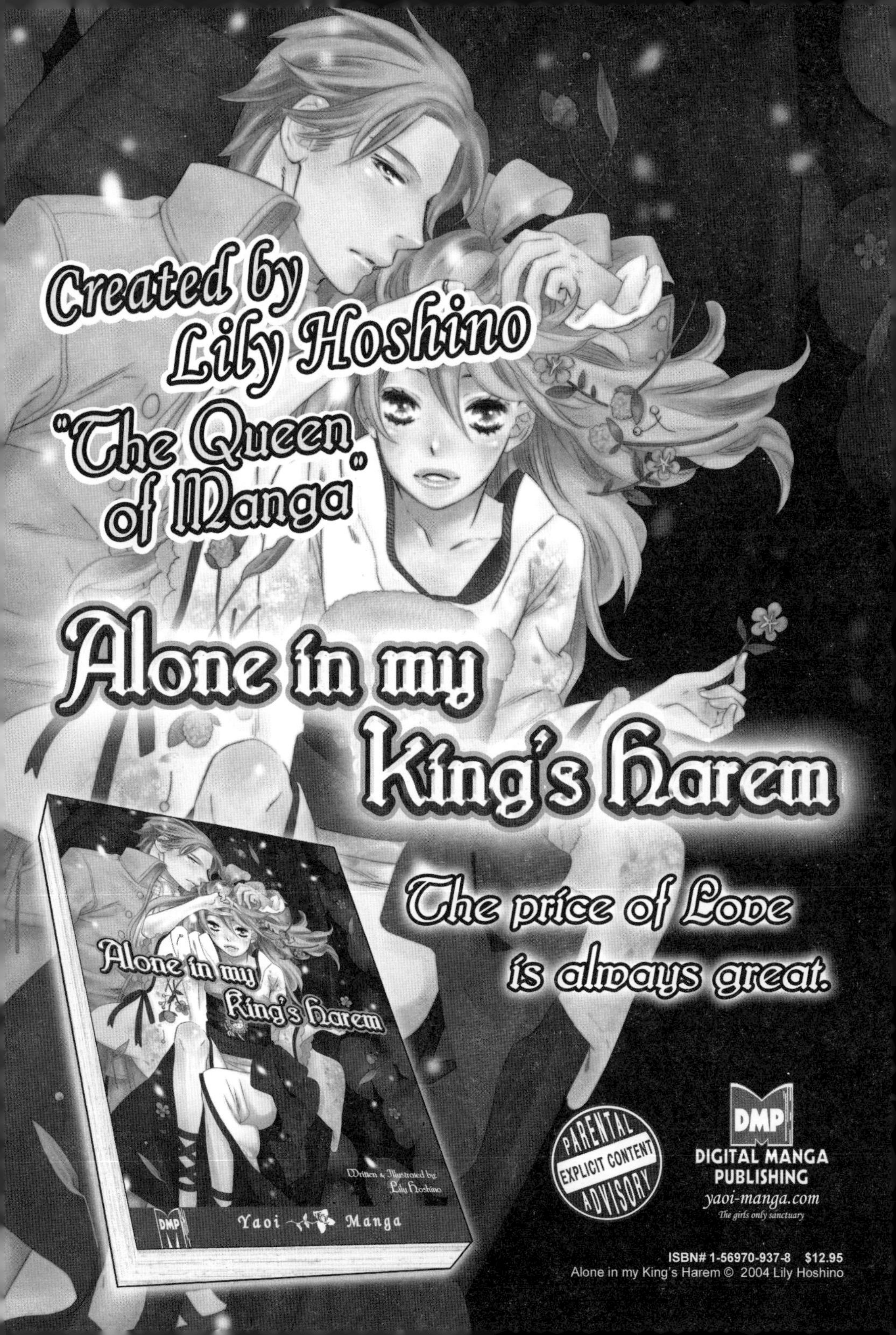
Created by Lily Hoshino
"The Queen of Manga"
Alone in my King's Harem
The price of Love is always great.
Alone in my King's Harem
Written & Illustrated by Lily Hoshino
DMP
Yaoi Manga
PARENTAL EXPLICIT CONTENT ADVISORY
DMP
DIGITAL MANGA PUBLISHING
yaoi-manga.com
The girls only sanctuary
ISBN# 1-56970-937-8 $12.95
Alone in my King's Harem © 2004 Lily Hoshino

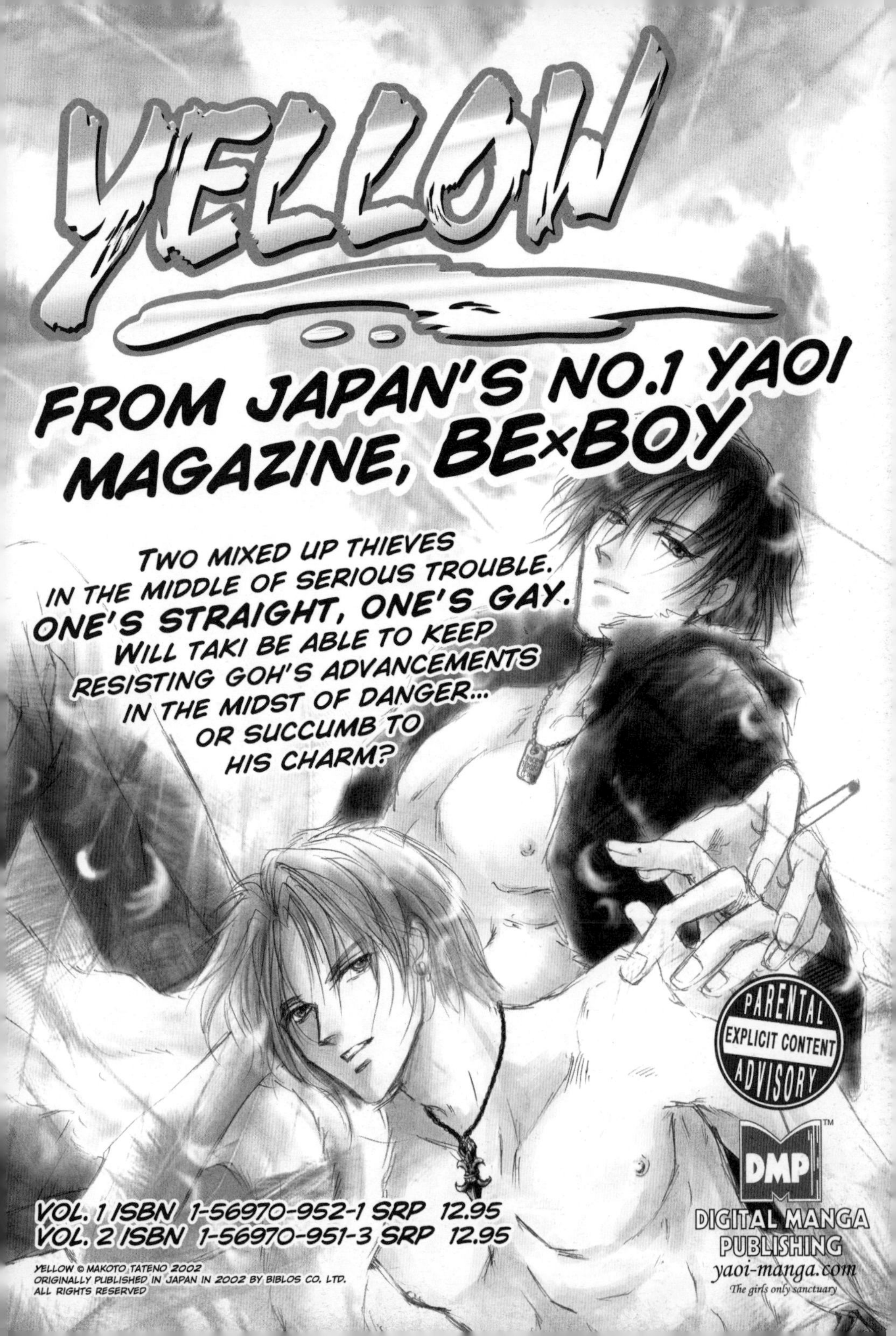
YELLOW
FROM JAPAN'S NO.1 YAOI
MAGAZINE, BE×BOY
TWO MIXED UP THIEVES
IN THE MIDDLE OF SERIOUS TROUBLE.
ONE'S STRAIGHT, ONE'S GAY.
WILL TAKI BE ABLE TO KEEP
RESISTING GOH'S ADVANCEMENTS
IN THE MIDST OF DANGER...
OR SUCCUMB TO
HIS CHARM?
PARENTAL
EXPLICIT CONTENT
ADVISORY
DMP
DIGITAL MANGA
PUBLISHING
yaoi-manga.com
The girls only sanctuary
VOL. 1 ISBN 1-56970-952-1 SRP 12.95
VOL. 2 ISBN 1-56970-951-3 SRP 12.95
YELLOW © MAKOTO TATENO 2002
ORIGINALLY PUBLISHED IN JAPAN IN 2002 BY BIBLOS CO. LTD.
ALL RIGHTS RESERVED

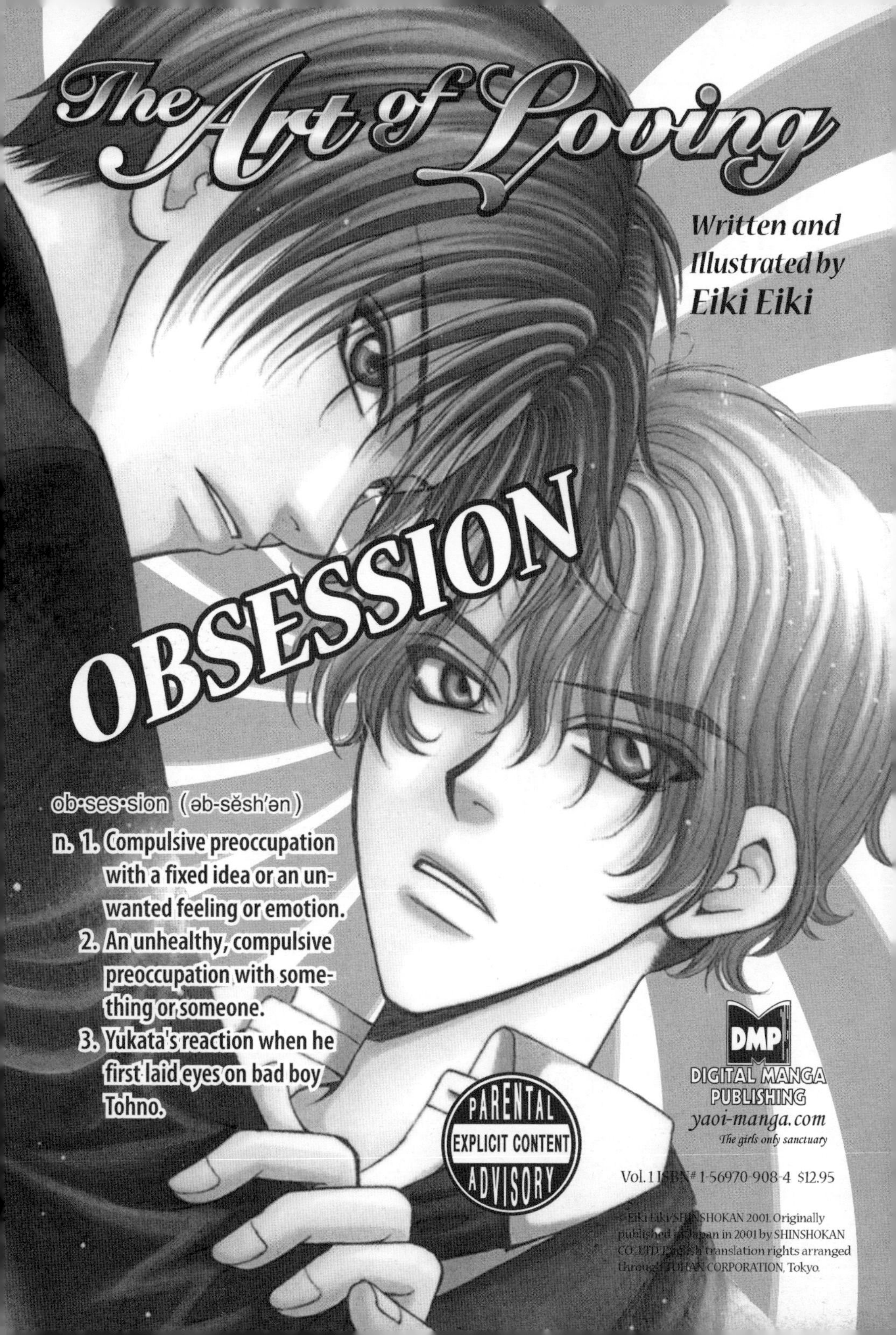
The Art of Loving
Written and Illustrated by Eiki Eiki
OBSESSION
ob·ses·sion (əb-sĕsh′ən)
n. 1. Compulsive preoccupation with a fixed idea or an unwanted feeling or emotion.
2. An unhealthy, compulsive preoccupation with something or someone.
3. Yukata's reaction when he first laid eyes on bad boy Tohno.
DMP
DIGITAL MANGA PUBLISHING
yaoi-manga.com
The girls only sanctuary
PARENTAL
EXPLICIT CONTENT
ADVISORY
Vol.1 ISBN# 1-56970-908-4 $12.95
© Eiki Eiki/SHINSHOKAN 2001. Originally published in Japan in 2001 by SHINSHOKAN CO., LTD. English translation rights arranged through TOHAN CORPORATION, Tokyo.

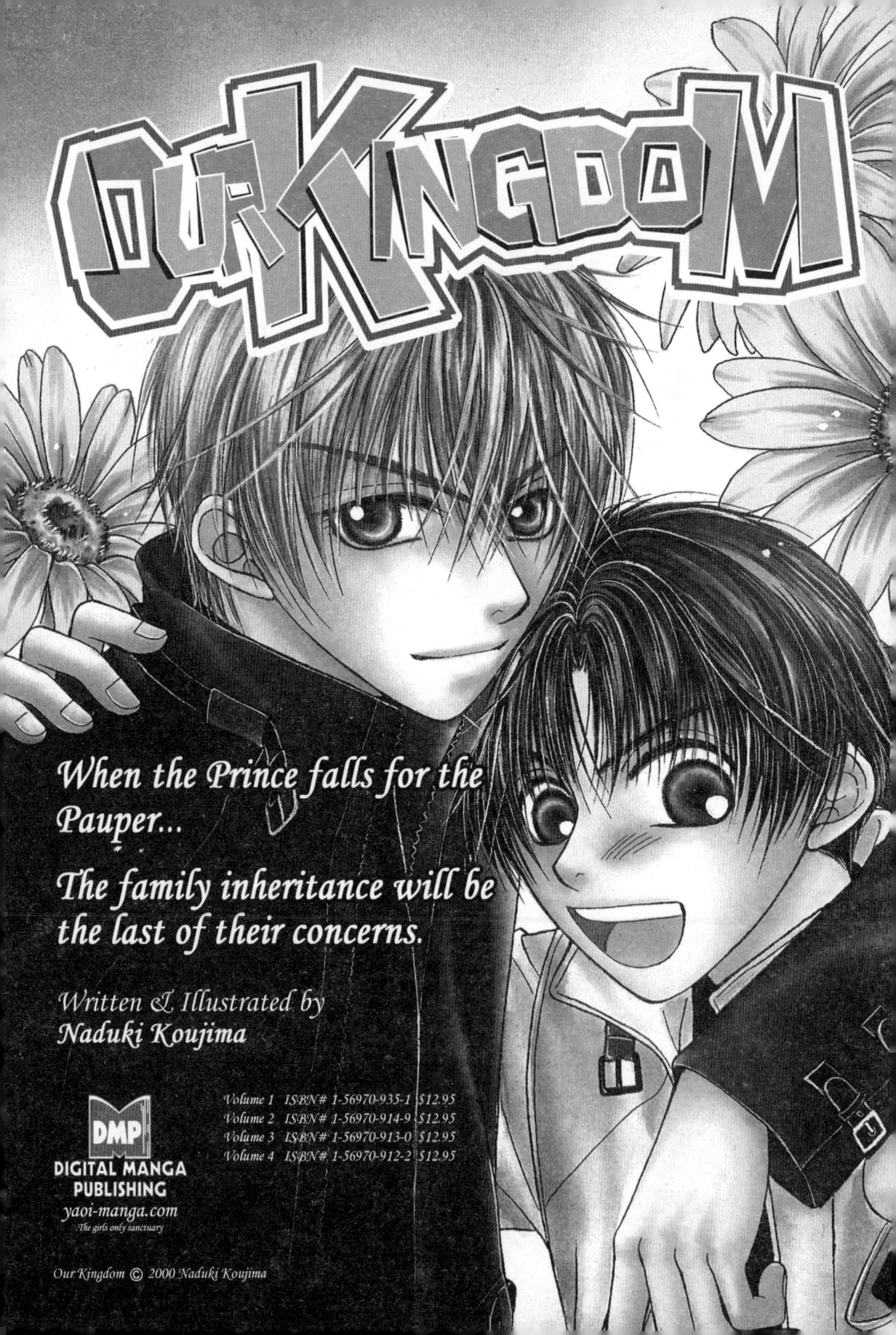
OUR KINGDOM
When the Prince falls for the Pauper...
The family inheritance will be the last of their concerns.
Written & Illustrated by
Naduki Koujima
Volume 1 ISBN# 1-56970-935-1 $12.95
Volume 2 ISBN# 1-56970-914-9 $12.95
Volume 3 ISBN# 1-56970-913-0 $12.95
Volume 4 ISBN# 1-56970-912-2 $12.95
DMP
DIGITAL MANGA PUBLISHING
yaoi-manga.com
The girls only sanctuary
Our Kingdom © 2000 Naduki Koujima

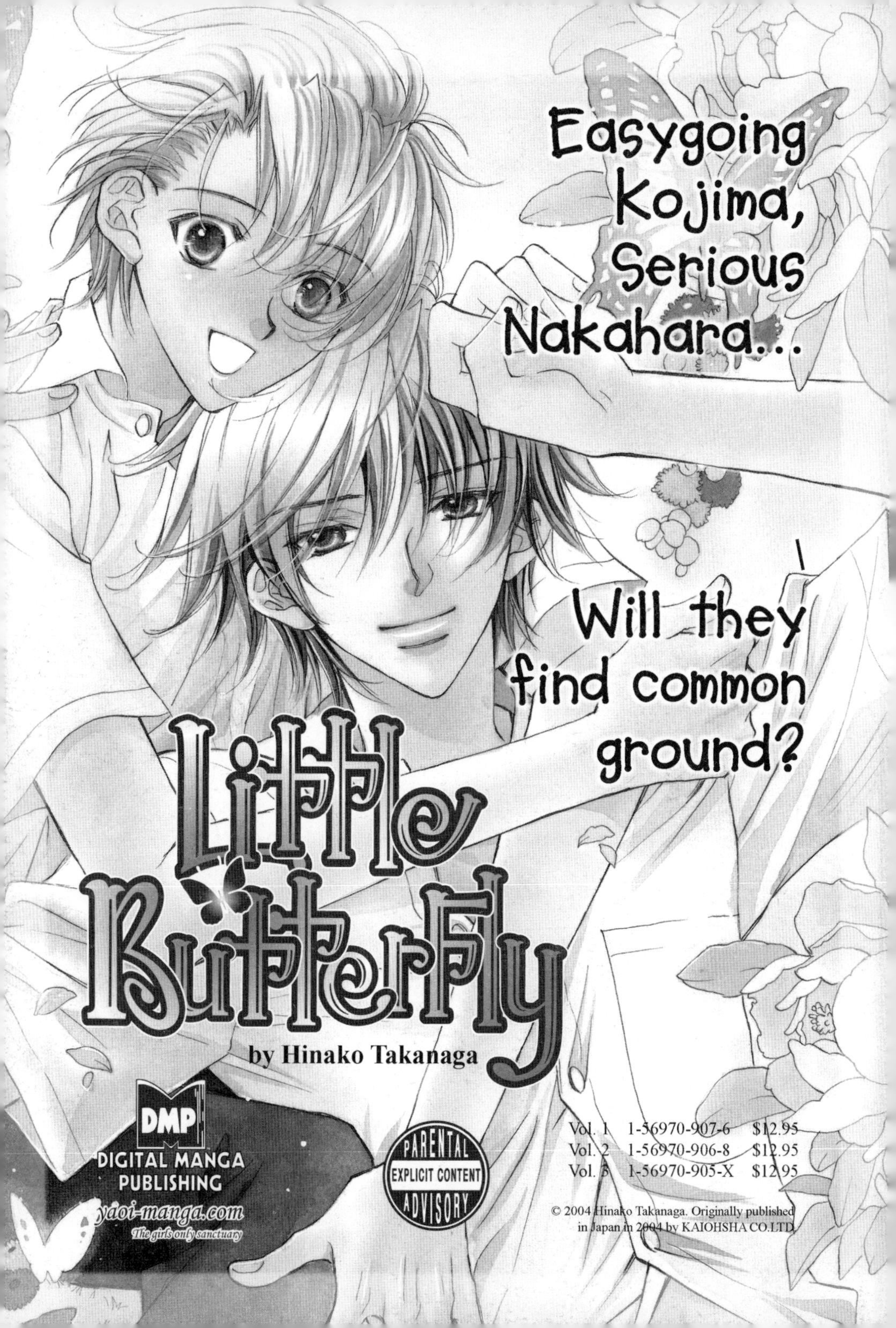

Easygoing Kojima, Serious Nakahara...
Will they find common ground?
Little Butterfly
by Hinako Takanaga
DMP
DIGITAL MANGA PUBLISHING
yaoi-manga.com
The girls only sanctuary
PARENTAL ADVISORY EXPLICIT CONTENT
Vol. 1 1-56970-907-6 $12.95
Vol. 2 1-56970-906-8 $12.95
Vol. 3 1-56970-905-X $12.95
© 2004 Hinako Takanaga. Originally published in Japan in 2004 by KAIOHSHA CO.LTD.

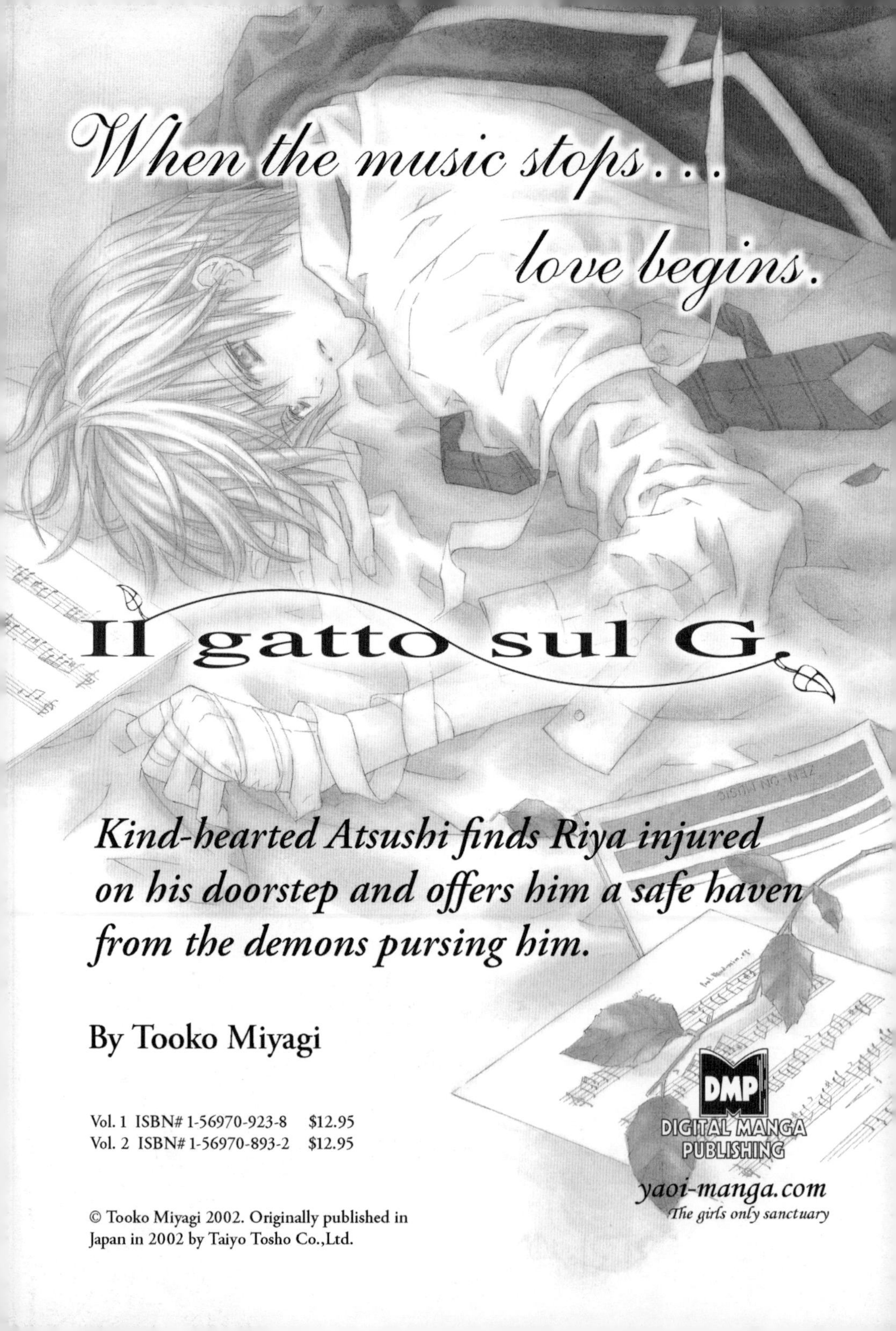
When the music stops . . .
. . . love begins.
Il gatto sul G
Kind-hearted Atsushi finds Riya injured on his doorstep and offers him a safe haven from the demons pursing him.
By Tooko Miyagi
Vol. 1 ISBN# 1-56970-923-8 $12.95
Vol. 2 ISBN# 1-56970-893-2 $12.95
© Tooko Miyagi 2002. Originally published in Japan in 2002 by Taiyo Tosho Co.,Ltd.
DMP
DIGITAL MANGA PUBLISHING
yaoi-manga.com
The girls only sanctuary

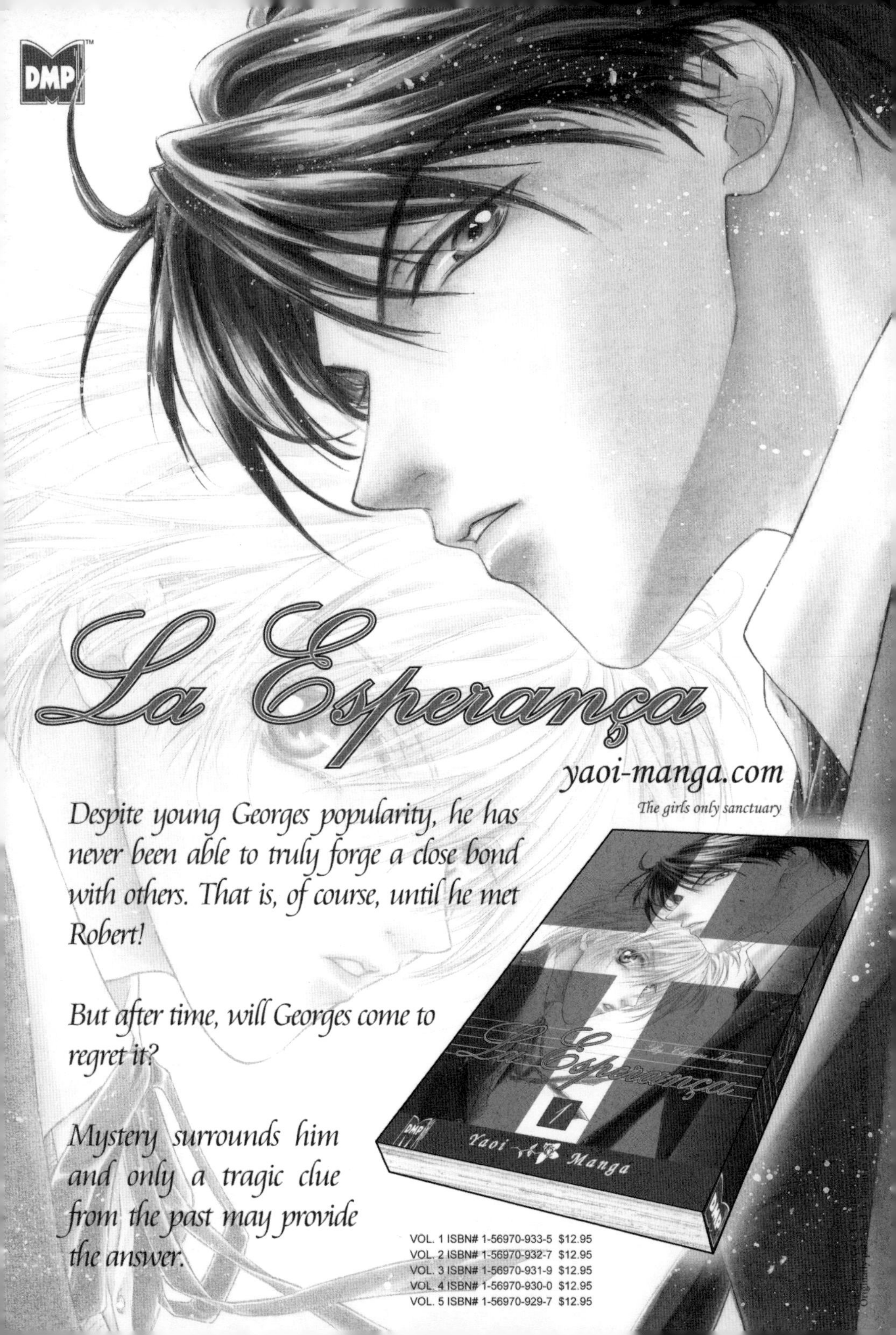
DMP
La Esperança
yaoi-manga.com
The girls only sanctuary
Despite young Georges popularity, he has never been able to truly forge a close bond with others. That is, of course, until he met Robert!
But after time, will Georges come to regret it?
Mystery surrounds him and only a tragic clue from the past may provide the answer.
La Esperança
Yaoi Manga
VOL. 1 ISBN# 1-56970-933-5 $12.95
VOL. 2 ISBN# 1-56970-932-7 $12.95
VOL. 3 ISBN# 1-56970-931-9 $12.95
VOL. 4 ISBN# 1-56970-930-0 $12.95
VOL. 5 ISBN# 1-56970-929-7 $12.95

STOP

This is the back of the book! Start from the other side.

NATIVE MANGA readers read manga from *right to left*.

If you run into our *Native Manga* logo on any of our books... you'll know that this manga is published in it's true original native Japanese right to left reading format, as it was intended. Turn to the other side of the book and start reading from right to left, top to bottom.

Follow the diagram to see how its done. *Surf's Up!*

NATIVE MANGA

READ RIGHT TO LEFT